H
C
C
S

Harvard Contemporary China Series, 16

The Harvard Contemporary China Series is designed to
present new research that deals with present-day issues
against the background of Chinese history and society. The
focus is on interdisciplinary research intended to convey
the significance of the rapidly changing Chinese scene. This
volume received support from the "New Perspectives in Chinese
Culture and Society" program, which is made possible by a grant
from the Chiang Ching-kuo Foundation for International Scholarly Exchange to the American Council of Learned Societies.

D1350604

One Country, Two Societies

Rural-Urban Inequality in Contemporary China

Edited by

Martin King Whyte

Harvard University Press

Cambridge, Massachusetts

London, England   2010

Library of Congress Cataloging-in-Publication Data

One country, two societies : rural-urban inequality in contemporary
China / edited by Martin King Whyte.

    p. cm.

  Includes bibliographical references and index.

  ISBN 978-0-674-03630-7 (cloth : alk. paper) —

  ISBN 978-0-674-03632-1 (pbk. : alk. paper)

  1. Cities and towns–China. 2. Villages–China. 3. China–Rural
conditions. 4. Rural-urban migration–China. 5. China–Social
conditions—1949– I. Whyte, Martin King.

  HT147.C48O62 2010

  307.2'40951–dc22

2009024812

Contents

Preface

This volume of essays and analyses on the rural-urban gap in contemporary China is the product of a complex and lengthy process that the Chinese would refer to as "fermentation" *(yunniang)*. The original impetus came from my colleague at the Fairbank Center for Chinese Studies, Merle Goldman, who has been involved in many of the previous volumes of the Harvard Contemporary China Series (HCCS). Merle had some funds left in a Fairbank Center account, and in 2003 she offered these to me as "seed money" to use to plan a conference on a topic of my choosing that would, we hoped, lead to another HCCS volume. Because at the time I was involved in a major research project in China focusing on inequality trends and was also teaching a graduate seminar on that topic, I decided to use the funds Merle provided to organize a conference planning workshop. The purpose of the planning workshop was to help me sort through the broad terrain of research issues regarding Chinese inequality trends in order to find the best focus for a conference, as well as to suggest names of scholars who were actively engaged in research on inequality-related topics. I also asked an informal grouping of my Fairbank Center colleagues—Elizabeth Perry, Tony Saich, and Merle—to advise me on how to organize the planning workshop as well as the eventual research conference.

The conference planning workshop was held at the Fairbank Center in June 2003. The outside specialists who attended were Thomas Bernstein (political science, Columbia), Deborah Davis (sociology, Yale), Ching Kwan Lee (sociology, then at the University of Michigan, now at UCLA), Albert Park (economics, then at the University of Michigan, now at Oxford),

Dorothy Solinger (political science, University of California-Irvine), and Wang Feng (sociology, University of California-Irvine). Each participant presented ideas on what some of the most important and controversial issues involving inequality trends in China were as well as names of researchers known to be actively working on such questions. I was fortunate to have a number of local China specialists sit in for at least part of the planning sessions, including Regina Abrami (political science, Harvard Business School), John Giles (economics, Michigan State, who was visiting Harvard that year), Gary Jefferson (economics, Brandeis), Charlotte Ikels (anthropology, Case Western Reserve), Liz Perry (political science, Harvard), Heng Quan (economics, Shanghai Academy of Social Sciences, also a visitor that year), Tony Saich (political science, the Kennedy School, Harvard), and James Watson (anthropology, Harvard).

An extended process of thinking and consultation then ensued that finally produced my decision to focus the planned conference on China's contemporary rural-urban cleavage as the most important, paradoxical, and controversial aspect of inequality in China today. It was then necessary to apply for funding for the research conference itself. I prepared a brief statement describing the planned focus of the conference as "Rethinking the Rural-Urban Cleavage in Contemporary China." I issued tentative invitations to a range of researchers from around the world who were known to be conducting research on various aspects of China's rural-urban cleavage and the status and treatment of urban migrants. On the basis of these preparations, in 2005 I applied for funding from the American Council of Learned Societies, through their program "New Perspectives on Chinese Culture and Society," as well as to the Fairbank Center, the Weatherhead Center for International Affairs, and the Asia Center at Harvard, and these applications were successful. I am grateful to the ACLS for agreeing to be the main funder of the conference, and to the Fairbank, Weatherhead, and Asia Centers for providing supplementary funding.

The conference on "Rethinking the Rural-Urban Cleavage in Contemporary China" was held on October 6–8, 2006, at the Fairbank Center. I am grateful to the staffs at the Fairbank Center, Weatherhead Center, and Asia Center, and particularly to Wen-hao Tien and Melanie Wang, for organizing the conference with flawless efficiency. In addition to the authors of the chapters included in this volume, the following scholars participated in the conference, either as paper-presenters or discussants:

Chih-jou Jay Chen (sociology, Academic Sinica, Taiwan), Xiaoneng Chen (sociology, Princeton), Vanessa Fong (anthropology, Harvard), Merle Goldman, Wilt Idema (Chinese literature, Harvard), Arthur Kleinman (anthropology, Harvard), John Logan (sociology, Brown University), Roderick MacFarquhar (political science, Harvard), Albert Park, Liz Perry, Mark Selden (history and sociology, Binghamton University), Ivan Szelenyi (sociology, Yale), Ran Tao (economics, Oxford), and Wen Tiejun (agricultural economics, People's University, Beijing). My thanks also to Winnie Yip, who did not attend the conference but agreed to provide a chapter on the rural-urban gap in access to medical care and health, and to Fei-Ling Wang, who attended as a discussant and subsequently agreed to provide the chapter that concludes this volume. Finally, I want to thank Lei Guang for sharing with me another paper he had written on recent debates about rural problems in China, a paper I liked so much that I persuaded him to include it as a second chapter of his in this volume.

Finally, I want to thank Mary Quigley in the Department of Sociology for office assistance at every stage of both the conference and the preparation of this volume, and Kathleen McDermott and Kathi Drummy at Harvard University Press for shepherding the volume through the publication process.

One Country, Two Societies

MARTIN KING WHYTE

1 | The Paradoxes of Rural-Urban Inequality in Contemporary China

One Country, Two Societies: Rural-Urban Inequality in Contemporary China reports new research on the nature, extent, and sources of inequality between all things rural and urban in contemporary China. This introductory essay explains why this volume, and the conference on which it was based, may have something new and important to say about the nature of the world's most populous and dynamic society. Despite a substantial literature examining aspects of village life, cities, and rural-urban relations in China in both the Mao and the post-Mao eras, important myths, unexamined assumptions, and puzzles remain.[1]

It is now clear that the revolution led by Mao Zedong, which has conventionally been seen as dedicated to creating a more egalitarian social order, in actual practice created something very much akin to serfdom for the majority of Chinese citizens—the more than 80 percent of the population residing in rural villages who were effectively bound to the soil. Despite some weakening of the bondage and discrimination faced by rural residents in recent years, China is still struggling with the legacy of the system created during the 1950s. That a peasant army led by a son of the soil, Mao Zedong, established what might be called "socialist serfdom" for rural residents is one major paradox of the Chinese revolution. Before discussing the grounds for these claims and pondering how this situation came about and was sustained over time, it is worth considering how much this development varies from the dominant view of inequality trends in China since 1949.

Conventional Views on Inequality Trends in Post-1949 China

Arguably, China experienced two dramatic social revolutions after 1949: the socialist revolution launched by Mao Zedong and his colleagues during the 1950s and the market reforms and dismantling of most socialist institutions spearheaded by Mao's former lieutenant, Deng Xiaoping, after 1978. Both transitions involved fundamental reorganizations, with China's citizens buffeted and challenged by having to abandon and renounce former ways of life and embrace a new social order—socialism after 1955 and, after 1978, something that has come to look increasingly like capitalism.[2]

What impact did each of these social revolutions have on patterns of social inequality in China? The conventional discourse provides a straightforward answer to this question. In that discourse Mao and his colleagues came to power in 1949 dedicated to attacking the vast inequalities of the previous "feudal" society. Through class struggle and the creation of socialist institutions in the mid-1950s, they created a more egalitarian social order. Inequalities based on property ownership, ties to foreign countries and firms, and elite family backgrounds all disappeared in the face of a new socialist order in which everyone depended on some form of wage employment in state-run or state-controlled enterprises (including farmers in China's form of collectivized agriculture, with wages in the form of work points).

However, the struggle for social equality did not end there. After 1958, when Mao looked at the society that he and his colleagues had created (a creation based in large part on copying the socialist institutions of the Soviet Union), he became concerned that there was still too much social inequality and excessive individual and family pursuit of material gain (rather than of moral/political goals). In response to this concern, and with the way prepared by denunciations of "revisionism" in the USSR,[3] in 1966 Mao and his radical followers launched the Cultural Revolution. That mass campaign had many complexities and struggles, but one important aim was to transform Chinese society into an even more egalitarian society by eliminating many remaining material rewards and differentials.

As a result of Cultural Revolution changes, China in the closing years of Mao's rule appeared to be an extraordinarily egalitarian society, with minimal variation in styles of dress, housing quality, consumer possessions, and other indicators of social inequality. Indeed, some of the measures taken to combat and even reverse social inequality—such as the mobilization of millions of urban educated youths to settle in the countryside and take up farming in the decade after 1968 and the use of teams of ordinary workers and peasants to manage reopened schools and universities—were unprecedented. Thus in the conventional view the combination of the socialist transformation of the 1950s and the Cultural Revolution launched in 1966 made China an unusually egalitarian social order by the 1970s.

However, the conventional discourse also stresses that this energetic promotion of a more equal society had severe social and economic costs. Many of China's best and brightest were attacked and intimidated and, in many cases, even imprisoned or driven to suicide. At the same time, individuals who came from "revolutionary" social origins and were activist promoters of Mao's vision, or who were simply doggedly loyal to their radical political patrons, were given authority to make decisions and manage the lives of their fellow citizens. The pursuit of social equality thus interfered with and undermined the goals of promoting economic development, production efficiency, and professional competence. In other words, Chinese society of the late Mao era was "too equal" and thus fundamentally inequitable, in the sense that variations in skill, effort, and responsibility and thus in contributions to society were not properly acknowledged or rewarded.[4] If that was the case, then China's leaders, in their drive to kick-start the Chinese economy after Mao's death, had good reason to reverse gears and renounce Maoist egalitarianism, which is precisely what Deng Xiaoping and his colleagues proceeded to do after 1978.

In the conventional view, contemporary China's second social revolution, launched in 1978, has involved a fundamental shift in priorities from promoting social equality to promoting economic growth. In the pursuit of growth, socialist institutions have been dismantled, market coordination of economic activity has been promoted, foreign and domestic private ownership have once again been allowed, and in general any measures that are seen as promoting foreign direct investment, increasing export sales, and raising living standards are encouraged by the state, regardless of the impact such changes have on social inequality (at least until relatively recently).[5] One result of this second social revolution (counterrevolution?) is that China's economic growth since 1978 has been extraordinarily rapid, averaging close to 10 percent a year for three decades and producing dramatic improvements in the average living standards of Chinese citizens. However, at the same time China's society has gone from being unusually egalitarian to very unequal, with widening cleavages revealed not only in income distribution statistics[6] but also in dramatic differences in clothing, housing quality, access to medical care, vehicle ownership, and many other realms. So the conventional wisdom concludes that China's second social revolution, launched in 1978, transformed China once again into a very *unequal* society.

Although there is a certain amount of truth in this conventional account of patterns and trends in social inequality in post-1949 China, in some respects it is oversimplified and in others it is dead wrong. The conventional interpretation can be faulted for failing to examine and understand the nature of socialist institutions as well as for failing to fit the observed reality of trends in rural-urban inequality in China.

At the root of the conventional account are basic assumptions that are rarely questioned—assumptions that socialist institutions work to promote social equality even if they may not be very efficient economically and that, in contrast, market institutions tend to spawn increasing inequality even if they promote economic productivity. These are the assumptions used to justify welfare state programs in Western societies: capitalism by its nature generates more inequality than socialism, and it is the responsibility of governments to counteract and soften the inequalities that capitalist markets tend to generate—for example, by employing income redistribution and welfare benefits targeted at the poor and disadvantaged. These welfare state policies of the government help avoid the danger that rising inequalities generated by market competition will translate into social protests and even revolutionary challenges to the system. Almost by definition it is assumed that when the government intervenes, the goal is to reduce inequalities. In a society in which the government dominates all spheres of social life, as in China's centrally planned socialist system before 1978, it is therefore presumed that social equality would as a matter of course be promoted very systematically.

In reality, socialist institutions and the role of the state in a socialist society do not inevitably and everywhere foster increased equality.

Rather, state socialism means that differential property ownership and market forces are removed as the primary generators of social inequality and are replaced by the policies and priorities of the planners and bureaucratic decision makers of the centrally planned socialist system.[7] There are no substantial market forces operating to create inequality that have to be overridden by state actions. However, whether planners and other bureaucrats adopt and implement policies that foster equality or generate inequality depends on their goals, priorities, and perceptions of societal needs. The result may be that in a socialist society the state (that is, the bureaucratic arm of leaders and planners) may implement policies that *aggravate* rather than reduce existing social inequalities. So specifying the role of the socialist state in counteracting or aggravating any particular inequality is an empirical question, not something that can be assumed almost by definition (socialism = equality).[8]

The second major criticism of the conventional discourse is that it does not fit the reality of the changes over time in what has become China's foremost social cleavage—the rural-urban gap. What actually happened to China's rural residents was very different from the scenario of systematic promotion of equality under Mao, followed by widening inequality in the era of market reforms. As indicated at the beginning of this chapter, the actual trend looks much more like descent into serfdom for rural residents in the Mao era, with only partial liberation from those bonds in the reform era. In other words, in multiple ways the social status, mobility opportunities, ways of life, and even basic citizenship claims of China's rural versus urban residents diverged sharply under the socialist system that Mao and his colleagues created, producing a caste-like division that did not exist before 1949. Thus socialism in the Mao era produced a fundamental aggravation of the rural-urban cleavage, not the reduction implied by the conventional discourse. This is the first major paradox the present volume examines: how and why did China's rural revolutionaries in actual practice institutionalize such extreme forms of rural-urban inequality?

Since 1978, in China's second social revolution, the picture is more complicated. In some respects the rural-urban cleavage has been weakened and reduced, although in other respects it appears to have widened still further.[9] Most of the chapters in this volume are devoted to examining specific aspects of the rural-urban gap in the post-1978 period in order to draw conclusions about both the current size of this gap and whether it is widening or being reduced over time. What is clear, at least, is that the extraordinary status gulf between rural and urban residents in China—substantially a product of socialist policies and the practices and institutions of the Mao era—has left a legacy that has endured to the present. This persistence has occurred even as those socialist policies and institutions that were its basis have been increasingly dismantled and replaced by market distribution. Most theories lead us to expect that where markets are dominant, individuals should be hired and promoted primarily because of their education, talent, experience, and other personal qualities, rather than because of the ascribed social category to which they belong.[10] Yet there is still not much sign that rural origins are declining in salience in China today. This institutional inertia poses a second major paradox for the researchers represented in this volume: why has it been so difficult in the midst of so much other hectic change to dismantle the systems of urban privilege and rural discrimination that were originally embedded in China's form of socialism?

This inertia contrasts sharply with what happened to another very important caste-like division created by Mao-era socialism. All Chinese families were classified in the early 1950s into class-origin categories based on their economic standing, property, participation in labor, and other characteristics before 1949. These categories (for example, landlord, poor peasant, worker, capitalist) became the basis for a system of class-origin labels that persisted over time and were inherited in the male line. By the 1960s and 1970s a person's class label, by then based on past history rather than on current social position (for example, those with landlord labels had not owned any land since before 1953), had a strong influence over whether that person was favored or discriminated against in many spheres of life (access to higher education and good jobs, entry into the Party or the army, whom he or she could marry, and so on).[11] In 1979 China's reformers declared this system of class labels outmoded and harmful, required that they be removed from personnel dossiers and other identity documents, and forbid favoritism and discrimination based on class labels. Almost overnight this class-label caste system began to disappear from public consciousness, and it appears to play no significant role in influencing access to opportunities in China today.[12] Nothing comparable has occurred to China's rural-urban caste system. The present volume addresses the puzzles surrounding the durability of the caste-like division of China's rural and urban citizens in reform-era China in the midst of so much hectic change on other fronts.

The remainder of this chapter presents a brief summary of the specific policies and institutions that created something akin to "socialist serfdom" for rural residents in the Mao era, as well as a similarly brief overview of some of the important changes that have altered rural and urban social patterns and rural-urban relations in China since 1978. That discussion is followed by a brief overview of the chapters included in this volume.

The Mao Era: The Institutionalization of a Sharp Rural-Urban Cleavage

In late imperial times, and continuing after the 1911 revolution, China was anything but a "feudal" society. Although the economy was based primarily on agriculture, and more than 80 percent of China's population lived in rural areas, there were few legal or institutional barriers to geographical and social mobility. Poor villagers could and did leave their communities in droves to seek their fortunes in the cities or frontier areas, or even overseas, sending back a portion of their incomes as remittances if they could and perhaps returning periodically for family events and festivals. A system of household registration existed over the centuries, but its function was to keep track of where people lived, not to restrict their movement. A rural migrant who succeeded in finding employment and income in a city could readily submit to registration, rent or buy housing, and in general become a settled urbanite, although he or she could perhaps retain a strong sense of being an urbanite from a particular rural place of origin and therefore be different from neighbors from other places.[13] By the same token there were no aristocratic entitlements (outside of the imperial family before 1911) or caste barriers to prevent the rich from losing their fortunes, jobs, and/or land and descending into poverty and desperation. Given the high rates of upward and downward mobility and the relative freedom of movement of the Chinese population, over the centuries the status barrier between rural and urban residents was not large.

When the Chinese Communist Party (CCP) swept to national power in 1949, this general pattern did not change much at first. Indeed, the CCP victory produced a huge wave of rural-to-urban migration as the victorious revolutionary army, consisting largely of rural recruits and heretofore confined to relatively inhospitable rural base areas, moved into the cities and took over the management of all urban government offices and enterprises. Throughout much of the 1950s, substantial freedom of geographic and social mobility continued, with ambitious rural residents both recruited to, and, on their own accord, flooding into, cities to staff the growing offices and factories of the new socialist state. However, a series of interrelated institutional changes introduced in the years from 1953 to 1958 fundamentally changed this situation, replacing the relatively free movement of people with a regime of bureaucratic assignment and immobility that lasted until after Mao Zedong died in 1976.

From the outset China's revolutionary leaders were worried about their ability to control and manage China's cities, which until the late stages of China's civil war had been controlled by Chiang Kai-shek and the Kuomintang (and earlier by Japanese occupiers and by other foreign powers in treaty port concessions) and as such had been centers of private business; foreign influence; secret society penetration; and rampant crime, drug addiction, and other social problems—all forces threatening CCP rule. Free migration from the countryside into the cities was seen as aggravating the difficulties of bringing unruly Chinese cities under control. Thus even as the new government declared that Chinese citizens had the freedom to migrate and to live wherever they chose, they also criticized "blind" migration that did not serve national interests. They launched targeted attempts to pressure certain groups of migrants to return to the countryside.[14] Only after the socialist transformation of the economy and the introduction and elaboration of a range of additional control institutions during the 1953–1958 period was comprehensive control of individuals and their movements possible.

Just as the full control system was completed in 1958, it was massively disrupted by the launching of the Great Leap Forward, which led to active recruitment of an additional 20 million migrants from the countryside to fill the projected labor shortage of urban factories. After the collapse of the Leap, there ensued a mass deportation to the countryside on roughly the same scale. So it was only around 1960 that the "invisible walls" Mao and his colleagues had created around Chinese cities slammed shut their doors, effectively eliminating virtually all further rural-to-urban migration until the reform period.[15]

Despite their unfamiliarity with, and anxiety about, urban management when they came to power, and also despite the rural roots of the

Chinese revolution, Mao Zedong and his colleagues ended up pursuing a vision of socialism that was every bit as biased toward the cities and industrial development and against agriculture and rural residents as the versions promoted by Marx, Lenin, and Stalin before them.[16] The embodiment of socialism was seen, as in the Soviet Union, in large, vertically organized, capital-intensive industrial complexes located overwhelmingly in cities, complexes whose production and other activities were tightly controlled by the bureaucratic decisions of planners, with that control facilitated by the fact that Chinese socialism involved the elimination of markets not only for capital and land but also for labor. As in the USSR under Stalin, agriculture and the rural population were seen primarily as providing a source of extraction of resources to power industrial development in the cities.[17] The combination of a capital-intensive industrial development strategy and the failure of the Great Leap Forward convinced China's leaders that the labor power of rural residents, in the form of migration to take up urban jobs, was no longer needed or desirable in order to industrialize in the 1960s and 1970s. Indeed, during those years, efforts that were much more massive and successful than those undertaken during the 1950s resulted in millions of urbanites being mobilized to leave the cities and settle in the countryside—an unprecedented reverse mass migration.[18]

Because rural labor power was not needed to power urban industrialization, the countryside primarily served as a source of low-cost agricultural products to feed the urban population, with a portion also destined for export to earn foreign currency to finance technological acquisitions and other key activities. These strongly urban-biased economic priorities led to fundamentally different official distribution policies being adopted toward the cities and toward rural areas. Urban residents were provided with secure jobs, heavily subsidized housing, education, medical care, rationed allotments of food and consumer goods, and a broad range of benefits (such as paid maternity leave, disability pay, and retirement pensions), a combination one scholar refers to as the "urban public goods regime."[19]

Rural residents, in contrast, received no such guarantees, were outside of the state budget, and generally only received such compensation and benefits as their own labors and their local communities could provide.[20] Although direct taxes on farmers were relatively moderate, the obligation to meet grain procurement quotas and thus turn over a large share of the harvest to the state at artificially low, bureaucratically set (and relatively fixed) procurement prices—when combined with the rising cost of urban manufactured goods and even agricultural inputs, such as chemical fertilizer—produced a price differential "scissors problem" for residents in China's rural communes.[21] These price policies, combined with the minimal and generally declining rates of state investment in rural areas and in agriculture, produced a situation in which many rural communities remained mired in poverty throughout the socialist period.

The rural picture was not entirely bleak during the Mao period, because the state expended considerable effort to foster a variety of techniques and institutions designed to improve agricultural performance and presumably raise the incomes of rural residents. However, for the most part these efforts took the form of "unfunded mandates" to build reservoirs, plant new strains of crops, change local incentive systems used to reward farm labor efforts, and so forth, all in the spirit of "self-reliance," relying on local resources and labor power with minimal financial assistance from the state. Some of these initiatives from above, such as China's own version of the "green revolution" promoting new, higher-yielding strains of major grain crops, were quite successful, and state promotion of rural health care and village cooperative health insurance plans and rural education raised life spans and education levels very significantly during the socialist period. However, other interventions from above in agricultural affairs were less successful (as in the limits placed on crop diversification and free marketing of the 1970s) or even disastrous (as with the Great Leap Forward of 1958–1960 with its 30 million or more excess deaths, almost entirely a rural phenomenon). The result was a widening of the gap in incomes and standards of living between rural and urban areas over the course of the Mao era, not progress in pursuing the proclaimed goal of shrinking that gap. When local communities were not successful in their efforts at "bootstraps" agricultural development, residents had no alternative but to remain locked in poverty.[22]

In China before the 1950s and in other societies around the world, the traditional remedy for rural poverty is out-migration. Individuals flee poverty-stricken communities to seek better prospects elsewhere—in other villages, in the cities, and sometimes even abroad. If they are successful in gaining an economic foothold elsewhere, they may send back cash remittances that help family members and relatives left behind as well as foster chain out-migration to share new opportunities. In some cases they eventually return and buy farmland or start up a village business. The potential gains to poor villages from out-migration generally far outweigh the potential losses (the feared "brain drain"). In socialist China, this escape mechanism was effectively closed off after 1960. China's rural residents became bound to the soil through a combination of institutions centering on China's system of household registration—the *hukou* system about which so much will be said later in this volume.

As indicated earlier, the requirement starting as early as 1951 that urban households all be registered through the local police substation did not initially prevent rural-to-urban migration. However, increasingly after 1953 new registration regulations and edicts were passed aimed at making such migration more difficult, culminating in much tougher regulations promulgated in 1958, which essentially prohibited all voluntary, individually initiated migration to urban areas. Though the new rules were not effectively enforced until after the high tide of the Great Leap Forward, they put in place the institutions that made China's rural and urban sectors not simply areas of different economic priorities, but lower and higher castes.

At birth an individual inherited the household registration status of his or her mother (although China is a thoroughly patrilineal society by tradition)[23] and was classified as agricultural or nonagricultural, as well as by the level of city for anyone with nonagricultural *hukou*. Registration status was tied to a complex set of migration restrictions. Individuals could move voluntarily downward (to a smaller city or to a rural place) or horizontally (as when rural brides moved into the homes and villages of their grooms), but not upward. Permission to migrate upward in the system was granted only if the urban destination gave bureaucratic approval in advance, and that was granted only in relatively rare and special situations (for example, admission to an urban university, service in and then demobilization from the army as an officer,[24] or in a situation in which an urban factory had taken over rural land for plant expansion).

As noted earlier, urban registration status was not necessarily permanent, and over the years millions of urban residents were mobilized to leave and resettle in smaller cities or in the countryside, where their new rural registration status would normally prevent them from returning to their places of origin.[25] The burden of accommodating "rusticated" urbanites was an additional hardship for China's villages. Through such "rustication" mobilizations, China's cities could remain relatively lean demographically and economically, with virtually all able-bodied adults fully employed, as villages became places of concentration of the unemployed and underemployed.[26]

It was next to impossible for a determined rural resident who ignored the rules and wanted to move to the city without bureaucratic permission to do so. Other institutions (besides household registration and migration restrictions) that made China's caste system enforceable were extensive urban rationing and the associated bureaucratic controls over the essentials of life. After the 1950s, urban individuals were assigned to jobs in a bureaucratic fashion by local labor bureaus, rather than hired by firms and enterprises directly. Local urban registration status was a requirement, and most of those assigned were graduates of local middle schools and universities. There was no labor market, and no job fairs or personnel ads. In general, there was no way for someone from outside the city to compete for a job there.[27]

Urban housing was also bureaucratically controlled and allocated, again with no market for housing rental or purchase by the general public. After the 1950s individuals and families obtained access to housing predominantly through their work organizations, and urban housing was generally so cramped that informal rental to a migrant would have been out of the question even if it had been legal. Individuals and families obtained medical care through clinics and hospitals affiliated with their work organizations or neighborhoods, and they were referred to these clinics and hospitals when they needed medical treatment, making anything except emergency room care off-limits to those who lacked local urban registrations at a minimum. Needless to say, only those with urban *hukou* could enroll their children in city schools. In addition, many but not all basic food items and consumer goods were strictly rationed, so, again, at least a local urban registration and perhaps other qualifications were needed (along with cash) to make a purchase. The list varied somewhat from city to city and over time, but in general it was a long one, including grain and flour, cooking oil, pork, sugar, doufu, powdered milk, cotton cloth and garments, soap, "beehive coal" for heating and cooking, bicycles, certain furniture items, and so on. As a result of these extensive regulations and rationing, it was extraordinarily difficult for someone from a rural area, or even from a town or smaller city, to stay for any period of time in a Chinese city.[28] The rigidity of these institutional arrangements, and their strict enforcement, help to explain how the age-old remedy of flight from the village to seek opportunities in China's cities remained effectively closed for two decades after 1960.

The Reform Era: Plus Ça Change?

The story of China's dramatic about-face after Mao's death is now familiar. In what amounts to a new social revolution, many of the institutions and policies of China's socialist era were jettisoned after the reforms were launched in 1978, increasingly replaced by market distribution, openness to the outside world, and the frenzied pursuit of economic development along lines similar to what had occurred earlier in Japan, Taiwan, and South Korea. These reforms, many of them discussed in the chapters that follow, have changed many aspects of economic and social life in China's villages and cities and have altered the nature of the rural-urban relationship. However, some important institutions and practices have not changed, or have changed only around the margins, so that China entered the new millennium still sharply divided into two separate castes, rural and urban, with sharply different rights and opportunities in life.

The two most important institutional changes affecting China's rural residents and rural-urban relations are the de-collectivization of agriculture and the loosening of migration restrictions. The end of collective farming (in the period from 1978 to 1983) and the return to family farming through the household responsibility system mean that villagers are no longer under day-to-day command of local cadres and have much more autonomy to plan their economic activities and deploy their family labor power as needed. Provided that families meet their obligations to turn over the required grain procurements and agricultural taxes (the latter phased out recently, as noted below) on their contracted land, they can experiment with new crops, start a business, or even leave to seek work elsewhere. Although China's authorities have a strong preference that "elsewhere" be restricted to village factories or jobs in rural towns, migration to distant locales and large cities has now become common. Indeed, China's establishment starting in 1979 of Special Economic Zones along the coast, which rapidly grew into major urban centers, would not have been possible without large-scale migration from China's villages.

The new opportunities for rural people to augment or even replace reliance on growing grain with a much more diverse array of activities—growing specialized crops, engaging in handicrafts, marketing to consumers in towns and cities, starting a village business, working in a rural factory, or seeking wage employment in urban areas—helped spur an initial rapid improvement in rural incomes in the 1980s and a dramatic reduction in the proportion of rural residents mired in poverty. Indeed, the fact that China's rural reforms took off earlier than the reform of the urban economic system (generally in the late 1970s, rather than after 1984) contributed to a shrinking of the income gap between China's rural and urban residents during the first half of the 1980s (see Figure 5.1).[29]

However, some new developments of the reform era further disadvantaged China's villagers, rather than "liberating" them to pursue better opportunities. In particular, the rural health care system, which had done so much to foster better health and longer lives despite the material poverty of the Mao era, collapsed. Village cooperative medical insurance systems ceased to function in most villages, with rural residents having to seek medical care on a fee-for-service basis, and many of the rural paramedical personnel (the famous "barefoot doctors") and even some fully trained medical personnel left rural areas or left medicine entirely. Similarly, the financing, teaching, and attendance levels in rural schools were undermined by market reforms, leading to a sharp decline in the early 1980s in rural secondary school enrollments, with some recovery in later years. As a result, in terms of access to medical care and education, the gap between rural and urban widened in China in the early years of the reform period.[30]

The de-collectivization of agriculture, in combination with market reforms in the urban economy, unleashed waves of rural-to-urban migration in China, with estimates of the size of that country's "floating population" at any one time ranging from 80 million to 130 million or even many more. By the early 1990s urban rationing was phased out in the midst of the growing abundance available in urban markets, and Mao-era prohibitions against employing and renting housing to rural migrants were also relaxed. For individuals with agricultural household registrations, getting established and earning a living in a city went from being close to impossible to simply difficult.

In established large cities most of the migrants initially filled niches and took jobs that the urban population disdained (as the "three Ds," jobs that were dirty, difficult, and dangerous), particularly in construction, hauling, domestic service, and street-corner commerce.[31] However, the rapid growth of new factories and businesses, many of them based on foreign or private ownership, produced a rise in demand for labor across the board that could only be satisfied by hiring rural migrants. Most large cities in the 1980s and 1990s responded to the migrant "threat" by passing complex sets of regulations designed to prohibit migrants from being hired in particular occupations and in certain kinds of state enterprises and government agencies. However, the availability of masses of eager rural migrants, who were willing to work for modest wages and in many instances had had at least some secondary schooling, led urban firms to try to get around such regulations in order to hire migrants. After the mid-1990s, as reform of state enterprises accelerated and with large numbers of employees of such firms laid off or threatened with firm closure, rural migrants increasingly were competing with urban residents for employment opportunities.

Despite the expansion of opportunities for rural migrants in the cities, the situation is still very far from equal opportunity for all Chinese citizens. The key point is that the vast majority of rural migrants seeking opportunities in Chinese cities still retain their agricultural and nonlocal household registrations, no matter how long they have resided in an urban locale. There are some limited exceptions to this generalization. If rural residents manage to find stable employment and housing in low-level cities (at the township level starting in 1984 and at the county level after 1994), they can apply to obtain nonagricultural *hukou* status in that locale. Also, in some periods and in some cities, wealthy rural migrants willing to invest large sums in either businesses or housing purchases have been able to obtain "blue seal" local nonagricultural *hukou*.

In very recent times there have been experiments in a variety of Chinese cities to more fundamentally reform the *hukou*-based system of discriminatory access to urban facilities and opportunities, but, in general, throughout the reform period categorical discrimination based on the rural-urban cleavage has persisted. Indeed, some might say that the primary change since the Mao era is that there is now a *three*-caste system in China, rather than a two-caste system, with one's opportunities and treatment differing sharply for rural residents, rural-urban migrants, and urban *hukou* holders.[32]

As the intermediate caste in this conception, migrants have access to many more opportunities than the rural kin they leave behind. However, on many different fronts they are subject to inferior treatment and discrimination by both urban *hukou* holders and urban authorities, no matter how long they have been a de facto urban resident. For example, migrants not only tend to be concentrated in less desirable jobs with lower pay and benefits, but, even when they work in the same jobs as urban residents, they may not receive the same treatment. Indeed, many migrants have their wages docked so they can pay substantial fees and deposits to be hired in the first place, making them in effect bonded laborers until they can pay off their "debts." In addition, migrants have generally not been able to send their children to urban public schools unless they are willing to pay special high fees, requiring most to resort to inferior but less expensive private schools that cater to migrants (or have their children attend school back in their villages). From time to time, urban authorities have bulldozed suburban housing settlements catering to migrants, and they have also closed and padlocked some migrant schools as "substandard." Migrants are vulnerable to police arrest, detention, physical abuse, and deportation to their native village, particularly if they are not able to present acceptable proof of urban temporary registration and other identity documents.[33]

For their part many if not most urbanites continue to regard villagers as well as urban migrants as uncultured, backward, and, in general, less civilized than urbanites,[34] and they often blame migrants for the increasing congestion and crime they see around them. Given this institutionalized discrimination, it is not surprising that a number of scholarly studies note the striking parallels between the treatment of China's floating population and illegal immigrants in the United States and also with the former apartheid system in South Africa—ironic parallels given the fact that migrants are Chinese citizens supposedly entitled by their constitution to equal treatment.[35]

Nonetheless, compared with the Mao era, the present situation can be viewed as progress, because China's rural citizens are no longer bound to the soil like serfs. By the same token, however, it is somewhat misleading to view current migrants as a separate caste. The barriers facing a villager who wants to become a migrant are modest and mainly financial and logistical, rather than legal, but the barriers facing either villagers or migrants who want to become urban citizens remain much more substantial.[36] Viewed in this light, migrants and villagers are distinct subgroups or strata within China's subordinate rural caste, while urban citizens continue to occupy a higher caste position. At present it remains more accurate to view Chinese society as divided into two, rather than three, rural-urban castes.

Despite the many obstacles and forms of discrimination they face, migrants keep flooding out of the countryside and into China's urban areas. They constitute the great majority of the de facto population of newly arising export-oriented cities, such as Shenzhen in Guangdong. Even in China's established large cities, they often constitute 30 percent or more of the actual urban population at any one point in time. By the same token, the proportion of China's population residing in rural areas has declined sharply since the reforms were launched, from perhaps 80 percent at that time to roughly 65 percent or less today. If we focus on the nature of work rather than residence or *hukou* status, then early in the twenty-first century China reached a milestone, with less than half of the total labor force dependent on farming.[37]

It is generally acknowledged that migrants have played a vital role in the economic revitalization of the Chinese economy since 1978 and of the economies of Chinese cities in particular. Migrants provide vital labor and services on which urban *hukou* holders and enterprises have come to depend. The reestablishment of at least relatively free-flowing migration after a generation of urban closure also has the same potential benefits for rural villages and their remaining residents that characterized China in the 1950s and earlier—underemployed rural labor power and extra mouths to feed can be removed from poor villages, migrants can send cash remittances and gifts back to families left in the village, migrants can assist family members and others to join them in taking advantage of urban opportunities, and some proportion of migrants may return to the village with new skills and resources they may use to start businesses to enliven the local economy.[38]

Despite the positive gains unleashed by massive out-migration since the 1980s, China's villages continue to face serious development obstacles. State priorities still heavily favor urban and industrial development, with the lion's share of government investment funds expended in that direction, rather than on agriculture, despite the large size and pressing development needs of the rural sector. Similarly, the great preponderance of bank loans in China's state-directed banking system go to large industrial firms, and particularly to the remnants of China's once-dominant state-owned enterprises, with little credit available for either private business or farm investments. In addition, the way the government's administrative and financial policies in rural areas developed after 1978 accentuated some development difficulties faced by villages. Higher levels of government expected townships and villages to maintain and improve village public facilities, such as roads and schools, while meeting demanding targets in multiple areas, but without significant state funding— a continuation in altered form of the "unfunded mandate" approach of the Mao era. To pursue their ambitious agendas, many local governments levied a large number of local taxes and fees in order to meet such obligations (not to mention to pay the salaries of their growing staffs). The result was an aggravation of the peasant "burden problem" and rising rural discontent during the 1990s.[39]

There were, however, positive developments in the reform era with some potential for reducing the rural-urban gap. In an arguably more successful variant of the state's preference for "bootstraps" development with minimal state funding, rural residents and China generally profited from a boom in township and village enterprises (TVEs) after the early 1980s, with the number employed exceeding 120 million by the early 1990s. Local nonagricultural jobs in TVEs constituted the primary alternative to urban migration for villagers wanting to escape a life of farming. However, two features limited the impact of TVE development on rural economies. First, TVEs were very unevenly distributed, primarily concentrated in relatively prosperous rural areas along the coast and near sources of foreign capital and export markets, rather than in poor interior villages where alternative employment was most needed. Second, the changed economic climate in the 1990s made it much more difficult for TVEs to compete and grow, and total TVE employment has been fairly stagnant since, rising to only about 140 million in 2003. Nonetheless, some rural locales have benefited during the reform era from the availability of two important employment alternatives that were largely closed off during the collective era—rural industry[40] and migration to the cities—and despite the state's continuing bias toward urban development.

The changing opportunity structure after China's reforms were launched has enabled some rural families, and indeed entire rural villages, to become very prosperous. However, since the mid-1980s the most dynamic growth in the economy has been in urban areas, and the income gap between rural and urban residents has widened once again—to levels that are unusually large compared to other societies. (The size and sources of that gap early in the twenty-first century are the focus of the chapters in Part II of this book.) The combination of state favoritism toward cities and industry on the one hand, and the continuation of institutionalized discrimination toward China's rural citizens through the *hukou* system on the other hand, have apparently counteracted any tendency for market reforms to help close the rural-urban income gap. As a result of the reforms, the term "socialist serfdom" is clearly not applicable any longer, because rural residents are neither bound to the soil as they were in the commune system nor operating in an economic system organized on socialist principles. Nonetheless, both rural residents and rural migrants living in cities continue to suffer from institutionalized discrimination in China today.

Signs of Change? New Policy Initiatives in the Twenty-first Century

Although China's market reforms have not, to date, done much to reduce the disadvantages that come with being born in a village and bearing an agricultural household registration, two developments early in the new century provide a glimmer of hope that the institutions that have promoted such a sharp cleavage between rural and urban may eventually be reformed and the gap reduced. The first involves announced changes in state priorities in favor of rural areas, and the second involves increasing public discussion and debate about the injustices of the *hukou* system and experiments with that system's reform or even elimination. As it is too early to know whether these new initiatives will be followed by sufficient administrative implementation and new resources to finally overcome the wide cleavage between rural and urban that has characterized Chinese society since the 1950s, only a sketchy overview of some of the new initiatives will be presented here.

Conventional accounts of Chinese policy shifts are customarily framed in terms of the primary CCP leader in charge in different periods since the reforms were launched: Deng Xiaoping in 1978–1989 (but with considerable control and influence until his death in 1997),[41] Jiang Zemin in 1989–2002, and Hu Jintao since 2002. Already toward the close of the period of Jiang Zemin's leadership, the CCP decided to shift economic development priorities away from the previous primary emphasis on coastal development toward the interior, as symbolized by the campaign to

"Open up the West" launched in 2000. At around the same time, vigorous new efforts were made to address rural discontent arising from the excessive burden of local taxes and fees, efforts focused on instituting "tax for fee" reforms and providing increased state financial resources to rural communities.[42] These changes, combined with another round of increases in the procurement prices paid to farmers for their grain deliveries in the mid-1990s, were intended to redress China's widening regional and rural-urban income and consumption gaps.

Additional efforts along the same lines have characterized the team of CCP leader Hu Jintao and Premier Wen Jiabao, which assumed command after 2002. Hu has warned against the danger of social unrest—particularly in China's villages—and is promoting the slogan of China becoming a more "harmonious society." As part of this effort, beginning in 2004 the new leadership announced efforts to phase out agricultural land taxes and rural school tuition fees and to have the state provide an increased share of funding for rural schooling. At around the same time, experiments were launched to reintroduce a network of cooperative medical insurance systems in rural villages to reduce the barrier to obtaining treatment posed by medical fees. Also, various localities in China are experimenting with introducing a minimum income subsidy system for poor rural families (along the lines of the *dibao* system implemented earlier in Chinese cities),[43] as well as modest cash old-age payments to rural parents who do not have a grown son to support them.

The picture is not entirely upbeat, because rural areas in recent years have been wracked by rising protests stemming from another form of rural-urban tension—the confiscation of rural land for urban commercial and industrial development without adequate consultation and compensation. Indeed, an increasing number of rural residents are losing their land to encroaching cities and urban developers without obtaining the full urban citizenship and job opportunities they had been led to expect in return. Still, the range of recent policy initiatives designed to marginally shift priorities and resources toward China's rural areas seems a hopeful sign.

The other area of hopeful developments that could redress the rural-urban cleavage involves a rethinking of China's *hukou* system. Increasingly since the mid-1990s, Chinese authorities as well as intellectuals have recognized the fundamental unfairness of China's *hukou*-based caste system as well as the way in which this system interferes with the optimal mobilization of the talents and energies of all of China's citizens. Instances of abuse of both rural residents and urban migrants have been condemned in the media and on the Internet. Discussions have been aired about the need to promote a general sense of citizenship for all Chinese, regardless of where they were born. Regulations have been passed designed to give migrants equal treatment with urban *hukou*-holders in such realms as wages, fringe benefits, and schooling for their children. Some cities have repudiated their lists of proscribed industries and occupations, lists that had been used to restrict many urban jobs to those with urban *hukou*. Many localities have been experimenting with a variety of schemes designed to either make it easier for migrants to obtain permanent urban *hukou* or to reduce and eventually phase out some of the regulations designed to restrict access to urban resources and opportunities to natives of the city. At the time of this writing, these efforts are in an early stage and apparently still face stiff resistance from entrenched urban interests.[44] Indeed, in Chapter 15 Fei-Ling Wang points out that there have been multiple waves of proclaimed reforms designed to abolish the *hukou* system's injustices, each of which has passed with only minimal impact. There remains considerable fear that if *hukou* restrictions are removed, and particularly if this is done too suddenly, Chinese cities could be swamped by tidal waves of additional migration from rural areas, posing a serious threat to social and political stability. Nonetheless, the increasingly open debate and new initiatives launched in recent years provide some hope. Though the caste-like division the *hukou* system perpetuates has survived three decades of market reforms, perhaps its days are numbered.

Plan for the Volume

Most of the remaining chapters in this volume are revisions of papers presented at a conference held at the Fairbank Center for East Asian Research at Harvard University in October 2006. These chapters are organized into five parts, each of which is designed to address a particular aspect of the evolution and current operation of the rural-urban cleavage in contemporary China.

Part I provides broader contexts within which to place the subsequent chapters dealing with contemporary rural-urban relations in China. One issue is whether the relatively sharp, caste-like division between rural and urban Chinese today—a division that is the focus of the rest of the volume—should be regarded as a continuation of, or as a break with, the patterns of urban-rural relations in China in earlier centuries. Drawing on memoirs and other sources mostly from late imperial and Republican times, Hanchao Lu argues in Chapter 2 that most Chinese in earlier times tended to favor small towns and village life over large and congested cities and moved easily back and forth between the two. Hanchao Lu suggests that the current wide status gap between town and countryside is mainly a post-1949 development, a view echoed earlier in this chapter. A related issue is how to place China in the context of conceptions of citizenship and the development of citizenship rights in other societies. Chapter 3 by Wu Jieh-min is a thoughtful examination of the nature of China's *hukou* system through the lens of general theories of citizenship, offering observations about the prospects for, and obstacles to, extending full citizenship rights and treatment to rural residents and migrants.

Part II of the volume includes two chapters by economists that examine the size and trend of the difference in incomes between rural and urban residents in China in recent years. Although past research has documented the very large and widening gap in incomes between Chinese urbanites and villagers since the 1980s, there are contentious debates about many of the specifics, as well as about technical but important issues, such as how to measure Chinese household income in the most meaningful way. These two chapters represent the state of the art by researchers who have been at the forefront of research on this topic. Both Chapter 4 by Terry Sicular, Yue Ximing, Björn Gustafsson, and Li Shi and Chapter 5 by Li Shi and Luo Chuliang utilize data from the China Household Income Project Surveys, national studies conducted in 1988, 1995, and 2002 that were designed to be more comprehensive and accurate than the income surveys regularly reported by China's National Statistics Bureau. However, the two chapters differ in the modifications that they introduce. The chapter by Sicular and colleagues takes into account regional variations in costs of living (generally higher in cities) and includes income figures for urban migrants (generally lower than the incomes of urban residents), adjustments that somewhat *reduce* estimates of the size of the urban-rural income gap in 2002. The Li and Luo chapter makes another kind of adjustment, including estimates of the income equivalent value of subsidies in kind enjoyed by some Chinese citizens (much higher for urban residents). This adjustment leads to an *enlarging* of the estimated gap between urban and rural incomes. The chapters in this part give us an improved picture of the sources and nature of the contemporary income gap between urban and rural China while sharpening the debate about the specifics.

Part III consists of four chapters designed to examine other aspects of rural-urban inequality besides household income. Chapter 6 by Emily Hannum, Meiyan Wang, and Jennifer Adams focuses on the gap in access to primary and secondary schooling between rural and urban China in recent times. In a similar analysis, Winnie Yip examines the gap in access to, and funding of, medical care between rural and urban China in recent years. In both the education and the health realms, substantial gaps remain, with minimal signs of progress toward rural-urban equality, although perhaps with more improvement in the health gap than in the schooling gap. In Chapter 8 Rachel Murphy examines the pattern of the spread of information technology into the Chinese countryside—is the "digital divide" between China's rural and urban residents growing or shrinking? In the realm she considers things look a little more hopeful. Although urban residents earlier had a huge advantage in access to wireless phones, the Internet, and other communications technologies, in recent times the rate of access in rural areas has been growing more rapidly than in urban areas. In Chapter 9 Li Limei and Li Si-ming focus on a different dimension of inequality—where people actually live (as opposed to where they are registered) in China's increasingly complex urban landscape and how household registration status, income, and other factors shape who lives in the most and least desirable neighborhoods. Together these four chapters help us move beyond the customary focus on income in discussing the contours of rural-urban inequality in China today.

Part IV includes four chapters that focus on the subjective side of rural-urban inequality in China and the experience of discrimination, particularly as felt by urban migrants. Wang Feng's chapter uses national survey data from 2004 to examine how fair or unfair urbanites, migrants, and rural residents believe current rural-urban inequalities and institutionalized preferences for those with urban *hukou* to be. Chapter 11 by Lei Guang and Fanmin Kong utilizes ingenious quasi-experimental data to compare and contrast the discrimination experienced both by migrants and by women in China's emerging urban labor markets. Arianne Gaetano's chapter covers the same terrain of discrimination experienced by migrants and women in Chinese cities today, but examined now through rich ethnographic information on the trials and tribulations of a pair of migrant sisters she interviewed and observed over several years and stints of fieldwork. The final chapter in this part, by Xiaojiang Hu and Miguel Salazar, takes us to the far periphery of China and examines the experience of Han Chinese migrant small business operators in Lhasa, Tibet. The subjects of their study, although members of the dominant Han ethnic group, nonetheless experience much the same low status and stigma experienced by migrants in more-developed Chinese cities. Apparently the disadvantages of being a migrant outweigh the advantages of being a member of the ruling ethnic group. The analysis by Hu and Salazar is especially poignant in view of the ethnic riots that broke out in Tibetan areas of China in March 2008, in which many Han Chinese small businesses and business operators were the targets of violence unleashed by angry protestors.

The final part of this volume, Part V, examines recent conceptual and policy debates within China regarding the status and treatment of rural residents and urban migrants. In his second appearance in this volume, Lei Guang discusses the politics that have led to the current low status of all things rural in China, concluding with some thoughts on what policy and institutional changes would be required to redress rural neglect and disadvantage. Fei-Ling Wang, the author of an important 2005 book-length study of the operation of China's *hukou* system,[45] provides a concluding chapter on the politics of changing *hukou* policy in the PRC in the last few years, with thoughts and some rather pessimistic conclusions on whether the sharp rural-urban cleavage that was institutionalized during the period of Mao's rule can be eliminated in the future.

Taken together, the chapters in this volume provide new ideas and at least partial answers to the two paradoxes and one speculation that originally motivated the conference at which most of them were initially presented:

- How did a revolutionary regime dedicated to the promotion of social equality create institutions after 1949 that in fact produced a form of "socialist serfdom" for rural residents, with a resulting extraordinarily large rural-urban status cleavage?
- Why have the institutions of China's caste system, a product of socialist institutions, not crumbled despite three decades of hectic

market reforms, leaving rural residents and urban migrants still severely disadvantaged and stigmatized?

• What are the signs that the extraordinarily durable system of institutionalized favoritism and discrimination embodied in China's *hukou* system may be finally weakening, producing hope that in the future the legacy of socialist serfdom will eventually be overcome?

1 | China's Rural-Urban Gap: Setting the Context

2 | Small-Town China
A Historical Perspective on Rural-Urban Relations

In contemporary China, where urban areas are significantly more advanced than rural areas and the rural-urban gap seems to be virtually unbridgeable, it is hard for people to imagine that for most of China's history, cities and towns were not seen as decisively a better place than the countryside in which to live or work. Scholars have pointed out that there was a rural-urban continuum in China prior to the mid-nineteenth century in which towns and countryside were harmoniously integrated. There was no sharp contrast or gap between city and country; particularly in the social and cultural realms, "urban" was not a category to be sharply distinguished from "rural."[1]

To be sure, differences between towns and countryside existed long before the modern age. As elsewhere in the world throughout human history, rural and urban residents at times felt at odds with each other. Despising peasants for their simplicity and ignorance and ridiculing country rustics has always been part of Chinese popular literature.[2] Likewise, distaste for towns and townspeople was also a notable part of the peasant mentality.[3] But the discrimination that came from both sides was part of a greater, multifaceted, and dynamic culture, and neither side was so strong in its prejudices that they constituted a deep cleavage between the rural and urban sectors of traditional Chinese life.

This age-old structure was broken by China's slow but inexorable industrialization in the late nineteenth and early twentieth centuries. As cities industrialized, they started to provide jobs, prospects for wealth, modern amenities that made daily life more convenient and comfortable, and, in some cases, political asylum on a scale that China had never seen before. Meanwhile, economic and social deterioration in the countryside in the late Qing period and early twentieth century widened the gap between cities and the countryside, and the influence of the West, which was associated essentially with large cities, left the countryside further behind. Furthermore, and ironically, the victory of the peasant-based Communist revolution did not help narrow the rural-urban gap but instead widened it. As is now common knowledge, the Maoist social and economic policies separated the rural and urban societies in the People's Republic to the extent that the nation had never seen before.

Straddling the rural-urban gulf were China's many small towns, which were, depending on one's perspective, both rural and urban, neither rural nor urban, or part rural and part urban. Scholars have devoted decades of research to the socioeconomic history of late imperial and modern China, and in the process they have extensively studied China's small towns, particularly those in Jiangnan.[4] Building on that research, this essay looks at China's small-town heritage from a cultural perspective. It seems to me that there was an inborn sentimental attachment among the Chinese elite—in particular, literati—to small-town life. In modern China there has been a sort of small-town mentality or complex that was once strongly reflected in the life and mentality of the elite. Situated in the intermediate zone between cities and countryside, small-town China was the site of, to paraphrase Mary Wright's words, the "last stand of Chinese conservatism."[5] The small-town mentality may have hindered the nation's modern development, but it helped to preserve some of the core values that cities lost in modernization.

What Are Small Towns?

The term "small town" as used in this chapter corresponds to the Chinese expression *xiao chengzhen,* which is a widely used term that cannot be easily defined. In general, towns immediately below the county level in China's administrative hierarchy are regarded as *zhen* ("town"). Garrisons of troops that were called *zhen* became the centers of military control in local areas no later than the seventh century. Because commanders trying to strengthen their control of supplies imbued some *zhen* with the functions of markets, the term *zhen* later often came to mean a non-administrative town where marketing was more active than in ordinary rural periodic markets or country fairs such as *xu* and *shi*.[6] Although the *zhen* officially was not an administrative unit, sometimes officials known as "town supervisors" (*jianzhen guan*) were stationed in *zhen* to ensure public safety and tax collection (such as collecting the tax on alcoholic beverages). The term *xiao chengzhen* refers primarily to these *zhen*-level communities or geographic areas. To use the Skinnerian model of urban hierarchy, the small towns under discussion can include the "intermediate markets," "central markets," and, in some cases, "local cities" (mostly, county seats). By that standard, China in the late nineteenth century had about eleven thousand small towns.[7]

Although county seats, unlike *zhen,* typically were surrounded by a wall and were more often regarded as a local city than a small town, some county seats were smaller in population and less developed than the towns under their jurisdiction.[8] For example, in the early twentieth century, of all thirteen towns (*zhen*) in Baoshan county, Jiangsu, only one had a population smaller than that of the county seat. The town of Luodian had almost five times as many people as Baoshan.[9] The town of Nanxun in Huzhou county, Zhejiang Province, was another example. Nanxun was a "gigantic town" (*juzhen*) with close to forty thousand residents in 1860 and was much more prosperous than the county seat of Huzhou, which gave rise to a folk saying in the region that "the city of Huzhou is not even half of the town of Nanxun."[10] As yet another example, as early as the late fourteenth century, the town of Tongli in Jiangsu Province used to pay more sales tax than the town of Wujiang, the county seat.[11] Therefore, an urban center that had obtained administrative status as a county seat was not necessarily excluded from the small-town category. County or prefecture seats that had a population of fewer than ten thousand were usually regarded as small towns.[12]

The word *zhen* is frequently used in the compounds *shizhen* (market town), *chengzhen* (city and town), and *xiangzhen* (rural town). The first two imply the urban nature of *zhen,* and the last refers to its rural background—together they indicate the dual nature of *zhen.* Sociologist Fei Xiaotong, China's leading authority on small towns, summarized the situation in these words:

> There exists a kind of social entity that is higher than rural communi-
> ties. These social entities mostly have a nonagricultural population. In
> terms of geography, population, economy, and environment, they were
> characteristically different from rural communities. At the same time,
> they maintain an indispensable relation with rural society. We use a
> common name to describe such social communities: small town.[13]

Obviously, Fei could not define small towns in any authoritative, statistically based way; rather, his description of small towns is based on what
was usually considered common sense or simply what was practical. This
reflects the dubious nature of the job of defining small towns. In fact, the
ambiguity itself is revealing. It tells us of the dualistic and transform-
able nature of small towns themselves, which is precisely what makes small
towns an interesting and important subject for studying China's rural-
urban relations.

In the urban hierarchy of the People's Republic, small towns are categorized as "administrative towns" (*jianzhizhen*). Essentially, the term
means that the town so designated is officially recognized as a "town."
But the standard of what qualifies as a "town" has continued to change
through the half of a century of the PRC's history, and the changes have
often been decided arbitrarily by the State Council based on the political
needs of the time. The most recent trend is to encourage the development of small towns as a way to absorb rural surplus labor and to promote
urbanization and economic development in general. Although there are
doubts about, and criticism of, overexpansion and, possibly, the emergence of a "bubble" of small-town development, the trend continues. By
the end of 2003, China had 19,811 administrative towns, with an average
population of 32,309 per town.[14] This means that the number of small
towns has doubled in the past century, and today the average size of a
town equals that of a "gigantic town" about a century ago.

Returning to the Small-Town Heartland

For more than half a century, Nanxun, a town on the northern border of
Zhejiang Province near Lake Tai, was a center of silk production. In the
late 1840s more than half of the silk exported from Shanghai was produced in Nanxun. After a brief setback during the Taiping Rebellion,
which devastated the region in the early 1860s, Nanxun bounced back to
prosperity. By the Republican period before 1934, well over one-third of

the silk exported through the port of Shanghai came from Nanxun.[15] As a result, tremendous wealth was concentrated in this small town. Local people used a figure of speech to describe and distinguish the magnitude of wealth among the town's rich families. A family that had more than five million silver dollars was called an "elephant," a family that had between one and five million dollars was called an "ox," and a family that had between a hundred thousand and a million dollars was called a "dog." By that standard, Nanxun had "Four Elephants, Eight Oxen, and Seventy-two Dogs," which became a widely known metaphor in the region. The actual number of wealthy families was larger than the folk saying conveyed.[16]

However, despite the extraordinary wealth that had accumulated there for half a century from the 1870s to the 1920s, Nanxun remained a small town. Its population, including surrounding villages, did not exceed forty thousand until the late 1980s, and the physical size of the town remained largely unchanged over the years, at about 3.9 km^2 (1.5 sq. mi.).[17] The Great Depression of the 1930s and the invention of nylon dramatically reduced the demand for silk, undercutting the foundation of Nanxun's economy. The town declined in the early 1930s, and the wars and the Communist revolution that followed further impeded its development. Nanxun became an obscure rural town and remained so for half a century. Only the recent economic reform brought back some degree of prosperity as a tourist town. In 1992, Nanxun had a population of forty-three thousand, only slightly more than its population a century before.[18]

Nanxun is not a unique case in the development of small towns. As Philip Huang has pointed out, "Silk, cotton, and market rice powered a dramatic growth of towns and cities in the Yangzi delta in the Ming and Qing."[19] Essentially, this rapid urbanization was characterized not by the growth of big cities, but the proliferation of small towns. The number of zhen-level small towns increased throughout the Jiangnan region from the late seventeenth century through the early twentieth century, but the size of each town remained small. There were many small towns in Jiangnan whose wealth came from trade that linked them to national and international markets.[20] Few of these towns, however, developed into cities or county seats.

Of course, a small town with a robust economy does not necessarily have to develop into a city or an administrative center. Because there were many small towns that reached a broad market far beyond the local region and that had a great potential to develop into a city but did not, we must ask why. The general answer, mostly from an economic perspective, is that small towns were essentially the place where agricultural crops and handicraft products were traded. Chinese historians often call small-town-based commercialization in late imperial China "sprouts of capitalism" (or "incipient capitalism") and debate why full-grown capitalism did not develop.[21] Obviously, to return to the case of Nanxun, the wealth of that town was essentially based on the silk trade; once the silk trade declined, so did the town. The same pattern applied to other so-called specialized towns, the prosperity of which was based mainly on a local product or the trade in a particular commodity such as silk, cotton, grain, or porcelain.[22] Also, as far as the lower Yangzi valley region was concerned, the rise of Shanghai and its special status as China's leading treaty port drew investment from its vicinity and impeded the development of the towns and cities elsewhere in the region.

There was also a cultural reason for the arrested development of small towns. At a time when the rural-urban gap was widening, small towns provided a haven for some conservative members of the elite who wished to maintain certain types of culture and lifestyle. In the small-town setting they continued to exercise traditional gentry-style leadership, to invest their capital in the agrarian sector of the economy, and to spend their wealth on luxurious lifestyles and cultural pursuits. There was little room for industrial development in this environment, and indeed, those who led local society had no intention of promoting that development.

At the end of the nineteenth century, more than half of China's urban population lived in small towns (including county seats with populations below ten thousand).[23] Although they were categorized as "urban," small-town residents were a kind of "marginal people" caught in the rural-urban divide. It is common knowledge among scholars that small towns always had what could be called a supporting rural area, which can be defined by the Skinnerian model of a hexagonal network or the Chinese notion that vividly depicts the villages that surround each small town as the "country feet" (xiangjiao) of the town.[24] Peasants in the surrounding area regarded the residents of the nearby small towns as "people on the streets" (jieshang ren)—that is, townspeople, as the word jie or street conveys an image of a paved, shop-lined road, such as were typically absent from Chinese villages. The residents of bigger cities, on the other hand, usually did not differentiate small-town residents from villagers, but rather lumped them together simply as "country folk" (xiangxia ren). As a sense of urban superiority became a common mind set in modern

China, sentiments about rural-urban differentiation grew. Small-town residents were subtle in how they distinguished themselves from others. In a recent survey of small towns conducted by a group of historians and sociologists from Zhejiang University, nearly all the small-town residents surveyed emphasized the difference between small towns and the countryside. They regarded themselves as "townspeople" (*zhenli ren* or *jieshang ren*), not "country people" (*xiangxia ren*). At the same time, they hesitated, or rather were too timid, to call themselves "city people" (*chengli ren*). This sentiment can be found in the early twentieth century as well.[25]

But one can hardly find such a sentiment among the elite. Being higher on the social ladder and financially secure, the gentry and non-gentry elite were much less concerned about issues of rural-urban identity than were the common people. In fact, as industrialized cities grew and society became increasingly differentiated into urban and rural communities, the dual nature of the small town provided a refuge for a large portion of the conservative elite. Cities were always more diverse than small towns, and in large cities only the ultra-powerful, such as high-ranking officials, or the truly lawless, such as gang bosses, could rule. Although the traditional Chinese literati or well-to-do merchants often felt like "small potatoes" in a big city or were at odds with life in a modern city, back home in the small-town setting they found a comfortable niche.

The central figures in small towns were local "great families" (*ju xing da zu*). These were families that had produced degree holders in China's civil examination system before it was abolished in 1905 and local magnates who gained prominence through commerce, the so-called gentry-merchants (*shenshang*).[26] As an elite group, Chinese gentry "concerned themselves with the promotion of the welfare and the protection of the interests of their respective home areas," where "their cultural leadership encompassed all the values of Confucian society but was also materially expressed" in various local actions.[27] Here the "home areas" were not necessarily small towns, but small towns provided a natural and convenient center for exercising local leadership. Prasenjit Duara has argued that there was a "cultural nexus of power" in rural China that integrated a variety of organizational systems and principles:

> These include hierarchies of a segmentary or nested type found, for instance, in the organization of lineages and markets. Hierarchies may be composed of territorial groupings whose membership is based on

an ascriptive right, as in certain temple organizations; or they may be formed by voluntary associations, such as water-control or merchant associations.[28]

These types of local power were more effectively exercised in a small-town setting than in scattered rural villages.

Purchasing farmland was the principal way for the wealthy to invest their capital. Until the early twentieth century, the main guide for Chinese merchants in reinvesting their capital was "get rich with the incidental [that is, commerce], but keep your wealth with the fundamental [that is, farmland]" *(yi mo zhi fu, yi ben shou zhi).*[29] One always bought land in or near one's hometown; it provided the foundation for one's ascent to the ranks of the local elite. Often, small businesses and commerce were operated by landlords in central market towns *(zhen)*, as were philanthropic works, which were a major responsibility, either voluntary or involuntary, of the local elite. But the most tangible institutions or establishments that significantly distinguished towns from their surrounding rural areas were what might be called "cultural enterprises," such as temples, memorial arches, private gardens, art collections, libraries, schools, and academies. These enterprises, which were usually lavish and sometimes extravagant, were one of the most consuming and capital-draining types of spending to be found.

In late imperial China, the wealthy were usually extravagant in their spending but not keen on reinvesting (except in purchasing farmland). In addition to spending money on promoting their social status in the Confucian-based value system, including degree purchasing, philanthropy, and education, successful merchants—regardless if they were big-city residents or small-town dwellers—spent their fortunes on luxurious lifestyles and cultural establishments. China's mainstream culture values thrift and prudence. A lesser-known but sometimes potent thought in Chinese culture is that consumption can produce wealth. Lu Ji, a sixteenth-century scholar who lived in Songjiang, Jiangsu Province, once boldly clamed, "I often observe broadly the trend of the world, noting that, in general, if a place is accustomed to extravagance, then the people there will find it easy to make a living, and if a place is accustomed to frugality, then the people there will find it difficult to make a living. Why? Because this is caused by the trend."[30] His contemporary, a Suzhou resident named Gu Gongxue, commented on luxurious lifestyles in Suzhou at the time: "The luxury of thousands of people supports the livelihood of thousands of others. Should the former become thrifty, the latter will be eliminated."[31] Such thoughts justified the custom of spending and helped promote spending. They were also the product of the luxurious lifestyles that prevailed in the Jiangnan region at the time.

But more important, the social milieu that valorized luxury sprang from a deep-rooted cultural value "to bring glory to one's ancestry" (yao zu yang zong) and "to return to one's hometown with honor" (rong gui gu li) or, in a more descriptive proverb that connotes the same thing, "to return to one's hometown in embroidered silken robes" (yi jin huan xiang). This kind of passion for family and hometown could be expressed in any geographical environment, but it seemed to be most evident in a small-town setting.

For instance, the merchants of Huizhou, one the most prominent merchant groups in late imperial China, still considered Huizhou as home and themselves as "wanderers," even after generations of doing business in Yangzhou and officially changing their households to counties in the Yangzhou region.[32] They sent countless silver dollars back to their hometowns in Huizhou to build houses, temples, tombs, memorial arches, and schools and academies, making the region one of China's richest in cultural establishments. Despite the devastating damage to the region during the Taiping Rebellion in the early 1860s and, more recently, the Cultural Revolution in the late 1960s, Huizhou remains renowned for its traditional homes built on once-bustling streets.[33] Another example involves the courtyard homes of central Shanxi Province, which were mainly the legacy of Jinshang ("Shanxi merchants") who endured the hardship of life in Mongolia for the sake of business, often for an entire lifetime, but kept building homes in their hometowns. Many of these homes were lavish. A late Qing residence in Qi County known as the Qiao Courtyard had 20 courtyards, 313 rooms, and 140 chimneys. Some 1,300 Ming-Qing homes in the region survive to this day.[34]

In the Yangzi delta, traditional two-story, blue-tiled whitewashed homes built by rivers and creeks were characteristic of most of the small towns in the region. Many of these residences were built by returned literati-gentry or non-gentry elite who found the comforts of home in a small-town setting. These homes have been the subject of nostalgia in recent years, and some of them have been carefully preserved. Contemporary poet Bai Hua admitted that every time he saw old houses in a small town, "I wanted to cry, to sing. . . . They were like a dream, an illusion."[35]

The place that inspired his comment was a Ming dynasty residential neighborhood in Nanxun known as the "Hall of a Hundred Rooms," which was a common residential complex initially built with funds provided by scholar-official Dong Fen (1510–1595), a Nanxun native who served as the Minister of Works in 1562. As a poet, Bai Hua might be overly sentimental about cultural relics, but the appeal of these old homes is obvious. Nanxun, like dozens of other small towns in Jiangnan, attracts thousands of visitors daily, primarily because of its old homes.[36]

More dreamlike establishments were not ordinary homes, but elegant gardens, memorial arches, and temples. Tobie Meyer-Fong's recent research on Yangzhou attempts to find "the values associated with the physical construction and symbolic meaning of buildings" in the early Qing, of which gardens were an essential part.[37] On a smaller scale, the same approach can be applied to small towns like Nanxun. Nanxun covered an area of merely 3.9 km² (1.5 sq. mi.), but it had 24 elegant gardens, all of which can be located even today. In the Qing period alone, 160 private mansions, including 16 gardens, were built in the town.[38] Three generations of the Liu family, starting from Liu Yong (1826–1899), who initiated the family fortune, spent four decades (1885–1924) building a 27-*mu* (4.5-acre) family garden called the Little Lotus Manor. The construction of this garden in a way symbolizes the small-town mentality of the gentry and non-gentry elite at this time of tremendous transition. The Lius were real estate tycoons and owned hundreds of alleyway-style homes (*lilong*) as well as magnificent buildings in some of the most desirable areas of Shanghai, where many of the family's members lived. Ultimately, however, the family saw the Little Lotus Manor as their real home. Indeed, the Liu family genealogy contains a statement that in the generations to come, anyone in the Liu family who removed a tree or even a rock from the premises would not be a good son.[39]

The Little Lotus Manor was just one of many cultural enterprises the Liu family built in Nanxun. The garden was linked to a much more valuable cultural edifice, the Jiaye Library established by Liu Chenggan (1882–1951), Liu Yong's grandson who inherited most of the family property. In 1924, Liu Chenggan spent 120,000 silver dollars to found the library. In the following eight years, he used virtually all of the family's fortune to purchase and print rare books and manuscripts, giving the library one of the best rare book collections in the country. On several occasions he sold an entire subdivision of houses in Shanghai in order to purchase books. Writer Lu Xun (1881–1936) called Liu a "foolish son of a wealthy family" but acknowledged that only such foolishness helped preserve some of China's most valuable classics, including works banned by imperial dynasties for political reasons.[40] Liu's case was extraordinary but not unique. It was common for small-town residents to build a huge collection of books and artworks. During the late Qing and early Republic periods, in Nanxun alone, there were at least three other major private libraries with extremely valuable collections. After 1949, they all became part of the special collections in China's major libraries.[41]

Outside a family's home, decorated arches were the most visible marks of the elite's sentiment of "returning to one's hometown with glories." These structures, some of which were erected under the order of the imperial house as an honor bestowed by the emperor, were often created to commemorate major donations and philanthropic works of local magnates. Nanxun's two most elaborate arches, erected in 1895 and 1908, respectively, with the permission of the throne, were earned by the Liu family for its many works of charity and contributions to state famine relief programs. Almost 26 km (16 miles) west of Nanxun, in the town of Wuxing, a street about .8 km long (less than half a mile) has about fifty arches that were erected with imperial permission. These were made of stone; most wooden decorated arches have not survived.[42]

Building bridges was another way for the elite to leave a long-lasting legacy. Well-to-do families saw contributing to road or bridge construction as an elite's typical community service or philanthropic endeavor. In the Jiangnan region, where waterways were abundant, bridges were essential to small towns, and they were mostly constructed with funds raised within the community, primarily donations from local gentry or wealthy families. Japanese scholar Kawakatsu Mamoru has researched 373 stone bridges in 25 small towns in Jiangnan and found the ratio between government-funded (guanjian) and community-funded (minjian) bridges was 13:153.[43] Nanxun alone had 111 community-funded bridges in the mid-nineteenth century, most of which were well constructed. In 1947 writer Xu Chi (1914–1996) undertook a survey in Nanxun when the town was very much in decline and found there were still 88 bridges gracefully standing in the town.[44]

"Faint vines, old trees, and crow teats; small bridges, flowing waterways, and ordinary homes—all in the twilight of a sunset." Poetry such as this is frequently quoted to describe the scenery of small towns in Jiangnan.[45] In this picture of lyric imagination, there is little room for industrial development. For generations, China's old gentry and non-gentry elite gave concrete expression to, and cherished, the poetic small-town image through their patronage.

Small Towns versus Shanghai

The elite's love of small towns was to some extent inherited by the new generations of literati in the twentieth century. The latter usually did not have the financial means to "return to one's hometown with glories," and most Republican-era writers were urban-based and their writings were urban—and often big-city—oriented. Yet small-town sentiment still lingered in the minds of new generations of Chinese intellectuals. The May Fourth generation writers held some paradoxical views about life in small-town Jiangnan in comparison to that in cosmopolitan Shanghai, a subject that may shed some light on what can be called China's small-town mentality.

Small towns in Jiangnan were often situated on a hillside, or by a river bank, or on a lakeshore. It was not unusual to see an entire town straddling waterways, with many bridges connecting various parts of the town. Old Ming-Qing-style houses and traditional lifestyles were preserved in these towns up to the Republican era, in contrast to the rapid changes and modernization in Shanghai since the late nineteenth century. Many of China's most prominent writers in the Republican era hailed from such small towns. As youths they went to Shanghai for education or employment. Later they found a home and a career in the city. Some of them lived in the city long enough to be called a "Shanghai writer." Yet they took a critical view of the city, saw themselves merely as sojourners in it, and kept a lifelong affection for the small towns from which they hailed but had never lived in for any length of time in adulthood. This was, of course, a type of nostalgia, a common sentiment as expressed in the maxim that "home is where the heart is." However, because such nostalgia and home-loving sentiment were frequently expressed together with cynicism and disdain for China's most modernized city, it went beyond simple nostalgia to represent a value or a choice.

Yu Dafu (1896–1945) lived, published, and gained his fame in Shanghai, yet he called the city "the devil's capital" and described city life as "perverted and decadent," characterized by "a scramble for money, open crime, a wasting of spirit, and a rampage of carnality."[46] As an escape, he built a house in Hangzhou near his hometown of Fuyang. His work and intellectual life, however, continued to be based in Shanghai. Yu's contemporary, artist and writer Feng Zikai (1898–1975), shared the same view. In Feng Zikai's mind old Shanghai was full of fraud and swindles and "human hearts there were vicious."[47] The viciousness of the city was vividly captured by a popular quip in his hometown, which Feng apparently did not think was much of an exaggeration: Be careful not to yawn in public in Shanghai because your tongue could be cut off in a second![48]

In contrast, Feng described rural Jiangnan as an earthly Eden, "full of natural beauty and an abundance of poetic sentiment and picturesque scenery." His hometown, a small market town called Shimenwan ("Stone Gate Turn") in Zhejiang Province, fit right into that environment:

> My home is located in nature-bestowed and poetic surroundings. On the turn of the Grand Canal, there is a branch. About two to three hundred steps from its bank, there is a dye-works called Feng the Wealthy. Inside the workshop there is an old house called the Hall of Virtue. Behind the Hall is the town's marketplace. Behind the marketplace is a flourishing mulberry field, in which small bridges, little creeks, big trees, and long corridors are scattered, and there I go fishing. . . . [49]

In 1933, after years of living in Shanghai, Hangzhou, and elsewhere, Feng Zikai built a traditional courtyard house in Shimenwan behind the Hall of Virtue and settled his whole family there. Feng claimed that he "spent a mere six thousand dollars to build that house, but if the First Emperor of Qin wanted to trade my house with his Afang Palace, or Shi Jilun [249–300 CE, known as the richest man of his time] proposed to exchange it with his Golden Garden, I would definitely decline their offers."[50] Feng named his dream home the Hall of Destiny (*Yuanyuan tang*) and later used the name for the titles of his three anthologies.

Even when Feng lived in Shanghai, he and his family retained much of a small-town lifestyle. This was not unusual, for despite Shanghai's much-celebrated and publicized modernity, most Shanghainese lived a sort of small-town life in crowded *lilong* (alleyway home).[51] But for Feng, Shanghai's diversity and the freedom to choose one's lifestyle were the attractions of living in the city. He recalled life in his alleyway home: "Here was a small world of your own and you were free to choose whatever lifestyle and customs to follow. . . . We were from Shimenwan, Zhejiang, so here we spoke the Shimenwan dialect, ate Shimenwan food, and lived a Shimenwan lifestyle as we pleased. Since we were actually hundreds of miles away from Shimenwan, this was truly incredible!"[52] Still, he gave up this imitation of hometown life in Shanghai in favor of actually living in Shimenwan. Feng's biographer, Geremie Barmé, called Feng "an artistic exile" who was "caught between the left and the right, neither a progressive nor a reactionary, and artistically both a neotraditionalist and a reformer."[53] At least in the sense of physical setting, Feng found a balance to these dichotomies in his small-town home.

Feng represented a type or a trend of his time. In his essay "Two Homes," writer Xia Mianzun (1886–1946) uses a conversation between two men to depict the bewildering situation of those who straddled the big city and the small town. Both men worked in a company in the city (implicitly, Shanghai) and had their immediate families with them, but in their hometowns they had another home where they had grown up; they were caught in the obligations of both. Their old homes were not shrinking but growing.

"Many people made a fortune in the city and built big houses in their [rural] hometowns," one man said. "We have two homes. The one in the city is in the nature of industrial and commercial society; the other in our hometown is in the nature of agrarian society. . . . I don't understand why my father built that big new house in our hometown just a year before his death. He had been a merchant, not a farmer, and he did not want me to learn farming either."

"This is a contradiction caused by the society. We live in a time of transition," the other man tried to comfort him. But he was no more confident about coping with the situation than his friend and ended the conversation (or the author ends the essay) in a helpless tone: "You know, I'll never sell my house in our hometown. I only say that this is a contradiction and I don't know what to do about it. I dare say that we're not the only persons who have felt the pain of this contradiction."[54]

In fact, Xia's essay was based on his own experience. Having lived in Shanghai for years and having served as the editor-in-chief of Kaiming Books, a major Shanghai-based publisher in the Republican era, Xia was one of many people who had a strong attachment to small-town life and a keen awareness of what he called the "conflicts between city life and the family-lineage system" that was essentially rural-based.[55] In 1921 he built a simple three-room house in his hometown of Shangyu, Zhejiang, on the shore of Lake White Horse and moved back with his whole family. Xia regarded the home building a big event in his life and later named his major anthology *Occasional Essays in a Simple Dwelling*.

Another Zhejiang native, writer Xu Chi (1914–1996), used the word *crystalline (shui jing jing)* sixty-six consecutive times in his description of his hometown Nanxun. His love and affection for the town were so profound that he titled his autobiography *Small Town Jiangnan*, despite the fact that he had left Nanxun for Shanghai at the age of sixteen and subsequently for most of his life had not lived in "small town Jiangnan." Xu's wife, Chen Song, was also a native of Nanxun. In a visit to Nanxun in 1947, after living in Shanghai for ten years, Xu recorded a little incident in the old house where they had lived:

> One day at midnight, Chen Song heard an unusual sound like something slithering on the ground. She sat up in bed and listened: in the darkness the sound seemed to be moving slowly and softly. When she turned on the kerosene lamp and got up from the bed, she stepped on something soft, which quickly disappeared. It was a big snake—its body was as big as the diameter of a rice bowl. It was believed that the serpent was a "home snake," and it must have had an inkling that Chen Song was back home and hence paid her a visit. . . . I was surprised to see that Chen Song, who was usually timid about such things, was not even the slightest bit scared about encountering a snake in the bedroom. On the contrary, she seemed quite delighted and told everyone: "I saw a home snake today. I saw this one before when I was a child."[56]

Chen's joyful reaction to the snake might be a bit eccentric, for even in a river town like Nanxun where serpents were ubiquitous, a snake in one's bedroom was usually considered a nuisance rather than a pleasure. But Chen Song's reaction to the snake was spontaneous, and the "home snake" folklore reflects a genuine home-loving sentiment. Such sentiment can lead to some blind faith in things local. For instance, Huizhou people who sojourned in Shanghai had a tradition that if one got beriberi in Shanghai, he or she needed to go back to Huizhou immediately. Once the person reached the upper valley of the Qiantang River near Huizhou, the swelling of the feet (the main symptom of the disease) would dissipate, and the beriberi would be cured all by itself. In 1907, Hu Shi (1891–1962), who was born in Shanghai but whose family hailed from Huizhou, caught beriberi in Shanghai; he immediately followed tradition and rushed back to his family's hometown. Hu is well known as one of the most Westernized individuals of twentieth-century China, yet he had not the slightest doubt about the efficacy of this hometown tradition.[57] Artist Zhu Qizhan (1892–1996) reported the exact same folk belief in his hometown, Liuhe, a small town only 48.28 km (30 miles) north of Shanghai. In 1909, when Zhu was a college student in Shanghai, he suffered from beriberi and dutifully went back to Liuhe for an "automatic" cure.[58]

Those with a Jiangnan background were not the only ones who were sentimental about small towns (or who disdained Shanghai); some "outsiders" who never lived in Jiangnan felt the same way. Liang Shiqiu (1903–1987), a native of Beijing who visited Jiangnan in 1923, had an interesting comment on Shanghai and Jiashan, a small county seat about 80.47 km (50 miles) southwest of Shanghai that had only two streets. Although an authentic urbanite—Liang grew up in a literati-bureaucratic family in Beijing and was at the time attending the American-sponsored Tsing-hua University—Liang felt like a country bumpkin on the streets of Shanghai, and the city's "overflowing Westernization" made him extremely uncomfortable and cynical. In comparison, his comments on Jiashan were amiable: "Although the two streets were narrow and simple, I walked there with ease, for I was sure that there were no killing machines like cars and trolleybuses running after me. The small stores and simple houses on the streets looked like medieval relics; they were unprogressive in a modern age. However, it was most obvious to me that the residents here in the town were mentally comfortable and [like Confucius said] 'happy for just being in it.'" Liang concludes that "although I felt Jiashan was inconvenient in terms of material life, spiritually I was much more contented there than I was in Shanghai."[59]

Liang was not xenophobic when he commented on the Westernization of Shanghai—indeed, only a few months after his seemingly unpleasant visit to Shanghai, he left China to study at Harvard. Rather, his comments reflect a conservative view that favored small-town life over big-city life, which was rather common among Chinese intellectuals in the early twentieth century. Lin Yutang (1895–1976), who lived in Shanghai and graduated from the city's prestigious Episcopalian St. John's University, called Shanghai a "terrible city, very terrible" and as proof listed twenty-three aspects in which it was "terrible."[60] In contrast, Lin described his hometown in rural southern Fujian as an absolute wonderland. Lin, who was arguably one of the most influential writers on Chinese culture in the West, asserted that the mountains and rivers in his hometown formed the foundation of his outlook on life. As a teenager, he traveled on a small paddled boat to Xiamen to attend school, a trip that took three days. Later, when steamboats became available, the trip was reduced to merely three hours. But Lin said he never regretted spending days on these trips in and out of his small hometown area, for they were, in his words, "the richest possession in my spiritual world."[61]

Small-town sentiment was not just common among Chinese intellectuals, but in a way it was also shared by Chinese politicians. The notion of "returning to one's hometown at an old age" (*gaolao huanxiang*) could be applied to anyone who retired from a career outside his or her native place and went back home to live in peace. More often than not, however, the notion was used in politics in conjunction with a step-down, a forced retirement, or a tactical retreat. In various stages in their lives, both Yuan Shikai (1859–1916) and Chiang Kai-shek (1887–1975), two of China's most dominant figures in the early twentieth century, returned to their small-town homes out of political considerations. Because both men later came back to politics, their return to their hometowns was seen as entirely tactical. However, given the complexity and brutality of modern Chinese politics, at their political nadir neither man could look forward to the future with much confidence. And in their nadir, both men quite spontaneously revealed a few traces of small-town-loving sentiment.

In 1909, Yuan Shikai was compelled by Prince Regent Zaifeng (1883–1951) to go back to his hometown of Zhangde, Henan Province. In less than three years, however, Yuan returned to politics to play a critical role in the 1911 Revolution and later proclaimed himself emperor in the notorious Hundred Days Restoration of 1916. His retirement in Zhangde has therefore been interpreted simply as the maneuver of a cunning politician. A picture of Yuan sitting on a small boat and draped in a fisherman's straw rain cape that was circulated at the time was interpreted as Yuan's attempt to fool his enemies in the imperial court.[62] But there is evidence that Yuan originally had prepared for an elongated, if not permanent, retirement in Zhangde. According to the memoir of Yuan's daughter, Jingxue, Yuan was genuinely relaxed at the beginning of his seclusion. He often asked his concubine to personally prepare his favorite dish, smoked fish. When autumn arrived, Yuan brought his sons and grandsons to raise crabs in a pond, letting the children feed the crabs sorghum and sesame seeds.[63]

Chiang Kai-shek also took his hometown as an ultimate refuge. In two of his most severe political crises, Chiang Kai-shek retreated to his hometown, Xikou, a scenic town of about two thousand people located twenty miles southwest of Ningbo. Immediately after the Xi'an incident of 1936, in which Marshal Zhang Xueliang (1901–2001) kidnapped Chiang to force him to form a united front against the Japanese, Chiang rested in Xikou for three months and put Zhang under house arrest there. Evidently, Chiang considered his hometown as the best sanctuary for healing after the dangerous turbulence in his political life and as the safest place to hold his renegade subordinate.[64] In January 1949, at the last stage of the civil war when Chiang stepped down from the presidency, he again withdrew to Xikou. Chiang's life there resembles Yuan Shikai's pastoral retreat in Zhangde some forty years earlier:

> The sixty-two-year-old Generalissimo walked in the countryside, watching the birds and relishing the peace. His son cooked taro which he enjoyed. "He often looked at his grandson and smiled," Ching-kuo [Chiang's son] recorded in his diary. At the Lunar New Year at the end of January, Chiang paid tribute to his ancestors at the family temple. In the evening, lantern parties with dragon dances were held in his honour.[65]

One of his closest retinue also noted that Chiang ordered his favorite hometown food, preserved dried Chinese cabbages stewed with pork. For an entire week, he relished that simple dish at every meal.[66]

Anecdotes like these may be considered trivial, but they are intriguingly similar, and the similarity indicates a common mentality. The retirees' homes were not in a big city nor in a small village but in between, in a small town. This seemed to have become a pattern in Chinese politics. For example, despite their boldly claimed break with traditional culture, the Communists did not abandon the small hometown tradition, but took it as an unquestionable birthright. Both Peng Dehuai (1889–1974) and Liu Shaoqi (1898–1969), when they were in serious political troubles with Mao and were on the verge of being purged, asked to return to their small hometown as a solution to the discord. In both instances, however, the requests were rejected. Judging from what Yuan and Chiang had done in their seclusion, banishment of Peng and Liu to their hometown was simply considered too benign a treatment of the condemned leaders in the Maoist political environment. But their wish to return home indicates that despite their lifelong career as revolutionaries struggling to overthrow the "old society," these veteran Communists indeed did not reject the back-to-hometown tradition. It was reported that on September 12, 1975, Zhou Enlai (1898–1976), on his deathbed, told his wife, Deng Yingchao (1904–1992): "I am leaving soon . . . very soon. After that, you should, number one, not involve yourself in politics. Do not stay in Zhongnanhai, do not stay in Beijing. Go back to your hometown. . . . Remember this, be sure to remember this, so I can rest in peace."[67] Zhou's words had a practical basis: he was referring to Deng's hometown Guangshan, a remote county seat at the foot of Mt. Dabie in Henan Province. Although Deng was not born in Guangshan, her family had lived there for generations. Deng's parents' and grandparents' home, a Qing-dynasty-style courtyard house of $2,000 \, m^2$ ($21,528 \, ft^2$) and more than thirty rooms, was still there for her should she decide to seek refuge.

Today the hometown sentiment is evident in a very different but still critically important theme in Chinese politics: corruption. *People's Daily* recently published an article on the widespread phenomenon of favoritism for one's hometown. Officially, this is regarded as part of China's rampant corruption, which has been a severe social and political problem since the late 1980s. But the public does not always equate hometown favoritism with corruption. Rather, it is seen as a credit to successful people who bestow benefits on their hometowns, not unlike the Western tradition of honoring alumni who donate to their alma mater. The *People's Daily* article admits that the "most worrisome fact" is that "some cadres do not regard this [hometown favoritism] as shameful. On the contrary, they regard it as glorious. Hometown people regard those who are able to get special treatment for the town as 'capable leaders' or 'good cadres.'"[68] Apparently, the age-old tradition of "returning to one's hometown with glories" is alive and well.

Does the Rural-Urban Continuum Continue?

Although both the late Qing reformists and the Nationalists had planned to incorporate the below-county-level townships into the official administrative system, it was the Communist regime that effectively projected state power down to the town and village level. After the establishment of the *hukou* system nationwide in early 1958, an official status as a town resident was a privilege that hundreds of millions of Chinese rural residents longed for but could not have. A town *hukou* carried with it, among other things, a cash-paying job and a secure, state-subsidized food ration, known as "commercial food grains" *(shangpin liang)*. These were denied to rural residents.

Because under the *hukou* system the state had the burden of subsidizing the food and other daily necessities of urban residents, there was an incentive to reduce the size of the urban population and thus ease the burden. Also, starting from the late 1950s, the radical policy of rural collectivization and the "unified purchasing and sale" policy had greatly decreased the need for commerce and hence the importance of small towns. Finally, Mao's strategic plan for preparing for a war that he thought was inevitable further validated the policy of discouraging urban development. The solution to all of these problems was mainly administrative: many small towns were reclassified as villages, and their residents automatically became "peasants." As early as 1955, the State Council reclassified 32 percent of China's administrative towns.[69] The policy of reducing the size of the urban population continued in the 1960s and 1970s. Between China's two censuses in 1953 and 1982, the number of small towns dropped 54 percent, from 5,400 to 2,900.[70] From 1961 to 1965 alone, China's small-town population decreased by more than 6 million. A few small towns that were chosen as headquarters of people's communes maintained a modicum of prosperity, but the level of prosperity in a great majority of small towns unmistakably declined. Prior to the economic reforms launched in late 1970s, run-down neighborhoods, poor infrastructure, empty store shelves, and enervated periodic markets were typical small-town scenes all across the country. The diminution of small towns was so widespread and obvious that one hardly needs statistics to verify it; suffice it to say that the average ratio of nonagricultural population in small towns to that in cities dropped by more than 50 percent between the two censuses.[71]

Three decades of frozen social mobility between villages and towns resulted in a massive division between rural and urban societies that China had never seen before.[72] However, the post-Mao reforms, starting from the countryside, have gradually reduced the gap. To be sure, there is still a rural-urban gap; in fact, it constitutes one of the most difficult crises facing China, which is the premise of this volume. But rural-to-urban mobility has greatly increased. Although during Mao's time, there was a virtually unbridgeable gulf between rural and urban societies in China, today the gap between the two is more a matter of the development of the rural society lagging behind that of the urban society. From a long-term historical perspective, economic development in China today is making the three decades of the absolute rural-urban division under Mao appear to be an interruptive break with the traditional rural-urban continuum.

Historian Linda Grove has meticulously documented a century of rural industrialization in a north China town, Gaoyang. Through the case study she has indicted a strong continuity of rural industrial practice and entrepreneurial spirit in twentieth-century China.[73] Rural industrialization in the late twentieth century, including both the commune-run small factories during Mao's time and the much more diversified small enterprises and businesses in the post-Mao era, has turned literally hundreds of millions of peasants into urbanites. Between 1985 and 2000, China added 210 million people to its urban population. In the period from 1993 to 2002, every year an average of 10 million peasants settled in small towns.[74] In 1998 the Third Plenary Session of the Fifteenth Central Committee of the CCP proclaimed that developing small towns is a "great strategy" in China's struggle for economic and social development. The Tenth Five-Year Plan, which was made public in March 2001, also claims that "the time for China's urbanization is maturing" and developing small towns is "key to the strategy of urbanization."[75] To underscore the significance of China's urban development, in recent years the Chinese media have quoted the 2001 Nobel Prize–winning economist Joseph Stiglitz (1943–): "The urbanization in China and the high-tech development in the United States will be the two keys to influence the human development in the 21st century deeply."[76]

Historians in general are not inclined to predict the future, nor are they expected to. But the past historical trajectory can help us speculate about future trends. At first glance, in today's high-stakes contest for a place in urban China, it does not seem right to say that a rural or small-town life is attractive. The spectacular evidence of China's fast-growing economy has been found mainly in urban areas, and it is there that hunger to share a piece of the economic pie is most insistent. Yet there are growing signs that indicate that China's urbanization may contribute to a resurgence of the rural-urban continuum in which small towns play a central role.

The current trend of urbanization is characterized not only by a large number of peasants migrating to big cities but also by the practice of "leaving the land without leaving one's hometown" *(li tu bu li xiang)*. Many farmers straddle villages and towns, taking nonagricultural jobs in a nearby town while keeping their homes and farmland in the village. These "peasants" frequently, if not daily, commute between the two, earning them the sobriquet of the "amphibious population" *(liangqi renkou)*. Their impact on the towns is such that it is now common to see small towns bustling during the day and empty at night. There are seasonal differences as well. During busy farming seasons, towns that are full of activity at other times of the year become virtually "empty." Meanwhile, industry also has moved directly to villages, blurring the boundary between rural and urban lives and creating a situation in which, as a new popular saying puts it, "Every village looks like a town, every town looks like a village."[77] Such a phenomenon is not unlike what sociologist Charles J. Galpin (1864–1947) described as "rurban" or the "rurbanism," in which "the open country is an element in the clustered town, and the town is a factor of the land, and the civilization, culture, and development of rural people are to be found in conjunction with town and small city, and not apart."[78]

A recent case study led by sociologist Andrew Walder of Zouping, a rural county in Shandong Province, found a dramatic increase of industry in the county, which grew from several hundred enterprises in 1980 to more than six thousand in the early 1990s, but the "rapid shift from agriculture to industry did not lead to the urbanization of the county: industry, instead, moved to the villages."[79] This trend has been more evident in the affluent coast of south China, which started the reform earlier. A case study of a village named Wanfeng in the Pearl River Delta found that although the 2,035 villagers were officially categorized as "peasants," the village was indeed an industrial town, with only 2 percent of its economy coming from agriculture. The various enterprises in Wanfeng employed about 40,000 workers from outside the area, many from other provinces. The village was indeed a sizable "town," with a good infrastructure, electricity, running water, and a bus line that operated along a major road through the village. The 6.8 km² (2.63 sq. mi.) of the village roads were cement-covered and tree-lined. A cinema with more than 1,000 seats, a public library with more than 15,000 titles, a park of more than 200 *mu* (33 acres), a hospital with operating rooms and 60 inpatient beds, a kindergarten with a capacity for 200 children, and a 17-gallery museum of village history were some of the amenities of the village. The village had not received a penny in government subsidies: whatever was in the village was a "natural" development based entirely on the initiative of villagers themselves.[80]

Under circumstances such as these, it is evident that an official town residence permit is now far less attractive than it was in the early stage of the reforms, not to mention in Mao's time. This is largely because once the reform toward a market economy was in full swing in the 1990s, peasants flocked to cities and towns to live and work on a long-term, if not "permanent," basis without having to worry much about obtaining daily essentials such as food and lodging. The rigid wall separating rural from urban Chinese was thereby breached. Today's rural migrants are no doubt still a disadvantaged group, with an inferior standard of living in virtually every category compared to that of regular urban residents, but now the issues that concern rural-to-urban migration are for the most part not about survival but about civil rights and inequality. At the lower level of migration—that is, peasants moving from villages to nearby small towns—the attractions of "urban" life have significantly faded, and the division between rural and urban residency is blurred. This is particularly noticeable in more developed areas. For instance, a 1999 survey conducted in a variety of small towns and villages near Shanghai garnered the following information on peasants' intention of moving into town and seeking an urban *hukou* status:

24 percent would have very much liked to have a nonagricultural *hukou*
12 percent would haved liked to have a nonagricultural *hukou* only if it is free
59 percent did not mind having either one
5 percent preferred an agricultural *hukou*[81]

What is most noteworthy about this survey is that the majority (59 percent) did not regard rural or urban residency as a concern, and there was even a group of people who preferred rural resident status. This indifference among peasants regarding *hukou* status was not limited to areas near Shanghai. About the same time that the survey was conducted, the town of

Daiyao in Xinghua, a rural county in Jiangsu Province, posted a note on the streets announcing that by paying 2,000 yuan local farmers could obtain a permanent town *hukou;* however, few people responded.[82]

The rapid growth of cities (in particular, large cities) in recent years has widened the rural-urban gap, a phenomenon that has been frequently noted. Indeed, to some extent most of the chapters in this volume discuss the issue of the rural-urban gap and inequality. A less-noted fact is that the widening rural-urban gap is largely a matter of the pace of development, that is, overall the countryside is lagging behind cities in making progress, rather than stagnating in an absolute sense. There is also a great regional variety in this matter. Most important, the reform has made rural-urban relationships fluid. Not only have millions of rural people made their way to the city—the majority have survived, and some have even thrived—but at the lower end of urban spectrum, in particular in more developed coastal areas, towns and villages have become fairly indistinguishable. From a historical perspective, the emerging trend that "every village looks like a town, every town looks like a village" may foretell the resurgence of the traditional pattern of a rural-urban continuum or, to use a trendy Chinese expression, *Chengxiang yitihua* (integration of city and countryside).[83]

Conclusions

Industrialization and the growth of modern cities in China led to the prevalence of the sense of urban superiority. The notion that the city is better than the countryside had long been a tradition, if not a cliché, in the West, but this notion started to stimulate the imagination of the common people in China only after the rise of treaty-port cities in the nineteenth century. For centuries Chinese peasants, who were, of course, the great majority of the population, saw cities as a place of taxation, lawsuits, crimes, and market rackets. In time, however, the obvious advantages that modern cities offered in employment, education, material comfort, and cultural life made cities attractive to common people and made living there seem a privilege.[84]

However, there have been reactions against urban life. The literati and other old elite groups frequently found large cities to be alienating and themselves uncomfortable expatriates. After whatever they might have managed to gain from the city—most commonly, wealth and literary fame—they tended to return to the small towns, where they could comfortably play the role of local leaders, exercise time-honored values, and preserve traditional culture. Although the mainstream culture that views big cities as superior and desirable overshadowed the sentimentality about small towns, the latter acted as a balance in modern China's increasing differentiation between urban and rural society.[85]

In a way this small-town sentiment has both universal appeal and practical application in the modern world. Ebenezer Howard's idea of a "garden city," among other schemes, aimed to build urban centers that preserve the beauty of nature and enhance social life while offering job opportunities.[86] To some extent this echoed China's small-town tradition, but the latter was more spontaneous and less prompted by utilitarian considerations (Howard's garden city scheme was motivated by the desire to improve the material conditions of the English working class through the provision of suitable homes and the building of new communities.) Even the target population Howard had in mind for his garden city, which was about thirty thousand people, resembles the size of an average Chinese *zhen* or small town.[87] More recently, the notion of Desakota, which describes a pattern of settlement that is neither urban nor rural but contains features of both, also dovetails with China's small-town tradition. The Indonesian-Malayan roots of the coined expression "desakota," which derived from the Bahasa Indonesian words for village *(desa)* and town *(kota)*, suggest the commonality of such a pattern in Asia.[88]

Today, the small-town sentiment of China's old gentry class and its like is largely gone, leaving only some lingering nostalgia for the "good old days." Nonetheless, recently small towns have gained new momentum. Since the early 1980s, the idea that small towns constitute a big issue *(xiao chengzhen, da wenti)* has been recognized in government economic policy making, and the number of officially categorized small towns *(jianzhizhen)* has increased dramatically, from 2,874 in 1980 to 19,780 in 2000. More than one-third of China's urban population now lives in these towns.[89] There are also signs that traditional culture and customs are vigorously resurging in small towns across the country.[90]

The small-town mentality of the literati elite in the past appears to be irrelevant to townspeople today, nearly all of whom are peasants (or former peasants) who are making a living in towns through nonagricultural activities. There is strong pressure to keep up with the tide of economic changes in daily life, and there is no room for idle sentimentality. But the practice of "leaving the land without leaving one's hometown" in the current rural-to-urban transition is more than just the result of carrying out the government goal of urbanizing the countryside without necessarily moving people into the city. Rather, it has its roots in history. In the current social milieu, the old gentry's mentality is remote and dated, but it may come back some day. A small but revealing sign was a retirement home called "Seniors' City" established in Nanxun in 1997. It attracted more than 140 retired people from Shanghai and overseas. These were well-to-do people who gave up their residences in the United States, Shanghai, and elsewhere in favor of a small-town home. As in old literati tradition, this retirement home, a 50-million-yuan establishment, is a haven for intellectuals. It has become the designated retreat for the Shanghai Higher Education Retirement Committee and one of China's top research institutions, Jiaotong University.[91]

History is not always about the past; it can also be a prologue. Like Howard's "garden city" scheme, which grew beyond its original concern for British workers and exerted a powerful influence on twentieth-century American middle-class suburban neighborhoods and the notion of green towns,[92] as China's urbanization advances, the old elitist small-town sentimentality, interrupted by the revolution and its chaos, will likely once again find its place in the lands outside big cities and reach the newly emerging Chinese middle class, which resides in that space between the city and the countryside.

3 | Rural Migrant Workers and China's Differential Citizenship

A Comparative Institutional Analysis

In March 2003 a young college-educated man from inland China, who worked in Guangzhou, was detained and tortured to death by local authorities. Personnel from a local detention and deportation station hunted down the victim, Sun Zhigang, on the streets of Guangzhou to face charges of failing to carry an ID card and temporary residence permit. The agents asserted that they were carrying out the state-sanctioned "Measures of Detaining and Repatriating Floating and Begging People in the Cities."[1] The local government covered up the incident until it was reported in the *Southern Metropolis News (Nanfang Dushi Bao)* a month later. Other news media rushed to follow the story, and heated discussions on the Internet accelerated the spread of the news. Because the victim was college educated and not an ordinary migrant worker, the tragic event outraged the nation and sent immediate shock waves to the central government. Amid the protests, three brave private lawyers turned in an appeal to the People's Congress requesting a review of the rules' constitutionality.[2] Within a few months, the State Council annulled the notorious measures and replaced them with a less severe "relief system." Detention and deportation stations across the country were replaced with shelter-style relief houses available to migrants who "choose to stay there."[3]

The death of Sun Zhigang and the central government's swift response revealed that discrimination against and mistreatment of migrants had become a grave social problem. During the post-Mao, open-door globalization era, migrants lived in the cities as pariahs or, at best, second-class citizens. The strict household registration (*hukou*) system was a keystone of social control in Mao's era and has remained a pillar of China's political system. The linking of *hukou* and citizenship rights has created tremendous problems for the country. Indeed, today migrants, mostly from rural areas, are still not considered to be citizens of places where they are employed. Migrants' civil rights at a basic level— including the right of movement (or migration) and residence, the right to free choice of employment, the right to place children in urban public schools, due process of law, and so on—are seriously infringed. In addition, the right to equal treatment in the distribution of welfare benefits in the cities where migrants work is also truncated. Although these problems have been widely reported since the early 1990s, the state has not been able to solve them. The truth is that all Chinese citizens are not treated equally despite the fact that the Chinese Constitution guarantees equal and universal protection of all citizens. In practice, citizens and citizen rights are categorized hierarchically according to birthplace, household registration, and employment status. In this chapter, this pattern of segmented and differentiated allocation of citizens' rights and entitlements will be referred to as *differential citizenship*.

Managing internal as well as international migration has always been awkward for developing nations. In the socialist world, the Chinese system of household registration parallels the *propiska* (residence permit system) in the former Soviet Union. The *propiska*, together with an "internal passport," was used to control the flow of migrants into central cities.[4] The purpose of the "managed migration"—embodying a system of differential resource allocation—is similar to what Dorothy Solinger has found in China, where the urban public goods regime is shored up by way of the *hukou* system.[5] The *hukou* is at the core of Chinese citizenship rights allocation, without which the state would not have been able to curb rural-to-urban migration; the *hukou* is used to maintain the urban unit (*danwei*) system, to extract agricultural surplus (especially during the high Maoist period), and to enforce rigorous birth control measures (in the reform era), among other policy goals.[6]

In Russia and several successor states of the Soviet Union, the *propiska* has been declared unconstitutional, but in fact it has continued to play an important role. The freedom of migration is seriously infringed by officials who utilize the *propiska* to control migrants while also making personal fortunes by collecting economic rents. Naturally, this has caused discrimination, bribery, extortion, illegal detention, and state violence.[7] Likewise, China's *hukou* system has persisted and evolved into an even more complicated matrix of governance during the market transition years. From a comparative perspective, the problems involving Chinese *hukou* are perhaps more intractable and tenacious than those caused by the *propiska*, because in China the huge number of migrants has an impact on almost every aspect of the protected urban regime and challenges the state's social control capacity on a national scale.

The evolution of the "Measures of Detaining and Repatriating" is a case in point. When the decree went into effect in 1982, its original purpose was to repatriate urban homeless citizens back to their hometowns in order to maintain a façade of clean, modern cities. However, as increasingly prosperous cities attracted a huge "floating population" from the countryside, these "peasant workers" injected dynamism into the urban economy while at the same time competing for urban public goods, bringing to a crisis the state's system of providing exclusive benefits to urban residents.[8] Thus, in 1991 the "Measures of Detaining and Repatriating" were extended to apply to newcomers. Migrants in the cities who did not have ID cards, temporary residence permits, or work permits were constantly at risk of being arrested, detained, and deported back to their home counties. In return for release, many detainees were forced to pay a variety of "fees" (actually ransoms), which local officials took to fill their "little coffers."[9] The migrants thus became victims of officials' predatory behavior and arbitrary state violence.

The central government is hardly unaware of the problems caused by the *hukou* system. Apparently, the government took advantage of the momentum of the Sun Zhigang incident to remove the "Measures of Detaining and Repatriating." As a matter of fact, since the 1990s the central government has tested various reform proposals. The state adopted measures loosening the rural-to-urban and transprovincial population flows and partially recognized peasant workers as a special form of workers who ought to be subject to the same state regulation and protection as "workers proper"—urban residents holding state-sector jobs—employed in urban units.[10] Ironically, "orderly floating," an official catch phrase since the late 1990s, coincided with soaring social contradictions, precipitated by the rural-urban divide, the keystone of China's dualistic governance and "emblem of citizenship."[11]

It is extremely difficult and politically dangerous for the center to change the household registration system in a fundamental way, for it is inter-locked with other institutions, such as social insurance and educational system, that define differential citizenship. In addition, localities are often keen on outwardly obeying the center's orders while secretly ignoring them if the orders run against their interests. Given their spatial constraints and limits to providing public goods, it is expected that the large cities would tend to support the existing rural-urban dualism. The cities want migrant labor but also try to preserve the hierarchy of rights and benefits that exclude migrants.

Even a minor change of policy could invite conflict and defiance. Local officials complained that the abolition of the "Measures of Detaining and Repatriating" was inimical to public security. The director of civil affairs in Guangdong Province embraced the center's goals:

> The relief house should be opened up, and iron doors and windows should be torn down. No traces of police detention stations or even prisons should be left. The internal management structure should be overhauled. The original detention, discipline, and deportation stations that were modeled after detention houses should be closed, in order to establish a genuine social relief system.[12]

However, he then proceeded to pose security issues:

> But some people think it is a hasty move to shift from a policy of detention and deportation to one of relief, and it is necessary to link public security up with detention and deportation. This mentality must be changed. . . . The new rules should have been proposed much earlier. The new policy is human-centered and is designed to protect citizens' personal freedom.[13]

The criticism above clearly shows the difficulties involved in reforming the governance of the migrant population. It is not easy to change the mentality and inertia of the bureaucracy, long relying on *hukou*-centered controls to preserve order and hierarchy. In the wake of Sun Zhigang's death, there have been repeated reports of imminent restructuring of the *hukou* system. In November 2005 the *New York Times* published a report headlined "China to Drop Urbanite-Peasant Legal Differences."[14] However, the story made it clear that the changes did not go as far as the headline suggested. It reported only that eleven provinces were experimenting with new measures for granting township and small city *hukou*. Similar stories about fundamental change in the *hukou* system have appeared every few years, but all of them have proved to be rumors or erroneous reports.[15]

The Chinese "Post-Speenhamland" Citizenship Transformation

Far from disappearing, the *hukou* system is being retooled for the present era of market liberalization and mobility. Since the late 1990s, the central government has put forward several measures designed to improve the status of peasant migrants in the cities without eliminating the dual structure. These are differentially implemented in the localities. This chapter considers whether the gap between the rights and treatments of various citizens' groups is widening or narrowing and whether differential citizenship is merely a short-term phenomenon of a transition economy.

The notion of modern citizenship is a good point of departure to explore these questions. In his classical statement, T. H. Marshall used British experience to illustrate modern citizen rights development under market capitalism: from civil rights in the eighteenth century, to political rights in the nineteenth century, finally arriving at social rights in the twentieth century.[16] Although he stated that this pattern of citizenship progression is "dictated by history even more clearly than by logic,"[17] it has been widely accepted that there is a universal logic of citizenship extension from civil to political to social rights along with capitalist development.[18]

However, Dorothy Solinger has observed the problem in the Chinese context: "[C]itizenship does not come easily to those outside the political community whose arrival coincides with deepening and unaccustomed marketization. . . . [C]apitalism, rather than promoting citizenship, may be antagonistic and detrimental to it, especially when it appears on the heels of a system of governmentally granted benefits."[19] The research presented in this chapter tries to ferret out new clues in China's development of citizenship to dialog with Solinger's findings and arguments.

In the following sections, I will define the concept of differential citizenship in contrast to that of universal citizenship and provide a mapping of differentiated citizen groups based on the concept. Next, I will analyze the citizen rights practices in China by comparing migrant groups to other groups, notably urban *hukou* holders. In doing so, I will borrow a few concepts from studies on international migration and apply them to the case of domestic migration. The conclusion, which begins with a re-visit of T. H. Marshall's classic thesis of the progression and limits to citizenship universalism, will consider several theoretical implications. The data I use in the article were mostly gathered from fieldwork and in-depth interviews, during 2004–2006, in various places in China, including the Pearl River Delta area, the Greater Shanghai area, and Southern Jiangsu Province.

To begin with the conclusions: First, there is no clear evidence of "devaluation of urban citizenship" in China even though a new group of "denizens" is emerging from the recent *hukou* system readjustments.[20] Second, since 1949, China has not merely experienced a "non-linear" development of citizenship rights, but apparently it has also experienced a non-Marshallian path of change, in which the *differentiating principle* serves as a driving force in lieu of the *universalizing principle* widely recognized in the context of typical market capitalist societies.

Finally, China's trajectory of citizenship transformation can be better construed as a pattern of post-Speenhamland transition under current waves of globalization. Pressures under globalization have further forged hierarchies of citizenship rights in China. The use of "post-Speenhamland transition" in this context is a heuristic device for historical-comparative understanding. In Karl Polanyi's groundbreaking work, *The Great Transformation*, the Speenhamland system of poor relief (installed in 1795) was construed as a last-ditch resistance against the advance of industrial capitalism.[21] The Speenhamland system guaranteed subsistence-level living to the dwellers on poor relief in the countryside. This system authorized a parish to administer relief within its territorial jurisdiction, which hindered the formation of a national labor market.[22] Its breakdown therefore facilitated the "free movement" of labor force to the cities and their "right to work" in the manufacturing sector based on a social relation of "contract" rather than "status."[23] Hence, England in the nineteenth century witnessed an epochal formation of a modern working class.[24]

In the context of the People's Republic of China (PRC), the commune system (established in 1958), before its complete breakdown in the early 1980s, strictly controlled rural-to-urban migration, paralleling the legacies of the manorial system and the Speenhamland regulation of the movement of labor. The Chinese commune institutions used to guarantee, at least in theory, a minimum livelihood to villagers who were bound to the soil in their hometowns. The rural-urban cleavage hinged on the severe regulation of *hukou* and internal migration; and the legacies of this dualism continue to shape the formation of the migrant working class to this day. In this way, the current post-Mao transformation in China can be interpreted as a case of post-Speenhamland transition in historical comparison.

Differential Citizenship in Action

The interlocking of *hukou* with citizenship rights is the most conspicuous element of China's citizenship system. Several historical-structural factors have contributed to the current system. First, China's rural-urban dualism was created in the 1950s when China collectivized agriculture, nationalized industry, and launched its first Five-Year Plan modeled on the Soviet Union. Dual governance of the population helped to control rural-to-urban migration and to extract agrarian surplus from rural areas by locking the peasants to the soil.[25] "The PRC *Hukou* Registration Statute" of 1958, in conjunction with other laws, formally initiated this dualism. But it totally collapsed during the Great Leap Forward (1958–1960) with vast unregulated urban migration. During this brief period, a large number of peasants entered the urban industrial sector, but at the end of the movement, they were repatriated back to the countryside. In the 1960s this policy disaster, combined with the horrendous famine, led the state to lock the dualistic system in place. Since the 1970s, the *hukou* system has been further utilized to enforce a stringent birth-control policy. In addition, widespread local protectionism throughout the country helps to exclude nonnatives from the urban public goods regime. The institutions and practices generated by differential citizenship embody a distinctive marriage of modernity and traditionalism, an expression of China's "communist neotraditionalism," as Andrew Walder phrased it.[26]

More than a half-century ago, the Chinese social anthropologist Fei Xiaotong coined the term *chaxu geju* (differential mode of association) to interpret social relationships in traditional China.[27] The concept of differential citizenship is relevant to Fei's articulation in two ways. First,

China traditionally lacked a system of citizenship granting universal and equal rights for all, as in a typical, modern, Western society. Second, a social relationship is traditionally defined by the distance to, and affiliations with, one's family line and relatives. A consequence of this mode of association is the ambiguity of one's rights and obligations. My approach differs from Fei's on one critical point: because a differential mode of association refers to the "traditional, peasant society," as opposed to "Western society," it suggests certain "pre-modern" and "pre-capitalist" social conditions, though not necessarily with a pejorative connotation.[28] Although I have been influenced by Fei's interpretation of Chinese culture, my understanding of differential citizenship is located in a state that has embarked on a modernization campaign to push rapid industrialization.[29] I emphasize the fact that the Communist ruling apparatus, a modernizing state, has played and continues to play a pivotal role in creating institutional inequality with its ever-increasing infrastructural power.[30] A "status" or "right" ascribed to an individual citizen or social group is superimposed by the state as well as being generated from indigenous social rules. Dual forces exert pressure on underprivileged persons and groups, so that the concept of differential citizenship does not rest simply on a spontaneous social order, as suggested in the notion of "association" by Fei's *chaxu geju* and his English translators. In short, the Communist regime established an institutionalized order that differentiated rural and urban citizen status along lines unseen before 1949.

Proponents of multiculturalism use the term "differentiated citizenship" to describe desirable, special treatments offered to disadvantaged citizen groups.[31] My usage of differential citizenship, in contrast, connotes a discriminating mechanism both inherent in the social system and imposed by the state. This definition is consistent with what Marshall observed long ago: "Status was not eliminated from the social system. *Differential status*, associated with class, function, and family, was replaced by the single uniform status of citizenship, which provided the foundation of equality on which the structure of inequality could be built."[32] The "Western" style of class inequality has emerged from an ideal type of unitary citizenship, whereas in today's China, class inequality is building on a non-single, nonuniform status of citizenship around the *hukou* system.

As defined above, the principle of differential citizenship takes root in both traditional and contemporary China. The institutionalized category of peasants under the commune system anticipated the emergence of migrant peasant workers (*nongmingong*, or *mingong* for short) during the reform era. *Mingong* literally means "private worker," in contrast to the urban *state*-employed worker.[33] In a sense, rural migrants in the reform era represent a new, invented social category, given its size and significance in the formation of a new working class, in contrast to the privileged state-sector workers under Mao's regime.[34]

Differential citizenship causes a multilayered mechanism in which rural migrant workers are situated at the bottom of the power structure in a locality. Table 3.1 illustrates the patterns of inequality generated by differential citizenship within a typical newly industrialized factory town. The analysis develops from my earlier fieldwork on "Shewei Village" (coded name) in Guangdong. Like many villages undergoing rapid growth and demographic changes in South and East China, Shewei had actually become an industrial town or small city by the mid-1990s.[35] There are three categories of inequality operating in the local citizenship regime based on three types of status distinction—urban vs. rural, cadres vs. non-cadres, and native residents vs. nonnative migrants—as shown on the top row of the table. A stratification of socioeconomic groups—cadres and elders, native residents, and migrants—is shown in the left columns. A mark is checked on the intersecting cell where a relative deprivation or differential treatment exists.

Table 3.1 Differential citizenship and hierarchies of status in China's factory town

		Relative positions of deprivation and disadvantages		
		(A) Cities vis-à-vis countryside	(B) Cadres vis-à-vis non-cadres	(C) Natives vis-à-vis nonnatives
Stratification	(1) Cadres and lineage elders	X		
	(2) Native villagers	X	X	
	(3) Migrant peasant workers	X	X	X

The first category (A) is the distinction of rural-urban residency through the *hukou* system, which rigorously regulates rural-to-urban migration and household registration and thus controls conditions of migration, labor, and rights in the cities. The second category (B) is a distinction among native villagers. The state delegates power to rural cadres for the management of collective assets; as a rule, the power is usually grasped by lineage elders or strong families with party ties in the villages. The third category of status differentiation (C) is embodied in the extremely unequal distribution of benefits between native and nonnative residents. This asymmetry is caused essentially by the notion of "collective ownership,"[36] a rural counterpart to the urban public goods provision regime. Outsiders without local *hukou* are deemed noncitizens of the village and are therefore ineligible for the benefits provided to natives. This is an important instance of how the collectivist institutions in the Mao period have influenced the market reform era.

Hence, three socioeconomic strata based on the above patterns of differential status can be identified. The first group includes cadres and lineage elders. Sitting at the top of the power hierarchy in the village, this group, disadvantaged only in comparison to the urban state sector, enjoys political and economic superiority through its control of village collective properties, including land and village enterprises. Many "rural entrepreneurs" have emerged through their superior power positions within the community.

A second stratum is composed of non-cadre native villagers. In most instances, they are the nominal "shareholders" of collective ownership and entitled to receive collective benefits, but they lack the power to control collective enterprises. In communities with large numbers of migrants, such as many Guangdong villages, villagers in this category have turned themselves into small landowners or "rentiers" or have left the soil to work as self-employed persons.

The migrant peasant workers occupy the lowest position in the newly industrialized town, just as they do in the city. Legally, they have to apply for a temporary residence permit from the public security bureau in order to be hired, a process usually handled through the factories that employ them. In fact, many migrant workers are not registered with the local authorities and become members of a "ghost population," partly because the factories can save a variety of "head taxes," including social insurance expenses, with the tacit permission of the officials.[37] Ironically, the widespread usage of the term "peasant worker" itself symbolizes an extreme form of "one nation, multiple systems" in the Chinese labor regime. The migrants' citizen rights are deprived in each of the three layers of the status differentiation. Furthermore, they are physically bound within the factory town by the *hukou* and the public security apparatus, working long hours at minimum wages and under inferior conditions.[38]

Migrants thus constitute a distinct category of subjects ruled by the state. They are caught in a predicament: they are neither rural nor urban, and neither peasants nor workers, but "peasant workers." The migrants are citizens *(gongmin)* of the PRC only when they stay in their native places, that is, the place of their *hukou* registration. Once they leave, they are transformed into "aliens" or, more accurately, "alien nationals."

It should be noted that all three groups fall under the official label of "peasant" in the *hukou* system. All the inequalities generated by the hierarchy of village citizenship and noncitizenship—discrimination, domination, and exploitation—occur within each category. The cadre peasants dominate the non-cadre peasant villagers; native peasants enjoy widespread rights and benefits unavailable to migrant peasant workers. Therefore, the differentiating principle of citizenship, which has evolved along with the emerging market economy, applies not only to the well-known *rural-urban divide*, but also to a *rural-rural divide*. This internal differentiation results in a status hierarchy. By contrast, the universalizing principle of citizenship, a touchstone of the Marshallian historical approach, appears at best feeble in China.

Table 3.2 examines the practices of differential citizenship in urban areas. In lieu of the usual dichotomy of urban citizen/noncitizen, I propose a spectrum ranging from urban citizen to "ghost worker" to capture the significant nuances between the different statuses. The wide range of noncitizens points to the fact that there is a complicated class stratification within the migrant population and that it is a long, bumpy road for a migrant to achieve full urban citizenship, a road that few travel.

Urban Citizens

The above analytical framework shows how the differentiating principle operates within an urban *hukou* regime. Only citizens with urban *hukou*

Table 3.2   Between citizen and ghost worker in China's urban citizenship regimes

Citizen	Denizen	Legal transient ↔	Ghost worker
Full membership	Partial membership	Limited membership	No membership
Native *hukou* holders, "naturalized" migrants	(a) Blue-seal *hukou* (*lanyin*) (b) Long-term residence permit holders (*juzhuzheng*)	Documented temporary residents	"Illegal," undocumented, or falsely registered migrants
	(c) Nonnatives temporarily employed in state units	(a) Migrant workers living in enclave-like factories (b) Self-employed workers living in slums, ghettos, or "city villages" (*chengzhongcun*) (c) "vagrants and beggars"	

are entitled to enjoy full urban membership. Native *hukou* holders typically, but not always, constitute the majority of the urban community. During the Mao era, urban citizenship was not a secure and stable status, because people could be sent down to the countryside for "reeducation" during political campaigns, returned to their villages to work during the Great Leap famine, or sent to the Third Front to contribute to the defense infrastructure in mountain and border areas. In each of these instances, they were stripped of their urban *hukou*.[39] Such arbitrary infringement of civil rights/*hukou* rights has been lessened in the reform era.

Under the current urban regime, only a small and select group of migrants can obtain full citizenship. These include those immigrants who are employed in urban units and allowed to transfer their *hukou* to the host city, people whose parents were sent down from the city to the countryside during the Cultural Revolution and now reclaim their urban membership as "returnees,"[40] and people with high skills or special talents who are eligible to be "naturalized" as full members. This group, along with the native residents, constitutes the core of the urban *hukou* regime.

Urban Denizens

A second tier of urban membership is primarily composed of (a) non-natives temporarily employed in the urban state units; (b) blue-seal *hukou* residents; and (c) long-term residence permit holders. I call them *denizens* with partial membership in the urban regime. The significance of the temporary state-sector employees, however, has been waning with the decline of the unit system and the privatization of many state enterprises. The blue-seal system was a product of the Jiang Zemin era, during which an expansionary financial policy and booming real estate market encouraged well-to-do migrants to buy private homes in the cities; the government awarded them a special *hukou* status called *lanyin* (blue seal). A blue-seal resident (similar to a permanent resident status in international migration) can apply for *luohu* (akin to "naturalization") after a certain period of residency.[41] The system operates like the "commercial immigration" programs in countries such as Canada, where wealthy migrants who invest a certain sum in real estate or enterprises are granted immigrant status. But it should be noted that the blue-seal *hukou* is effective only within the locality where it is issued. In this way, the freedom of migration that a blue-seal holder actually enjoys is limited.[42] Shanghai granted the blue seal to approximately forty-two thousand people between 1994 and 2001, among whom 88 percent acquired the status through purchase of real estate.[43] The central government curbed the blue-seal system in the early 2000s as the real estate bubble burst on a national scale and the blue seal was thought to add fuel to the overheated housing markets.[44] However, those who had already acquired the blue seal at that point were allowed to retain their status and apply for local *hukou*.[45]

A new long-term residence permit system (*juzhuzheng*) was put into effect in the early 2000s. This new policy has been implemented to varying degrees at the local government level, depending on a locality's population control target and capacity in public goods provision. Overall, the new system has refocused the granting of urban *hukou* from attracting economic capital to bringing in human capital. As a result, acquiring a full urban membership has become more difficult; being a *nouveau riche* is not sufficient to buy a *hukou* in the central cities under the blue-seal system. Take Shanghai, for example. The city launched a new residence permit policy to facilitate a "soft flow of talented people" in 2002. Eligible applicants were redefined as "persons with a college diploma or higher education, or persons with special talents."[46] According to one Shanghai scholar, as of September 2004 approximately fifty thousand people held residence permits.[47] The new system also paired with a reduction of quotas for naturalization. Only twenty-four thousand people were granted permanent *hukou* (citizens proper) in Shanghai in 2004; the quota was further reduced to twelve thousand in 2005, of which two thousand were reserved for returnees whose parents were intellectuals who had been sent down during the Cultural Revolution.[48] Notably, due to the rapid expansion of higher education in recent years, Shanghai produces more than thirty thousand college graduates annually; and since 1996, the government has no longer guaranteed urban employment positions to the graduates by assignment. Thus, one can imagine how intensely graduates, many of whom originate outside Shanghai, have been competing with one another for Shanghai *hukou*.

I have adopted the term *denizen* from international migration theory, which defines the word as an extrapolitical member of the community enjoying wide-ranging social and economic rights. In the original context, what distinguishes denizens from citizens is that the former do not or cannot participate in political life as the latter do; usually, there is no significant difference in the domain of civil and social rights.[49] However, in China, denizens are not granted the franchise even at the grassroots level. Another line separating denizens from citizens is the extent to which new immigrants can receive urban public goods. As a rule, social security coverage and welfare benefits are not as comprehensive for denizens as for citizens.

Compared with migrants on temporary residence status, denizens are *privileged noncitizens,* but the ubiquitous problem of policy uncertainty in China has made the status of denizens vulnerable and less desirable than that of their counterparts in Western Europe and North America. As one Shanghai resident noted:

> Even if you find a decent job in Shanghai and get the residence permit (*juzhuzheng*), you are still subject to review regularly, say every three to five years. And it is very likely that when the applicant gets old, the government would not approve the renewal and would force him to return to his hometown. Moreover, there are no compulsory provisions for medi-

cal insurance for them. It is left to the employer. . . . The policy is similar in Shenzhen, but more loosely implemented. All of the problems are caused by local protectionism.[50]

Based on the above findings, we conclude that Chinese urban denizens are at best partial members of the urban regime. Their status as privileged noncitizens is fluid, insecure, and vulnerable. They still have strong motivation to seek formal citizenship, however difficult, because citizen status alone guarantees permanent rights to live in the city. Therefore, in China's local communities we have not observed the phenomenon of "devaluation of (urban) citizenship," as documented in Europe and North America. Urban citizenship remains a precious, highly sought-after good.

Legal Transients—Documented Temporary Residents

Rural migrants occupy a substantial and growing proportion of the population in the developing coastal areas. Shangai is an example. At the end of 2005, the city hosted about 5.8 million migrants, with a 13.6-million permanent *hukou* population.[51] In other words, 30 percent of the city's total population were migrants. At the end of that same year, in Kunshan, Jiangsu Province, there were 655,000 citizens and 689,000 registered noncitizens;[52] more than half of the total population were migrants. In the manufacturing region of South China, where the need for laborers is great, the ratio runs much higher. In 2005 in Dongguan, Guangdong Province, 78 percent of the total 7.5-million population came from outside that province.[53] A year later, Shenzhen of Guangdong Province accommodated 6.5 million migrants, and the city's *hukou* residents were 1.9 million.[54] All of the above estimates are based on governmental statistics, which tend to underestimate the numbers of migrants.

By "legal transient," I mean a migrant with the status of documented temporary residence. This status is dissimilar to the urban denizen (blueseal or long-term residence permit holder) in several ways. First, unlike the more stable residence permit, temporary residence status is short-term, often under constant inspection, and requires regular renewal. Sun Zhigang fits into this category, for when he was arrested on the street for failure to carry an ID card, he had been working legally as a temporary resident in Guangzhou. This incident demonstrates that even a documented transient may face high risks and official abuse. Second, a denizen has better social security coverage and is entitled to more urban benefits than a temporary resident.

Third, a class line distinguishes many transients from denizens. Although denizens compose a tiny fraction of the emerging middle class, the bulk of transients constitute the new working class. Thus, a gulf exists between denizens and transients in terms of class position and living conditions. If denizens resemble quasi "free citizens," transients represent the *metics* in ancient Greece. Metics, originally referred to as "freed slaves," worked in the Greek polis without the right to become citizens. These non-citizens, or resident aliens, were exposed to dangers because they were a disenfranchised, alienated, and racially defined underclass.[55] Chinese migrant workers have almost all of the characteristics of the metics, except that they are not racially differentiated. Nonetheless, in principle Chinese urbanites attain urban citizenship on the basis of *jus sanguinis,* so this ethno-cultural foundation for granting urban *hukou,* in conjunction with the traditional pejorative attitude toward peasants, has made "urban Chinese generally view rural Chinese as ethnically distinct."[56]

Yet transients are not a uniform, homogenous social group. There is a fine line among them—the *legality* of their status as transients. Where and for whom a migrant works is not a good indicator of whether one is a "legal" dweller. Migrants may work in foreign- or domestic-owned factories; in the service sector as nannies, waiters, or salesclerks; or at construction sites. They may be self-employed, running small shops or restaurants. Similarly, where they find shelter is also not a good indicator of legal status. To simplify, migrants tend to live in two primary types of housing: (1) enclave-like factory dormitories or densely populated factory towns or (2) urban slums or ghettos, such as Zhejiangcun in Beijing or *mingong dayuan* (migrant slums) that are ubiquitous in many cities.[57] These categories do not include homeless "vagrants and beggars." An important line between "legal" and "illegal" is whether a migrant has registered with the host government for *temporary residence status* and filed related paperwork. A documented status of temporary residence usually did not make much difference to the migrants during the early years of the reform era, but it has been gaining significance since the late 1990s, when the central government began adopting policies that were intended to improve migrants' working and living conditions. Legal status is no longer trivial, because a documented status now gives access to certain benefits, however limited. For example, the new social insurance program is designed to provide migrants with retirement pensions, unemployment benefits, health care and injury insurance, and birth subsidies.[58] However, it should be noted that the social insurance benefits enjoyed by documented transients are significantly less than those enjoyed by denizens.

In addition, the right to move and work is better protected under temporary residence status. During the 1990s, complaints about excessive and irregular fees charged for securing documented status soared. Since the early 2000s, especially following the Sun Zhigang incident, the center has cracked down on official corruption tied to issuing temporary residence cards.[59] As early as 1999, the Guangdong Provincial People's Congress passed an act that allows a legal migrant to apply for a local permanent *hukou* after seven consecutive years of residence.[60] Yet, this apparently liberal provision has not attracted a single applicant from among Guangdong's huge migrant population. According to one Guangdong scholar, this is because "no migrant is aware of the existence of the law."[61] A more plausible explanation may be that the red tape facing such a permanent status seeker is too cumbersome and the fees too high.

Compulsory education for migrant children is another domain under reform. China's urban public education systems have long discriminated against migrant children. In the 1990s it was almost impossible for them to enter public schools. These children had to enroll in low-quality and poorly equipped private schools. During that period, the center experimented with ways of encouraging public school enrollment, but in vain. In 2003 the State Council sent local governments an "opinion" on migrant children's education, jointly issued by six central ministries. This document required host governments to allocate funds for migrant children's compulsory education with equal treatment.[62] In several respects, this new policy was unprecedented in trying to extend education rights to migrants. Most importantly, the policy charged the public schools, which now were no longer allowed to charge extra fees, with an obligation to admit migrant children as long as they held valid documents. However, in practice, today migrants are still reluctant to send their children to public schools. First, many schools continue to charge exorbitant fees for migrant children by creating ingenious categories that circumvent the center's new policy. Second, migrant parents and children are daunted by the prejudices of teachers, classmates, and classmates' parents. Third, there are difficulties with institutional coordination in China's complicated and segmented education system, which is based on the principle of territorial jurisdiction. In general, migrant children must return to their *hukou* hometowns for education beyond junior high school. At the same time, because textbooks at guest schools differ from those in their hometowns, parents fear this might add to the burden of preparing for senior high school entrance exams.[63]

In July 2008 the State Council sent down a new document, demanding that migrant-receiving local governments provide free and accessible compulsory education to all migrant children who are legally registered.[64] Yet, the actual effects of this new policy announcement need to be watched closely in the coming years.

Ghost Workers: Undocumented Migrants

Registered migrants belong to the group with limited urban membership and are supposedly covered with minimal social insurance, whereas undocumented migrants enjoy no urban membership rights. They are invisible on official dossiers and statistical yearbooks; they are not participants in the social security system; and they are truly mobile and fluid, as suggested by government classification of them as the "floating population." They are like "ghosts" haunting the skies above and the earth beneath China's booming cities.

Huge numbers of undocumented migrants live and work in the prosperous coastal cities. For instance, from 2004 to 2005, an estimated 2.4 million undocumented migrants[65] and 5.8 million documented migrants lived in Shanghai.[66] In Dongguan, fewer than half of the total migrant population (estimated at 5 to 6 million) was registered with local authorities between 2001 and 2002.[67] In Shenzhen, 36 percent of the 10 million migrants were unregistered in 2005.[68] It is no exaggeration to infer that ghost workers have played a major role in China's industrial development. The above figures clearly show the magnitude of the undocumented migrant population. They also point to the unreliability of using official statistical yearbooks to calculate the number of migrants.

Two points should be noted. First, the boundary between "legal" and "illegal" transients is not as clear-cut as that between transients in general and denizens. There is ample space for these two categories to overlap. The distinction between transients and denizens is primarily a class difference, although that between legal and illegal transients is more tactical than class-based. Many migrants deliberately misinform their employers or local authorities. In the same vein, employers and local officials often hide real numbers, for economic reasons or other motivations.[69]

Second, "illegal," undocumented, or falsely registered migrants are the most alienated of the urban alien nationals. Bereft of all state benefits, including social security, their status makes them vulnerable to merciless exploitation, bribery demands, and other abuse by officials. Table 3.3 provides a sketch of the differential citizenship rights and treatments in a local community. I call it a "Marshallian checklist" for historical as well as cross-societal comparison. In this Chinese context, the category of urban citizens is taken as a benchmark or ideal for comparison because it represents the best attainable treatment offered to Chinese citizens. Undocumented ghost workers sit at the bottom in every aspect of citizenship rights.

Dialectics of Pure Transiency

Given the above considerations, we should not overlook the Janus-faced situation of undocumented migrants. Certainly, illegal status may expose a migrant to imminent dangers, but, as is evident in Sun Zhigang's case, even a person with legal status could face fatal abuse. Bureaucracies can, of course, easily find fault with even legal transients. Therefore, transiency is essentially a fluid situation, rather than a fixed identity; and urban noncitizens may even take advantage of transiency under certain circumstances. First, ghost workers, hiding information from local authorities, can escape surveillance and corrupt demands. For example, many female migrants have shunned pregnancy tests. Being invisible can shield one from perils as well as deny one benefits.

Second, migrants may use fake IDs to enter the labor market. "ID services" (banzheng) are ubiquitous in China today, especially in urban slums or suburban factory towns that are densely populated by migrants. It is easy to obtain fake IDs, diplomas, certificates, or licenses, all of which a newcomer needs in order to pass the urban gate.

Third, the use of fake documents has had an important effect on social security. In field interviews, I often hear complaints by employers that migrant workers themselves do not want to participate in the social insurance program. This seems not entirely a pretense. Migrant informants explain: "If I can't stay here for a long time, I can't take the personal account

Table 3.3 A Marshallian checklist of differential citizenship rights in a local urban polity in China

	Citizen	Denizen	Legal transient	Ghost
Civil rights	Freedom of residence and occupation basically protected	Freedom of residence and occupation basically protected	Freedom of residence and occupation partially protected	Seriously deprived; exposed to official abuse
Political rights	Eligible to participate in grassroots—level elections	None	None	None
Social rights	Complete coverage of welfare benefits	Access to more or less complete coverage of welfare benefits	Partially covered with lesser benefits; urban public goods provided with higher prices	None

(of the retirement pension) with me when I leave the factory." In short, the insured's personal account does not migrate with the migrant, especially in the case of transprovincial movement.[70] Migrants in general do not trust the government because of policy uncertainty. Thus many decline insurance in order to save their portion of the contribution. Of course, this is welcomed by employers. Exploring deeper, I found that many uninsured workers used fake IDs or did not apply for temporary residence so they were by default excluded from the umbrella of the urban citizenship regime.

Above all, a central issue is how migrants enter the urban labor market and with what status. Ghost workers are elusive because, unlike the registered transients, they cannot be pinned down easily by the state surveillance apparatus. They are "unregulated" by the government and "really free," without even a temporary residence status. In this sense, they are purely transient—invisible, unruly, and ungovernable.

Theoretical Implications

It is time to bring T. H. Marshall back into the arena of domestic migration. Students of international migration have applied his ideas to immigration studies. Recently, a debate has grown about the applicability of his concepts to the current world system under globalization. For example, "immigration is one reason why Marshallian citizenship universalism is no longer plausible today."[71] In the literature of international migration, the contemporary Marshall is forced to deal with the problem of closure and exclusion by the citizenship mechanism across national borders. By contrast, the classical Marshall was concerned with the evolution of citizenship within the boundaries of a nation-state tackling the issue of "how citizenship, and other forces outside it, have been altering the pattern of social inequality."[72] Problems of social inequality and domestic migration in China make it necessary to revisit Marshall's ideas.

Marshall made the classical statement about the progression and limits of citizenship universalism more than a half-century ago. His original observation on British development of citizenship rights remains a valid point of reference for this research. Modern citizenship presupposed a new form of contract between free and equal subjects, which was a departure from feudal status institutions. Universalism has established itself as a principle, at least ideally within the liberal circle, for the advocacy of citizenship and democracy since the nineteenth century.

Citing H. S. Main, Marshall argued that in the early stage of modern citizenship development, the single uniform status of citizenship "was clearly an aid, and not a menace to, capitalism and the free-market economy, because it was dominated by civil rights, which confer the legal capacity to strive for the things one would like to possess but do not guarantee the possession of any of them."[73] Contrary to a common reading of Marshall, that he wholeheartedly espoused a unilinear, progressive perspective of citizenship development under the rise of market capitalism—from civil to political to social rights—Marshall *did* reflect on the problem of formalism in civil rights, especially freedom of speech and property rights. True, he recounted the development of citizenship from the seventeenth to the twentieth centuries in an orderly, even linear fashion.[74] Nevertheless, he unequivocally stated that "blatant inequalities are not due to defects in civil rights, but to *lack of social rights,* and social rights in the mid-nineteenth century were in the doldrums."[75] Lack of social rights makes civil rights a void doctrine. As yet, the lack of civil rights (particularly the *hukou*-centered infringements of rights) makes social rights unattainable to most Chinese migrant workers.

Valuable Urban Membership under Differential Citizenship

Drawing on Marshall's classical argument and the findings of my research, I propose several points with theoretical implications. First, what has distinguished China's development of modern citizenship from that prevailing in most Western countries is the *differentiating principle of citizen status and rights.* A single uniform status of citizenship did not exist in the Mao era.[76] Nor has it established itself during the subsequent market transition. On the contrary, Chinese capitalism has been thriving in the soil of differential citizenship and "a system of governmentally granted benefits," which in turn has aggravated social inequalities and systematic bias against underprivileged citizen groups. Solinger has observed that "through the mid-1990s it was official policy that 'citizens' not in possession of a local *hukou* were to be prevented from receiving urban public goods."[77] Although the state has tried to improve its infrastructural capacity in providing public goods, and more migrants are now granted limited access to the urban public goods regime, the structural inequality caused by the interlocking of *hukou* and citizenship has not changed in any fundamental way. In addition, the principle of territorial jurisdiction on *hukou* has continued to be an unrelenting force in local governance. The state is merely ameliorating the problem on the surface, leaving intact the fundamental pattern of inequality.

Therefore, I observe no clear indication of "urban citizenship devaluation" in China, in contrast to the postnational membership in the European context.[78] Urban citizenship, particularly in the major cities, is still a precious good under intense competition. As one Chinese sociologist points out:

> The *huji* [that is, *hukou*] system has been loosened since the 1980s, but as the phasing out of the old 'unit system' and consequently the retreat of its social integration function, the *huji* status is becoming more significant to the social members, particularly to the urban dwellers. Under the old unit system, [a small number of] agricultural *hukou* holders were allowed to enter the urban enterprises and acquire corresponding unit membership and occupational status. However, the current immigrants are basically excluded from the urban organizational system, and they enter the urban labor market as cheap laborers.[79]

Furthermore, the term "peasant worker" has become a distinct social category. It is reproducing itself in social practice and in public life so effectively as to create a "hereditary status effect"—the term "peasant worker's children" has been adopted as an official category in public policy.[80] This category serves to legitimize government differential treatment. Inequality thus reproduces itself through official categories.[81]

Non-Marshallian Path of Change and Beyond

Since the late 1990s, the central government has advocated a policy of "orderly floating" and has begun to recognize migrant workers as "a new form of labor army, emerging from China's advance toward open reform, industrialization, and urbanization," on the condition that their rural *hukou* remain unchanged.[82] At the same time, there have been changes in the urban regime on two fronts: On the one hand, urban citizens who were accustomed to privileged distribution of public goods now have to accept the discipline of the "market." The state has significantly withdrawn from the social welfare sphere and allowed market forces to march into it, particularly in housing and medical care. On the other hand, migrants who have long been excluded from the urban regime are now granted a few opportunities of becoming denizens or offered access to a shoddy version of the social security program. What is the significance of the state's retreat from welfare benefits in the state sector, alongside a strategy of piecemeal incorporation of nonurban citizens into social security? This question leads to another important observation on China in historical perspective.

During the Mao years, China experienced a non-Marshallian path of change. The urban sector was securely protected and controlled by a Soviet-style, quasi-Bismarckian welfare system. It guaranteed basic social rights to urbanites through the "unit system." Meanwhile, in the vast countryside, a minimum level of social security was arranged by the commune system. The "five guarantees" provided a pittance for the poorest.[83] But most relied on their own and family earnings, and retirement was out of the question. And the number and types of available welfare resources depended on the prosperity of the village as well as on local decisions about allocation. In both sectors, civil liberties were severely restricted and political participation primarily meant state mobilization for mass struggles against class enemies or for leap-forward movements.

The post-Mao transition has fashioned a slow, incremental, yet uncertain expansion of civil rights, particularly the rights to speak, work, and migrate. Note that many of these rights have not been sanctioned by the state, but have mostly been achieved by the rural population through unorganized collective actions such as the influx of migrant workers into townships and cities, which has forced the government to acquiesce or accommodate. The fragmented authoritarian regime is indeed on the defensive. Migrants are good at using the weapons of the weak. They know how to evade population control policies by taking advantage of the segmented structure of the territorial jurisdiction system. There is no doubt that the Chinese people now enjoy a measure of de facto freedom from the state unseen in the Mao era. However, the withering of the state welfare system and rampant market forces are making a twist of the progress in citizenship rights. Will the rise of a market economy in China eventually give birth to universalistic citizenship?

There is no clear sign that universal citizenship in China is following a linear development. Quite the contrary, differential patterns of citizenship appear to be creeping into, and even dovetailing with, the marketized urban regime. As Western history demonstrates, lack of social rights makes civil rights a void doctrine. Here is a paradox of the Chinese case: Under the multiple trends of uncertain, unsteady expansion of civil liberties under a seemingly resilient authoritarian regime,[84] rampant state-bureaucratic capitalism, and unwieldy globalized market forces, will China experience one more time the Marshallian path of change in human history, if the nation is able to overcome the legacies of differential citizenship?

I will try to clarify the problem from a historical-comparative perspective. The *hukou* problem lies at the heart of any meaningful transformation. The huge pressures of China's enormous population are an inescapable precondition, and China's demographic structure profoundly shapes the postsocialist context in distinctive ways. A brief comparison with Soviet Union/Russia will suffice.

In 1988, a few years before the Soviet Union disintegrated, the first sector (agriculture and forestry) constituted 20 percent of the total labor force; the second sector (industry and construction) 38 percent; and the third sector (transportation, communications, distribution, and other service jobs) 42 percent. In the same year, two-thirds of total population lived in towns and cities.[85] The Soviet Union had long become an industrialized and urbanized country before its successor states embarked on "capitalist revolution" in the early 1990s.

In comparison, in 1978, on the eve of China's market reform, the first sector constituted 70.5 percent of the labor force; the second sector 17.3 percent; and the third sector 12.2 percent. In 1982, 20.6 percent of total population lived in towns and cities. China was still an agrarian nation. After twenty-five years of market transition, 49 percent of the total labor force was still employed in agriculture in 2003; two years later, 43 percent of the total population lived in towns and cities.[86] In terms of urbanization, China in the late 1970s approximated the Soviet Union in 1917, the year of the Communist revolution; China today is slightly behind the level of Soviet urbanization in 1961. In terms of employment, China is still less industrialized than the Soviet Union was in 1989. The numbers tell us several things. First, although China and Russia are in the midst of similar postsocialist transitions, the structural characteristics respectively appear to be divergent. Russia faces an institutional transition from a socialist system to a capitalist system, whereas the Chinese state is simultaneously facing two issues: industrialization and urbanization, and an uncertain institutional transformation. Second, although both countries have encountered the problems of domestic migration and both have adopted similar controls, Chinese *hukou* reform is profoundly difficult from an institutional perspective. Third, Russia had formed a modern labor force before it joined the global capitalist game, but China is enduring an unprecedented, demographic shift in a squeezed time-space transformation. The issue of labor force formation in the postsocialist context leads to my final point.

China's Post-Speenhamland Transition under Globalization

It might be tempting to argue that the Chinese state's withdrawal from the welfare sphere parallels the current neoliberal developments of Western market economies and coincides with new waves of globalization. However, macro-historical comparisons suggest otherwise. Given China's structural characteristics, the nation is undergoing a process of modern working-class formation with semi-feudal characteristics, as the state-employed labor force steadily phases out and an army of rural migrant workers arises. If this interpretation is plausible, then it appears that China is striding on a path comparable to that of early Western capitalism, in which a Polanyian "fictitious labor market" is being manufactured on a national scale. Consequently, China's trajectory of citizenship transformation can be construed as a Chinese version of a post-Speenhamland transition under current waves of globalization. Over the last three decades, global restructuring in division of labor has made China the world's new "manufacturing center," which has required a huge cheap and disciplined labor force. The dismantling of the commune system and the loosened migration controls came in time to "free" the "socialist serfs" and shoveled them into the urban sector.[87]

Incorporation in the globalized market coincides with a discriminatory treatment of migrant workers under conditions of differential citizenship. The differentiating principle in the allocation of citizen rights, with the *hukou* system as its core, is used by central and local governments and beneficiaries of the urban regime as a defense against the demands of aspiring migrant workers. In essence, globalization helps forge hierarchies of citizenship rights in China.[88]

Therefore, differential citizenship is both a precondition and a byproduct of China's road to capitalism. A category of "alien nationals" must be created and contained in the *hukou* system to promote "primitive accumulation." Chinese peasants now have the right to move, entering the cities and becoming peasant workers, or metics, without adequate welfare protection. In the short run and on the system level, there seems no feasible way for the state to solve the *hukou* problem. This explains why the State Council unequivocally recognized the migrant workers as an important labor force but fell short of securing for them the full rights of urban citizens.[89]

China's current industrialization, arguably, is the second great world transformation since the English Industrial Revolution. Viewed through Marshallian eyes, advocating a single uniform status of citizenship is "clearly an aid, and not a menace to, [good] capitalism and the [genuinely] free-market economy."

II | China's Rural-Urban Income Gap

TERRY SICULAR
YUE XIMING
BJÖRN A. GUSTAFSSON
LI SHI

4 | How Large Is China's Rural-Urban Income Gap?

Studies of China's inequality almost universally find that the gap between urban and rural household incomes in China is large, has increased over time, and contributes substantially to overall inequality. According to most estimates, household per capita income in urban China is more than triple that in rural areas, giving China one of the highest urban-to-rural income ratios in the world. The size of the gap has received attention in the Chinese media and in official government and Communist Party reports, and concern about the gap underlies major policy initiatives, such as the "Build a Socialist New Countryside" campaign.[1]

Is such concern justified? This depends on the true magnitude and importance of China's rural-urban income gap. Measuring the income gap is difficult, and all existing estimates contain some biases. One difficulty is that available data do not adequately capture certain components of household income. An important component that is missing in most Chinese income data is housing-related income, which includes subsidies on publicly owned rental housing and the imputed rental value of owner-occupied housing. Housing-related income is relevant to measurement of China's rural-urban gap because it differs systematically between rural and urban areas; in addition, its contribution to the income gap has likely changed since the implementation of urban housing reforms in the mid-1990s.[2]

Another missing component is the value of household consumption of goods and services paid for or subsidized by the government. Although many types of government subsidies have been reduced or eliminated during the reform period, subsidies of public services such as education and health care continue. Some researchers argue that contributions to social insurance programs such as pension and medical insurance by the government, employers, and employees should also be counted in income, although there is some disagreement on this point. Government subsidies accrue disproportionately to urban residents, and so if they are not fully counted in income, China's rural-urban income gap will be understated.[3]

Bias also arises because of pricing. The costs of living in urban areas are higher than in rural areas. Consequently, estimates that do not correct for geographic price differences will overstate the size of the rural-urban income gap. Few past studies of inequality in China adjust for geographic differences in the cost of living. This is understandable, as systematic information on spatial price differences has been scarce.[4]

Most studies of China's rural-urban income gap are based on surveys that do not adequately capture unregistered rural migrants living in cities. Migrant income is on average lower than that of the registered urban population and higher than that of the rural population. Exclusion of migrants therefore causes overstatement of the urban-to-rural income ratio. Proper treatment of migrants in calculations of the income gap has become increasingly important as the reforms have allowed greater geographic mobility and migration. The treatment of migrants is also important from a conceptual standpoint, because migration can be a key mechanism for narrowing rural-urban income differentials.

With these considerations in mind, in this chapter we present new estimates of China's urban-to-rural income ratio and of the rural-urban income gap's contribution to overall inequality in China. For the analysis we have used data for 1995 and 2002 from the China Household Income Project (CHIP) surveys, which are large, have broad regional coverage, and provide a wide range of detailed information about households and individuals. These data are particularly useful for our purposes because they contain information on housing-related income components and, for 2002, include a sample of rural-to-urban migrants.

Using the CHIP data as a starting point, we have made three adjustments in the calculation of the urban-to-rural income ratio. First, we use a fuller measure of income that includes housing-related components of income. Second, we have adjusted for geographic differences in the cost of living. Third, using the CHIP migrant subsample, we have calculated estimates of the urban-to-rural income ratio that include migrants. Although these three adjustments do not eliminate all bias, they bring measurement of the gap closer to international best practice.[5] Along the way we have considered broader methodological issues related to the measurement of China's urban and migrant populations, and we discuss some of these issues below.

With these three adjustments, China's urban-to-rural income ratio is substantially reduced and markedly lower than the standard estimates. Urban income per capita is approximately double, rather than triple, that in rural areas. Furthermore, between 1995 and 2002 the urban-to-rural income ratio remained fairly constant, and the income gap's contribution to overall inequality rose only slightly. These results raise questions about the widely held perception that over time China's rural-urban income gap has become an increasingly serious problem.

Note that this volume's Chapter 5 provides alternative estimates of China's urban-to-rural income ratio that more fully incorporate government subsidies to households. In principle all government subsidies on the consumption of public services should be included in income, but due to difficulties measuring the value of these subsidies, most studies do not include, or only partially include, them. In addition to adjusting income for housing components of income and geographic price differences, as we do here, in Chapter 5 Li Shi and Luo Chuliang include in income their estimated values of government subsidies for public health and education. They also include contributions by employers and employees to pensions, medical insurance, providence funds, and certain other social insurance programs. Disagreement exists over whether such contributions should be counted as part of income; our estimates include the benefits from, but not the contributions to, such programs.[6] Estimates in the two chapters also differ in years of coverage and treatment of migrants. The analyses in these two chapters provide different but complementary information on China's rural-urban income gap.

Definitions and Data

The data used for our analysis come from the 1995 and 2002 rounds of the CHIP survey. The CHIP surveys were directed by a team of Chinese and international researchers under the auspices of the Institute of Economics of the Chinese Academy of Social Sciences. The research team oversaw the design of the survey instruments and sampling. The Household Survey Teams of the Chinese National Bureau of Statistics (NBS) carried out the survey. A detailed description of the survey and data are available elsewhere; here we highlight key features of the data that are relevant to our analysis.[7]

Regional coverage of the survey changed somewhat between 1995 and 2002. To ensure comparability, we use a subsample with the property that each provincial-level unit was present in the survey for both years. In our analysis the rural sample covers Anhui, Beijing, Gansu, Guangdong, Guizhou, Hebei, Henan, Hubei, Hunan, Liaoning, Jiangsu, Jiangxi, Jilin, Shaanxi, Shandong, Shanxi, Sichuan, Yunnan, and Zhejiang, and the urban sample covers Anhui, Beijing, Gansu, Guangdong, Henan, Hubei, Jiangsu, Liaoning, Shanxi, Sichuan, and Yunnan.[8]

The CHIP survey oversampled urban residents in 1995 and undersampled them in 2002, so their shares in the survey sample do not reflect the relative sizes of the urban and rural populations in China's total population. For calculations that combine the rural and urban samples, therefore, we use population shares based on China's Annual National Sample Survey on Population Changes as published in recent issues of the NBS *China Statistical Yearbook*. These population data are widely used and have the advantage that they count rural migrants resident in cities for six months or longer as part of the urban population.[9]

The 2002 CHIP survey includes a special sample of migrants, making it possible to calculate household per capita income for this important group in that year. Below we discuss the migrant sample and also discuss China's urban and migrant population statistics, as these are relevant to estimation of the rural-urban gap and inequality.

The target variable for this study is household per capita disposable income. Disposable income counts all forms of cash and in-kind income, including, for example, the value of farm products produced by rural households and retained for self-consumption, in-kind subsidies and transfers received by urban households, and earnings (both in cash and in kind) from assets such as real estate. Government taxes and fees are subtracted.[10]

Studies of income and inequality for China typically use household income data collected by the NBS in its annual urban and rural household socioeconomic surveys. The definition of income used in the NBS surveys captures most, but not all, components of disposable income. A notable weakness is its treatment of housing-related income. Housing-related income should include subsidies on subsidized rental housing occupied by the household, rent earnings from rental property owned by the household, and the imputed rental value of owner-occupied housing. The NBS household income data do not include housing subsidies and do not include imputed rental income from owner-occupied housing.[11]

The CHIP survey data contain information on these forms of income, making it possible to include them in our analysis. The measure of income used here, then, is equal to the NBS measure of household disposable income plus housing subsidies and imputed rent. Including these components makes our income numbers higher than those obtained using the NBS income measure. Including these components of income also widens the rural-urban income gap, because urban households on average have higher housing subsidies and own more valuable housing than rural households.

Our analysis treats the individual as the unit of analysis. The survey data, however, contain income for households, not for individuals. To obtain individual income, we follow common practice and simply divide household income by the number of household members. This approach abstracts from intra-household allocation issues.[12]

Price levels have changed over time and differentially among provinces and between rural and urban areas. The NBS publishes separate price indices for rural versus urban areas in each province. When comparing incomes across time, we use these price indices to convert incomes into constant prices. Using these price indices allows the deflation factors to capture price trends specific to urban and rural areas within and among provinces.

Prices can differ spatially at any point in time, and, in principle, analyses of inequality should adjust incomes to correct for geographic differences in the cost of living. Studies of China typically do not correct for geographic price differences because regional price data have not been available. Fortunately, recent work by Loren Brandt and Carsten A. Holz provides estimates of spatial price indices for China. We use their spatial price indices to control for differences in purchasing power among provinces and between urban and rural areas.

The Brandt-Holz spatial price indices have some limitations. One weakness is that their estimates of housing costs are based on the costs of construction materials, and the difference in the costs of construction materials between urban and rural areas is typically smaller than the difference in costs of housing services. Consequently, the Brandt-Holz indices likely understate the true price differential between urban and rural areas. Also, Brandt and Holz only have raw price data for 1990. They use a basket of consumption quantities for 1990 to calculate baseline spatial cost of living indices for 1990, and then they extrapolate to later years using the NBS provincial urban and rural consumer price indices. Here we are extrapolating a fairly long way, from 1990 to 2002.

Despite these limitations, the Brandt-Holz spatial price indices provide an opportunity to correct, albeit imperfectly, for geographic differences in the cost of living, and to understand how such corrections affect measurement of the urban-to-rural income ratio. In view of the limitations of these price indices, we present estimates calculated with and without geographic price adjustments. The differences between the two sets of estimates are substantial. This is not surprising as Brandt and Holz's numbers imply that in 1995 prices in urban areas were, on average, 36 percent higher, and in 2002 were 39 percent higher, than in rural areas.

The Rural-Urban Income Gap, Excluding Migrants

To show the impact of the different adjustments, we look at them sequentially. We begin with unadjusted estimates of the urban-to-rural income ratio. Table 4.1 gives average household per capita disposable income, with and without the housing components of income discussed above, for all of China and separately for urban and rural households. The statistics in this table are in current prices with no spatial price adjustments, and they do not include the migrant subsample, which will be discussed in "The Rural-Urban Gap, Including Migrants," later in this chapter.

The top half of Table 4.1 gives mean household per capita incomes calculated using the NBS definition, which excludes housing subsidies and imputed rent on owner-occupied housing. The bottom half gives incomes calculated using our broader definition of income, which includes these income components. Whether these income components are included or not, in both years the urban-to-rural income ratios in Table 4.1 are close to or exceed 3.

Adding in the housing-related income components increases incomes in both rural and urban areas, but more so in urban areas. Consequently,

Table 4.1 Mean household per capita disposable incomes and the
urban-to-rural income ratio (yuan, current prices)

	1995	2002
Without housing subsidies and imputed rent (NBS income definition)		
National	2,396	4,770
Urban	4,429	8,038
Rural	1,564	2,673
Ratio of urban to rural	2.83	3.01
With housing subsidies and imputed rent		
National	2,921	5,826
Urban	5,635	10,004
Rural	1,810	3,145
Ratio of urban to rural	3.11	3.18

Note: Income without housing subsidies and imputed rental income on owner-occupied
housing is calculated according to the NBS income definition. Income with these
components equals NBS income plus housing subsidies and plus the imputed rental value of
owner-occupied housing. All tables hereafter include these components in income.

All income and inequality estimates in this and later tables are calculated using the CHIP
household survey data. The income estimates calculated using the NBS income definition
reported here differ somewhat from those published by the NBS, because CHIP is a
subsample of the larger NBS household socioeconomic survey sample. The NBS estimates for
the urban-rural income ratio are 2.7 for 1995 and 3.3 for 2002. See NBS, *China Statistical
Yearbook, 2003* (Beijing: China Statistical Press, 2003).

The CHIP survey oversampled urban households in 1995 and undersampled urban
households in 2002. To correct for this, we calculate national mean incomes using weights
that reflect the shares of the urban and rural populations in China's total population as given
by NBS survey-based population data (see Table 4.5). Migrants are not included here.

this adjustment enlarges the urban-to-rural income ratio, by 10 percent
in 1995 and by 6 percent in 2002. We conclude that the standard NBS
definition of income leads to understatement of the urban-to-rural income
gap. In ensuing discussion, we confine our attention to estimates based on
our more complete measure of income.

Our next step is to adjust for geographical differences in the cost of living. The income estimates in Table 4.2 have been adjusted for these differences and are expressed in terms of national average consumer prices
over both urban and rural areas. These numbers reflect differences in
the real purchasing power of households in different locations. We refer
to them as Purchasing Power Parity (PPP) incomes.

Table 4.2 Mean household per capita disposable PPP incomes and the urban-to-rural income ratio (yuan, current prices except where noted)

	1995	2002	Change from 1995 to 2002 (%, constant 1995 prices)
National	2,584	5,139	76.2
Urban	4,259	7,798	62.2
Rural	1,899	3,434	60.2
Ratio of urban to rural	2.24	2.27	1.3

Note: Incomes in this table include housing subsidies and imputed rental income on owner-occupied housing; migrants are not included.

All incomes in this table are expressed in terms of Purchasing Power Parity (PPP), that is, they are adjusted for geographic price differences and reflect the nationwide average cost of living. PPP adjustments are based on cost of living estimates from Brandt and Holz, "Spatial Price Differences in China." We calculate the nationwide average cost of living index by applying current population shares (see Table 4.5) to Brandt and Holz's mean urban and rural cost of living indices.

Changes over time are calculated in constant 1995 prices. Incomes from 2002 are deflated to 1995 prices using NBS consumer price indices for each provincial urban and rural location.

As costs of living are higher in urban areas, adjusting for spatial price differences substantially reduces the income gap. With spatial price deflation, the relative gap declines markedly, from more than 3 to about 2.25 in both years.

The last column of Table 4.2 shows changes over time in PPP incomes and in the urban-to-rural PPP income ratio. Changes are calculated using constant 1995 prices. Between 1995 and 2002 both urban and rural incomes increased by about 60 percent, and the urban-to-rural income ratio increased only slightly, by a mere 1.3 percent. This result contradicts the conventional view that the rural-urban income gap widened during this period, but the conventional view is based on data that are adjusted neither for housing-related income nor for geographic price differences. These two adjustments eliminate the apparent widening of the gap, because from 1995 to 2002 the gap between urban and rural areas in housing-related income narrowed, and the price differential between urban and rural areas expanded. Note, however, that although the urban-to-rural income ratio remained relatively constant, the absolute difference between urban and rural incomes rose.[13]

Our adjustments for income definition and pricing have, on balance, reduced the size of the urban-to-rural income ratio, but they have not eliminated it. What explains the remaining gap? To some extent it reflects differences in the characteristics of urban and rural households. For example, urban households have higher levels of education and fewer dependents per working-age adult than do rural households. Several studies have investigated the extent to which the income gap is explained by differences in such characteristics. In general, they find that differences in characteristics are only part of the story. For example, Sicular, Yue, Gustafsson, and Li, using the CHIP data and making the same adjustments as shown here, find that in 2002 about half of the rural-urban income gap was explained by differences in the characteristics of urban and rural households. This implies that if rural households had the same characteristics as urban households, the urban-to-rural income ratio would be 1.6 rather than 2.3, as reported in Table 4.2. In other words, even if urban and rural households had the same characteristics, urban incomes would still exceed rural incomes by about 60 percent. This "unexplained" 60-percent income gap can be interpreted as the pure benefit of being an urban resident.[14]

China's rural-urban gap is not uniform regionally. The urban-to-rural income ratio is highest in the West, well above 4 before price adjustments (Table 4.3). Adjusting for spatial price differences greatly reduces the gaps in all regions, especially in the West, which has the highest differential in the cost of living between urban and rural areas. Even in PPP terms, however, the West's urban-to-rural income ratio exceeds 3, as compared to around 2 in the Center and East.

Changes over time in the rural-urban income gap differ markedly among the three regions. Between 1995 and 2002, the gap rose in the West and the Center, reflecting relatively slow growth of rural income. In contrast, the gap declined in eastern China, where rural income growth outpaced that in urban areas. Trends in the East, China's most developed region, hint that in the long term widening of the rural-urban income gap is not inevitable. Growth and development of the nonrural economy, combined with linkages that allow for positive spillovers to the rural sector, can stabilize and possibly narrow the rural-urban gap.

Table 4.3 Regional differences in the urban-to-rural income ratio

	1995		2002		Change in the PPP ratio from 1995 to 2002 (%, constant 1995 prices)
	Unadjusted	PPP	Unadjusted	PPP	
West	4.25	3.33	4.32	3.49	4.8
Center	2.68	1.95	3.02	2.23	14.4
East	2.99	2.05	2.88	1.89	−7.8

Note: The note to Table 4.2 applies.

For each region, mean income is calculated using weights that reflect the proportion of urban-to-rural individuals within that region as given by the NBS population data.

Western provinces are Sichuan (including Chongqing), Guizhou, Yunnan, Shaanxi, and Gansu. Central provinces are Shanxi, Jilin, Anhui, Jiangxi, Henan, Hubei, and Hunan. Eastern provinces are Beijing, Hebei, Liaoning, Jiangsu, Shandong, Zhejiang, and Guangdong.

The Rural-Urban Gap and Inequality, Excluding Migrants

How important is the rural-urban income gap to overall income inequality in China?[15] The standard view is that the rural-urban income differential is a major factor underlying inequality. Most studies attribute nearly half of nationwide inequality to the rural-urban gap. The standard view, however, is based on analyses using unadjusted NBS income data. Our adjustments, especially those for geographic price differences, greatly change the story.

Table 4.4 shows estimates of income inequality in China calculated with and without adjustments for geographic price differences. The first row of the table shows the level of inequality. Using PPP incomes reduces the overall level of measured inequality by more than 25 percent. In other words, about one-quarter of inequality in China as commonly measured is due to spatial price variation and does not reflect real differences in purchasing power among households. Note that here inequality is measured by the Theil L inequality index (also known as the Mean Logarithmic Deviation or MLD). Calculations of overall inequality with and without price adjustments using other common measures, such as the Gini coefficient and Theil T index, give similar results.

Adjusting for prices greatly alters the contribution of the rural-urban income gap to overall inequality. With unadjusted incomes, the rural-

Table 4.4   The urban-to-rural income ratio and inequality

	Unadjusted		PPP	
	1995	2002	1995	2002
National Inequality (Theil L)	.363	.368	.264	.275
Contribution of the gap to overall inequality (%)				
Nationwide	41	45	28	30
West			51	53
Center			28	36
East			23	22

Note: The note to Table 4.2 applies.

For more detailed results and an explanation of the methods used to calculate and decompose inequality, see Terry Sicular, Yue Ximing, Björn Gustafsson, and Li Shi, "The Urban-Rural Income Gap and Inequality in China," *Review of Income and Wealth* 53, no. 1 (2007): 93–126.

urban income gap contributed 41 percent of total inequality in 1995 and 45 percent in 2002. One would conclude, based on these numbers, that the rural-urban gap was a major, and increasing, source of inequality. After adjustment for geographic price differences, the gap's contribution to inequality is markedly lower, roughly 30 percent in both years. Less than one-third of overall inequality in PPP incomes is due to the rural-urban gap; in addition, the gap's contribution to overall inequality changed only slightly between 1995 and 2002.

Disaggregating by region provides additional information about the rural-urban income gap's contribution to inequality. The contribution of the rural-urban PPP income gap to inequality varies substantially among China's three regions. In the West the rural-urban income gap contributes roughly half of total inequality within the region, as compared to less than a quarter in the East.

Indeed, the rural-urban income gaps in the East and Center do not generate much inequality. In these regions, inequality is primarily attributable to income differentials within urban and within rural areas. The situation is different in western China. Overall inequality is markedly higher in the West, and the numbers in Table 4.4 indicate that the reason for this, and indeed the distinguishing feature of inequality in the West, is the high level of inequality between urban and rural areas.

Efforts to reduce the rural-urban gap, then, should concentrate on western China.[16]

Urbanization and Migrants: Some Data Issues

In recent decades China's urban population has experienced unprecedented growth. The expansion of China's cities holds implications for analysis of China's rural-urban income gap. Estimates of national average income and nationwide inequality depend on the shares of the rural and urban populations in the national population and so are sensitive to the level of urbanization. As urbanization is partly the result of rural-to-urban migration, the treatment of migrants in calculations of the urban-to-rural income ratio is also relevant.

Table 4.5 gives NBS statistics on the size of China's urban population. Between 1990 and 2002, the urban population increased by about two-thirds, and its share of the national population rose from roughly 25 percent to about 40 percent. This growth in the urban population was the result of three processes: (1) natural increase in the urban population due to births and deaths among urban residents, (2) reclassification of formerly rural locations (and their resident populations) as urban, and (3) rural-to-urban migration.

Of these processes, migration appears to have been most important. Kam Wing Chan and Hu Ying report that the urban natural rate of increase has been low. They estimate that in the 1990s it contributed only about one-third of the total growth in the urban population. They also calculate the contribution of place reclassification, which by their estimates accounted for 22 percent of urban population growth in the 1990s. In principle, analysis of China's rural-urban income gap should make adjustments to control for place reclassification, but the information required to hold place classifications constant is unavailable.[17]

The major source of urban population growth has been rural-urban migration, which by Chan and Hu's estimates contributed 55 percent of urban population growth in the 1990s. Most studies of China's rural-urban income gap, however, do not include migrants or do so inadequately, because they are based on the NBS annual urban and rural household socioeconomic surveys (as distinct from the NBS annual sample surveys on population changes), which have used sample frames based on place of registration, not place of residence. With many migrants not registered

Table 4.5 Urbanization in China

	Urban population	
Year	Number of persons (millions)	Proportion of national population (%)
1990	302	26.4
1995	352	29.0
2000	459	36.2
2001	481	37.7
2002	502	39.1

Note: Urban population numbers and proportions are from NBS, *China Statistical Yearbook 2003* (Beijing: China Statistical Press, 2003) 97. These statistics are based on the NBS population censuses and annual sample surveys on population changes. Note that these numbers include unregistered rural migrants residing in urban areas for six months or longer.

in the cities in which they live, they have been underrepresented in the NBS urban socioeconomic survey samples. This group is also missed in the rural samples, because the socioeconomic surveys only count individuals who reside at home for a substantial portion of the year (more than six months) or are the primary source of income for their rural households.[18]

The CHIP urban and rural subsamples follow the NBS sampling frame, and so they also underrepresent migrants. In order to improve coverage of migrants, in 2002 the CHIP researchers added a special survey of rural migrants resident in urban areas. The CHIP migrant subsample contains 2,005 households and 5,327 individuals. It covers all of the provinces, although not all of the cities, in the regular CHIP urban survey. CHIP's choice of cities and their sample sizes reflect the concentration of rural-urban migrants in large cities. Specifically, the CHIP migrant survey includes the two provincial-level municipalities (Beijing and Chongqing), all of the provincial capital cities, and one or two middle-sized cities in each of the provinces. The sample contains 100 migrant households in each of Beijing and Chongqing, 200 migrant households from each of the coastal and interior provinces, and 150 migrant households in each of the western provinces. Within each province, 100 migrant households reside in the capital city and the rest are in other cities. Within cities, the migrant households were selected from within the same urban resident committees used for sampling in the regular urban household survey. Selection into the migrant survey sample is not affected by place of origin or length of residence in the city, but the household head must be registered as rural, not urban.[19]

The CHIP migrant subsample is large and has broad geographical coverage, but it is not strictly representative of the migrant population nationwide. As the sampling frame is based on urban residential neighborhood committees, the CHIP migrant sample excludes migrants who were not living in residential neighborhoods, such as those living in construction sites, factories, and on the street. Included are migrants who live in urban residential neighborhoods, that is, migrant individuals and families that live in apartments or other urban housing or who are lodging in such buildings. This group includes both short- and long-term migrants but likely contains a disproportionately high share of long-term migrants and also of migrant families. With these limitations in mind, we use the migrant subsample to explore the effects of including migrants in analysis of the rural-urban gap.

In order to incorporate the migrant sample in our analysis, we must assign a weight to the migrant sample that reflects its share of the national population. Estimates of the size of China's rural-to-urban migrant population vary considerably. Rather than rely on a single estimate, we identify an approximate range that reflects the range of estimates in published studies. The lower end of the range is based on a study by Liang Zai and Ma Zhongdong using data from China's 2000 census, which counted migrants as urban residents if they had lived at their place of urban residence for six months or longer. Using the census data, Liang and Ma estimate the total migrant population in cities as equal to 13 percent of the total urban population. This number includes urban-to-urban migrant households and so overstates the share of rural-to-urban migrants. The number of migrants likely increased between 2000 and 2002, the year of interest here.[20]

The higher end of the range is based on a study by Mo Rong that provides estimates for 2002 drawn from a special, nationwide survey of rural households that included detailed questions about labor movement. Mo's study reports that rural migrant workers resident in cities equaled 16 percent of the urban population. This population share counts only workers and not dependents, so we adjust it to include dependents using information from the CHIP migrant sample, in which 24 percent of the members of migrant households are dependents. The adjusted migrant population share, including dependents, is equal to 21 percent of the urban population. This estimate is high, as the CHIP migrant subsample likely includes a disproportionately large number of dependents.[21]

Although individually imprecise, these numbers can serve as upper and lower bounds for the share of rural migrants in the urban population. In our analysis below, we assume that in 2002 the migrant share in China's urban population fell between 13 and 21 percent. In most of our calculations we use the midpoint in this range, 17 percent. We conduct sensitivity analyses to explore how the choice of the migrant population share affects the findings.

The Rural-Urban Gap, Including Migrants

Table 4.6 shows mean per capita incomes in 2002 incorporating rural-to-urban migrant households. Mean income for migrants is the average per capita income in the CHIP subsample of migrant households. Mean urban income including migrants is the weighted average of incomes for the urban registered and migrant subsamples, with migrants assumed to constitute 17 percent of the urban population.

Not surprisingly, mean per capita income of migrants falls between the incomes of urban registered and rural households. Specifically, it is 60 percent lower than that of urban registered households and 40 percent higher than that of rural households. It follows, then, that including migrants reduces mean urban income and reduces the urban-to-rural income ratio. For both unadjusted and PPP incomes, including migrants reduces the ratio by about 10 percent. With migrants, the ratio of PPP incomes is 2.12; without migrants (see Table 4.2), the ratio is 2.27.[22]

Table 4.7 gives the level of inequality and the contribution of the rural-urban gap to inequality, with and without migrants. For purposes of comparison, these estimates are given with and without geographic price adjustments. Including migrants has an indeterminate effect on the level of overall inequality. Table 4.7 reports the level of inequality measured using the Theil L index, which declines slightly when migrants are included. Inequality measured using a different inequality index, the Theil T, increases slightly. These apparently contradictory outcomes simply reflect the fact that including migrants has both inequality reducing and inequality increasing effects. For example, including migrants reduces overall inequality by narrowing the urban-to-rural income ratio, but it increases inequality within the urban sector. Different inequality

Table 4.6 Mean household per capita disposable income and the urban-to-rural income ratio including migrants, 2002 (current yuan)

	Unadjusted	PPP
National	5,566	4,942
Urban	9,337	7,293
Urban registered	10,004	7,798
Urban migrant	6,083	4,831
Rural	3,145	3,434
Ratio of migrant to registered urban	0.61	0.62
Ratio of migrant to rural	1.94	1.41
Ratio of urban to rural	2.97	2.12

Note: Population weights are rural 60.91%, urban nonmigrant 32.445%, and urban migrant 6.645%. As discussed in the text, these shares maintain the official urban-rural population shares for 2002, with migrants constituting 17% of the urban population.

Price adjustments are explained in the note to Table 4.2.

See the text for a discussion of the migrant sample.

measures assign different weights to such countervailing effects. In any case, the impact of including migrants on the level of overall inequality is small.[23]

How does including migrants affect the rural-urban income gap's contribution to inequality? Including migrants reduces the gap's contribution by about four percentage points. This result is the same regardless of whether incomes are in PPP terms (see Table 4.7).

Table 4.7 The rural-urban income gap's contribution to overall inequality in incomes, with and without migrants, 2002

	Unadjusted		PPP	
	Without migrants	With migrants	Without migrants	With migrants
National Inequality (Theil L)	.368	.354	.275	.268
Rural-urban income gap's contribution to inequality (%)	44.6	41.1	30.0	26.1

Note: The note to Table 4.6 applies.

Table 4.8 gives the results of sensitivity analyses that demonstrate how using different migrant shares in the urban population affects these results. All numbers in this table are calculated using PPP incomes. We use the following migrant shares in the sensitivity analysis: 0 percent, the share implicitly assumed by analyses that do not include migrants; a low estimate of 13 percent; a mid-range choice of 17 percent; and a high estimate of 21 percent. We also show results for a yet higher migrant share of 25 percent so as to demonstrate the possible impact of further growth in the migrant population.

As expected, the urban-to-rural income ratio falls as the population share of migrants increases. At one extreme, with zero migrants the income ratio is 2.27. At the other extreme, with a migrant share of 25 percent, the income ratio falls to 2.06.

Also as expected, the contribution of the rural-urban gap to overall inequality declines steadily as the migrant share rises. The effect, however, is surprisingly small. A near doubling in the migrant population share from 13 percent to 25 percent causes the contribution of the rural-urban income gap to fall by fewer than 4 percentage points, from about 27 percent to 24 percent of overall inequality.

These numbers demonstrate that although including migrants influences measured patterns of inequality, the impact is not overly large. This is true even when assuming a high migrant population share. One reason why the effect may be small is that migrants tend to have characteristics similar to those of urban residents (younger, better educated, smaller households). Consequently, movement of this subset of the rural population does not reduce the rural-urban gap as much as would movement of "average" rural residents.[24]

Table 4.8 The rural-urban income gap and its contribution to inequality, 2002: Sensitivity analysis using alternative migrant population shares

	Migrant share of the urban population				
	0%	13%	17%	21%	25%
Urban-to-rural PPP income ratio	2.27	2.16	2.12	2.09	2.06
Contribution to inequality (%)	30.0	27.0	26.1	25.1	24.2

Note: This table shows results for PPP incomes. The note to Table 4.6 applies.

The modest impact of migrants on overall inequality also reflects that migrants fall in the middle of the income distribution. Their inclusion increases the proportion of middle-income households in the population and has little effect on income differentials between the richest and poorest households. Commonly used inequality measures like the Theil index are most sensitive to changes at the high and low extremes of the income distribution, rather than changes in the middle.[25]

Conclusion

In our analysis we have reexamined China's rural-urban income gap, with careful attention to several measurement issues, specifically, the definition and measurement of income, geographic differences in costs of living, and treatment of urban-to-rural migrants. Of these, geographic differences in the cost of living are most important. Correcting for geographic price differences greatly changes the size of the rural-urban gap and its contribution to overall inequality, far more so than the other adjustments. The study of income inequality is motivated by concerns about real differences in incomes, not apparent differences that merely reflect prices and the cost of living. Geographic price adjustments are therefore needed in order to obtain a meaningful measure of the rural-urban income gap.

Several key findings emerge from our analysis. Incomes in urban China are roughly double, rather than triple, those in rural areas. We note, however, that even after recalculation, China's urban-to-rural income ratio remains high by international standards. Robert Eastwood and Michael Lipton give ratios for other Asian countries in the 1990s that fall between 1.3 and 1.8, with the Philippines a high outlier at 2.17. John Knight and Lina Song give urban-to-rural ratios for income and consumption in twelve countries in Asia, the Middle East, and Africa and most of which are well below 2.0. The estimates for other countries reported in these sources generally include housing subsidies and imputed rent, and they count migrants in urban areas, but they are not adjusted for geographic price differences. Our equivalent calculations for China give a ratio of almost 3, well above the reported estimates for all the other countries in these sources except Zimbabwe and South Africa.[26]

By our estimates, the rural-urban income gap is not the major source of income inequality in China. The rural-urban income gap contributes one-quarter of China's overall income inequality. Although this contribution is not trivial, it is smaller than the contributions of inequality *within* rural areas and *within* urban areas, which account for the remaining three-quarters of China's national inequality. Policy measures to reduce inequality, then, should not neglect income differences within sectors.

The rural-urban income gap and its contribution to inequality differ markedly between the East, Center, and West. The income gap is very large in western China, as is its contribution to inequality. In eastern China the size and importance of the rural-urban income gap is relatively small. These regional differences suggest that efforts to bridge the rural-urban divide should target the West. Further research is required to identify what sorts of targeted interventions would be most effective, but some recent analyses provide evidence on this question. Studies by Fan Shenggen, Zhang Linxiu, and Zhang Xiaobo, and by Zhang Xiabo, and Fan Shenggen examine the impact of public investments on regional poverty and inequality in GDP per capita. Their findings suggest that public investment targeted to western China, especially in rural education and in agricultural research and development, would have the most impact.[27]

With respect to trends over time, and excluding migrants due to lack of migrant data for 1995, we find that the rural-urban income gap has widened only slightly between 1995 and 2002. The more-or-less stable trend in the national gap masks noticeably different trends in eastern, central, and western China. Between 1995 and 2002, the gap widened in the West and Center and narrowed in the East. These regional differences suggest the need for policies designed to address the particularities of each region, rather than nationwide measures that cut with a single knife (*yi dao qie*).

Urbanization and migration are significant factors underlying inequality in China, but migration is unlikely to eliminate the rural-urban income gap. Our calculations show that increasing the share of migrants in the urban population does not greatly reduce the rural-urban income gap. Such calculations capture only part of the story, but other evidence points to the same conclusion. In principle, migration's effect on the rural-urban income gap works through labor markets. As workers move from the countryside to the cities, wage differentials should decline. Much of the rural-urban income gap in China, however, is due to nonwage income. For households in the CHIP samples, nonlabor income accounts for nearly half of the absolute difference between urban and rural incomes. The most important types of nonlabor income are housing-related income components and pensions, which together account for 30 to 40 percent of the absolute income difference.[28]

Migration's effect on the gap also depends on the characteristics of the urban versus rural population. If urban residents continue to be better educated, have fewer dependents, and so on, compared to rural households, then the gap will persist. In addition, the gap will be less likely to narrow if migration is characterized by self-selection, that is, if the individuals who choose to migrate are better educated, younger, and have smaller families than the general rural population.

Clearly, multiple factors underlie China's rural-urban income gap. Some of those factors are substantive; others are not. Careful measurement of the gap is a necessary first step toward identifying the substantive factors and, where needed, developing appropriate policies.

LI SHI
LUO CHULIANG

5 | Reestimating the Income Gap between Urban and Rural Households in China

China is a society with an enormous income gap between rural and urban households. The income gap has changed over time, but it has shown a monotonically rising trend since the late 1990s. According to the official definition of household income (defined by the National Bureau of Statistics, or NBS), the urban-rural income ratio went up from 2.47 in 1997 to 3.23 in 2003.[1] In addition, if China is placed in an international context, the rural-urban income gap in China is much larger than in most other countries.[2] If the gap continues to widen, some researchers predict that China's rural-urban income gap will be larger than that of any other country.[3] The widening income gap has recently attracted increasing attention from researchers and policy makers, domestically and internationally. At the same time, arguments about estimates of the rural-urban income gap have become intense. There are two contrasting opinions. One opinion argues that the official figures on the rural-urban income gap are overestimated because regional living costs are not taken into account. Given the fact that living costs are higher in urban areas than in rural areas, the actual income gap between urban and rural households should be smaller than is shown by official statistics if household income is adjusted by regional living costs. The second opinion is that there is a significant underestimation of the rural-urban income gap because the NBS's definition of household income does not take into account some income components, especially subsidies in kind provided to urban residents but not to rural residents.[4] If these income components are included in total household income estimates, the income gap becomes much larger than is stated in the existing literature. Some scholars even declare that the actual income ratio of urban to rural households is more than 5 to 1.[5]

The argument involves how to define household income in both rural and urban areas. As there are considerable differences between urban and rural households in terms of income sources, income components, consumption structure, and social protection, it is much more difficult in China than in other countries to obtain comparable urban and rural household income estimates. This is a big challenge facing researchers in understanding the rural-urban income gap in China.

The data used in this chapter come from the household survey conducted in the early 2003 for the reference year 2002. In all, 9,200 households and 37,969 individuals were selected from 120 counties in 22 provinces in rural areas and 7,000 households and 20,632 individuals from 72 cities in 12 provinces in urban areas. The is referred to as the CHIP (China Household Income Project) survey. Li Shi, Chuliang Luo, Zhong Wei, and Ximing Yue provide a detailed description of CHIPs 2002.[6] Based on the dataset from CHIPs for 2002, we try to correct the biases in the estimation of the income gap between urban and rural households. Using the same data, Terry Sicular, Yue Ximing, Björn Gustafsson, and Li Shi, in Chapter 4 of this volume, reestimate the income gap between urban and rural households in 2002. Their study makes two new contributions compared to simply using the income definition of NBS. First, the Sicular et al. study extends the income definition by including in-kind subsidies of public housing and imputed rent of private housing. Second, the differences in living costs between urban and rural areas are taken into account in deriving household income. Our study in this chapter attempts to go further in the first direction followed by Sicular et al.,[7] with a focus on estimation of the disguised subsidies gained by both urban and rural households and how including these affects estimates of the rural-urban gap. As our reestimation also leads to revised estimates of income inequality within each sector, we also report these new estimates of income inequality within both urban and rural areas and for China as a whole.

The second section of the chapter sketches the income gap between urban and rural areas based on the NBS income definition, providing a background and starting point for our study. The third section discusses the methodology of estimating disguised subsidies gained by urban residents. The fourth section shows the distribution of disguised subsidies and revised estimates of the urban-rural income ratio and of income inequalities within urban and rural areas and in China as a whole after incorporating simultaneously all three types of income adjustments: the disguised subsidies gained by both urban and rural households, spatial price differences in urban and rural areas and in provinces, and imputed rent of self-owned housing attributed to household income. The last section offers concluding remarks.

The Income Gap between Urban and Rural Areas: Using the NBS Income Definition

Most studies on the income gap between urban and rural China use the income definition of the NBS, which includes different income components for rural households and for urban households. NBS has used the concept of net income for rural households since it started to conduct household surveys in the early 1980s. That net income consists of two major components, cash income and home products for self-consumption after deduction of production costs, although NBS does not clearly document how the self-consumed products are valued. Rural net income can also be expressed as individual wages, family business income, property income, and transfer income, categories usually reported separately in China's statistical yearbooks. It is obvious that the concept of household net income misses an important income component: imputed rent of private housing. As estimated by A. R. Khan and Carl Riskin, the imputed rent of private housing accounts for 11.6 percent and 13.5 percent of household income in rural areas in 1995 and 2002, respectively.[8] Obviously, if this component is included as part of household income, the average income of rural households will be higher than the figures published by NBS.

There are even more serious problems with NBS's income definition for urban households. First, the definition of household disposable income adopted by NBS does not include imputed rent of private housing, the same omission as for rural households. Given the fact that more and more urban residents have become private housing owners through either purchasing commercial apartments or privatization of public housing, the problem of underestimation of household income due to exclusion of imputed rent of private housing has become very serious. The second major problem is that many in-kind subsidies and social security benefits are not computed as parts of household income for urban residents. This would not be so problematic if everyone were equally entitled to the same social protection in a society. However, China is obviously not such a society. Therefore, the market value of social security benefits should be considered if income comparisons are made between urban and rural households, as these programs are only provided to urban households. During the last decade, the social security system was reformed in a direction of increasing the contribution of both employees and work units to social insurance programs. These contributions in terms of monetary value should be regarded as a part of household income, but they are excluded from household income by NBS's income definition. In this chapter we have estimated the monetary value of the contributions to social security programs by individual employees and work units. There is no doubt that income per capita would be raised sharply for urban households if these disguised subsidies were included in household income calculations, as would the urban-rural income ratio.

The last major problem is that the household income estimates calculated in most studies are not adjusted for differences in living costs (regional purchasing price parity, or PPP), which differ in urban and rural areas and across provinces. As in other developing countries, living costs in China are by and large higher in urban areas than in rural areas. The large differences in living costs between urban and rural China plausibly result in underestimation of rural household income or overestimation of urban household income when making income comparisons. Therefore, without taking regional living costs into account, the estimates of the urban-rural income ratio would be upward biased.[9] In sum, the NBS income definition diverges notably from the well-being actually enjoyed by urban and rural residents.

Some studies have noticed these problems and have tried to rectify these biases one way or another. For example, Khan and Riskin redefined the income definition by adding imputed rent of self-owned housing into household income. Irma Adelman and David Sunding made efforts to estimate the disguised subsidies obtained by urban residents in a particular year in order to revise the underestimated income gap between urban and rural households. Sicular et al. re-computed the income gap between urban and rural by using the regional cost-of-living index derived by

Loren Brandt and Carsten A. Holz. Sylvie Démurger, Martin Fournier, and
Li Shi used the same index for reestimating changes in income inequality
in urban China over the period from 1988 to 2002. Martin Ravallion and
Shaohua Chen used the regional living costs of poor households to make an
adjustment for household income in both urban and rural areas.[10] However, none of these studies deals with these three biases simultaneously.
The major contribution of this chapter is its consideration of these biases
together in estimating the urban-rural income ratio in China.

Before presenting our estimates of the urban-rural income ratio, it is
worth examining the changes in the gap based on the NBS's income definition since the beginning of economic reforms in the late 1970s. Figure
5.1 plots the income ratio of urban to rural residents since 1978. Before
the mid-1980s, the income ratio decreased significantly, with faster income growth of rural households occurring as a result of the spread of
agricultural reforms throughout the countryside. The ratio reached 1.82
in 1983, the lowest level in the last three decades. However, since the middle of 1980s, the basic trend has been for the income ratio to keep increasing, although it decreased in specific years. The income gap has increased
more rapidly since 1997. According to NBS figures, in 2003 the income
ratio of urban to rural households reached 3.23, perhaps the highest level
in the history of the PRC.

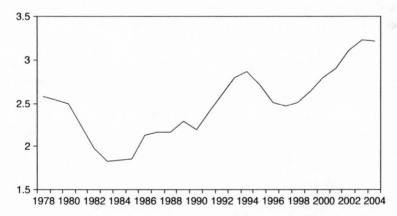

Figure 5.1   China's income ratio (urban/rural), 1978–2004. Authors' calculation
based on *China Statistical Abstract 2005* (Beijing: China Statistics
Press, 2005).

Meanwhile, the urban-rural income ratio accounts for a growing proportion of income inequality in China as a whole. Using the Theil index, the inequality in the entire country can be separated into three parts: inequality within urban areas, inequality within rural areas, and inequality between urban and rural areas. According to the three waves of household surveys from CHIPs, the share of inequality between urban and rural areas as a proportion of overall national inequality increased from 38 percent in 1988 to 43 percent in 1995 and approached 47 percent in 2002.[11]

Methods of Estimating Disguised Subsidies

Review on the Methods Applied in the Existing Studies

As pointed out above, many researchers have noticed that the income ratio based on the definition of NBS cannot reflect the differences in real well-being of urban and rural residents, and they have made efforts to get more comparable income for both population groups. Adelman and Sunding estimated that in-kind subsidies received by urban households were equivalent to 82 percent of their monetary income in the mid-1980s.[12] The World Bank estimated that the corresponding percentage in 1995 was 72 percent.[13] NBS has calculated the size of the housing subsidy, medical and traffic subsidy, price subsidy, and in-kind income. The methods adopted in NBS's estimation varied for different subsidy items. For instance, they simply estimated the housing subsidy as 25 percent of the average wage in those employed in urban areas,[14] derived the medical and commuting subsidies by subtracting "pension" and "other income of staff & workers from state and collective owned units" from "social insurance and welfare funds," obtained the price subsidy by subtracting some items included in wages from "government price subsidies," and assumed the in-kind income amounted to 5 percent of the "per capita income available for living," according to some surveys. All of these indicators can be found in the *China Statistical Yearbook* in 1995. Cai Fang and Yang Tao followed this method to calculate nonwage income, but their estimated size of nonwage income was different from what NBS obtained.[15] Housing subsidies were obtained by subtracting the rent paid by individuals from fixed assets investment in housing per capita in urban areas. We view these estimation methods as flawed and will attempt to present more reasonable estimates.

Disguised Subsidies Received by Urban Residents

Although in-kind income from self-produced consuming is included in the net income of rural residents, disposable income does not include the in-kind income earned by the urban residents. Because of the urban-rural division, rural areas are excluded from most social security programs, such as medical insurance and unemployment insurance. The expenditure on social security programs is excluded from personal income estimates. Because the fees for social security programs are usually shared between individuals and work units, the work units pay part of the fees for the individuals, but such payments are always neglected in previous personal income estimates. Social security programs are closely related to work units and employment status. If job opportunities were open equally to all the members of society, the well-being generated from these programs would be distributed randomly and with equal probability to all members. However, urban and rural areas in China are sharply divided, and formal employment is restricted to urban residents, while rural residents have no chance to obtain such jobs.[16] Therefore, rural residents and even most migrants cannot benefit from the social security programs of urban areas. These social security programs are only enjoyed by urban residents and become an important source of the real income gap between urban and rural areas.

During the economic transition, urban residents can still obtain some in-kind income. Additionally, some urban residents can still obtain some distributions at lower prices than the market value. For example, some public housing was leased to urban residents at rents below the market value, and the government provided educational subsidies so that urban residents did not have to pay much for schooling. All of these subsidies became parts of the actual income of urban residents, although they are disguised. We refer to these as disguised subsidies. Without such subsidies, urban residents would have had to pay more from their income to get the equivalent utility. The disguised subsidies include the following:

Public Housing Subsidies

If residents live in a public apartment and pay a below-market rent, they receive a public subsidy. Even in the mid-1990s, the majority of urban households lived in public housing either owned by local governments or by work units. The data from the CHIPs 1995 indicates that 57 percent of urban households lived in such public housing in that year. Using the same data, Wang Lina and Zhong Wei estimated the housing subsidy for urban households living in public housing and obtained 10 yuan per month per square meter.[17] The subsidy is the difference between the market rent and the rent paid by a household. From their estimation, we can compute the housing subsidy as about 1,296 yuan per capita for all urban households in 1995. However, the housing reform changed the structure of housing property rights dramatically. Table 5.1 shows that the proportion of urban households living in public housing decreased from 57 percent in 1995 to 16 percent in 2002, while privately owned housing increased from 43 percent to 80 percent. The housing reform led to a considerable increase in private ownership of residential housing in urban China.

The housing subsidies in 2002 are valued as the difference between the market rent and the rent actually paid by households. The information of market rents was provided by respondents.[18] Some households did not report the market rent of their public housing, and in those cases we assign a predicted rent value. The predicted value is derived from a regression model in which the reported market rent is treated as the dependent variable and living area, location, and housing condition as independent variables. The regression analysis uses a sample restricted to households living in public apartments and responding to the market rent question. In this manner we obtain the mean value of housing subsidies as 1,358 yuan per capita in urban areas in 2002.[19]

Table 5.1 Structure of housing property rights in urban China, 1995 and 2002

	1995		2002	
	Households	Percentage	Households	Percentage
Public housing	3,935	56.75	1,064	15.57
Private ownership by housing reform	NA	NA	4,199	61.43
Privately owned housing	2,952	42.57	1,263	18.48
Others	47	0.68	309	4.52
Total	6,934	100	6,835	100

Source: CHIPs 1995 and 2002.
NA: not available

Medical Subsidies

We estimate the medical subsidies for urban residents only, because there were few rural residents covered by any type of public health care in 2002.[20] The medical subsidies for urban residents are derived directly from a question included in the 2002 urban household survey, "How much did the government and your work unit pay for your health care in 2002?" The 2002 data indicate that 4,718 urban individuals got their medical expenditure reimbursed either by a public health scheme or their work units, with an average reimbursement of 1,283 yuan If the medical subsidy is averaged over the total urban population, the medical subsidy per capita is 293 yuan.

Educational Subsidies

It is widely recognized that there is a notable difference between rural and urban residents in terms of educational attainment, educational opportunities, and the quality of education. On average, rural people are provided with less opportunity and lower-quality schools than their urban counterparts. In addition, the financial system for education differs in urban China and in rural China, leading to more public subsidies to education provided by local governments for urban residents.[21] We think the subsidies to education should be counted as a part of household income when the urban-rural income comparison is made. However, it is not possible to estimate this kind of subsidy from a household survey, because in most cases respondents have no idea what the subsidies are. What we can get from the 2002 household survey is school fees paid by households, from which we can calculate the total amount of school fees paid by rural and urban households separately. We can also get the total expenditure on education separately in both urban and rural areas. Logically, the disguised educational subsidy is equal to the total educational expenditure minus total school fees paid by households.[22]

The educational subsidy is related to the educational level. The educational subsidy per capita in urban and rural areas is derived as follows: first, we compute the educational subsidy per student for each category of student for urban and rural areas separately, and then we weight the subsidy per student by the proportion of each category of student in the total population.

Enrollment is another factor affecting the magnitude of educational subsidies in urban and rural China. Even though the subsidies per student at the college and professional school level are assumed to be indifferent to where the student comes from, the opportunity to receive these levels of education is different for urban and rural residents. Obviously, the chance for a rural youth to enter into college or professional school is much lower than for an urban youth, and this produces a gap in educational subsidies between urban and rural households. In 2002, we estimate, the size of the overall total of educational subsidies was 482 yuan and 282 yuan per capita for urban and rural residents, respectively, as shown in Table 5.2. Apparently in that year an urban resident received 70 percent more in educational subsidies than a rural resident did.

Contributions to Social Security Programs

Social security programs have an urban bias in China. Urban employees are entitled to several types of social security that are beyond the reach of rural people. However, the value of social security contributions is not

Table 5.2   Educational subsidies, 2002

	Ratio of the students at each level to the total population		Subsidy per student (yuan)		Subsidy per capita (yuan)	
	Urban	Rural	Urban	Rural	Urban	Rural
College	0.0239	0.0066	8,810.95	8,810.95	210.58	58.15
Professional school	0.0056	0.0084	3,194.14	3,194.14	17.89	26.83
Senior high school	0.0388	0.0228	3,122.63	1,626.37	121.16	37.08
Junior high school	0.0441	0.0672	1,610.20	872.85	71.01	58.66
Elementary school	0.0622	0.0932	1,254.02	713.61	78.00	66.51
Total					498.64	247.23

Source: *China Statistical Yearbook of Educational Expenditure* and *China Statistical Yearbook*, 2003.
   Note: Ratios of the students at each level to the total population are calculated based on the relevant information in the 2002 household survey.
   In the *Statistical Yearbook of Educational Expenditure*, the educational expenditure and school fees are combined for urban and rural areas. We set the ratio of educational subsidies per student for the senior high school in urban to rural as 1.92:1, as the ratios for the junior high school and elementary school are 1.84 and 1.76, respectively.

counted as household income in the NBS income definition. In this case, one question is raised: if social security program coverage could be purchased in the market, how much would each program cost? In other words, the social security coverage enjoyed by urban employees should be valued and taken into account in computing their household income. In the NBS income definition, contributions to social security programs both by individuals and work units are subtracted from household disposable income. However, these contributions should be considered as part of the household income. The reason is that these contributions are a kind of (forced) savings intended to give employees a way to deal with uncertainties in the future. Up to 2002, social security programs were almost totally absent from rural areas, although a new cooperative medical insurance scheme and dibao (minimum income subsidy program) have been on trial in some rural areas since 2002. The urban social security programs were of several different types:

Housing Accumulation Fund

The Housing Accumulation Fund started experimentally in Shanghai in 1991 and was widely implemented in urban China as a whole in 1994. According to the *Guideline of Housing Accumulation Fund Management* issued in 1995, the fund comprises contributions from both individual employees and their work units. The contribution is equal to a proportion of the average monthly wage in the previous year and is the same for the individual and work units. The proportion varies from 5 percent to 20 percent across provinces. In principle, the *Housing Accumulation Fund* covers all urban employees. Because the 2002 survey collected information on Fund contributions made by each urban employed person, we use this information for our estimation of the contribution, which should be added to household income.

Pension Scheme

Before pension reforms, the government and work units took full responsibility for providing pensions for urban retirees. Retiree pensions were not financed by worker contributions before they retired. During the economic transition, the pension system was reformed to share contributions to pension funds between employees and their work units. According to new regulations, a work unit and an employee should contribute 28 percent of the employee's total wage payment to the pension fund, with the work unit contributing 20 percent and the employee 8 percent.

The 2002 household survey contains information on the individual contributions of each worker to his or her pension fund. With this information, we derive the total contribution by multiplying the individual contribution by 3.75, with the resulting total counted as a part of household income.

Pension reform has only taken place in production enterprises. Employees in the government sector and nonproduction organizations are still covered by the old pension system. They do not explicitly contribute to their pension funds, but they receive even higher pensions after retirement. Data from the 2002 household survey indicate that the average pension for retirees who were once employed in the government sector or in institutions is 1.84 times that of those who retired from production enterprises. Therefore, we derive the pension contribution of employees in the government sector and in institutions by multiplying the pension contributions of enterprise employees by 1.84.

Contributions to Medical Insurance

Contributions to medical insurance are also shared by individuals and their work units for those employed in production enterprises. Work units should contribute 6 percent of the total wage of each employee and the employee should contribute 2 percent. Because the 2002 survey gives us the total wage for each worker, we simply derive the benefit each worker obtains from medical insurance by multiplying his or her total wage by 8 percent. Although those employed in the government sector and in institutions do not contribute to medical insurance individually, we apply the same procedure to find their benefit from public medical insurance.

Unemployment Insurance

In 1998 the government published *Decree of Unemployment Insurance,* which set up an unemployment insurance fund. The fund is raised in two parts, with contributions from both employees and work units. The former pay 1 percent of their total wage, while the latter pay another 2 percent. That means an augmenting of the income of urban employees by 3 percent if the total contributions to the unemployment insurance fund are counted as a part of their income. Up to 2002, all urban employees, either in enterprises or in the government sector and other institutions, were covered by unemployment insurance.

The 2002 household survey inquired directly about all contributions to social security programs by individual employees, but some respondents did not answer these questions. Therefore, we replace the missing values with predicted values. To predict how much these respondents actually contribute to social security programs, we regress the contribution of employees with positive values on their personal characteristics. The regression model includes wage level, work experience, employment sector and provincial dummies as independent variables. With the coefficients of the independent variables available, we then assign each of the respondents with missing social security program responses with the values predicted by our regression model.[23]

Table 5.3 reports the descriptive statistics for all the items of social security contributions that we consider part of individual income. The value of all of the contributions in urban China is 1,933 yuan per capita. The contribution to the pension scheme is the largest proportion, accounting for 53 percent of the total value. The standard deviation and Gini coefficient columns in Table 5.3 show that the distribution of each contribution within the urban population is highly unequal.

Income in Kind

Income in kind is calculated directly from the 2002 household survey, in which respondents were asked about in-kind income (noncash income) corresponding to various items of consumer goods. The items of consumer goods include food, such as meat, fish, vegetables, and fruits; clothes;

Table 5.3 Descriptive statistics for payments to social security in urban areas, 2002

	Mean	Stand. Dev.	Percentage	Gini index
Housing funds	474.47	625.18	24.54	0.5878
Pension scheme	1,021.68	1,044.03	52.85	0.5033
Medical insurance	332.81	320.72	17.22	0.4744
Unemployment insurance	99.25	119.85	5.13	0.5361
Others	4.91	51.79	0.25	0.9829
Total payments of social securities	1,933.13	1,848.92	100.00	0.4706

Note: The number of observations is 20,632, the sample size of individuals in the 2002 urban survey.

Table 5.4 Descriptive statistics for the disguised subsidies gained by urban residents

	Mean	Stand. Dev.	Percentage	Gini index
In-kind housing subsidies	1,358.35	1,823.67	31.77	0.5824
Medical subsidies	293.43	2,311.61	6.86	0.9412
Educational subsidies	498.57	762.53	11.66	0.6874
Total contribution to social securities	1,933.13	1,848.92	45.22	0.4706
In-kind income	191.64	857.30	4.48	0.7953
Total disguised subsidies	4,275.12	4,157.03	100.00	0.4159

Note: All of the observations—20,632, the sample size for the urban survey—are calculated for each kind of subsidy.

and other daily consumer goods. The mean of in-kind income is 192 yuan in 2002, with the Gini coefficient being 0.80.

The Size of Disguised Subsidies Gained by Urban Residents

Table 5.4 shows descriptive statistics for the disguised subsidies received by urban residents. The largest subsidy is the contribution to social security programs, amounting to 45 percent of the total. The second largest is housing subsidies in kind, which amount to 32 percent. All of these subsidies are highly unevenly distributed. Putting all of the items together, we obtain the total of disguised subsidies as 4,275 yuan, which is much higher than the per capita income of rural households. The distribution of the total amount of the disguised subsidies, with a Gini coefficient of 0.42, is more unequal than that of personal income in urban areas[24] but is more equal than any one of the individual subsidy items.

Reestimating the Income Gap and Income Inequalities

Using estimates of all types of disguised subsidies received by both urban and rural households, we recalculate the income gap between urban and rural households and income inequalities within urban and rural areas and in China as a whole. In addition, to make an adjustment for household income by considering differences in living costs between urban and rural areas and across provinces, we apply the spatial price indices generated by Brandt and Holz.[25]

Table 5.5 presents the income per capita in rural and urban China in 2002 and urban-to-rural income ratios using different income definitions. If household income is not adjusted for spatial price indices, the income ratio of urban households to rural households is 3.12 using NBS's income definition. The ratio is almost the same as the estimate published by NBS, which has been widely cited. However, the ratio rises to 4.35 if disguised subsidies are included in household income, while the ratio falls slightly to 4.28 if the imputed rent of private owned housing is also taken account.

In addition, the results in the lower panel of Table 5.5 also indicate to what extent the income gap between urban and rural households changes if household income is adjusted by spatial price indices. Although the urban-rural income ratio is sharply reduced by this adjustment, the gap is still very large when disguised subsidies are considered. As shown in Table 5.5, the urban-rural income ratio increases from 2.24 to 3.1 when the income definition shifts from Income I to Income II.

Table 5.6 shows the estimates of Gini coefficients for rural and urban China and for the country as a whole using different income definitions. If household income is not adjusted by spatial price indices, the Gini coefficients in urban and rural areas are .32 and .37, respectively, using NBS's income definition and .457 in China as a whole. National income inequality becomes considerably wider, with the Gini coefficient jumping to more than .50 if disguised subsidies are included in household income, although the addition of disguised subsidies has only a slight impact on estimates of inequality within urban and within rural China.

Table 5.5 Income gap between urban and rural households by different income definitions (yuan)

	Urban	Rural	Urban/Rural
Unadjusted			
Income I (NBS definition)	8,083.65	2,591.83	3.12
Income II (income I+subsidies)	12,358.77	2,839.29	4.35
Income III (income II+imputed rent)	14,081.29	3,289.18	4.28
Adjusted with PPP			
Income I (NBS definition)	5,487.53	2,452.57	2.24
Income II (income I+subsidies)	8,340.35	2,686.53	3.10
Income III (income II+imputed rent)	9,502.62	3,109.93	3.06

Table 5.6 Income inequalities within urban and rural areas and in China as a whole by different income definitions

	Gini coefficient		
	Urban	Rural	National
Unadjusted			
Income I (NBS definition)	0.320	0.367	0.457
Income II (income I + subsidies)	0.323	0.351	0.507
Income III (income II + imputed rent)	0.323	0.349	0.504
Adjusted with PPP			
Income I (NBS definition)	0.299	0.364	0.399
Income II (income I + subsidies)	0.296	0.349	0.442
Income III (income II + imputed rent)	0.296	0.345	0.438

Turning to the lower panel of Table 5.6, the estimates of Gini coefficients after adjustment of household income by spatial price indices, we find that the adjustment has more impact on urban inequality than on rural inequality, with the largest impact on national inequality. As illustrated in Table 5.6, using Income I, the Gini coefficient in China as a whole decreases by nearly 6 percentage points after adjusting for variable prices; using Income II, it decreases by 6.5 percentage points. However, it is worthy noting that the Gini coefficient for China as a whole after adjustment for spatial price differences and including disguised subsidies is only slightly lower than for that with no adjustment and correction (.438 versus .457). This result indicates that the two factors (price differences and disguised subsidies) counteract one another in correcting the biases of the official figures on income inequality in China.

Conclusion

Assessment of the income gap between urban and rural households in China is largely dependent on how household income is defined. Given the striking differences between urban and rural people in terms of monetary income, accessibility of public services, and living costs, it is difficult to get urban and rural household income estimates that are fully comparable. This chapter attempts to reestimate the income gap between urban and rural China by taking both disguised subsidies and spatial price differences into account (along with imputed incomes from housing). Although income in kind in the form of consumer goods such as apples, fish, and pork has decreased significantly in urban areas since the end of the 1980s,[26] the monetary value of disguised subsidies in terms of social security and public services, to which only urban residents are entitled, has increased over the same period. As urban residents are privileged in terms of entitlement to social security programs, public housing, and other public services, we estimate much higher disguised subsidies received by urban households than by rural households. This calculation leads to a significantly wider income gap between urban and rural China than is usually reported. Although the adjustment of spatial price differences works in the other direction and results in a narrower gap, the gap is still at a very high level if disguised subsidies are taken into account. Including the disguised subsidies also leads to a higher estimate of income inequality in China as a whole.

III | The Rural-Urban Gap in Access to Social Resources

EMILY HANNUM
MEIYAN WANG
JENNIFER ADAMS

6 | Rural-Urban Disparities in Access to Primary and Secondary Education under Market Reforms

Education has an increasingly important role to play in ameliorating or exacerbating rural-urban inequality in China. By the turn of the twenty-first century, a person's access to education had begun to matter a great deal to his or her lifetime economic security.[1] Returns to education in urban China have been rising since the onset of the market reform period in the late 1970s; returns nearly tripled during the period from 1988 to 2003, rising from 4.0 to 11.4 percent.[2] In rural areas, by the year 2000, an additional year of education increased wages by 6.4 percent among those engaged in wage employment, and education is becoming the dominant factor that determines whether rural laborers are successful in finding more lucrative off-farm jobs.[3]

Historically, children in rural areas have faced substantial disadvantages in securing education, but the trend in recent years, as incomes, inequality, and educational costs have all risen, is unclear. In this chapter, we review policies that have been put in place to address the urban rural gap in recent years, we employ the China Health and Nutrition Survey[4] (hereafter CHNS) to illuminate recent changes in urban-rural educational disparities, and we analyze a sample from the 2000 census for a more detailed description of rural-urban disparities.

Data Sources

We draw on longitudinal, individual-level data on education from the 1989 through 2004 waves of the China Health and Nutrition Survey (CHNS), a multipurpose panel survey conducted by the Chinese Academy of Preventive Medicine and the Institute of Nutrition and Food Hygiene, in collaboration with the Carolina Population Center at the University of North Carolina. The CHNS used a multistage cluster process to draw a sample from eight geographically diverse provinces that differ by level of economic development, public resources, and health indicators. The provinces covered in 1989 were Liaoning, Jiangsu, Shandong, Henan, Hubei, Hunan, Guangxi, and Guizhou. In 1997, Liaoning was replaced by Heilongjiang; thereafter, both provinces were included in the sample. Replacement households and communities were added to the sample in some survey years.[5] Counties in each of these eight provinces were stratified by income level and randomly selected based on a weighted sampling scheme. In addition, the provincial capital and a lower-income city were selected. Villages and townships within the counties and urban and suburban neighborhoods within the cities were selected randomly.[6] We use data from the CHNS to investigate the trend in educational disparities over time.

We also present descriptive and multivariate analyses of enrollment using unit-record data from a .95 per thousand microsample from the 2000 China population census. Although we are unable to look at changes with the census data,[7] the census sample offers two features that complement some of the shortcomings of the CHNS. First, the census covers all provinces, which is important for our purposes, given the possible high degree of regional disparity in education. Second, the census allows us to consider minority status in conjunction with rural residence. Measurement of ethnicity in the CHNS is limited,[8] and the provincial coverage of the CHNS also makes representing the experiences of minorities problematic.

We focus on children in two overlapping age groups: "compulsory age," or seven- to sixteen-year-olds, and "secondary age," or thirteen- to eighteen-year-olds. The compulsory age range is meant to approximate the "at-risk" group for a nine-year cycle of compulsory education. The secondary age range is intended to pick up children who have reached a level of schooling where fees become significant, at least in the time frame covered by the datasets employed here.

There are also logistical reasons for this choice. First, children in these age ranges, and especially in the younger compulsory ages, are likely to still be in their families of origin, and thus urban-rural differences in attainment are less likely to be affected by migration. Second, although it might be ideal not to select overlapping age ranges, we opted to allow an overlap due to the small sample size in the CHNS. For the sake of consistency, we adopted the same approach with the census data. We do not consider the educational position of rural children of migrant parents in cities—we are not able to pick up all of these individuals in the CHNS or in the census.[9]

Education Policies and the Rural-Urban Split

From the perspective of educational access, among the most important education reforms in recent decades have been the 1985 Decision on the Reform of the Education Structure (hereafter the 1985 Decision) and the 1986 compulsory education law that followed. The 1985 Decision was issued as a part of public finance reforms developed to ease the transition to a market economy. The Decision included many initiatives, such as nine years of compulsory education, the expansion of vocational education, the strengthening of educational leadership, and increased local financing of education. A shift of financial responsibilities from the central government to local levels was the foundation of the reform.[10]

Local levels of government were given the responsibility for raising and spending educational revenue. In practice, provincial governments took on the provision of higher education and transferred the responsibility for the financing of compulsory education to lower levels of government. A major objective of finance reform in education was to mobilize new resources for education, and the 1985 reform specified that multiple methods of financing should be sought.[11]

Several months later, in early 1986, the National People's Congress passed the Law on Compulsory Education, designating nine years of education, six years of primary and three years of lower secondary, as compulsory for all children.[12] Timetables were set for different regions to achieve full compliance with the law. However, the law fell short of guaranteeing the funding for education, and many schools, particularly those in poor rural areas, financed local education by collecting either tuition or miscellaneous school fees. Thus, decentralization and privatization created new barriers to access for the poorest children, even as families, on average, had many more resources to invest in their children and the reforms effectively mobilized these resources.

The Chinese government has responded to concerns about access problems under the decentralized system with a series of equity-oriented policy proclamations issued throughout the period. For example, the Education Law of 1995 affirmed the government's commitment to equality of educational opportunity regardless of nationality, race, sex, occupation, property conditions, or religious belief.[13] It also specified that the state should support educational development in minority nationality regions, remote border areas, and poverty-stricken areas.[14] The central government launched a massive education project for children living in poor areas between 1995 and 2000 with a total investment of US$1.2 billion, the most intensive allocation of educational funding in the last fifty years.[15] The *Action Plan for Revitalizing Education in the 21st Century*, released in 1999, confirmed a commitment to implementing compulsory education across the country.[16]

The focus on problems of rural poverty has intensified in the twenty-first century. In 2003, the State Council held the first national working conference since 1949 to formulate plans for the development of rural education, with a focus on protecting access to and improving the quality of compulsory education in rural areas.[17] Among the ideas to emerge from the conference were plans to establish an effective system of sponsorship for poor students receiving compulsory education, such as by exempting poor students from all miscellaneous fees and textbook charges and offering them lodging allowances by the year 2007.

In March 2004, the State Council approved and circulated the *2003–2007 Action Plan for Revitalizing Education*, called the *New Action Plan*.[18] One of the strategic priorities of the *New Action Plan* is the implementation of compulsory education in rural areas. In 2005 it was announced that the government would spend 218 billion yuan to help improve education in rural areas in the subsequent five years.[19] A mechanism would be established to ensure the wages of rural middle and elementary school teachers, and by 2007, the government committed to eliminating educational tuition and fees and providing free textbooks and subsidies for needy rural students in compulsory education.[20]

Although the impact of any one policy is difficult to establish, Ministry of Education official data show favorable trends in enrollment and retention at the stage of compulsory education. For example, in 1990, five-year retention rates for primary school[21] were around 71 percent; they rose to 95 percent by 2000 and 2001 and rose again to 99 percent in 2002 and 2003.[22] The official transition rate from primary to lower secondary was 88 percent in 1995 and had reached 92 percent in 2001.[23] Three-year retention rates for middle school (chuzhong) rose from 83 percent in 1990 to 92 percent in 2003.[24] Whether these findings in government education data dovetail with evidence from population-based surveys, and whether the access gap between urban and rural areas is closing, are questions that we address in the next section.

Trends in Rural-Urban Disparities

We begin by investigating enrollment and years-of-schooling measures among children ages seven to sixteen, ages at which the nine-year target for compulsory education established in the mid-1980s should be in play. Table 6.1 shows the percentage enrolled and years of education attained by age group, year, residence status, and sex. The top panel focuses on seven- to sixteen-year-olds and suggests higher levels of access among the samples in later years. Table 6.2 tests this trend with panel models of enrollment that account for province of residence and age. Models 1 and 2 constitute baseline comparison models, with and without provincial controls. Model 3 adds an interaction between year and rural residence to test for significant changes in the scope of rural disadvantage. Model 1 shows that, on average, the odds of being enrolled are lower for rural residents, net of other variables in the model, and lower for girls than for boys. Odds are significantly higher in 2004, compared to 1989. Model 2 shows that the scope of rural disadvantage is stable with or without incorporating these geographic differences into the model. Model 3 adds a series of indicators of rural-year interactions to test for change in the scope of rural disadvantage across survey years. Together, the year, rural, and year-by-rural indicators indicate that the overall level of enrollment is rising, but they do not indicate that the difference in odds of enrolling between urban and rural areas is narrowing. Of course, this finding must be placed in the context of very high enrollment rates at compulsory ages: even though rural children are much more likely to be the ones not enrolled, very few children in this age range are not enrolled.

Table 6.1 Enrollment rates and years of education completed by age group and survey year

7- to 16-year-olds

Year	Enrollment rate (%)				Rural/urban (%)		Years attained				Urban-rural years	
	Rural boys	Urban boys	Rural girls	Urban girls	Boys	Girls	Rural boys	Urban boys	Rural girls	Urban girls	Boys	Girls
1989	88.22	91.07	83.84	89.30	96.87	93.89	4.35	4.93	4.28	4.83	0.58	0.55
1991	90.78	93.46	86.48	93.20	97.13	92.78	4.51	4.91	4.70	4.92	0.40	0.22
1993	89.45	95.62	84.63	93.51	93.55	90.50	5.31	5.57	5.53	5.97	0.26	0.44
1997	93.25	96.81	93.28	95.96	96.32	97.21	4.76	4.97	4.87	5.36	0.21	0.50
2000	92.41	95.44	90.15	95.94	96.83	93.97	5.67	6.24	5.80	6.01	0.57	0.21
2004	96.46	97.21	94.89	98.90	99.23	95.95	5.43	6.45	5.74	5.80	1.03	0.06

13- to 18-year-olds

Year	Enrollment rate (%)				Rural/urban (%)		Years attained				Urban-rural years	
	Rural boys	Urban boys	Rural girls	Urban girls	Boys	Girls	Rural boys	Urban boys	Rural girls	Urban girls	Boys	Girls
1989	60.51	70.83	55.18	61.38	85.43	89.91	6.86	7.65	6.43	8.10	0.79	1.67
1991	65.36	74.17	59.19	76.35	88.12	77.52	7.21	8.36	7.02	8.19	1.15	1.17
1993	63.88	78.99	58.90	78.87	80.88	74.67	7.40	8.53	7.55	8.65	1.13	1.11
1997	74.51	87.28	71.11	83.93	85.37	84.73	7.94	8.63	7.93	8.93	0.68	1.00
2000	72.90	89.62	70.15	87.50	81.35	80.17	8.16	8.77	8.29	8.97	0.62	0.68
2004	75.56	87.58	80.45	94.69	86.27	84.96	8.55	9.36	8.48	9.32	0.81	0.85

Source: Carolina Population Center and the Chinese Center for Disease Control and Prevention. N.D. "China Health and Nutrition Survey" (Computer files). Project website: http://www.cpc.unc.edu/projects/china.

Table 6.2 Random effects logistic regression models of enrollment, 7- to 16-year-olds

	(1) Base model		(2) Base model, province controls		(3) Rural change test	
Age	2.441	(18.15)**	2.441	(18.09)**	2.441	(18.08)**
Age squared	-0.114	(20.03)**	-0.114	(19.94)**	-0.114	(19.93)**
Rural (1=Yes)	-0.728	(7.64)**	-0.755	(7.88)**	-0.434	(2.56)*
Female (1=Yes)	-0.332	(4.51)**	-0.336	(4.54)**	-0.337	(4.57)**
Year						
1991	0.292	(2.75)**	0.302	(2.82)**	0.489	(1.99)*
1993	0.130	(1.26)	0.103	(1.00)	0.620	(2.43)*
1997	0.932	(7.79)**	1.004	(8.17)**	1.321	(4.79)**
2000	0.658	(5.71)**	0.681	(5.78)**	1.075	(3.93)**
2004	1.602	(9.36)**	1.639	(9.43)**	2.187	(5.12)**
Year × Rural Interactions						
1991 × Rural					-0.232	(0.85)
1993 × Rural					-0.625	(2.24)*
1997 × Rural					-0.390	(1.28)
2000 × Rural					-0.482	(1.61)
2004 × Rural					-0.669	(1.44)
Province dummies			×		×	
Constant	-8.948	(11.95)**	-8.608	(11.28)**	-8.862	(11.48)**
Observations	12,432		12,432		12,432	
Individuals	6,355		6,355		6,355	

Source: Carolina Population Center and the Chinese Center for Disease Control and Prevention. N.D. "China Health and Nutrition Survey" (Computer files). Project website: http://www.cpc.unc.edu/projects/china.

Note: Absolute value of z statistics in parentheses

* significant at 5%; ** significant at 1%

Given the high level of participation in compulsory ages in the CHNS sample, we turn now to an analysis of the secondary age range. A more striking story of persisting rural disadvantage with rising levels of enroll- ment emerges. Here, enrollment rates in the lower panel of Table 6.1 show a rising trend overall, but they also indicate a persistent enrollment gap that is actually wider in the sample in the early 2000s than in 1989. We test the trend in Table 6.3. Models 1 and 2 (without and with provin- cial controls) show that the odds of enrollment are significantly lower for rural than for urban children. More to the point, in Model 3, significant negative coefficients on the year-by-rural interactions indicate that, on average, the gap was significantly wider in 2000 and 2004 than in 1989, which is consistent with the descriptive findings.

Investigating years-of-schooling outcomes for the same age group in the lower right panel of Table 6.1 and Table 6.4 reveals significant in- creases overall and a persistent urban-rural gap. Table 6.4 shows that, on average, the rural disadvantage was about 0.8 years, whether or not prov- ince differences were incorporated (Models 1 and 2). Table 6.4 suggests that, by 2004, controlling for age, sex, and location of residence, on aver- age, children were attaining more than one-and-a-half years more educa- tion than in 1989 (Models 1 and 2). Model 3 shows that there is no signifi- cant interaction between rural residence and year, suggesting no evidence of rural children either catching up or falling further behind in years of education.

Urban-Rural Disparities in the Year 2000

We next turn to an analysis of census data from all provinces in the year 2000 to provide a more comprehensive description of the nature of rural- urban disparities in education. Earlier work with the 1990 and 2000 censuses has confirmed the expansion of compulsory education through the 1990s.[25] By the year 2000, entry into primary school even among rural youths ages ten to eighteen had reached 99 percent for China as a whole.[26]

Overall, in the 2000 census, among compulsory-aged children ages seven to sixteen, about 94 percent of children in urban areas were en- rolled, compared to about 89 percent in rural areas. For secondary-aged children, corresponding figures were 76 percent and 61 percent (see Table 6.5). Multivariate logistic regression analyses of enrollment for both

Table 6.3   Random effects logistic regression models of enrollment, 13- to 18-year-olds

	(1) Base model		(2) Base model, province controls		(3) Rural change test	
Age	-0.704	(1.58)	-0.677	(1.51)	-0.661	(1.48)
Age squared	-0.009	(0.63)	-0.010	(0.69)	-0.011	(0.72)
Rural (1=Yes)	-1.197	(12.36)**	-1.236	(12.67)**	-0.822	(4.67)**
Female (1=Yes)	-0.290	(3.71)**	-0.297	(3.79)**	-0.300	(3.81)**
Year						
1991	0.432	(4.09)**	0.430	(4.06)**	0.594	(2.60)**
1993	0.300	(2.69)**	0.277	(2.47)*	0.702	(2.82)**
1997	1.141	(9.26)**	1.201	(9.57)**	1.505	(5.81)**
2000	0.978	(8.32)**	1.015	(8.46)**	1.728	(6.55)**
2004	1.539	(10.49)**	1.578	(10.53)**	2.184	(7.05)**
Year × Rural Interactions						
1991 × Rural					-0.218	(0.85)
1993 × Rural					-0.545	(1.96)
1997 × Rural					-0.399	(1.37)
2000 × Rural					-0.905	(3.09)**
2004 × Rural					-0.791	(2.27)*
Province dummies			×		×	
Constant	14.924	(4.37)**	15.245	(4.44)**	14.815	(4.31)**
Observations	8,907		8,907		8,907	
Individuals	5,730		5,730		5,730	

Source: Carolina Population Center and the Chinese Center for Disease Control and Prevention. N.D. "China Health and Nutrition Survey" (Computer files). Project website: http://www.cpc.unc.edu/projects/china.
Note: Absolute value of z statistics in parentheses
* significant at 5% ** significant at 1%

Table 6.4 Random effects regressions of formal education completed, 13- to 18-year-olds

	(1) Base model		(2) Base model, province controls		(3) Rural change test	
Age	2.457	(16.92)**	2.487	(17.18)**	2.488	(17.25)**
Age squared	-0.061	(12.61)**	-0.062	(12.83)**	-0.062	(12.88)**
Rural (1=Yes)	-0.816	(14.88)**	-0.836	(15.46)**	-0.736	(7.81)**
Female (1=Yes)	0.053	(1.10)	0.050	(1.07)	0.050	(1.06)
Year						
1991	0.216	(5.13)**	0.207	(4.94)**	0.317	(3.75)**
1993	0.488	(10.06)**	0.466	(9.64)**	0.618	(6.38)**
1997	0.892	(15.37)**	0.881	(15.13)**	0.950	(8.37)**
2000	1.316	(21.78)**	1.298	(21.39)**	1.391	(11.98)**
in 2004	1.690	(23.92)**	1.636	(23.03)**	1.690	(13.12)**
Year × Rural Interactions						
1991 × Rural					-0.146	(1.51)
1993 × Rural					-0.202	(1.84)
1997 × Rural					-0.094	(0.72)
2000 × Rural					-0.127	(0.96)
2004 × Rural					-0.067	(0.45)
Province dummies			×		×	
Constant	-15.606	(14.44)**	-15.512	(14.36)**	-15.597	(14.48)**
Observations	8,742		8,742		8,742	
Individuals	5,303		5,303		5,303	

Source: Carolina Population Center and the Chinese Center for Disease Control and Prevention. N.D. "China Health and Nutrition Survey" (Computer files). Project website: http://www.cpc.unc.edu/projects/china.

Note: Absolute value of z statistics in parentheses

* significant at 5% ** significant at 1%

Table 6.5 Percentage enrolled by age group, residence, sex, and minority status, 2000

	7–16 population			13–18 population		
	Total	Urban	Rural	Total	Urban	Rural
Total	90.16	94.06	88.51	66.26	76.10	60.82
By . . .						
Sex						
Male	91.14	94.43	89.77	67.89	77.44	62.86
Female	89.07	93.65	87.12	64.51	74.74	58.56
Minority Status						
Han	91.07	94.18	89.69	67.50	76.23	62.37
Male	91.94	94.52	90.80	69.17	77.63	64.43
Female	90.11	93.81	88.46	65.71	74.81	60.07
Minority	81.97	92.29	79.43	55.45	74.28	49.83
Male	83.97	93.02	81.80	56.79	74.70	51.65
Female	79.81	91.54	76.84	54.01	73.86	47.84
Region						
North	91.85	95.12	90.38	68.73	80.16	62.16
Northeast	88.67	93.87	84.23	63.90	77.93	49.70
East	91.26	94.22	89.80	68.20	77.06	62.25
Central-South	90.94	93.63	89.85	65.94	71.62	62.98
Southwest	86.09	93.35	84.20	61.07	77.06	55.46
Northwest	89.60	94.54	88.13	67.93	79.23	64.04

Source: National Bureau of Statistics. "2000 Census Microsample" (Computer file). Beijing: National Bureau of Statistics.

groups indicate a significant rural disadvantage, after accounting for regional effects, minority status, age, and sex, for both age groups (see Tables 6.6 and 6.7, Model 2).

Our analysis suggests that at the compulsory ages, urban enrollment rates vary little across China's macro-regions, hovering between about 93 and 95 percent. Rural rates range from 84 to 90 percent. At the secondary ages, urban rates range from 72 to 80 percent, and rural rates range from 50 to 64 percent (see Table 6.5). Multivariate analyses indicate some significant differences in the effects of rural residence across macro-regions, compared to the North region, especially at the secondary level (Tables 6.6 and 6.7, model 5). Consistent across the two age groups is the

Table 6.6 Logistic regression models of enrollment, 7- to 16-year-olds, 2000

	(1) Baseline	(2) Main effects	(3) Rural-minority interaction	(4) Rural-female interaction	(5) Rural-region interaction
Age	-0.599	-0.609	-0.610	-0.610	-0.611
	(100.82)**	(101.39)**	(101.44)**	(101.37)**	(101.41)**
Rural (1=Yes)	-1.008	-0.972	-0.914	-0.853	-1.013
	(44.88)**	(42.01)**	(38.10)**	(27.11)**	(14.63)**
Minority (1=Yes)		-0.760	-0.271	-0.761	-0.757
		(28.35)**	(3.59)**	(28.34)**	(28.19)**
Sex (1=Female)		-0.267	-0.268	-0.085	-0.268
		(16.47)**	(16.48)**	(2.15)*	(16.52)**
Region					
Northeast		-0.515	-0.516	-0.517	-0.285
		(12.98)**	(12.99)**	(13.01)**	(3.34)**
East		-0.222	-0.216	-0.222	-0.288
		(7.19)**	(7.01)**	(7.20)**	(3.97)**
Central-South		-0.146	-0.139	-0.146	-0.395
		(4.74)**	(4.53)**	(4.74)**	(5.37)**
Southwest		-0.646	-0.634	-0.646	-0.382
		(19.20)**	(18.84)**	(19.20)**	(4.26)**
Northwest		-0.170	-0.164	-0.170	-0.166
		(4.15)**	(4.00)**	(4.15)**	(1.54)

	(1)	(2)	(3)	(4)	(5)
Rural × Northeast					−0.347
					(3.60)**
East					0.086
					(1.08)
Central-South					0.314
					(3.88)**
Southwest					−0.303
					(3.13)**
Northwest					−0.003
					(0.02)
Rural × Female				−0.229	
				(5.29)**	
Rural × Minority			−0.569		
			(7.07)**		
Constant	10.777	11.394	11.350	11.307	11.441
	(121.77)**	(121.66)**	(120.71)**	(118.81)**	(104.83)**
Observations	217,431	217,431	217,431	217,431	217,431
Prob>chi^2	0.0000	0.0000	0.0000	0.0000	0.0000
Pseudo R^2	0.2269	0.2434	0.2440	0.2437	0.2444

Source: National Bureau of Statistics. "2000 Census Microsample" (Computer file). Beijing: National Bureau of Statistics.

Note: Robust z statistics in parentheses

* significant at 5%; ** significant at 1%

Table 6.7 Logistic regression models of enrollment, 13- to 18-year-olds, 2000

	(1) Baseline	(2) Main effects	(3) Rural-minority interaction	(4) Rural-female interaction	(5) Rural-region interaction
Age	-0.768	-0.779	-0.780	-0.780	-0.782
	(140.72)**	(141.16)**	(141.17)**	(141.48)**	(140.94)**
Rural (1=Yes)	-1.416	-1.421	-1.385	-1.324	-1.563
	(61.38)**	(60.42)**	(57.54)**	(42.28)**	(24.54)**
Minority (1=Yes)		-0.482	-0.141	-0.482	-0.481
		(17.00)**	(1.98)*	(17.00)**	(16.89)**
Sex (1=Female)		-0.249	-0.249	-0.118	-0.245
		(14.09)**	(14.07)**	(2.99)**	(13.81)**
Region					
Northeast		-0.501	-0.500	-0.500	-0.253
		(12.07)**	(12.05)**	(12.07)**	(3.27)**
East		-0.223	-0.217	-0.224	-0.279
		(6.90)**	(6.73)**	(6.93)**	(4.13)**
Central-South		-0.234	-0.228	-0.235	-0.606
		(7.42)**	(7.25)**	(7.50)**	(8.96)**
Southwest		-0.483	-0.471	-0.483	-0.288
		(13.22)**	(12.87)**	(13.22)**	(3.27)**
Northwest		0.039	0.046	0.039	-0.150
		(0.94)	(1.12)	(0.95)	(1.50)

	(1)	(2)	(3)	(4)	(5)
Rural ×					
Northeast					−0.493
					(5.43)**
East					0.076
					(1.00)
Central-South					0.547
					(7.22)**
Southwest					−0.239
					(2.49)*
Northwest					0.258
					(2.35)*
Rural × Female				−0.193	
				(4.44)**	
Rural × Minority			−0.437		
			(5.66)**		
Constant	13.630	14.225	14.201	14.176	14.372
	(149.55)**	(146.36)**	(145.97)**	(144.14)*	(131.17)**
Observations	125,579	125,579	125,579	125,579	125,579
Prob>chi²	0.0000	0.0000	0.0000	0.0000	0.0000
Pseudo R²	0.2381	0.2465	0.2469	0.2467	0.2493

Source: National Bureau of Statistics. "2000 Census Microsample" (Computer file). Beijing: National Bureau of Statistics.
Note: Robust z statistics in parentheses
* significant at 5% ** significant at 1%

finding that, compared to the gap in the North, the rural-urban gap appears wider in the Northeast and Southwest.

Our analysis also underscores the importance of ethnicity. Table 6.5 shows that rural minorities are highly disadvantaged in enrollment rates. For example, at the compulsory ages, about 77 percent of rural minority girls are enrolled, and at the secondary ages, about 48 percent are enrolled. These numbers compare to about 92 percent for urban minority girls ages seven to sixteen, and about 74 percent for urban minority girls ages thirteen to eighteen. Multivariate analyses confirm the disadvantaged position of minorities, overall (Tables 6.6 and 6.7, Model 2), and show that there is a significant interaction with rural residence, such that the difference in educational opportunities associated with urban versus rural origins is substantially greater for minorities than for the majority Han (Tables 6.6 and 6.7, Model 3). Finally, the census data shows that, on average, rural residence has a somewhat more negative impact for girls than for boys, in both age groups (Tables 6.6 and 6.7, Model 4).

Exclusion

Finally, we turn to a discussion of exclusion. One logical definition of "excluded children" refers to those not meeting current government policy targets for nine years of compulsory education. Defining exclusion as not being currently enrolled and having less than a junior high school education, among thirteen- to eighteen-year-olds in the CHNS sample, there has been a precipitous drop. In 1989, about 22 percent of the children in the CHNS sample were excluded. By 2004, exclusion had dwindled to near nonexistence in the CHNS sample: just 4 percent of the sample, or thirty-four children, were excluded.[27]

The census samples are large enough to investigate exclusion in greater detail, by employing different definitions of exclusion and by looking at the composition of excluded children compared to all children. Table 6.8 shows the percentage of children ages thirteen to eighteen among different groups who are out of school with either less than primary or less than junior high school education. Primary exclusion remains an issue only in rural areas, and only substantially among minorities, among which group 4.5 percent of males and almost 9 percent of females fit into this category. In terms of region, it is only the rural Northwest and Southwest that have a significant struggle with numbers of children excluded from primary school—just over 3 percent in the Northwest and 4.5 percent in the Southwest.

At the junior high school level of exclusion, the census figures suggest that about 13 percent of rural youth, but less than 4 percent of urban youth, meet this category of exclusion. For rural Han females, the number is about 13.5, and for males about 8 percent. For rural minorities, the situation is much more dire: more than one-fourth of rural minority males and more than one-third of rural minority females meet the junior high school exclusion criterion. By region, the rural Northeast, Northwest, and Southwest are the worst off, with the most disadvantaged Southwest showing one in four children meeting the junior high school exclusion criterion.

Table 6.8   Indicators of exclusion, 13- to 18-year-olds, 2000

| | Percentage not enrolled and . . . | | | |
| | Less than primary attainment | | Less than junior high school attainment | |
	Urban	Rural	Urban	Rural
Among all	0.25	1.31	3.75	13.17
Among males	0.26	0.91	3.39	10.56
Among females	0.24	1.76	4.11	16.06
Among Han	0.24	0.59	3.51	10.73
Among Han males	0.25	0.41	3.12	8.28
Among Han females	0.23	0.79	3.89	13.46
Among minority	0.44	6.48	7.11	30.37
Among minority males	0.47	4.51	7.15	26.76
Among minority females	0.41	8.64	7.06	34.31
Among North	0.21	0.41	2.58	9.04
Among Northeast	0.21	0.51	3.14	16.26
Among East	0.18	0.47	2.97	8.31
Among Central south	0.25	0.31	4.18	10.36
Among Southwest	0.56	4.46	6.43	26.43
Among Northwest	0.32	3.43	4.91	17.27

Source: National Bureau of Statistics. "2000 Census Microsample" (Computer file). Beijing: National Bureau of Statistics.

A different way to illustrate the problems of exclusion is to show the characteristics of excluded children, compared to the characteristics of all children in the age range. Figure 6.1 shows the percentages of rural, minority, and female children; the percentage in each region for children in both definitions of exclusion; and the percentage for all children. This figure shows, unsurprisingly, that the vast majority of the few children who meet the primary exclusion criterion are rural (90 percent), as are 86 percent of those children who meet the junior high school exclusion criterion. Minorities are strongly overrepresented among excluded children: they are just 10 percent of the general population but 56 percent of the children excluded by the primary criterion, and 26 percent of the children excluded using the junior high school criterion. Girls are somewhat overrepresented for both definitions of exclusion relative to their share in the population. The Southwest and Northwest regions are quite overrepresented: 8 percent of children live in the Northwest, but 22 percent of primary exclusions are in the Northwest, as are 11 percent of junior high exclusions. The Southwest is where the differences are most striking: this region is home to 14 percent of children, 51 percent of primary exclusions, and 30 percent of junior high exclusions.

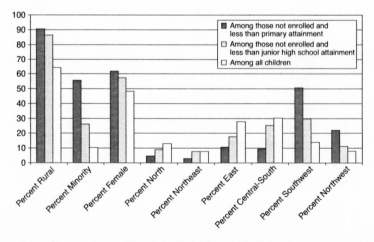

Figure 6.1 Characteristics of "excluded" children and all children ages 13–18 in 2000. Source: National Bureau of Statistics. "2000 Census Micro-sample" (Computer file) (Beijing: National Bureau of Statistics).

Summary

Analyses show that the level of education in rural and urban areas is increasing rapidly and that a large majority of urban and rural compulsory-age children are now enrolled. Among the few children who remain locked out of access to compulsory education, the vast majority are rural; minority children and children in western regions are disproportionately represented;[28] and girls are slightly overrepresented. Our investigation of secondary-age children shows that although rural access to secondary level schooling has risen, so has urban access, such that a rural penalty persists.

There are significant geographic and ethnic disparities in the level of rural access and in the urban-rural gap. Specifically, the enrollment penalty for living in a rural area varies across regions, particularly at the secondary level. In addition, our census analyses indicate that on average, the enrollment penalty for living in a rural area is somewhat greater for girls than for boys and substantially greater for minorities than for Han, at both the compulsory and secondary ages. Moreover, not only are minorities experiencing a disproportionate penalty for rural residence, they are also disproportionately likely to be living in poor regions and in rural areas. For example, among seven- to sixteen-year-olds, 20 percent of minorities and 31 percent of Han live in urban areas. More strikingly, 50 percent of minorities, but only 18 percent of the Han, live in the impoverished Northwest and Southwest regions.

Discussion and Conclusions

In this chapter, we have considered rural access to basic and secondary schooling overall and relative to urban access. Our findings attest to notable successes in raising access to education in rural areas—a trend that will bring important benefits to rural society via improved literacy and numeracy skills. From an absolutist perspective, the trend in access for rural students in recent decades is unambiguously positive.[29]

Less clear is whether the degree to which the relative position of rural residents has changed in a material way with educational expansion. Our analyses of the China Health and Nutrition Survey yielded no evidence of a significant narrowing of the rural-urban gap in enrollment or years of schooling attained by youth, and our analyses of enrollment in the 2000 census confirmed penalties for rural residence. A similar insight of absolute improvements and persisting inequalities emerges from our discussion of exclusion. The numbers excluded from education have dropped precipitously; this is an accomplishment that must not be minimized. However, exclusion from education before attaining compulsory education continues to exist and is almost entirely a rural problem. In addition, exclusion falls disproportionately on rural minority children, in the poor western regions of the country.

Ensuring basic educational access in poor rural areas is a focus of intense government activity at present. During the Tenth National People's Congress, Premier Wen Jiabao pledged to "eliminate all charges on rural students receiving 9-year compulsory education before the end of 2007."[30] Nearly four months later, in June 2006, the Standing Committee of the National People's Congress approved the Amendment to the Compulsory Education Law that was to go into effect September 1, 2006.[31] Considered a strategic part of developing a "new socialist countryside," one of the goals in the latest Five-Year Plan, this law aims to give rural children the same educational opportunities as their urban counterparts, and arrangements are being put in place that seek to address significant finance and human resource problems in rural schools.[32]

Initiatives in place to address problems of rural poverty will partly address the barriers faced by rural minorities. But additional policy attention has targeted minority areas specifically in recent decades, with a growing network of laws intended to advance the interests of historically disadvantaged ethnic groups.[33] In education, policy makers have supported increased protection of language rights; subsidies for minority students; the establishment of minority boarding schools and affirmative action policies for matriculation into colleges and universities; special classes to support minority matriculation into colleges; and subsidized nationality schools and colleges, including ethnic minority teacher training colleges.[34] In recent years, domestic and international projects have also sought to support nine-year compulsory education for minorities.[35] Given the significant access barriers that rural minority children continue to face, the success of programs seeking to improve the absolute—and relative—position of rural minorities will be a critical determinant of future ethnic stratification in China.

We have highlighted here the large impact of rural residence on enrollment for one group of rural children—minorities. Due to data limitations, we have not considered another group of rural children who may be at high risk for exclusion: children of rural migrants in China's cities. Until very recently, migrant children have had limited access to the urban state school system, and a series of laws and regulations have been implemented to increase access, including the Amendment to the Compulsory Education Law that went into effect on September 1, 2006.[36] Recent estimates of enrollment rates for this group range widely, which is unsurprising given the difficulty of identifying a sampling frame for this group.[37] The little-known scale of exclusion among this group of rural children is a significant gap in our understanding of rural-urban educational inequality in China.

Finally, we close by highlighting the point that our analyses have focused on questions of access and exclusion at the base of the educational system. Of course, this is just one piece of the overall picture of educational stratification. From the perspective of understanding education and larger patterns of urban-rural inequality in China, an equally important issue is rural student access to upper secondary and higher education. The bottleneck faced by children at the upper secondary level has intensified, with widening access to middle school, and tuition remains a significant barrier to poor families at this level. There is little evidence available about the rural-urban sorting and selection that goes on at this stage of education.

Higher education has expanded rapidly during the last decade, with many new options across the spectrum of cost, institutional type, and institutional quality. On the other hand, the long-standing university exam system, together with skyrocketing tuition and fees, is a higher barrier to rural students, on average, compared to urban students. Using the 2004 College Students' Economic Status Survey, Li Wenli found that approximately 32 percent of university students were from rural areas during the period between 2000 to 2003, compared with 68 percent from urban areas.[38] Similarly, Liu Jingming's work using 2003 data from the general social survey in China demonstrated that young people who lived in municipalities reporting to the government and those who attended key secondary schools had an enrollment advantage for baccalaureate education when compared with rural youth.[39] Both Li and Liu argue that rural-urban inequality in higher education has decreased as opportunities for higher education have expanded, but definitive empirical research on this issue is not available.[40] Complicating the picture is the great and growing diversity of institutional types within the higher education system in China. In-depth analysis comparing four-year universities to adult higher education suggests that rural youth are benefiting from more access to lower-status adult education, while urban residents are increasing their relative advantage in four-year higher education.[41] To better understand the contribution of education to rural mobility and rural-urban inequality, researchers need to address an important dearth of information about both overall gaps in access to higher levels of education and about the quality of education being accessed by urban and rural youth.

Rural-urban disparities are not well theorized in studies of stratification and mobility, but they are significant structural elements of educational inequality in many countries—elements that often intersect with class and ethnicity. Spatial dimensions of inequality in human development, including rural-urban dimensions, are commonplace in developing and transitional economies.[42] In addition, cross-national studies of student achievement in both Africa and industrialized countries indicate poorer educational performance of rural students, compared with urban students.[43] A full picture of social stratification in China, as in many countries, requires more systematic attention—empirical and theoretical—to the scale and mechanisms of urban-rural educational disparities.

7 | Disparities in Health Care and Health Status

The Rural-Urban Gap and Beyond

China built an enviable health-care system in the 1950s after the Chinese Communist Party came to power. Following the Russian Semenkov model, China extended basic health care to most of its population by relying on prevention, primary care, and a limited drug list, delivered by low-cost and modestly trained health-care providers. Expensive high-technology medicine, specialty care, and brand-name drugs received low priority. This strategy enabled China to make significant progress in enhancing well-being, particularly among the poor, as well as in protecting people from catastrophic medical expenses. The health of the population improved substantially. From 1955 to 1982, infant morality fell from 200 to 34 per 1,000 live births, and life expectancy increased from about 35 to 68 years, all while the government spent only about 3 percent of gross domestic product (GDP) on health care.[1]

When China embarked on its economic reform in 1978, it adopted a position of benign neglect toward the health sector. The Chinese leaders focused their full attention on economic growth and did not develop a coherent health policy, leaving the health system vulnerable to repercussions from the economic transition process. Since this time, individuals' access to care has become dependent on ability to pay and vulnerable to the increasingly for-profit market behavior of health-care providers, which has led to rapid cost escalation. In less than two decades, China's health-care system has transformed from one that provided prevention and affordable basic health care to all to one plagued by inequality in access to care and in health status and one in which many families are driven into poverty due to large medical expenses.[2] Rural areas and the West and Central regions, where economic progress lags behind, have been particularly hard hit.[3]

In this chapter, I first describe China's health policies before and during the economic reform. Next, I present evidence on the gaps in health care and health status between urban and rural populations and across different socioeconomic groups. I then describe and discuss the latest government initiatives to address these gaps. The final section of the chapter discusses conclusions.

Development of China's Health-Care Systems

Pre-Reform Institutions and Their Demise

China's health protection system in the pre-economic reform period was built on three pillars: a public delivery system with substantial government subsidies; price controls for medical services and inputs; and universal coverage through the Cooperative Medical Scheme (CMS) in rural areas and the Government and Labor Insurance Schemes (GIS/LIS) in urban areas.

Under Communist rule, China developed a three-tiered organization for the delivery of health care. In rural areas this consisted of village health posts, township health centers, and county hospitals, while in urban areas it was comprised of employee clinics operated by enterprises, community health centers, and city hospitals. In rural areas, practitioner training varied from one year after junior high for village doctors (who were assisted at the grassroots level by even more minimally trained "barefoot doctors") to fully qualified physicians at large county hospitals. Although urban health services were similarly organized, they were staffed with more qualified health professionals. The larger cities also had specialty hospitals and medical centers affiliated with medical schools. This three-tiered system provided a structure for efficient patient-referral for treatment of health problems.

Health facilities, like nearly all other enterprises at the time, were publicly owned. The government subsidized about 50 to 60 percent of their recurring costs, calculated to pay for the salaries of health personnel. The remaining revenue came from fee-for-service activities under a government-controlled price schedule, where prices were set below cost in order to make services affordable and accessible even for the poor and uninsured. Input prices were similarly controlled. Health-care workers, like other employees in state-owned enterprises, were paid on a salaried basis, with low cash remuneration.

Almost-universal insurance coverage was provided by the Cooperative Medical Scheme (CMS) in rural areas and the Government Insurance Scheme (GIS) and Labor Insurance Scheme (LIS) in urban areas. The CMS was primarily financed by the welfare fund of the farming collective (generally the brigade level within the rural people's commune structure). It organized health stations, paid village doctors to deliver primary care, and provided drugs. It also partially reimbursed patients for services received at township and county hospitals. At its peak in 1978, CMS covered 90 percent of China's rural population. However, CMS also suffered from problems of poor management that contributed to the downfall of these systems after the initiation of agricultural reforms in the early 1980s.

In urban areas, the GIS, financed by government budgetary funds, covered government employees, retirees, disabled veterans, university teachers, and students. The LIS, financed by each enterprise's welfare fund, covered that enterprise's employees, their dependents, and retirees. There was no risk pooling across governments or across enterprises, meaning that an individual's medical benefits were directly linked to the profitability of his or her employer. Consequently, when economic reforms swept through in the 1980s and 1990s, severely eroding the financial capacity of provincial governments and state-owned enterprises, workers not only faced job insecurity but also were unable to have their medical expenses reimbursed, leaving them practically uninsured.

Under this health-care system, there was relatively equal access to basic health care for the majority of Chinese citizens. Despite an extensive provider network and subsidized universal coverage, centrally controlled health service prices and modest health worker salaries resulted in a relatively low level of overall health spending. In 1981 health expenditures were still just over 3 percent of GDP, as noted earlier. Except for high-ranking officials, however, access to advanced medication and technology was limited.

Economic Transition and Its Consequences for Health Care

Economic reform impacted the health-care system through two major channels. First, a large proportional decline in government revenue constrained state capacity to finance health care. This trend, together with the subsequent perverse incentives that providers were subject to, has led to rapid cost escalation and unaffordable health care. Second, as the CMS collapsed and the GIS/LIS became financially unsustainable, health insurance coverage dropped drastically. Because of the government's differential responses toward urban versus rural areas, major disparities in health insurance coverage arose.

Reduction in Government Capacity to Finance Health Care

Governments of all transitional economies have faced serious fiscal difficulties. Despite sustained economic growth, China followed a similar pattern. Tax revenues for all levels of government declined from 35 percent of GDP in 1980 to a low of 11 percent in the period from 1995 to 1996.[4] The immediate effect of this decline in revenues was a drastic reduction in government subsidies to health facilities. Government subsidies as a share of total hospital and health center revenues decreased from more than 50 percent in the pre-reform era to approximately 10 percent in the 1990s.[5] This change seriously eroded public facilities' ability to provide subsidized care.

To keep health care affordable, the government maintained its strict price control by setting prices for basic health care below cost. At the same time, the government wanted facilities to survive financially, so it set prices for new and high-tech services above cost and allowed a 15-percent profit margin on drugs. These policies created perverse incentives for providers who had to generate 90 percent of their budgets from revenue-generating activities, a situation that turned hospitals, township health centers, and village doctors into profit-seeking entities. Equally important, this price-setting approach has created a leveraging effect whereby a doctor has to dispense seven dollars' worth of drugs to earn one dollar of income. As a result, providers overprescribe drugs and profitable tests. Seventy-five percent of patients suffering from a common cold are prescribed antibiotics, as are 79 percent of hospital patients—more than twice the international average of 30 percent.[6] This gross trend of overprescription has led China's health-care expenditure to grow at 16 percent per year for the past two decades[7]—that is 7 percent faster than the growth of GDP and probably the fastest rate of increase in the world.

Another consequence of providers' profit-seeking behavior has been the collapse of the three-tier referral system. Once providers realized that the more people they treat, the higher their profits, they began to compete with one another for patients, leading to overcrowding in large hospitals and underutilization of lower-level facilities. This situation has also contributed to the expenditure inflation.

Reduction in Health Insurance Coverage

The introduction of the Household Responsibility System in rural China led to the disintegration of the communes that had formed the basis of CMS financing. The government adopted a laissez-faire policy, and these organized financing schemes collapsed. CMS coverage shrank precipitously, covering only 10 percent of the rural population throughout the 1990s. As I explain later, it was not until 2003 that the Chinese government began to address this problem. Despite recent efforts, access to health care in many areas is still governed by the ability to pay, and many Chinese villagers cannot afford health care.

In contrast, the government strategy toward insurance coverage for the urban population has been much more cautious and proactive. There were several reasons for this. First, fulfilling the LIS commitment to their employees imposed a heavy financial burden on enterprises, seriously hampering their ability to compete in a competitive market economy. Because of the health-care cost escalation, the 11 to 14 percent of wages that the enterprises set aside for medical expenses often proved insufficient, so profits had to be used to supplement the shortfall. Compounding the problem further was the lack of risk pooling across enterprises or local governments. As an enterprise began to run a deficit under the new market economy, it became unable to reimburse its employees' medical bills; as a result, workers were in effect uninsured and the government was concerned that their discontent would threaten social stability. Finally, state employees were promised lifelong security in exchange for low monetary wages. To allow a deficit-running state enterprise to go bankrupt, the government first had to ensure urban workers continued health care, pensions, and other securities not tied to the enterprises.

In December 1998 the Chinese government announced a major policy decision: the establishment of a social insurance program for urban workers to replace the flagging LIS and GIS systems. The new program combines individual Medical Savings Accounts (MSAs) and social risk pooling at the city level. It is financed by premium contributions from employers (6 percent of an employee's wages) and by employees (2 percent of each employee's wage). It covers all urban workers, including government employees and employees of both state and non-state sectors. The self-employed, workers for small scale businesses, workers' dependents, and migrant workers, however, are not covered; as a result, 50 percent of the urban population is uninsured.

The rapid escalation of health-care costs, accompanied by shrinkage in health insurance coverage, has led to a rapid increase in patients' out-of-pocket health expenditure. Between 1978 and 2003, patients' out-of-pocket health expenditure grew at an average rate of 15.7 percent,[8] accounting for 60 percent of total health expenditure in 2003.

Trends in Rural-Urban Disparities

The Chinese government's policies toward its health-care sector since it embarked on its economic reform left access to health care dependent on a resident's ability to pay, while health expenditure escalation was not put in check. In this section, drawing on different data sources, I examine disparities in government spending on health care, the financial burden imposed on households by health spending, access to health care, and health status between and within the rural and urban populations up to 2003 and 2004, when China embarked on major efforts aimed at reversing the growing disparities.

Total and Government Spending on Health Care

Table 7.1 shows that total health expenditure per urban resident is on average roughly four times that per rural resident. Meanwhile, government spending is five to six times higher in urban than in rural areas, leading to a greater share of government expenditure out of total health expenditure in urban areas. This disparity is primarily because government spending on health is through direct subsidies to health facilities; because most of the large hospitals are located in urban areas, they receive the bulk of government funding. Over time, government spending as a share of total health expenditure dropped to a mere 7.5 percent in urban areas and 5.3 percent in rural areas. The government's underinvestment in rural health care, combined with the lack of insurance coverage in rural areas, imposes a major financial burden on the rural population.

Table 7.1 Per capita total and government health expenditure (RMB)

Year	National			Urban			Rural		
	THE	Gov't.	Gov't./THE	THE	Gov't.	Gov't./THE	THE	Gov't.	Gov't./THE
1991	77	8.2	10.6	188	24.2	12.9	45	3.8	8.5
1995	178	14.9	8.4	401	40.3	10.0	113	7.0	6.2
1998	295	20.0	6.8	626	52.7	8.4	195	9.1	4.7
1999	322	22.0	6.8	702	57.3	8.2	203	9.9	4.9
2000	362	23.9	6.6	813	61.8	7.6	215	10.6	4.9
2001	394	27.4	7.0	841	69.3	8.2	245	12.2	5.0
2002	451	30.5	6.8	987	73.7	7.5	259	13.8	5.3

Source: Data from *China Health Statistical Yearbook*, 2006. Government expenditure from Zhao Y., Wan Q., Tao S., et al., "Analysis and Result on China Health Account Assessment for the Year of 2002," (in Chinese) *Chinese Health Economics* 23 (2004): 5–10.

Financial Burden on Households

Based on findings from the National Health Survey,[9] Table 7.2 shows the financial burden of health care on households. Between 1993 and 2003, health expenditure as a share of household income increased, on average, from 8.2 percent to 10.7 percent in rural areas and from 6.0 percent to 7.2 percent in urban areas. This comparison shows that although income has grown, health-care spending has grown even faster. Within the rural and urban areas, there exist income disparities in the health financial burden, with rural residents in the lowest income quintile spending the highest percent of their income on health care.

Table 7.3 further illustrates the financial risk that individuals are subject to when faced with illnesses. In 1993, the cost of an episode of hospitalization was about 74 percent of a rural resident's income and 80 percent of an urban resident's income. In 2003, for both the urban and rural samples, the cost was two times as high as an individual's annual income. However, within urban and rural areas, the risk is particularly severe for individuals in the lowest income quintiles. In rural areas an episode of hospitalization can cost as much as six times an individual's income, and in urban areas, the cost is about four times an individual's income. These findings highlight the consequences of a health-care system that relies on ability to pay and the huge disparities in financial risk protection across different income groups within the rural and urban areas.

Access to Health Care

Table 7.4 shows the results of these financial barriers on access to health care. In rural areas, 23 to 24 percent of the population refused to be hospitalized due to financial reasons, and in urban areas this number was 16 percent in 2003, up from 10 percent in 1993. Among those who were hospitalized, nearly one-third (32 percent) of rural Chinese discharged themselves against their doctors' advice because they could not afford to stay. Only 18 percent did so in urban areas. In 1993, 12 percent of rural residents did not seek care when ill because of the cost of that care. This rate increased to 17.7 percent in 2003. Interestingly, the increase was even larger in urban areas, possibly due to a more rapid increase in health-care costs there, as shown in Table 7.3. In addition, the current

Table 7.2 Per capita out-of-pocket health expenditure as a percentage of income

| | Urban | | | | Rural | | | |
| | Income level | | | | Income level | | | |
Year	Lowest quintile	Middle quintile	Highest quintile	Total	Lowest quintile	Middle quintile	Highest quintile	Total
1993	14.1	6.9	4.0	6.0	19.7	10.1	5.0	8.2
2003	10.8	8.1	5.6	7.2	26.7	11.4	7.7	10.7

Source: National Health Services Survey, 2003.

Table 7.3 Financial burden of care (expressed in 1993 values)

	Urban				Rural			
	Income level				Income level			
	Lowest quintile	Middle quintile	Highest quintile	Total	Lowest quintile	Middle quintile	Highest quintile	Total
Outpatient expenditure per visit (RMB)								
1993	33	48	55	47	21	25	25	22
2003	114	196	342	204	72	81	128	88
Inpatient expenditure per admission (RMB)								
1993	1,244	1,457	2,039	1,598	489	483	661	535
2003	3,981	6,366	9,163	7,098	2,080	2,233	3,729	2,542
Per capita annual income (RMB)								
1993	739	1,677	3,848	1,942	223	546	1,596	724
2003	946	2,809	8,135	3,462	333	885	2,839	1,201

Source: National Health Services Survey, 2003.

urban health insurance program covers only 50 percent of the urban population.

Table 7.4 also shows that the poor have less access to care than the rich do, regardless of whether they live in rural or urban areas. In 2003, 23 percent of those living in the poorest rural areas refused to be hospitalized due to financial reasons, compared with 18 percent in the richest areas. The trend is similar in urban areas, with more than 21 percent of those in less-developed cities refusing hospitalization because of cost, compared with 15 percent in the most developed cities. The same holds true for outpatient care: in both urban and rural areas, the percentage of people not seeking care due to financial reasons increases as socioeconomic status declines. It is important to note that the disparities in access between income groups and within rural and urban areas have increased significantly over time.

Health Status

This section presents evidence on inequalities in health status between urban and rural areas as well as across income groups. There are many measures of health status. This chapter presents three measures: infant mortality rates, maternal mortality rates, and height. The mortality rates are indicators of how well a health system delivers basic health care, and height is a summary measure of health status commonly used in the health and development literature.[10]

Infant and Maternal Mortality Rates

Figures 7.1 and 7.2 show that over time the rural-urban gap in infant and maternal mortality rates has diminished, although significant disparities still exist, especially in the maternal mortality rate. This reduction of inequalities can be attributed in part to changes in maternal and child health-care utilization: gaps in the percentage of deliveries occurring in a health-care facility and utilization of both pre- and postnatal care have diminished over time. Figures 7.3 and 7.4 further examine inequalities in infant and maternal mortality rates by showing variations across provinces. Provinces are ranked in ascending order according to their GDP per capita. It can be seen that both mortality rates differ significantly across provinces, with provinces with higher GDPs performing better.

Table 7.4 Access to care

				Urban			Rural			
	Total	Urban	Rural	Large city	Medium city	Small city	Type 1	Type 2	Type 3	Type 4
Refused to be hospitalized due to financial reasons (%)										
1993	20.4	10.4	23.9	NA	NA	NA	NA	NA	NA	NA
2003	20.7	15.6	22.8	15.0	11.1	21.5	18.0	20.3	27.0	23.0
Requested early discharge from hospital due to financial reasons (%)										
2003	27.7	18.3	31.6	NA	NA	NA	NA	NA	NA	NA
Did not seek care when ill due to financial reasons (%)										
1993	12.1	7.9	12.4	7.9	6.1	8.2	10.6	12.6	12.3	14.3
2003	18.7	20.7	17.7	17.8	20.9	23.0	14.5	14.6	19.2	21.1
Average per capita income (yuan)										
2003	3,302	6,565	2,175	8,292	6,607	4,589	3,163	2,187	1,938	1,187

Source: National Health Services Survey, 2003.

NA: not available

Note: The divisions in this table are based on an index of socioeconomic conditions. Cities are divided into three classes—large, medium, and small—with large cities having the highest level of socioeconomic development. In rural areas, towns, and villages are grouped into four types, with Type 1 areas having the highest level of development.

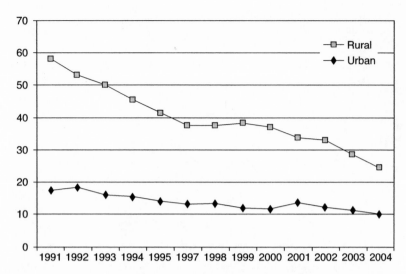

Figure 7.1 Infant mortality rate (per 1,000). *China Health Statistic Yearbook,* 2006.

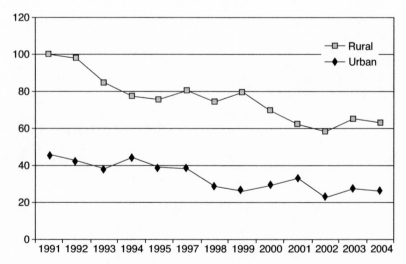

Figure 7.2 Maternal mortality rate (per 100,000). *China Health Statistical Yearbook,* 2006.

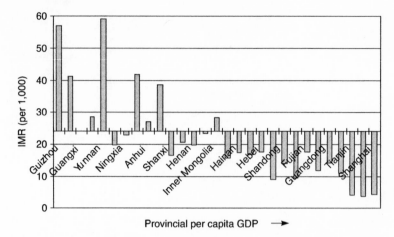

Figure 7.3 Infant mortality rate, 2000. Author's calculations using birth- and death rates from China 2000 Population Census Assembly (online at http://www.chinadataonline.org).

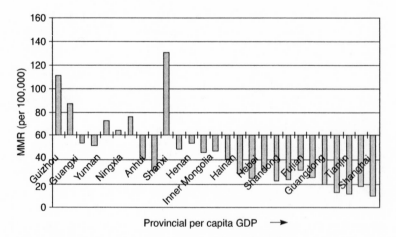

Figure 7.4 Maternal mortality rate, 2002. *China Health Statistical Yearbooks*, 2006.

Height

Using the China Health and Nutrition Survey (CHNS), I conducted regression analyses to examine inequalities in height between urban and rural areas, as well as across provinces and different income groups. The CHNS collected longitudinal data for eight provinces spread across different regions of China for 1989, 1991, 1993, 1997, 2000, and 2004. I focus on children between two and ten years old and adolescents between eleven and eighteen years old and perform separate regressions for males and females. The results are shown in Table 7.5.

For children between two and ten years old, height increased significantly over the fifteen years from 1989 to 2004. For example, controlling for income, girls in 2004 were 2.5 percent taller than girls of the same age in 1989 and boys in 2004 were 4 percent taller than boys of the same age in 1989. Overall, both boys and girls living in the rural areas are 1.9 percent shorter than their urban counterparts. Those who lived in households with higher incomes are taller. However, the greatest disparities in height exist across provinces. The regression results show that girls and boys in Guizhou are 5.2 percent and 5.6 percent shorter, respectively, than those in Liaoning, Jiangsu, Shandong, and Heilongjiang. Similar patterns were found for adolescents. Rural girls are 1.3 percent shorter and rural boys are 1.9 percent shorter than their urban counterparts. Again, those who live in higher-income households are taller. Similarly, there are major disparities across provinces. I also tested for changes over time in the gaps between the urban and rural areas, across income quintiles, and across provinces, but did not find any significant differences.

Table 7.5   Differences in height by rural-urban and income groups

	Girls (2–10)	Boys (2–10)	Girls (11–18)	Boys (11–18)
Rural compared with urban	−1.9%**	−1.9%**	−1.3%**	−1.9%**
Compared with Income Quintile 1				
Income Quintile 2	0.3%	0.0%	0.2%	0.3%
Income Quintile 3	0.8%**	0.4%*	0.6%**	0.6%**
Income Quintile 4	0.9%**	0.1%	1.0%**	0.7%**
Income Quintile 5	1.1%**	0.6%*	1.2%**	1.4%**
Observations	3,088	3,529	3,618	3,936

Note: Results based on random-effect regression of log heights on age, age squared, year, and province dummy.

$**p < 0.01$, $*p < 0.05$

China's Latest Reform Initiatives

The Chinese public has expressed their discontent with unaffordable access to health care and medical impoverishment (*kan bing nan, kan bing gui*; getting medical care is difficult and expensive) and with the rural-urban gap in government spending and policy attention through thousands of organized protests throughout the country in recent years; these protests receive frequent media attention.[11] At the same time, current Chinese leaders are giving greater priority to social development and to trying to build a more equitable society. In October 2006, the Chinese government announced that its new guiding principle is that development should be *people-centered*: it will strive to build a harmonious society by balancing economic and social development and urban and rural development.[12] Under this principle, health has been identified as a top social priority. President Hu Jintao promised a "bigger government role in public health, with a goal for everyone to enjoy basic health care service to continuously improve their health and well-being."[13] This new attitude, together with growing tax revenue generated by a thriving economy, have led to the introduction of several major reform initiatives.

Establishing New Cooperative Medical Schemes

In rural areas China's proposed solution to its health care problems has been to establish a "New Cooperative Medical Scheme" (NCMS)—a government-run voluntary insurance program initiated in 2003. The primary objectives of NCMS are to reduce rural-urban inequality in health care and to insure rural residents against catastrophic health expenses. Both the central and local governments subsidize each farmer 20 yuan (US$2.50; a total of US$5 per farmer) in the western and central provinces, with the farmer paying an additional 10 yuan (US$1.25) as an annual premium to enroll in NCMS. Government subsidies for eastern provinces are half of those for western and central provinces. By 2006, NCMS covered 50 percent of the rural population and was targeted to reach 100 percent by 2008. Local governments are free to choose the benefit packages and administrative arrangements of their NCMS according to local conditions, as long as they follow two policy guidelines: voluntary enrollment and coverage of catastrophic illnesses.[14]

Establishing Community Health Centers in Urban Areas

In an attempt to assure all urban residents basic health care and to redirect urban patients' reliance on hospital services toward primary care, in 2005 the government announced the establishment of community health centers (CHCs) to provide prevention, primary care, home care, and rehabilitative services.[15] CHCs will eventually be set up in every urban neighborhood in the hope that they will substitute for hospitals' expensive outpatient services and curb the unnecessary use of hospitals as convalescent homes. Whether these goals will be realized remains to be seen. Evaluations of the effectiveness and impact of CHCs have been limited.

New Government Funding for Universal Basic Health Care

Among all of the initiatives, perhaps the most important is the Chinese government's commitment to substantially increase its investment in health care. With a significant increase in tax revenue from a booming economy, China plans to inject an additional US$25–US$38 billion of government funding—the equivalent of 1 to 1.5 percent of GDP—into health with the goal of providing universal basic health care to urban and rural residents alike. This commitment represents a tripling of government spending on health and clearly signals the government's increased role in financing health care.

Conclusions

During almost two decades of benign neglect, China's health-care system was transformed from one that provided affordable basic health care to all people to one plagued with inequality in access to health care. Many families, especially the poor, now bear a heavy burden in paying for medical expenses. In particular, China's preferential treatment of the urban population in terms of providing health insurance coverage led to huge gaps between the urban and rural areas. This disparity in coverage led to disparities in access to care. Of interest is the fact that although the rural-urban gaps in several measures of access to care (refusal to be hospitalized due to financial reasons, not seeking care when ill due to financial reasons) have narrowed, ironically, the narrowing was not due to improvements in the conditions of the rural population but, rather, to a worsening of the conditions for the urban population. This trend can be attributed to the fact that recently health-care costs have been increasing at a faster rate in urban areas than in rural areas.

The record for health status, as measured by the infant mortality rate, maternal mortality rate, and the height of children and adolescents, is more favorable. Like other transition economies, such as the Czech Republic, the Slovak Republic, Hungary, Poland, and Slovenia, which did not suffer from major economic contractions or a total collapse of the health-care system during economic transition, China's infant mortality rate and life expectancy at birth have improved moderately. In particular, the rural-urban gap in infant mortality rates experienced a marked reduction in the 1990s. This trend may be due to improvements in maternal and child-care services nationwide that occurred during this period. Nonetheless, significant gaps remain. It would also be premature to conclude that remaining rural-urban disparities in health-care access have little impact on health outcomes. Health outcomes such as the infant mortality rate and life expectancy are affected by a number of complex factors outside of the health system. Further investigations of health outcomes that are more sensitive to health-care access, such as disease-specific health outcomes, may reveal a different picture.

Beyond the rural-urban gap, the evidence in this chapter also highlights the fact that significant disparities in health care and health status exist across provinces and income groups and that these are often of a greater magnitude than the disparity between urban and rural areas. There are two plausible explanations for these trends. One obvious explanation is that in a health-care system where access to care is largely determined by ability to pay and where health-care costs are increasing rapidly, those who will be most adversely affected are low-income individuals. Another explanation lies in the unique way in which China divides its fiscal responsibilities between the central and local governments. In 2003 only 8 percent of total government health appropriations came from the central government.[16] The rest were financed by local governments. By placing the majority of expenditure responsibilities on local governments, China left financing and provision of health care highly vulnerable to local economic conditions.

Recent government initiatives and the new commitment to significantly increase government spending represent a giant step toward reducing health-care inequalities between urban and rural areas and toward assuring a basic level of care for all. The extent to which these initiatives can effectively reduce the remaining gaps remains to be seen.

8 | The Narrowing Digital Divide
A View from Rural China

The literature on information communication technologies (ICTs) in China emphasizes the existence of a pronounced digital divide between the urban haves and the rural have-nots. Some of this literature explains that when funding infrastructure construction and devising pricing and product options, ICT providers have historically given priority to the preferences of the politically vocal and prosperous urban elite.[1] Other studies use weighted maps and figures to demonstrate that China's interior and rural regions have been largely excluded from the expansion of information technologies, such as the fixed-line phone and the Internet.[2]

This chapter examines a phenomenon so far neglected in the literature—the shrinking of China's rural-urban digital divide. The shrinking of this divide has been overlooked by scholars for at least three reasons. First, academic research and publishing has not yet caught up with the rapidity of the expansion of ICTs into rural areas. Second, in focusing on fixed lines and the Internet, researchers have failed to notice the expansion of cheap mobile phones.[3] Finally, in identifying only Internet density or the numbers of users as indicators of communications distribution, scholars have overlooked the intermediate role of local government organizations and schools in disseminating more widely information obtained via the Internet.

This chapter draws on Chinese-language secondary data, yearbooks, and media reports, as well as interviews and observations conducted in Rivercounty, a rural settlement located in Ji-angxi Province, in 2000, 2004, 2006, and 2007, using these sources to show that, contrary to the conventional wisdom, the digital divide be-tween rural and urban areas is shrinking. The first section of this chapter, which addresses the expansion of telecommunications into China's rural interior, presents figures to illustrate the rapidity and extent of the expan-sion of fixed phones, mobile phones, and Internet connections into Chi-na's rural interior. The next two sections move beyond the dichotomy of the urban informational haves and the rural informational have-nots to explore a crucial dimension to the shrinking of the divide: the burgeon-ing of the rural informational Have-Less. The second section of this chapter documents the rise of Have-Less technologies and services in rural areas. The third section explores rural peoples' growing demands for and use of these budget ICTs in order to participate in translocal so-cial and economic networks in a world characterized by the increased movement of labor, goods, and capital.[4] The fourth section examines the intermediate access to the Internet that state agencies at county and township levels facilitate through their information-service provision-ing. This is a crucial dimension of the narrowing of the digital divide, one that is glossed over in aggregate figures on the occupational back-grounds and geographic locations of Internet users. The fifth section considers the contribution of rural schools and recent curriculum inno-vations in reducing digital disadvantage among the next generation of rural residents. The conclusion reflects on why the rural-urban gap has been narrowing with regard to ICTs while at the same time remain-ing entrenched in other aspects of social resource provisioning, such as health and education.

Expansion of Telecommunications into China's Rural Interior

Fixed Phones and Mobile Phones

There has been a rapid increase in rural people's access to ICTs. As shown in Table 8.1, the proportion of people in rural China with access to a fixed-line phone has been growing. The percentage of administrative villages with a fixed phone connection has also increased, from around 60 percent in 1995 to 83 percent in 2001 to 91 percent in 2004 to 100 percent by the end of 2006.[5] A caveat, though, is that an administrative village comprises several natural villages; where these are geographically dispersed, residents in more remote hamlets may still experience difficulties in getting access to a phone.

More dramatic than the increase in fixed phones is the increase in mobile phones. In 2004 the number of mobile phones per hundred people in China exceeded the number of fixed-line phones,[6] a situation observed in some other low- and middle-income countries.[7] In rural China, the growth in the numbers of people using mobile phones has been pronounced in poor and remote areas that have been too isolated to benefit from fixed phone connections. For instance, in 2005 Jiangxi China Mobile extended its GSM digital network to 120 villages that had had no prior form of phone connection whatsoever. This much-publicized gesture enabled the Jiangxi government to proclaim at the end of 2005 that 100 percent of administrative villages had access to a phone.[8] Rural people also favor mobile phones for the same reasons of convenience as urban customers, and this growing preference for mobiles explains in large part the fall in fixed phones between 2003 and 2004 (Table 8.1). Table 8.2 demonstrates the pace of increase in mobile phone density in Jiangxi Province, yet even these remarkable figures likely represent only a fraction of actual mobile phone usage, because many people share mobile phones.

Communications Expenditures

A further indication of the growing usage of communications by rural people is the increase in rural expenditures on transport, post, and telecommunications, shown in Table 8.3. The rise in rural expenditure on communications partially reflects the effects of policy efforts in the early 2000s to improve rural incomes, including reductions in the farmers' tax

Table 8.1 Percentage of China's urban and rural households with fixed phones

Year	% of urban households with a fixed phone	% of rural households with a fixed phone
2000*	NA	26.4
2003**	95.4	36.6
2004**	96.4	34.9

Source: *China Statistical Yearbooks* (Beijing: China Statistical Press, 2001* and 2005**).
NA: not available

Table 8.2   Ownership of mobile phones per 100 households in Jiangxi Province

Year	Rural ownership per 100 households	Town ownership per 100 households	City ownership per 100 households
2000*	1.43	14.37	16.33
2003**	18.73	78.06	81.29
2004**	30.69	95.22	99.80
2005***	64.82	136.26	
2006***	78.04	147.22	

Source: *Jiangxi Statistical Yearbook*, (Beijing: China Statistics Press, 2001*, 2005**, and 2007***.).

burden, subsidies for grain production, and the encouragement of labor migration. A large survey of phone ownership conducted in rural Sichuan, Jiangsu, and Shandong at the end of 1997 reveals the importance of income increases in propelling phone ownership, identifying a threshold of 2,000–3,000 yuan annual income per capita before connections occur.[9] Yet, as Zhuangqun Hu and Chuanwu Huang have noted, higher incomes are not the sole factor behind rising rural expenditure on communications.[10] That other factors are involved is suggested by the fact that in 2004 the annual income of rural residents was equivalent to the 1993–1994 income of urbanites, yet the expenditure of rural people on communications in 2004 was double that of their urban counterparts in 1993–1994. Other factors influencing these expenditures include a decline in the cost of handsets, the elimination of fixed phone connection fees, and rural peoples' increased demand for ICTs, a dimension of the narrowing of the digital divide, which is discussed in the third section of this chapter.

Internet

Just as with phones, rural areas are not being left out of Internet access. In Rivercounty in the late 1990s, Internet cafes opened in the old and new county seats,[11] and in 2005–2006 they opened in several townships. Some rural households have even obtained Internet connections: according to China Telecom, households in rural Jiangxi with an Internet connection increased from zero in 2000 to five hundred thousand in 2006.[12] If we assume that each of these households comprises two Internet users, that would mean the presence of approximately 1 million Internet users in rural Jiangxi. But this figure may be somewhat optimistic given that a

Table 8.3 Urban and rural residents' expenditures on communications,
             post and transport

Year	Residents' income (yuan)		% of expenditure on communications, post and transport	
	Urban	Rural	Urban	Rural
1992	2,027	784	2.64	NA
1993	2,577	922	3.82	NA
1994	3,496	1,221	4.65	NA
1995	4,283	1,578	4.83	NA
1996	4,839	1,926	5.08	NA
1997	5,160	2,090	5.56	NA
1998	5,425	2,162	5.94	3.84
1999	5,854	2,210	6.73	4.38
2000	6,280	2,253	7.90	5.57
2001	6,860	2,476	9.30	6.32
2002	7,703	2,936	10.4	7.03
2003	8,472	2,622	11.1	8.39
2004	9,422	2,936	11.8	8.83

Source: Zhuangqun Hu and Chuanwu Huang, *Analysis of China's Telecom Development* (Beijing: Social Science Academy Press, 2006), 145.
NA: not available

survey conducted by the China Internet Research Centre in 2006 reported fewer than 3 million Internet users in Jiangxi,[13] a province that has nearly 17 million urban residents and more than 26 million rural residents. In addition, across China only 0.4 percent of Internet users are farmers.[14] Although the media may have exaggerated the figure for Internet connections, there has nevertheless been rapid growth in Internet connections in lower-order and semi-urban settlements, such as county seats and township towns, as well as in some villages, usually those located close to counties and townships.

The Rural Information Technology Have-Less

The rise of Have-Less ICTs in China's rural hinterlands is a crucial dimension to the narrowing of the rural-urban digital divide. The term "Have-Less" mentioned at the beginning of this chapter was initially coined by

Carolyn Cartier, Manuel Castells, and Jack Linchuan Qiu to examine the informational stratification that exists in the overlooked grey areas of the digital divide in China's cities.[15] Even though Cartier et al. formulated the concept to analyze the characteristics of low-end ICTs in the cities as well as the backgrounds and behaviors of poor urban customers, I maintain that the term is equally useful for describing low-end ICTs and their users in rural areas.

A mix of factors has contributed to the rise of Have-Less ICTs among people from lower socioeconomic backgrounds. A factor emphasized by Cartier et al. is bottom-up demand and agency. Indeed these authors go so far as to argue that the absence of assistance from either the state or corporate players has been critical in forcing people from lower socioeconomic backgrounds to push for access to budget ICTs.[16] Yet while grassroots demand—explored in detail in the third section of this chapter—is undoubtedly central to the rise of Have-Less ICTs, this current section demonstrates that the state and telecommunications companies have also played a decisive enabling role.

State commitment to achieving the goal of national connectedness during the 1980s and 1990s helped China to achieve the most rapid construction of a fiber-optic cable network in world history. In addition, owing to the strategic importance of the sector, the then state regulator—the Ministry for Post and Communications—required China Telecom to increase its investment in infrastructure in rural areas and to cross-subsidize China Post's operations in poorer areas.[17] Subsequently, in 1994, to generate a commercial impetus for accelerating the expansion of telecommunications goods and services, the State Council ended China Telecom's monopoly by authorizing the formation of the mobile company Unicom. This was followed in 1998 by the merging of the Ministry of Electronic Industry and the communications networks of the Ministry of Radio, Film, and Television; China Aerospace; and China Aviation Corps to form the new Ministry of Information Industry. At the same time the new State Administration for Film, Television, and Radio was created, and in 1999 this Administration established an Internet and cable television company, China Cable Corps,[18] which caused ChinaNet (via China Telecom) Internet subscription charges to fall. Meanwhile, China Telecom, owned by the former Ministry of Posts and Telecommunications, was divided into China Telecom with fixed phone and Internet operations, and China Mobile, with mobile phone operations.[19] China Telecom was relieved of the burden of subsidizing the post office, though this concession failed to compensate for the losses incurred on account of exclusion from the ascendant field of mobile phones.[20]

The telecommunications companies initially responded to the new competitive situation by trying to recruit more urban customers. But by the early 2000s the urban market for many telecommunications products and services had become saturated. With much encouragement from relevant state ministries, the companies therefore increasingly turned their attention to the countryside. The mobile companies invested substantially in infrastructure in rural areas—in particular, in the hardware for advanced signal engineering. For instance, during the early 2000s in Jiangxi's counties, both mobile companies raced to upgrade from GSM to CDMA, the latter offering five times the host capacity of the former as well as superior signal quality,[21] and by the end of 2008 most administrative villages had obtained CDMA coverage. China Telecom also increased its investment in rural areas. Again in Jiangxi Province, China Telecom offered free installations of fixed-line phones in selected villages, ostensibly as part of its contribution to building a new socialist countryside, a policy approach advocated since 2006 to denote increased attention to rural public goods and services and the removing of barriers to rural-urban linkages.[22] In the mid-2000s ChinaNet, seeking to mark its turf for Internet services via China Telecom, extended cable connections to townships throughout Jiangxi, partly in anticipation of future moves by county cable television companies to diversify into Internet services.

Have-Less Mobile Goods and Services

Once the infrastructure was in place, mobile companies were able to set about devising a range of cheap products to attract rural customers. In Rivercounty in 2003 China Mobile launched its economy line called All China, which included the "masses phone card," the "Jiangxi mountain and river leisure card," and the "fields and gardens card." The same year Unicom introduced its economy phone card line called "Wishes in Hand." Then, in July 2006, the Rivercounty branch of Unicom also launched the "home garden card," which undercut the rates of China Mobile's "fields and garden card." Through their cheap rates—for instance, 500 minutes of listening time for around 6 yuan per month and 0.3 yuan per minute for nationwide dialing—this new market in budget phone cards enabled large numbers of rural people to afford communication technologies. Indeed, the numbers of people in less affluent areas across China who have signed up for cheaper charges in recent years have been of such magnitude that mobile companies' monthly revenue per user has even started to fall.[23]

The mobile companies have also tried to attract rural customers by devising services that meet their needs for information and for maintaining networks. For example, in Rivercounty in October 2005 both mobile phone companies launched a service whereby individuals pay to have airtime credit transferred from the mobile phone of a village-based agent to their own mobile phone. The China Mobile service is referred to as Adding Value by Remote, while the Unicom service is called Mobile Petrol Station. This service saves villagers from traveling to the township branch of either China Mobile or Unicom and is particularly valued by customers in remote villages.[24] As another example, in 2005 China Mobile and the Department of Agriculture launched a service across Jiangxi Province that sends informational text messages called *nong xin tong* (rural bulletins). Depending on their selection, subscribers can opt to receive specialist information on fruit cultivation, animal husbandry, urban training and employment opportunities, market opportunities, and agricultural produce prices. According to the manager of the Rivercounty branch of China Mobile, his branch has seven thousand *nong xin tong* subscribers, most of whom are village cadres, specialist producers, or *getihu* (small business operators).[25] As a final example, during the mid-2000s, China Mobile joined forces with China Post to offer a service whereby text messages are sent to villagers to notify them when remittance funds from city kin have arrived. This service has become especially important in poor and remote townships: across China post office branches in remote localities have closed, in part because China Post no longer receives subsidies from China Telecom.[26]

Internet Cafes

Internet cafes based in rural townships are a further expression of the emergence of Have-Less ICTs. These cafes began to appear in Rivercounty in 2005 and offer online access at between 1 and 2 *yuan* per hour, a rate affordable for most potential rural consumers. The cafes have come about through two developments. One is the fall in connection prices that has occurred as a result of market competition. In 2004 the Rivercounty Broadcasting and Television Company challenged China Telecom's monopoly on Internet business by offering combined cable and Internet access. Then in 2005 Railcom, a phone company that operates mainly in county seats also offered Internet services. These new entrants forced China Telecom to halve its fee, and across South China the company continues to be the main provider.

The second development has been the emergence of rural individuals who have a knowledge of, and interest, in the Internet and have the money to establish Internet cafes. In some senses their emergence corresponds with Cartier et al.'s finding for China's cities: that providers in the Have-Less ICT economy originate from lowly socioeconomic backgrounds. In Rivercounty's old and new county seats, both of which are bottom-rung urban settlements, Internet cafes were established by laid-off state sector workers as well as by some demobilized soldiers. In Rivercounty's townships, which are rural-designated settlements, most Internet cafes were established by high school graduates with previous migration experience. The Bureau of Culture requires that Internet cafe operators have at least a high school education, a requirement that reflects Party-state efforts to regulate the Internet sector and prevent unhealthy usages. Yet even though township Internet cafe owners have an education level that is higher than that of the average rural resident, they are far from privileged. They are individuals who have turned to labor migration as a way out in an environment that, despite their graduation from high school, has offered few prospects for a better life.

Township Internet cafes play a key role in helping to transfer awareness about the Internet from the urban ICT Have-Less sector to an incipient counterpart sector in rural areas. There is, however, an important caveat pertaining to the role of migration in promoting the Internet as a Have-Less technology in rural areas: the positive selection effects of out-migration reduce the numbers of potential Internet cafe customers, and this loss is difficult to compensate for because the Internet has a higher "educational" barrier to usage than phones. Cheap rates alone are therefore inadequate to attract the volume of users needed to sustain the Internet businesses. The effects of migration on Internet learning and the rural business experiences of Internet cafe owners are illustrated in their testimonies. One Internet cafe owner in RH Township, Rivercounty, told me:

I worked for three years in Guangzhou, and this is when I came into contact with computers. I worked in a warehouse and had to enter details about left-over stock into a computer. I also went to internet cafes in my spare time; there were many of them in the city. On returning home I did not want to farm but had nothing else to do. So my wife and I borrowed around sixty thousand *yuan* from friends and relatives. Most of our customers are middle and high school students. Some students want to go online to look up their exam results. There are also some returned migrant customers, especially at Spring Festival. They use the webcam to talk with siblings and friends who are migrants in the cities. Most of them play games and chat. Some people who work in nearby work-units also go online from time to time. It is difficult to do business because most young people are in the cities. Parents don't let their children come and the older people don't understand it. I hope to break even.[27]

Another Internet cafe owner located in GP Township, Rivercounty, explained:

I went out for 6 months but didn't like it. Whilst there, I met a master worker *(shifu)* who taught me how to install computers. I invested around sixty thousand *yuan* to set up here with twelve computers. I also need to pay around 800 *yuan* per month in electricity expenses. To help earn a livelihood I also farm 10 *mu* of land with my family. The rural market is not so good for trying to develop an internet business, and the cafe alone could not support me. I've been running the cafe for three months now and hope things get better.[28]

Admittedly, these entrepreneurs face immense difficulties operating in the rural environment, but their activities nevertheless help to reduce the gap between the urban ICT Have-Less and the rural ICT Have-Less.

Have-Less Networks and Demand

In an increasingly mobile and economically diversified environment, rural people's growing demand for and daily usage of Have-Less ICTs constitute a further major dimension to the narrowing of the digital divide. Since the disbanding of the communes, the return to household farming, and the rise of the market economy in the early 1980s, translocal networks have assumed increased importance in enabling rural people to obtain the resources and information they can use to reduce their livelihood risks and pursue economic and other opportunities. As Cartier et al. point out, social networks are not new in China, but networks are changing in their function, form, and durability.[29] ICTs have become central to rural peoples' strategies for maintaining and negotiating these networks, in part because the alternatives such as post or travel are costlier and more time-consuming.

In many areas in South China, including in Jiangxi Province, patrilineal kinship networks are an example of relationships that are being sustained and reinvented, in part, through phones. Since the late 1980s, large numbers of patrilineal kinship groups have been updating or compiling their genealogies, which provide conceptual maps of male membership of the group. Phones have facilitated this process, and they have also made it easier for rural people to use correspondence, exchange, and reciprocity to activate in real life the conceptual blood ties that are mapped out in the genealogies. For instance, in some cases the members of large surname groups use the Internet and phones to mobilize patrilineal kin living in a range of rural and urban settlements, and even in other countries, to contribute funds for building monuments, roads, and schools and for arranging festivals or other activities.

In this era of market reforms, rural people have also been keen to maintain ties with affines and with individuals who have the status of "fictive kin," such as former schoolmates and workmates who commonly refer to each other as "brother," "sister," and "aunt." Some scholars have argued that lower-level urban settlements, such as towns and county seats, help to dissolve rural-urban boundaries in the sense that many rural people have kin, relatives, or friends who work part time or full time in these settlements, and rural people themselves often traverse the village and semi-urban or lower-order urban settlements in daily life.[30] Family members or other contacts who work in local government or institutions, such as schools or hospitals or in business, can be important sources of help when individuals need to obtain access to permits or to better-quality public goods and services. Rural people use phones to maintain these relationships and to contact individuals when need or opportunity arises.

ICTs also enable rural people to maintain contact with friends and relatives who are migrant laborers in large coastal cities. As Cartier et al.

observe, even though much elite commentary on labor migrants refers to them as moving "blindly" or "floating," "the reality is that exchange of information usually precedes and accompanies human movement," thereby maintaining and extending existing social networks.[31] For instance, when returning to their villages for Spring Festival, migrants keep abreast of social and economic developments in the city by phone, as indicated by the high sales volume of the discount Spring Festival dialing cards sold at township mobile company branches at this time of year.[32] By talking with city-based siblings and former classmates in Internet cafes or on the phone, most rural young people obtain an accurate understanding of urban living and working conditions. Much migration occurs through "chain migration" whereby rural people from particular localities use the information feedback mechanism from pioneer migrants to move to the same destination areas and occupational sectors; these chains multiply over time to cover more diverse locations and forms of employment.[33] Phones, and mobile phones in particular, play a role in this process. For instance, sociologists Raymond Ngan and Stephen Ma have documented how actual and intending migrant workers have used their phones and social networks to identify more attractive employment opportunities, thereby enhancing their bargaining position with employers during periods when labor shortages prevail.[34]

As has been observed of poor people in other developing countries,[35] rural people in China have been creative in adapting their use of phones to the reality of their economic circumstances. Some elderly people I met in Rivercounty had a phone that had been purchased by their migrant adult children; to save money, they used the phone primarily for receiving calls. Another strategy used by poorer people is to keep calls short. For instance, in one survey of 142 children living in poor areas of Northwest China's, the authors report that in 88 percent of the cases migrant parents maintained contact by phone and that the calls occurred on average twice a month for less than five minutes each time.[36]

Rural people also use ICTs for building and maintaining the translocal networks necessary for trading and entrepreneurship. Villagers I encountered in rural Jiangxi commonly described those who were adept at making money and who had social and economic networks outside the village as having "ability." At the higher end of the "ability" spectrum are so-called white-collar entrepreneurial farmers. I visited the premises of one such white-collar farmer in Shangrao, which is one of thirty-six nationwide pilot information districts. He raised several thousand pigs, and in his office behind the pig barns, there was a computer with bookmarks for pig production Web sites.[37] Yet even though some media reports envision a countryside full of such informational farmers, the reality is that the vast majority of farmers do not use virtual networks or information sources to plan their economic activities.[38] In fact, there is much concern in elite circles that the rural Have-Less use the Internet to partake in distinctly unproductive activities—for instance, online gambling.[39]

Most ordinary farmers use mobile phones, rather than the Internet, as the main tool for maintaining and extending economic networks. Phones help to alleviate the information asymmetry and vulnerabilities that farmers face when trying to price and sell their goods or seek new opportunities. Phones are also the means by which farmers scattered in different villages and different counties can coordinate their sales. Rather than each individual trying to find a buyer for a small amount of produce, farmers can attract a buyer and negotiate a higher price by offering a larger volume of produce. For example, Mr. Nie is a specialized duck and chicken farmer who lives in WX Village in Rivercounty. He learned poultry-raising skills by working with his maternal uncle who lives on the outskirts of the small city of Zhangshu more than 60 km (more than 37 miles) away. Mr. Nie maintains regular phone contact with his uncle as well as with a couple of experienced farmers in the Zhangshu area. He also keeps in touch with a Guangzhou-based purchaser whom he met during a previous visit to Zhangshu. Mr. Nie obtains his fertilized eggs from specialist producers located in both Zhangshu and Guangzhou, and he often sells the fully grown birds via these same people. In an institutional environment in which purchase chains can be unreliable, the phone helps Mr. Nie in negotiating poultry-raising agreements with individuals in different locations. This strategy minimizes the risks he incurs because of traders who supply fertilized eggs but then refuse to buy the birds and traders who offer an amount less than the previously agreed-on price.[40]

Rural people also use ICTs to obtain information and help from sources that lie outside their own social and economic networks. One example is the recent dial-to-order service that China Post has offered following its loss of China Telecom subsidies. China Post hires rural agents, usually notable local people, to whom farmers can phone in their orders for pesticides, fertilizer, seeds, and daily goods, which are then delivered to their door.[41] One agent, a village doctor, told me that his agency had a turnover of 100,000 yuan per year. He also explained that farmers benefit not only from the convenience of telephone ordering, but also from the reliability of the China Post brand in a market rife with fake inputs.[42]

It is thus far clear that rural people use Have-Less ICTs to participate in ever wider social and economic networks and to obtain information and support from ever more diverse sources. But stratification processes that affect rural people's involvement in social and economic networks also affect their access to ICTs. One example is occupation. In River-county members of less prosperous households engaged primarily in sub-sistence agriculture said to me, "Why do we need phones in the fields all day?" One village cadre offered a similar view, explaining, "Only people with 'ability' have a mobile phone. Those without ability don't need one." Another example is gender. Again in Rivercounty, several married women in their thirties to fifties replied to my questions about mobile phone ownership by saying, "My old man [husband] has one." When I inquired further, I learned that in many instances the husband had the mobile phone because he was thought to do the outside economic work such as trading or odd jobs, whereas the wife was thought to be largely based at home—this despite the fact that many women worked locally on building sites in the county seat and in nearby towns. A final example is education. When I asked villagers living near townships if they ever went to the local Internet cafe, common responses included "We don't understand it," "We have no culture," and "Why would a farmer go online?" The ways in which stratification affects both societal and individual perceptions of ICT entitlement and relevance have been referred to by some scholars as the "second level digital divide" (the first being the distribution of the technology itself).[43] But even though some Have-Less ICT users have more and others have less, it remains that unprecedented numbers of rural people are now using ICTs.

Intermediate Access to the Internet and the Narrowing Digital Divide

Another dimension of the narrowing of the rural-urban divide is the role of government institutions in providing rural people with intermediate access to the Internet. The central government has actively encouraged officials in lower-level government institutions to use and promote infor-mation services in rural areas. This is because information is seen as necessary for developing the economy. Whereas in an agrarian society added labor input raises yields, and in an industrial society new machines raise yields, in an informational society communicated information about varieties and prices raises not only yields but also profitability.[44] The priority given to "informationalization" can be seen in key national policy documents. Informationalization *(xinxi hua)* was the thematic focus of the Tenth Five-Year Plan (2001–2005)[45] and was featured in the Action Plan of the Rural Information Service, which was launched in 2001 through the Chinese Ministry of Agriculture.[46] In 2006, informationalization was identified as central to the construction of the New Socialist Countryside, the development priority of the Eleventh Five-Year Plan (2006–2011).[47]

Wider institutional restructuring is a further factor that has helped to encourage information activities among officials at lower levels of government. An ongoing program of laying off state personnel was initiated in 1998 and intensified in 2002 and 2006, with the reduction and then eradication of rural taxes and a corresponding fall in extra-budgetary funds.[48] Bureaucracies have therefore had to deal with heavy work burdens from top-down policy mandates on the one hand and limited fiscal and personnel resources on the other. ICTs have helped local institutions to adapt to such an environment. One adaptive strategy has involved moving away from labor-intensive modes of work centered on quota enforcement. Quotas have habitually been enforced in a range of areas, including crop production to reach GDP targets and population regulation in order to reduce the number of above-quota births.[49] There has instead been a shift toward service-oriented work whereby local officials use information to support rural people in their efforts to regulate their own behavior in conformity with wider Party-state objectives. Local bureaucracies have also increasingly incorporated ICTs into their ongoing efforts to locate economic projects and to promote entrepreneurialism and revenue generation.

Informational Government

Officials have been assisted by various programs in their efforts to use ICTs in their work. In 1999 China Telecom launched a program called Government Online in coastal cities as part of an effort to expand the company's client base.[50] Government Online also resonates with the government institutions' own aspirations for technological advancement.[51] In Jiangxi in 2006, more than 90 percent of county governments were now online.[52] In the case of Rivercounty, a Government Information Center was established in 2003, and its Web site was set up in April 2004.[53]

A further initiative that has increased local officials' awareness of the Internet is training classes. The Organisation Bureau, responsible for managing Party cadres, requires Party members to attend several short training sessions at the county Party School each year. Although study in ideology and Party policy continues to be central, the topic of Internet use has been integrated into the curriculum so that "modern civil servants" learn how to find practical information on pertinent subjects, such as the implications of WTO regulations for pesticide usage.[54]

Nonproduction Institutions

Nonproduction institutions *(shiye danwei)* are key vehicles for facilitating farmers' intermediate access to the Internet. These institutions are involved in areas of work such as service delivery, research, standards, testing, and inspection; they have titles such as station, institute, center, school, or association; and they fall under the jurisdiction of a relevant administrative bureau or department responsible for coordinating work within a sector.[55] As these units employ almost half of state personnel and take up a major portion of state expenditure,[56] they face particular pressures to increase their "efficiency," with informationalization being one key approach. One of many such institutions in Rivercounty that uses the Internet is the Agricultural Information Service Center, which falls under the jurisdiction of the County Bureau for Agriculture. The Center was founded in Rivercounty in September 2003. It overlaps with the pre-existing Agricultural Extension Depot *(nong ji zhan)* and employs six graduates from agricultural colleges.[57]

In 2002 the earlier incarnation of the Rivercounty Agricultural Information Service Center, the Agricultural Extension Depot, established an agricultural hotline. Such hotlines had appeared in other parts of China in 2000–2001.[58] In 2005 the Rivercounty hotline was incorporated into a province-wide, computerized, voice-activated answering system that invites a caller to select from a menu of options.[59] In 2005, 280 calls came into the hotline, and by 2008 this number had increased to 489.[60]

When a caller's problem cannot be solved by the automated menu, the caller is transferred to a member of the County Service Center. The Center member often uses the Internet to help the caller with technical and sales matters. One example of a technical matter happened in 2004, when large amounts of one village's chili crop began to shrivel. The Center worker e-mailed the Nanchang Vegetable Research Institute, which in turn sent a technician to investigate and give advice on appropriate use of pesticide. An example of a sales matter involved a farmer who phoned to say that he needed to sell 8,000 birds. The Center staff duly placed an advertisement on an agricultural Web site, which was seen by outside purchasers who subsequently bought the entire stock. In another example, farmers in a village had several thousand kilos of unsold pears. They were worried that the pears would quickly rot in the hot July climate. The Center placed an ad on the Internet. Some customers from Guangdong subsequently arrived and paid between 0.5 and 0.7 yuan per catty (0.5 kilo or 1.10 pounds), which was more than the local price, because at that time in their marketplace, there were few watermelons, and apples from Beijing had not yet arrived.[61]

An additional route for enabling rural people to have intermediate access to the Internet is the Center's bimonthly "Agricultural Information Fast Bulletin" newsletter, which prints a selection of the hotline inquiries, solutions, and follow-up stories. The Bulletin was founded in the latter half of 2002, and it is sent free of charge to township and village government offices and to specialist producers. Additionally, some of this information is disseminated yet again by being transferred to bulletin boards in the township market squares and government offices and to the walls of village offices.

Schools and Narrowing the Digital Divide

A final dimension of the narrowing of the digital divide is the role of rural schools in educating children about computers and the Internet. Since the late 1990s, educators and policy makers in China have grown ever more vocal about the need to move away from a focus on rote memorization for examination subjects such as Chinese and mathematics in favor of promoting the all-around competencies of children. The most recent Compulsory Education Law (2006) follows a series of previous policy documents that require teachers, schools, and education agencies to give priority to enriching the curriculum. This drive to promote quality (su-zhi) education reforms has overlapped with a parallel commitment to informationalization. Hence, during the 2000s in both rural and urban schools an Information Class has been added to other non-exam subjects, such as physical education, music, and art.

Certainly there are big differences between rural and urban schools with regard to their capacity to provide ICT training. Legal education scholar Ran Zhang has highlighted rural-urban inequalities in relation to facilities by asking, "While good schools in urban areas have already had 'world-class' facilities such as gyms, swimming pools, and up-to-date computer labs, how can a small rural school with rundown buildings enter the game of *suzhi* education?"[62] Ran Zhang has also noted that owing to the high exam scores required for progression to good schools and the strong exam culture that determines both students' and teachers' life chances, Information Class and other enrichment classes are often replaced by further teaching in examination subjects, a practice that seems to be most pronounced in rural areas.[63] Furthermore, there is the question of inequalities in teachers' technical proficiencies; urban-based teachers generally have higher educational qualifications and more training than rural-based ones.[64]

Yet despite rural-urban educational inequalities, rural schools are still helping to close the rural-urban digital divide. In 2007 I visited two village primary schools located in Rivercounty. I learned that since 2005 a bi-weekly information class had been added to the school timetable. Admittedly, the computers in the classroom were not networked, and the headmasters confessed that they taught the minimum amount required to satisfy upper-level directives. But even so, third graders at these schools were learning how to use PowerPoint, Word, and other programs. In addition, at the middle and high school levels students were learning on networked computers, and some schools had subscribed to "Sunshine Net," an educational intranet established in 2004 by China Telecom in conjunction with the Bureau of Education to provide students with healthy information free from moral threats.[65]

Teachers also nurture students' familiarity with ICTs by using the Internet in their teaching preparation and practice. In Rivercounty in 2007 a long-distance education project among rural primary and high school teachers was launched whereby each school established a dedicated distance education training room that contained a networked computer; each teacher was issued a log-in card from the Rivercounty Department of Education. Yet, as one primary school headmaster explained, "Most teachers don't really use the distance education facilities because they already have a computer at home."[66] It is possible, however, that in situations in which teachers must live in a village rather than in a nearby town that the distance education rooms would be used more. Even in circumstances in which the distance education rooms are largely redundant, their presence makes explicit to teachers the desirability of using the Internet in their teaching preparations. Indeed, in conversation several teachers told me that sometimes in lessons they would talk to students about items that they had read online, a process that would arguably increase students' familiarity with the idea of the Internet.

Conclusions

Owing to the dominance of the concepts of "rural-urban divide" and "digital divide," the shrinking of the digital divide in China has so far been overlooked by researchers. Yet as this chapter has shown, the rural-urban digital divide in China has been narrowing. This is evident with regard to the expansion of infrastructure into rural areas; the unprecedented availability of Have-Less ICTs in rural areas; the growing demand for and daily usage of Have-Less ICTs by rural people; the intermediate access to the Internet facilitated by local government institutions and schools; and the role of schools in reducing the barriers that constitute the "second level" digital divide.

Why is it that the rural-urban divide has been narrowing in relation to ICTs while remaining entrenched with regard to other social resources, such as health and education? One reason is that with ICT provisioning, the pertinent factor is the hard capital of infrastructure, which, when in place, enables large numbers of people to use the resources. With health and education provisioning however, the soft capital of human resources, administration, and ongoing training are crucial to sustainability and efficacy. Although it is true that telecommunications engineers need to make periodic visits to rural areas to maintain the infrastructure, it is not the same as requiring large numbers of well-trained teachers, doctors, and nurses to live in rural areas for years at a time, something that more qualified and experienced ones are reluctant to do.[67] In addition, human resources require ongoing funding: the remuneration and working conditions of health and education professionals are strongly influenced by local economic conditions and fiscal resources,[68] and so the provisioning of these social resources is affected by constraints that do not apply to the provisioning of ICTs.

Second, market incentives are central to generating the impetus for investment in ICT infrastructure and for providing cheap products and services in rural areas. As several telecommunications engineers told me, market demand in the countryside is so strong that as soon as signal coverage is established in an area, hundreds of new customers appear. Mobile phone branch managers also acknowledged their responsiveness to market demand and explained to me that they were aiming to make a profit on volume of customers rather than on price. Indeed a handset of around 200 yuan and charges of around 20 yuan per month were deemed affordable for most rural households. The managers also told me that they anticipated that gradual improvements in rural incomes would propel parallel increases in the proportion of rural subscribers to higher cost options. In fact, owing to their recognition of the potential of the rural market, in Rivercounty in 2006 both China Mobile and Unicom appointed their first-ever rural advertising agents. However, while market incentives are potent in propelling growth in the ICT sector, such incentives are not suited to driving the provision of health and education services. This is because health and education are public goods, and systems of provisioning that rely on payment by users are widely recognized to exacerbate inequalities and to disadvantage the poor.[69]

Third, in an environment where translocal networks are increasingly important for reducing risks and for maintaining economic and emotional well-being, phones have become an essential component of everyday sociality and integral to everyday strategies for pursuing livelihoods. Phones offer Have-Less users several advantages. They amplify the benefits of other connections, such as roads and electricity, by reducing labor and transaction costs and increasing purchasing power.[70] They are more convenient and affordable than mail or travel. Their usage patterns can be adapted to limited budgets. Their usage is relatively unimpeded by second-level digital divide factors, such as education. A phone is enough for a rural resident to benefit from the same possibilities for communicating across distance as an urban resident. Admittedly, phones do not eliminate the manifold disadvantages and hardships faced by rural people, such as their vulnerability in negotiating contracts or their protracted separation from loved ones on account of labor migration. However, phones do help rural people in coping with these difficulties.

Fourth, ICTs are tools for disseminating information to wider audiences, and information itself is a diffuse and multifaceted resource. The use of ICTs by institutions that have the capacity to assemble and provide information resources permits far more people than those with immediate access to the technology to benefit. In the case of rural China, all levels of the Party-state apparatus have been instructed to incorporate information into their strategies for promoting economic development and enhancing efficiency. At the same time, telecommunications companies have been keen to recruit organizations, such as county and township governments, non-production institutions, and schools as clients through projects such as Government Online, agriculture information sites, Sunshine Net, and distance education schemes. The rapid increase in mobile phone density among rural people has been indispensable in facilitating rural peoples' intermediate access to these informational sources. This form of access to information has helped to narrow the rural-urban digital gap in ways not visible in statistical data on the regional distribution of Internet users. Such intermediate provisioning is not, however, feasible for health or education because the delivery of these public goods requires the physical co-presence of the beneficiaries and the relevant professionals. Even so, there are pilot projects whereby the Internet is harnessed to help in improving the competencies of teachers and health professions who work in poor and remote regions.[71]

Finally, schools play a role in reducing the digital disadvantage of rural children and teenagers. In Information Class students gain hands-on experience with computers, and in general lessons teachers sometimes refer to items that they have read online. Even though rural peoples' perception of the relevance of ICTs for their lives will continue to be affected by wealth, gender, generation, and occupation, education is likely to mitigate the barriers presented by some of these inequalities. Indeed, a nationwide survey of Internet usage finds that whereas in the past most Internet users had a BA degree, in recent years the proportion of users with a high school education or with one or two years of middle school education has been increasing.[72]

Clearly, the digital divide is a dimension of rural-urban inequality in China that is distinctive because it has been narrowing, rather than remaining entrenched or growing. This trend has been encouraged by and has fed into other processes of change, including market reforms, economic diversification, labor migration, administrative restructuring and the implementation of mass compulsory education. The narrowing process has been occurring in several ways, some of which are directly observable—for instance, in the rapid increase in mobile phone usage—and some of which are less observable—for instance, through increased intermediate access to the Internet among farmers and reductions in the effects of the second-level digital divide among the younger generation of rural residents. The narrowing of the digital divide is undoubtedly a fundamental, though overlooked, dimension of change in patterns of rural-urban inequality in China, the ramifications of which await scholarly investigation.

LI LIMEI
LI SI-MING

9 | The Impact of Variations in Urban Registration within Cities

The Chinese *hukou* system is believed to be one of the most important components contributing to the social divide between urban and rural areas in China.[1] Combined with the *danwei* (work unit) system in the city[2] and the people's commune system in the countryside,[3] the *hukou* system constructed an invisible wall between city and countryside in the Mao era and it thereby determined how Chinese lived and shaped China's sociopolitical structure and socioeconomic development in many domains. Urban residents could enjoy relatively high levels of social welfare, such as the provision of basic food, lifetime employment, higher incomes, subsidized public housing, and the right to free education, medical care, social security, pensions, and so on. Peasants were tightly tied to the land in order to feed urban residents and supply raw materials for industrial development in the city. The *hukou* system was so powerful that it not only strongly deterred migration from rural areas to the cities, but it also restricted the population flow from small and medium cities to big cities. It triumphantly distributed and fixed people of various socioeconomic statuses into different places. As a result, almost everyone lived where he or she was registered.

Economic reforms since 1978 have compelled the impregnable *hukou* system to relax the barriers to travel, prompting an influx of migrants from the interior to the coastal cities and from villages and small and medium cities to big and megacities. Although a valid residency permit technically requires an individual to live in the area designated on his or her permit, in practice the system has largely broken down. It is now possible for someone to unofficially migrate and get a job without a valid permit. Although geographic mobility and change of employment have become much easier, the social concomitants of *hukou* status still persist.[4] The conversion of *hukou*, either from rural to urban, or from low-level to high-level cities, is still difficult, although the stringent *hukou* system has undergone various stages of reform and relaxation since the 1980s. Many of these migrants have been de facto urban residents for years but do not have proper urban or nonagricultural *hukou* registrations. With the development of a market-oriented economy in China, more and more people can be found outside their place of formal *hukou* registration. In 1982 the population whose registered place and actual residence had been separated for more than one year was 6.6 million. In 1990 the figure increased to 21.4 million, and in 2000 the number of migrants whose registered *hukou* place and actual residence had been separated for more than half a year reached 105 million. According to the 2005 China 1 percent population survey, the total floating population in Chinese cities reached 147.4 million, occupying 11.3 percent of the total population.[5]

The above figures, which include both inter-provincial and intra-provincial migrants, still tend to underestimate the de facto migration volume. If we scale down to examine an individual city, the magnitude of the separation of registered *hukou* place and actual residence *(renhufenli)* would be much more prominent. To put it in a simpler way, *renhufenli* refers to the situation in which the registered *hukou* place differs from the actual residence site. The basic place of *hukou* registration in a Chinese city is the street office, town, or township (*jiedao banshichu, zhen, or xiang*).[6] Thereby *renhufenli* can be operationally defined as the condition in which the registered street office/town/township is different from the person's actual street office/town/township of residence. This separation is caused by both intercity migration and intraurban population movements. Table 9.1 shows the composition of migrants in Beijing, Shanghai, and Guangzhou in 2000 and in 2005. Migrants account for more than 30 percent of the total permanent population in all three cities (the percentage of migrants in Guangzhou is even more than 40 percent). Beijing and Shanghai have experienced a steady increase in the number of migrants from 2000 to 2005. Quite a substantial proportion of the migrants can be attributed to intraurban migration. Because cities accommodate most of the migrating population, this chapter will focus on the *renhufenli* phenomenon within a city.

Specifically, *renhufenli* can be subdivided into two types. The first type of *hukou* is one in which is registered but the person is not present *(huzai renbuzai)*, which is usually found in places of population outflow. The second type is one in which the person is present but the *hukou* is not registered *(renzai hubuzai)*, which is often observed in places of population inflow. From a macro perspective, the interior areas of China can be regarded as the origin places of much population out-migration, where "registered but not present" is prevalent. The coastal areas of China can be seen as the destination of much migration, where "present but not registered" is the norm among the migrants. From the micro angle, *renhufenli* can also be observed within a city, especially in big cities. Besides the large quantities of inbound migrants, intraurban movement is also salient. Along with urban renewal, development of new urban districts, and heightened residential mobility of urban residents,[7] population tends to disperse from the inner city to suburban areas, although the reverse movement is not uncommon.[8] Population relocation within a city does not necessarily involve the change of *hukou* registration place. Therefore *renhufenli* within a city is increasingly common in contemporary Chinese cities. The number of Beijing *hukou* holders who do not live in their registered places reached 2.29 million in 2005, occupying one-fifth of the total locally registered population. Among these people, 52.3 percent had moved to another street office/town/township within a given urban district/county, while the rest had moved to a street office/town/township of another urban district/county.

Large quantities of intercity and intracity migration have resulted in a changing demographic map, a trend that presents a challenge to the Chinese state and makes the *hukou*-based governmental planning regime irrelevant. With the proliferation of *renhufenli* phenomenon within a city, there arise questions about the implications for urban dwellers and urban management in Chinese cities. This chapter seeks to analyze the magnitude and features of this phenomenon and to examine the influences it exerts on urban residents. The empirical portion of the research is based on a household survey in Guangzhou, the largest city in southern China and the capital of Guangdong Province. As a result of the past thirty years of social and economic reforms, and also partly due to a higher level

Table 9.1 The composition of migrant population in selected cities in 2000 and 2005

	Permanent population (million)		Interurban migrants (million)		Intraurban migrants (million)		The percentage of migrants in permanent population (%)	
	2000	2005	2000	2005	2000	2005	2000	2005
Beijing	13.57	15.38	2.57	3.39	2.17	2.29	34.95	37.0
Shanghai	16.41	17.78	3.87	4.63	2.25	2.44	37.30	39.7
Guangzhou	9.94	9.49	3.42	NA	0.97	NA	44.19	43.0

Source: 2000 China population census, see Beijing Municipal Bureau of Statistics, *Beijing Shi 2000 nian Renkou Pucha Ziliao* [Beijing 2000 Population Census Assembly], Beijing: China Statistics Press, 2002; Shanghai Population Census Office, *Shanghai Shi 2000 nian Renkou Pucha Ziliao* [Shanghai 2000 Population Census Assembly], Beijing: China Statistics Press, 2002; Guangzhou Population Census Office, *Guangdong Sheng 2000 nian Renkou Pucha Ziliao Huibian* (Guangzhou shi) [Guangdong Population Census Assembly (Guangzhou)], Guangzhou: Guangdong Economy Press, 2002.

2005 China 1% population survey, see Beijing Municipal Bureau of Statistics, *2005 nian Beijing Shi Baifen Zhiyi Renkou Chouyang Diaocha Ziliao* [Beijing 2005 1% Population Survey Data Assembly], Beijing: China Statistics Press, 2007; Shanghai Municipal Bureau of Statistics, *2005 nian Shanghai Shi Baifen Zhiyi Renkou Chouyang Diaocha Ziliao* [Shanghai 2005 1% Population Survey Data Assembly], Beijing: China Statistics Press, 2007; Guangdong 1% Population Survey Office, *2005 nian Guangdong Sheng Baifen Zhiyi Renkou Chouyang Diaocha Ziliao* [Guangdong 2005 1% Population Survey Data Assembly], Beijing: China Statistics Press, 2007.

NA: not available

Note: 2005 Guangdong 1% population survey data assembly does not differentiate the inter- and intra-urban migrants.

of integration with Hong Kong, Guangzhou is among the top three largest urban economies in China today, along with Shanghai and Beijing. Rapid economic development and high population mobility have brought about enormous challenges to the *hukou* system. In 2005 there were 4.08 million residents, or 43 percent of the total population, living outside their officially registered places in Guangzhou (see Table 9.1). As such, the city provides a good laboratory to study the *renhufenli* phenomenon in China.

The remainder of the chapter is organized as follows: First, the sampling strategy of the household survey in Guangzhou is described. Second, the hierarchical structure of the urban *hukou* system is briefly portrayed. Then the magnitude and features of *renhufenli* are analyzed using the household survey data. Third, the differences in treatment, especially in terms of education provision, toward different urban *hukou* are examined to show the hierarchical structure of urban *hukou* within a city. Finally, the concluding section summarizes major findings and discusses the possible factors underlying the *renhufenli* phenomenon.

Data

The data were obtained through a household survey in Guangzhou conducted between August and December 2005.[9] The survey was administered to all household members eighteen years of age or older. In total 1,203 interviews were completed successfully. The contents of the questionnaire included current and previous *hukou* status and place of registration of household members as well as basic sociodemographic characteristics of the family.

There are ten urban districts and two county-level cities under Guangzhou's administration currently (see Figure 9.1).[10] The survey districts cover the former eight urban districts of Guangzhou and the northern part of Panyu (specifically, Dashi Town), the latter now constituting part of the contiguous built-up area of the city. A multilevel probability proportion to size (PPS) sampling strategy was adopted. The respondents were selected in proportion to the population of the urban districts, except Panyu.[11] The *juweihui* or residents' committee, is the lowest level in the urban administrative hierarchy in China. Therefore, it constitutes the basic spatial unit in the sampling design. A number of residents' committees were first selected according to PPS principle in every urban district. Then, the street addresses were used to select the sampled households.

Every selected residents' committee would include a target of twenty-five interviews.

The Civil Affairs Department in Guangzhou provided a household list for the year 2004, including both registered households and households with temporary residence status (residence for half a year or more). There

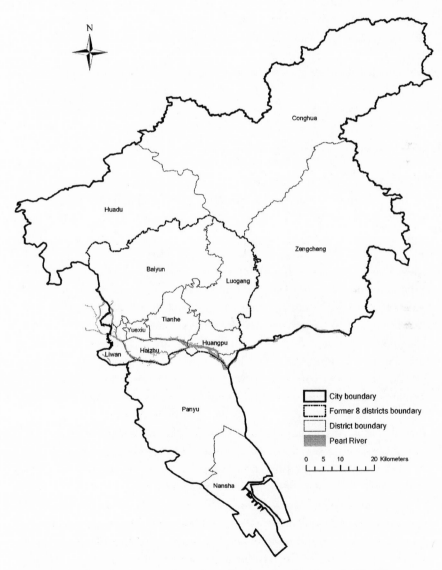

Figure 9.1 The administrative boundary of Guangzhou by the end of 2005.

were two main inferential problems in this list: first, it overestimated, in the place of origin, local residents who were living in other districts; that is, it overestimated the population in net out-migration districts. Second, it underestimated, in the destination, actual local residents who were living in other districts; that is, it underestimated the population in the net in-migration districts. To solve the problem, we first assigned a number of the cases to each stratum (district). The domain of stratification was the original eight urban districts. Then we applied weights derived from the 2000 population census and household registration data to the 2004 list to get an estimated number of households in every district (weight = permanent population/registered population in the 2000 census). This strategy could somewhat solve the problem of coverage bias discussed in P. F. Landry and M. M. Shen.[12]

The Hierarchical Structure of Urban *Hukou*

The People's Republic of China's (PRC) *hukou* system has caused a differentiation of people in each administrative unit based on their *hukou* type, namely, agricultural versus nonagricultural. It has also created a stratification of people across regions based on their *hukou* location, ranging from megacity, big city, medium city, small city, and town. The combination of these two stratifications has affected the allocation of resources, opportunities and life chances for every Chinese. Based on one's *hukou* type and location, Fei-Ling Wang sketches a pyramid structure of social stratification in China.[13] A majority of people (70.5 percent of the total population) classified as low class are at the bottom. These are rural *hukou* holders living in the rural areas. Urban *hukou* holders living in small cities and towns (18.2 percent) and rural *hukou* holders living in suburban areas of metropolises and provincial capital cities (3.4 percent) are categorized as middle class. Urban *hukou* holders living in medium cities (10.4 percent) are labeled as high class. On the top is the elite class (6.3 percent), composed of urban *hukou* holders living in the metropolises, provincial capitals, and large cities. A similar hierarchical structure can also be found within a city, although the composition may vary from one city to another. For instance, the local rural *hukou* holders of urban villages are probably endowed with many more benefits than are local urban *hukou* holders. As a result, many villagers are unwilling to convert their agricultural *hukou* to a nonagricultural one, which is the case of Guangzhou.[14]

As a consequence of large-scale and frequent population migration, the *hukou* composition of the urban population becomes rather complicated. Local and nonlocal *hukou* holders, urban and rural *hukou* holders, and agricultural and nonagricultural *hukou* holders coexist in a city. Table 9.2 shows the *hukou* composition of each urban district and county-level city under Guangzhou's administration. More than 40 percent of permanent residents do not hold Guangzhou *hukou*. In addition, the distribution of *hukou* types is uneven. The nonagricultural *hukou* holders are concentrated in the urban core. The outer suburbs accommodate most of the agricultural population and the inner suburbs lie in between. In general, local urban *hukou* holders enjoy many more benefits than do nonlocal *hukou* holders. Local urban *hukou* holders, however, are not a homogeneous cohort. Instead, they can be subdivided into holders of urban core, inner suburbs, and outer suburbs registrations. Due to uneven urban development in the city, the urban *hukou* holders of different districts are entitled to different benefits, even though this urban-suburban divide may be smaller than the urban-rural cleavage.

The hierarchical structure of urban *hukou* within a city can be told from the *hukou*'s different selling price. For example, in the *hukou* sales scheme for investors implemented in big cities since the mid-1990s, the requirements not only vary across different cities but also differ within a given city. For a set of three urban *hukou* (self, spouse, and one child) in one of the eight central districts of Beijing, one must be a private entrepreneur who has paid local taxes of more than 800,000 yuan a year for at least three years (or a total three-year tax payment that exceeds 3 million yuan) and must hire at least a hundred local workers (or at least 90 percent of the employees must be local *hukou* holders). However, if a household applies for the same set of *hukou* outside the eight central districts, the tax payments and employment requirements can be halved (400,000 yuan a year and fifty workers or 50 percent local hires). The required price in Shanghai is lower than that in Beijing. An investor of 1 million yuan who has been in operation for more than two years may apply for a blue seal *(lanyin)* Shanghai *hukou* for one of his employees.[15] In the five outer districts and the three counties of Shanghai, the requirement is lowered to 300,000–500,000 yuan in investment.[16] The different selling price of *hukou* indicates the different levels of administrative status of urban districts/counties and their different attractions to prospective residents.

Table 9.2 *Hukou* composition of total population in different urban districts of Guangzhou (%), by *hukou* location

	Local *hukou*	Nonlocal *hukou*	Pending	Going abroad
Dongshan	72.02	26.66	0.58	0.74
Liwan	70.15	29.09	0.29	0.47
Yuexiu	74.45	24.78	0.43	0.33
Haizhu	50.88	48.19	0.65	0.27
Tianhe	39.60	58.29	1.95	0.15
Fangcun	46.76	52.82	0.40	0.02
Baiyun	42.26	56.65	1.04	0.05
Huangpu	44.57	54.51	0.86	0.05
Panyu	51.69	47.33	0.96	0.02
Huadu	68.33	31.18	0.46	0.03
Zengcheng	72.20	24.60	3.19	0.01
Conghua	83.71	15.16	1.13	0.00
Total	55.66	43.07	1.13	0.14

Source: Guangzhou Population Census Office, *Guangdong Sheng 2000 nian Renkou Pucha Ziliao Huibian (Guangzhou shi)* [Guangdong Population Census Assembly (Guangzhou)], Guangzhou: Guangdong Economy Press, 2002.

Note: 2005 Guangdong 1% population survey data assembly compiles the data based on the adjusted administration system in Guangzhou. The geographical area of the new urban districts is not compatible with that of 2000 (see note 10). Considering that the general pattern of *hukou* composition is much the same over the span of five years, either by *hukou* location or by *hukou* status, we only present the 2000 census data here and in Table 9.3.

Hukou acquisition through the purchase of commodity housing is another case in point that shows the different values commanded by different urban districts' *hukou*.[17] According to the Management Regulation on Blue Seal *Hukou* of Guangzhou *(Guangzhou lanyin hukou guanli guiding)* issued in 1999, only those who buy an apartment ranging from 50 to 100 m² (538 to 1,079 ft²) in designated areas such as Baiyun, Fangcun, Xinjiao Town of Haizhu, the eastern periphery of Tianhe, and Guangzhou Economic and Technological Development Zone (ETDZ), which are all located at the inner suburbs of Guangzhou, can acquire one to three blue seal *hukou*. The blue seal *hukou* scheme is not applicable in the urban core. In contrast, the flat purchasers in Panyu, an outer suburb, can be directly granted Panyu *hukou*. The different entry per-

Table 9.3   *Hukou* composition of total population in different urban districts
of Guangzhou (%), by *hukou* type

	Nonagricultural		Agricultural	
	Number	Percentage	Number	Percentage
Dongshan	489,392	89.15	59,550	10.85
Liwan	418,355	88.78	52,875	11.22
Yuexiu	303,896	89.69	34,926	10.31
Haizhu	835,384	68.15	390,441	31.85
Tianhe	673,830	62.05	412,165	37.95
Fangcun	186,459	57.84	135,929	42.16
Baiyun	624,710	36.12	1,104,834	63.88
Huangpu	179,789	46.60	206,063	53.40
Panyu	433,312	26.84	1,181,237	73.16
Huadu	160,240	22.57	549,684	77.43
Zengcheng	180,407	20.71	690,498	79.29
Conghua	96,932	18.94	414,755	81.06
Total	4,582,706	46.69	5,232,957	53.31

Source: Guangzhou Population Census Office, *Guangdong Sheng 2000 nian Renkou
Pucha Ziliao Huibian (Guangzhou shi)* [Guangdong Population Census Assembly
(Guangzhou)], Guangzhou: Guangdong Economy Press, 2002.

mits to the *hukou* of different areas in a city also manifest the hierarchical structure of the *hukou* system. It can be concluded that in addition
to the dual division between urban and rural *hukou,* the urban *hukou*
itself is also differentiated under the economic reforms. There is a hierarchical structure of urban *hukou* within a city: with the urban core
hukou at the top, the suburb *hukou* next, and the urban *hukou* outside
the city at the bottom.

Most studies on the *hukou* system focus on the urban-rural cleavage,
one of the most important consequences of this system, and on its discrimination against outsiders. Such studies assume the homogeneity of
urban *hukou.* In this chapter we examine the urban-suburban divide
within a city as a result of the hierarchical composition of the *hukou* system. Specifically, we try to elucidate the different treatment toward people with urban *hukou* within a single city by the example of education
provision. We seek to augment and update our knowledge of the *hukou*
system by focusing on intraurban movement.

The Phenomenon of *Renhufenli* in Guangzhou

Despite its frequent administration adjustments, the basic spatial pattern of Guangzhou has not changed too much, and its total jurisdiction area remains the same. The following analysis adopts the division of old urban core, inner suburb, and outer suburb: Yuexiu, Liwan, Dongshan, and Haizhu are regarded as the old urban core, covering an area of 128.3 km² (49.5 sq. miles); Tianhe, Fangcun, Baiyun, and Huangpu are inner suburbs, with an area of 1,315.3 km² (507.8 sq. miles); and the former four county-level cities, namely, Panyu, Huadu, Zengcheng, and Conghua, are the outer suburbs, covering an area of 5,990.8 km² (2,313 sq. miles).

Magnitude of the *Renhufenli* Phenomenon

The 2005 Guangzhou survey provides data on *hukou* registration and movement. Table 9.4 compares the current residence and current and previous *hukou* place of the respondents. It can be seen that the number of actual residents is less than the number of registered persons in the urban core. On the other hand, the number of actual residents is larger than that of registered ones in both the inner and outer suburbs. Notably, about 10 percent of survey respondents currently hold non-Guangzhou *hukou*. If we trace the respondents' previous *hukou* location, the proportion of non-Guangzhou *hukou* holders is much higher, which shows that some migrants have obtained Guangzhou *hukou* successfully after they moved to the city. It can also be observed that quite a number of the urban core *hukou* holders who have moved out to the suburbs have not changed their *hukou* registrations accordingly. The phenomenon of the registered *hukou* location being different from the actual residence is quite prominent.

Let us take a closer look at the *renhufenli* subsample. Altogether there are 247 out of 1,203 respondents who live elsewhere than in their registered *hukou* location, occupying 20.5 percent of the total sample. About 52.6 percent of these separations are due to intraurban movement. Nearly 40 percent are registered in the urban core, but only 28.7 percent actually live there. About 38.5 percent reside in inner suburbs, but only 13.4 percent are registered there. The proportion of registration in the outer suburb is even lower, at 1.6 percent (see Table 9.5). In other words, "registered but not present" is much more likely to occur in the urban core

Table 9.4 Comparison of current residence and current and previous *hukou* place of the respondents

	Current residence		Current *hukou* place		Previous *hukou* place	
	Frequency	Percentage	Frequency	Percentage	Frequency	Percentage
Urban core	500	41.6	522	43.4	593	49.5
Inner suburbs	503	41.8	439	36.5	329	27.5
Outer suburbs	200	16.6	123	10.2	81	6.8
Outside Guangzhou	0	0.0	119	9.9	194	16.2
Total	1203	100.0	1203	100.0	1197	100.0

Source: 2005 Guangzhou household survey.

(71.5 percent), and "present but not registered" tends to be found in the suburban areas (71.3 percent—see Table 9.6). A large amount of *ren-hufenli* population movement originates from the urban core. Suburbs, especially the inner suburbs, have become the major destination of population relocation. It should be noted that similar spatial patterns are also shown in other cities, such as Beijing, Shanghai, and Nanjing.[18] The Beijing 1 percent population survey in 2005 indicates that nearly 60 percent of "present but not registered" population is found in the inner suburbs and another 28 percent is in the outer suburbs. The inner suburbs and urban core accommodate 49 and 28 percent of the "present but not registered" population, respectively.

The Urban-Suburban Population Relocation and *Hukou* Movement

Suburbanization took hold in China's major cities in the 1980s.[19] Moves to suburban locations were, in the main, less than voluntary. They were largely due to the construction of industrial development zones in the urban periphery, urban redevelopment, and population resettlement. Many empirical studies show that it was the state and *danwei* that played a leading role in relocating households from the inner-city core to suburban districts.[20] But self-initiated relocation from the inner core to the suburbs is on the rise along with the economic liberalization and housing marketization. Gaubatz documents the construction of suburban villa developments around Beijing, Shanghai, and Guangzhou, often in the form of gated communities.[21] Furthermore, no longer exclusive enclaves for the minority wealthy people, vast tracts of land and huge housing floor space in suburban areas are also open to the new middle class, due to increasing economic affordability and the availability of housing mortgages. Massive housing construction, especially in suburban areas, generates large numbers of residential moves and hence vacancy chains.

Panyu is a suburban district immediately adjacent to Guangzhou. With housing reform and transportation improvement, Panyu has witnessed large-scale real estate development and profound urban transformation since the end of the 1980s. The proliferation of commodity housing estates in Panyu has attracted large numbers of people relocating from the inner city. Voluntary moves are associated with substantial increases in housing space, as are higher income and better education. The out-migrants are

Table 9.5 Comparison of residence and *hukou* place of the *renhufenli* subsample (number of cases, row %, column %)

Hukou place	Residence														
	Urban core			Inner suburb			Outer suburb			Total					
Urban core	25	26.9	35.2	43	46.2	45.3	25	26.9	30.9	93	100.0	37.7
Inner suburb	7	21.2	9.9	10	30.3	10.5	16	48.5	19.8	33	100.0	13.4
Outer suburb	1	25.0	1.4	1	25.0	1.1	2	50.0	2.5	4	100.0	1.6
Outside Guangzhou	38	32.5	53.5	41	35.0	43.2	38	32.5	46.9	117	100.0	47.4
Total	71	28.7	100.0	95	38.5	100.0	81	32.8	100.0	247	100.0	100.0

Source: 2005 Guangzhou household survey.

Table 9.6 The spatial distribution of *renhufenli* in Guangzhou

| | Registered but not present | | Present but not registered | |
	Number of cases	Percentage	Number of cases	Percentage
Urban core	93	71.5	71	28.7
Inner suburbs	33	25.4	95	38.5
Outer suburbs	4	3.1	81	32.8
Total	130	100.0	247	100.0

Source: 2005 Guangzhou household survey.

dominantly young, upwardly mobile singles or dual-career couples in white-collar jobs with substantial incomes. The new arrivals settle down in the city and buy their first home in Panyu because of the better living environment and cheaper price in comparison to Guangzhou city.

The relocation from the central city to the suburban area does not necessarily bring a corresponding change in *hukou* registration. Household registration, which used to control rural-urban and inter-city migration, has become less significant in constraining intraurban migration.[22] Residents can change their household registration location from one urban district to another in the same city under certain conditions, such as marriage, change of residence, and moving in with relatives (see Table 9.7). A person can readily move his or her household registration place from any of the original eight urban districts to Panyu. However, the reverse is not common. Generally speaking, local governments with urban designation are allowed to adopt higher standards in constructing infrastructure. Although Panyu was designated as an urban district of Guangzhou in 2000, some public services are still managed independently from the original eight urban districts due to Panyu's former status as a county-level city. Panyu has yet to experience much improvement of urban infrastructure and amenities. For instance, there are two medical insurance systems in Guangzhou: one for the original eight urban districts, the other for the four suburban districts/county-level cities—Panyu, Huadu, Zengcheng, and Conghua. The medical insurance card of Guangzhou city is not applicable in Panyu or vice versa. The change of *hukou* place may cause inconvenience to residents. Therefore, many residents who hold *hukou* in the original eight urban districts are unwilling to change their household registration after their relocation to Panyu.

Those whose place of household registration was outside Guangzhou City had several options to deal with the situation. They could either move the place of household registration to Panyu through the purchase of commodity housing or leave it at the original place. "Buy a flat and gain a household registration quota *(goufang ruhu)*" was one of the measures that the local government once used to facilitate the sale of commodity housing. The quota gave the flat purchaser Panyu *hukou* status, calculated according to the flat size purchased. The larger the housing floor space, the more quotas one could get. In the case of Panyu, purchasing a flat with size of between 40 and 60 m² (430.5 and 645.8 ft²) allowed the buyer to name two persons to acquire Panyu *hukou*, while the purchase of a flat that was between 60 and 80 m² (645.8 and 861.1 ft²) allowed the buyer to name three. The specific procedures of the *goufang ruhu* scheme were rather costly and time-consuming. For instance, before October 2002, the commodity-housing purchaser who wanted to acquire Panyu *hukou* had to pay an "urban infrastructure construction fee" *(chengshi zengrong fei)* ranging from 3,000 yuan to 5,000 per person.[23] Even if one had paid the fee and submitted all the application materials, there was a chance that she or he might fail to acquire it. The worst thing was that the *goufang ruhu* policy was constantly changing. The Public Security Bureau has abolished and restarted the scheme several times. The latest one stipulates that the *goufang ruhu* measure is no longer applicable to those who bought commodity housing after January 1, 2004.[24]

Many households, especially those that held Guangzhou *hukou* (in the original eight urban districts), did not bother to change the place of household registration to Panyu after they moved to Panyu. About 47.82 percent of the residents held nonlocal *hukou* in Panyu in 2005. In the newly built commodity housing estates in the suburbs, *renhufenli* could be even more prevalent. Take the subsample of survey respondents in three commodity housing estates (Luoxi New Town, Riverside Garden, and Star River) in Panyu. Only 15.2 percent held Panyu *hukou* before they bought the commodity housing there. The resettlement in Panyu impelled some of the new suburban dwellers to change their *hukou* place. As a result, the proportion holding Panyu *hukou* increased to 44.8 percent. This was largely due to homebuyers whose original *hukou* places were outside of Guangzhou. But there were still 21.6 percent of the subsample holding *hukou* in places outside Guangzhou and 33.6 percent holding *hukou* in other urban districts in Guangzhou (see Table 9.8).

While a Panyu *hukou* possesses certain attractions to in-migrants, it does not mean much to Guangzhou *hukou* holders. The *hukou* system in contemporary China has lost its power in prevent population migration. However, an urban *hukou* still carries with it some privileges tied to urban services, especially education provision.

Table 9.7 Details for intraurban movement of *hukou* location in Guangzhou, by applicant categories

Eligible applicant (*hukou* holders of the ten urban districts of Guangzhou)	Documents required for application	One-stop *hukou* movement procedure (*yizhan shi*)
1. Marriage	*Hukou* booklets of the receiving party and the moving party I.D. card Marriage certificate	Go directly to the certificate issuing center of the public security bureau in the move-in *hukou* location to settle the move-out and move-in procedure.
2. House movement (purchase, inherited, self-built, *danwei* public housing)	*Hukou* booklets of the receiving party and the moving party I.D. card Housing deed or *danwei* housing certificate	
3. Family union (parents, spouse, and children)	*Hukou* booklets of the receiving party and the moving party I.D. card Kindred certificate	
4. Divorce, house sale, rented house taken back by the homeowner	*Hukou* booklets of the receiving party and the moving party I.D. card Divorce certificate Housing sale document Termination of housing leasing contract	

Source: Guangdong Provincial Public Security Department, *Guangzhoushi jumin banli yizhanshi shiqu hukou qianyi xuzhi* [A notice about the intraurban movement of *hukou* location in Guangzhou], http://www.gdga.gov.cn/hzzc/hzzcbs/hzywzn/t20050901_59245.htm, accessed August 27, 2006.

Table 9.8   Comparison of *hukou* place of the subsample of three commodity housing estates in Panyu

	Current *hukou* place		Previous *hukou* place	
	Frequency	Percentage	Frequency	Percentage
Urban core				
Yuexiu	7	5.6	9	7.2
Liwan	2	1.6	2	1.6
Dongshan	10	8.0	8	6.4
Haizhu	5	4.0	3	2.4
Sum	**24**	**19.2**	**22**	**17.6**
Inner suburb				
Tianhe	10	8.0	10	8.0
Fangcun	0	0	0	0
Baiyun	4	3.2	9	7.2
Huangpu	2	1.6	3	2.4
Sum	**16**	**12.8**	**22**	**17.6**
Outer suburb				
Panyu	56	44.8	19	15.2
Outside the survey area but in GZ	2	1.6	5	4.0
Sum	**58**	**46.4**	**24**	**19.2**
Outside GZ	27	**21.6**	57	**45.6**
Total	125	100.0	125	100.0

Source: 2005 Guangzhou household survey.

The Hierarchical Urban *Hukou* and Differential Treatment

The higher the administrative status of a city/urban district, the more benefits are attached to its *hukou*. Newcomers still have to tolerate certain suffering and inconvenience caused by not holding the local *hukou*. Local permanent *hukou* registration defines a person's rights regarding many activities in a specified locality (See Table 9.9).[25] Education provision is probably the most important benefit that is still tightly attached to the *hukou* system.[26] In this section we examine children's access to education as an illustration of the discrimination created by the hierarchical urban *hukou* system within a city.

Table 9.9 Selected discriminative treatments to nonlocal *hukou* holders

		Non-local *hukou* holders
Education		Pay a large lump of money, temporary enrollment fee (*jiedu fei*/*zanzhu fei*) to be admitted by public primary and junior middle school (which cannot guarantee final enrollment)
		Not eligible for admission to public senior middle school
		Do not allow to participate in the college admission examination outside the *hukou* registered place
Economic housing		Not eligible to buy the economic housing
Public rental housing		Not eligible to apply
Employment		Need to provide several certificates, such as work permit for migrants, Temporary residency certificate and certificate of family planning
		Some jobs are still reserved for local *hukou* holders
Social security		Not entitled to the urban social security
Certificates issuing	Birth permit certificate	Not eligible to apply these certificates outside the *hukou* registered place
	Family plan certificate	
	ID card	
	Marriage/divorce certificate	
	Passport	
Car license		Only those with a temporary residence certificate for more than one year can apply for a car license
Voting rights		Not eligible for voting outside of the *hukou* location

Note: for the detailed requirements of migrant employment, see L. Zhang, "Reform of the *hukou* System and Rural-urban Migration in China: The Challenges Ahead" (2000). http://mumford.albany.edu/chinanet/conferences/Zhang.doc, accessed September 2006.

Admission to Primary and Junior Middle Schools

In its Constitution (1982), China recognizes the right of every citizen to receive an education and in 1986 introduced legislation establishing nine years of compulsory education for every child, starting from age six or seven. Generally speaking, most children attend public school, enjoying the right to a nine-year compulsory education with free tuition. The *hukou* location determines where to receive education. A child cannot enroll in a place other than in his or her registered *hukou* place unless the family pays a very high "temporary enrollment fee" (*jiedu fei, zanzhu fei*).

Public schools in Guangzhou are to provide education to all school-aged children holding Guangzhou *hukou*. However, urban *hukou* holders of different urban districts in Guangzhou are given different treatment. The situations in the original eight urban districts and in suburban areas are quite different. The Bureau of Education of every urban district subdivides its district into many small enrollment areas (*xuequ*). Each public primary school will admit students from the mandated enrollment areas. The distribution of admission quotas in the original eight urban districts of Guangzhou is said to be based on the actual residence, the so-called "vicinity principle" (*jiujin yuanze*). Under this principle, children should attend primary school near their home, within a distance of less than 3 km (1.86 miles).

The government tries to establish an enrollment system that emphasizes "neighborhood schools," moving away from the prior system, which focused on examination scores for entering district or citywide "keypoint schools."[27] The practice of ranking based on the quality of education and facilities, however, still prevails, sometimes under names other than "keypoint." The current hierarchy of the primary and junior middle schools is parallel to the administrative structure; that is, provincial, municipal, district, county-level city, town, and village. A marked hierarchical system of school provision implies a high concentration of facilities in the original eight urban districts and lower-order facilities in the suburban areas. The education quality of the central urban districts is much higher than that of the suburban areas. For example, the original Dongshan District (now part of Yuexiu District) in Guangzhou accommodates the most prestigious schools. In 2005 the Guangdong Provincial Government proposed to stop ranking the schools that provide nine-year compulsory education within the next five years. But the hierarchy may persist for a much longer time, especially in the minds of parents.

To handle the excessive desire to be admitted to the most prestigious schools in the central city, *hukou* location has been used as an entry threshold for allocation of the uneven supply of education resource across localities. It is required that the residence be exactly the same as the registered *hukou* location.[28] In other words, only the local students who live right in their registered *hukou* place are eligible for public primary and junior school enrollment. Otherwise a student is not qualified even if he or she holds a Guangzhou urban *hukou*. Therefore, whether a child holds a local *houkou* or not is decisive in determining where that child goes to school.[29] As a consequence, a game of *hukou* movement for the sake of children's education is played by many urban residents. Those who have moved out of the district with better education provision are not willing to change their *hukou* registered place; at the same time, those who live in the district that provides lower-quality education would try hard to change their *hukou* to the desired place.[30] One leading way is to purchase commodity housing in the desired urban district so as to move the *hukou* location. The *Nanfang Dushibao* (a local newspaper in Guangzhou) has reported many cases of people spending large amounts of money to relocate their *hukou* in this way right before the primary school admission examination with the expectation that their children can get a better education and thereby have better opportunities in life. In many cases such activities result of separation of registered *hukou* place and actual residence.

The situation in the self-contained suburban commodity housing estates in Panyu is rather complicated. The developer has to pay an education infrastructure matching fee (*jiaoyu sheshi peitao fei*) amounting to 5 percent of the total real estate value to the government to qualify for public education provision. However, very few developers are willing to pay the matching fee. Instead, the developers themselves try to provide education facilities and services to the homebuyers. It is a common practice for developers to construct a number of private schools, including kindergartens, primary schools, junior middle schools, or even senior middle schools according to the population size in their subdivisions (see Table 9.10).[31] They may claim to set up a branch of a prestigious school located in the central city in order to promote apartment sales. But it is doubtful that the quality of the branch is as good as that of the parent school.

The Price Bureau of Guangzhou stipulated that all the public primary and junior and senior middle schools should implement the so-called uniform fee scheme *(yifei zhi)* starting in 2002.[32] Table 9.11 provides a list of standard fees charged by ordinary public schools, which are subject to upward adjustment of 10 to 25 percent by different ranks of schools. The tuition fees charged by private schools are many times higher than those in the public schools, although the specific price might vary among different private schools. For example, Clifford School charges 48,150 yuan per year for elementary students, ninety-five times the tuition fee of an ordinary public school. Considering that the annual disposable income of urban residents in Guangzhou in 2005 was only 16,884 yuan, the fee is rather high and is beyond the means of many homebuyers.

At the same time, the door of local public schools is closed to children of homeowners who move in from other parts of Guangzhou or from outside of the city unless a large temporary enrollment fee is paid. For instance, the children of homebuyers in Clifford Estates cannot go to the public school in Zhongcun Town (where Clifford Estates is located) even if they have a Panyu *hukou*. The reason given by the Bureau of Education of Panyu is that the children should go to the school located in the commodity housing estate according to the vicinity principle, regardless of whether the school is a public or private one. Besides, the local government has not received any education infrastructure matching fee from either the developers or the homeowners. Therefore, it has no responsibility to provide public schooling for them. Now that the housing price includes the education matching fee, it is the developer who should provide education service for the homebuyers. Thus children of the homebuyers of the estates are deprived of the right to attend public schools to receive nine-year compulsory education.

To overcome this dilemma, some of the homeowners have been trying hard to gain their children's admission to the public schools of the original eight urban districts by using their personal networks *(guangxi)* and paying extra money. It is also common for them to buy or rent an apartment in the central city in order to make their children eligible for admission to the desired public school. Otherwise, they have to bear the high cost of the private school in the commodity housing estate.

Table 9.10 Education facilities in selected commodity housing estates in Panyu

Commodity housing estates	Schools built by the developer	Estimated number of households	Nature
Luoxi New Town	Primary school of Luoxi New Town Junior middle school of Luoxi New Town	Nil	Public school
Riverside Garden	Lai'en Chinese and English School (primary and middle school)	10,000	Private school
Star River	Panyu Zhixin Jounior Middle school	3,000	Private school
Nanguo Olymics Garden	Experimental Primary and Junior School of Beijing Normal University	4,000	Private school
Guangdi Garden	Panyu Guangdi Puiching Experimantal primary and junior school	Nil	Private school
Clifford Estates	Clifford School (primary, junior and high school) Clifford Estate School (primary and junior school)	30,000	Private school
Huanan New Town	Panyu branch of the affiliated high school of South China Normal University	5,000	Private school
Huanan Country Garden	Primary school	4,000	Private school

Source: X. H. Yang, "Gongxiao meiyou le, xiangshui qu hanyuan" [Where to appeal in the absence of public school?], *Nanfang Dushibao*, October 12, 2004.

Table 9.11 Comparison of tuition fee between public and private school (RMB/year)

		Commodity housing estate in Panyu	Public schools in the original eight urban districts
Kindergarten	Tuition fee	28,890	130–420
	Mandatory miscellaneous fee	13,375	
	Total	42,265	130–420
Primary school	Tuition fee	34,240	0
	Mandatory miscellaneous fee	13,910	506
	Total	48,150	506
Junior middle school	Tuition fee	34,240	0
	Mandatory miscellaneous fee	15,910	800
	Total	50,150	800
Senior middle school	Tuition fee	23,000	1880
	Mandatory miscellaneous fee	7,200	
	Total	30,200	1880

Source: The homepage of Clifford school, http://www.clifford-school.org.cn/enro.htm, accessed August 22, 2006; the homepage of the Price Bureau of Guangzhou, http://www.gzwjj.gov.cn, accessed August 26, 2006.

Note: The Chinese government implements a policy of nine-year compulsory education. Under its guidance, the public primary and junior middle schools do not charge tuition but do charge a mandatory miscellaneous fee. The public senior middle schools, which are beyond the nine-year compulsory education scheme, charge both tuition and a mandatory miscellaneous fee.

Admission to Senior Middle School

According to the briefing document released by the Admission and Examination Committee of Guangzhou (*Guangzhou zhaosheng kaoshi weiyuanhui bangongshi*) in 2007, only Guangzhou *hukou* holders and a few approved non-Guangzhou *hukou* holders are eligible for admission to public senior middle schools. Interdistrict admission is allowed for senior middle school students, but with restrictions. Although private senior middle schools and all kinds of vocational high schools offer citywide admission, public senior middle schools are only open to students with *hukou* in designated areas. *Hukou* registration is still one of the enrollment requirements of public senior middle schools, together with the grades on the lower middle school graduation examination.

As a result of these regulations, *hukou* holders of different urban districts in Guangzhou have different choices. *Hukou* holders of the urban core (Yuexiu, Liwan, and Haizhu) have the greatest freedom to choose public senior middle schools anywhere within the seven urban districts of Guangzhou (the original eight urban districts). *Hukou* holders of the inner suburbs have more limited choices. Except for twenty-one so-called national model senior middle schools *(Guojiaji shifanxing putong gaozhong),* which are open to all students with *hukou* in both the urban core and the inner suburbs, they can only sign up for public middle schools located in their registered *hukou* district. *Hukou* holders of the outer suburbs have the least freedom. They can only enter public middle schools within the district where their *hukou* is located (see Table 9.12). If a student wants to attend a school located outside his or her *hukou* location, he or she is regarded as a non-designated student *(zexiao sheng)* and has to pay a selecting-school fee *(zexiao fei).* The collection of selecting-school fees in the admission of senior middle school students is approved by the Education Department of Guangdong Province. This practice is implemented with three limits set by the Education Department: the number of non-designated students, the amount of money paid, and grade. The higher the rank of the school, the higher the selecting-school fee. In 2007 those attending the most prestigious public senior middle schools could be charged up to 40,000 yuan per student each school year. The terms and conditions for admission to public senior middle schools also demonstrate the discriminatory treatment of *hukou* holders of different urban districts. The *hukou* holders of the urban core are the most favored, those of the inner suburbs are next, and those of the outer suburbs are at the bottom.

Generally speaking, outsiders (nonlocal *hukou* holders), especially rural migrants, are excluded from free admission to local public schools,[33] although the Education Bureau does give special favors in admission for eleven categories of nonlocal *hukou* holders *(zhengce jiedusheng),* such as descendants of martyrs, and returned overseas Chinese.[34] There is *hukou*-based institutional discrimination in both primary and middle school admission inside a city. Furthermore, discrimination exists not

Table 9.12 The qualification of admission to senior middle school in Guangzhou in 2007

	Hukou holders of seven urban districts		*Hukou* holders of outer suburban areas (Panyu, Nansha, Huadu, Conghua and Zengcheng)
	Urban core (Yuexiu, Haizhu and Liwan)	Inner suburban areas (Tianhe, Huangpu, Baiyun and Luogang)	
National model senior middle school (*Guojiaji shifanxing putong gaozhong*) (public)	Eligible for all seven urban districts	Eligible for all seven urban districts	Only eligible for *hukou* place
Other senior middle school (public)	Eligible for Yuexiu, Haizhu, and Liwan	Only eligible for *hukou* place	Only eligible for *hukou* place
Private senior middle school	No limitation	No limitation	No limitation
Technical secondary school, polytechnic, vocational high school	No limitation	No limitation	No limitation

Source: The Admission and Examination Committee of Guangzhou, *Guangzhoushi gaozhong jieduan xuexiao zhaosheng baoming redian wenti jieda* [The questions and answers about the admission of the senior middle schools in Guangzhou in 2007], March 14, 2007, http://www.gzzk.com.cn/html/10000210.html, accessed April 4, 2007.

only between urban *hukou* holders and rural migrants,[35] but also between urban *hukou* holders of the central city and suburbs. Local governments guarantee education of children, like all other social rights, only for their own constituents. Resources are allocated according to the number of registered residents in each jurisdiction.

Summary and Discussion

In the pre-reform era, the *hukou* system gave the Chinese people different identities, which were endowed with different privileges and resources. Population mobility was under strict control by the government, and people were fixed in different worlds by the powerful "invisible wall" dividing city and countryside. This system resulted in a sharp urban-rural divide, which has received much criticism and examination by scholars. The economic reform, however, has forced the *hukou* system to be relaxed and to soften its control on population mobility. But the rules or entry permit for obtaining urban *hukou* are still in force. The *hukou* system today is more of an economic barrier than a simple ban on migration. Change of residence does not necessarily bring about corresponding change in *hukou* status and location. The separation of registered and actual residence place is becoming more prominent with the progress of economic reform, caused not only by intercity migration but also by intra-urban movement.

The resources and opportunities are unevenly concentrated in several big cities in an unbalanced society.[36] The big cities have become the major destinations for migrants. There is differentiation between urban districts of the same city as well as the reification of the urban-rural division. Not only does cleavage exist between urban and rural *hukou*, but also the *hukou* of the urban center and that of the suburbs carry with them different benefits. The urban *hukou* categories within the city compartmentalize the different *hukou* holders into a hierarchical structure: with the urban core *hukou* at the top, the suburban *hukou* next, and the urban *hukou* outside the city at the bottom. To some extent, the hierarchical structure of urban *hukou* is like a microcosm of the urban-rural divide of the *hukou* system within the confines of a city.

Such a socio-spatial division is both a result and a cause of a grossly uneven distribution of political power and economic resources and opportunities. Market reform has greatly changed the "shortage economy" in Maoist era,[37] but the shortage in many important public services, such as education and medical care, has largely persisted. Resource distribution by *hukou* registration continues to be practiced in these fields, which endows *hukou* of different places within a single city with different values and attractions. The deficient and uneven supply of public service over space in the city is the underlying cause of the urban-suburban division of the *hukou* system. The lack or inferior supply of service in the newly developed urban districts (formerly rural areas) makes many urban core *hukou* holders unwilling to change their *hukou* location, even though they have actually moved to the suburbs. Free internal migration without corresponding resources to redistribute over space reinforces the role of *hukou* as an entry permit for certain public services. Many residents play a game of changing/keeping *hukou* to enjoy the benefits. The *hukou* and actual residence location differences will be maintained as long as benefits and services are still attached to *hukou* registration.

IV | The Experience of Being a Migrant in Contemporary China

10 | Boundaries of Inequality

Perceptions of Distributive Justice among Urbanities, Migrants, and Peasants

Inequalities are durable in a society because social categories and institutions, not individual preferences and volitions, create and maintain them.[1] The boundaries that delineate membership in a social category are physical as well as mental. Physical boundaries include those that are geographic, such as a common residential or employment location, or biological, such as skin color or gender. Boundaries are mental or cognitive because social categories are ultimately social constructs. For social categories to exist and to function, members of a social category must share a common recognition of collective identity, interests, and rights. Social psychologists who have studied categories in social cognition thus conclude that "the term category is commonly used to describe the totality of information that perceivers have in mind about particular classes of individuals (for example, Germans, plumbers, pastry chefs), and this knowledge can take many forms (for example, visual, declarative, procedural)."[2] Boundaries, in other words, are also symbolic, with their origins derived not only from material but also cognitive and communicative dimensions.[3] The case of the rural-urban divide in China, a divide that was created in a two-decade period but could hardly be closed through a three-decade effort, is but one prime modern example.

At the turn of the twenty-first century, the Chinese population is segmented into three broad but distinctive social groups. Urban and rural Chinese, whose statuses were institutionalized during the Socialist era of the 1950s to the 1970s, are now joined by a third group of citizens, rural-to-urban migrants. These migrants form an increasingly large segment of the population who leave their rural origins, who often move in circular forms between rural and urban China, and who mostly float on the surface of urban Chinese society. Nearly three decades into China's economic reforms, which were supposed to undo some of the economic and social injustices created under Socialism, clear differences in life chances and in quality of life persist among these three groups of the Chinese population. Categories created under Socialism have, in other words, formed a solid basis of durable inequality in Chinese society.

How does the Chinese population interpret a socially segregated China that already has a half-century history? In addition, to what extent do Chinese of different status perceive reality in a similar or a dissimilar way? On top of the social and economic categories that are in existence, are there also corresponding mental categories that both reflect and cement the social divide? These are the main questions I attempt to address in this chapter. I first establish that as a legacy of China's urban-rural divide under state Socialism, there are indeed three distinctive social groups today who compose the Chinese population. The differences separating these three categories are institutional, not geographical or simply occupational. Utilizing national survey data on perceptions of distributive justice, I then explore what differences, if any, exist among the three groups in their perceptions of the current social system and of economic inequality in China. I also show how different social groups perceive their social status in Chinese society today. Last, I examine how perception of inequality is socially bounded by identifying the unique role of social categories in perceptions of inequality, a role that is independent of the characteristics of individuals who form these three social groups. Socially bounded perception of inequality reflects the reality of social stratification; it also serves an important role in perpetuating existing social inequality.

One Country, Three Peoples

It is well known that the current state of the urban-rural divide in China has its institutional roots in Chinese Socialist practices of the 1950s to the 1980s (see the discussions in Chapters 1 and 3). Such a divide not only affected lives of Chinese in these two parts of the society, but also lives of scholars working on China. The first systematic sociological studies of the Chinese society under Socialism, for example, were conducted and published in separate volumes for rural and urban China.[4] Other studies of Chinese society similarly followed this tradition, focusing only on urban or on rural China.[5] Indeed, to study China as a whole sociologically became such a challenge that few scholars attempted it for fear of running the risk of being overly general or even superficial.

China's contemporary urban-rural divide differs from that society's past history and from other developing countries.[6] The difference is not so much in the manifested outcomes, namely, differences in standards of living or quality of life. The real difference lies in the institutional design and legacies, which make the differences in life quality long-lasting. China's state-engineered industrialization under its planned economy system dictated the need to squeeze peasants for capital accumulation, for cheap labor supply, and for cheap raw materials. The same program also dictated that welfare provision for direct participants of the industrialization program, those in cities, could not be extended to the vast rural population. To protect the state from overextending its capacity to provide welfare benefits, the state enforced a strict migration control policy between the late 1950s and the early 1980s. Relying on the *hukou* (household registration) system to differentiate entitlements between urban and rural residents and to control migration flow, an invisible wall separating the two populations was erected that resulted in different life chances and patterns of social mobility.[7] Under Socialism, China was effectively a "one country but two systems" state, with urban China governed strictly under a planned economy system with universal welfare provision and rural China under planning but largely through a collective self-reliance system. Punishing political enemies by stripping them of their nonagricultural household registration status and sending them back to the countryside further made rural China not only an economic wasteland, but also a political garbage dump. Being a rural Chinese, therefore, not only meant economic deprivation and social discrimination, but also political stigmatization.

During the two decades since the mid-1980s, a third category of Chinese was born. This is the category of domestic migrants, specifically those who migrate from rural to urban China, who now number in the neighborhood of 100 million or more. Following the government's lifting of migration controls in 1984, internal migration in China rose dramatically.[8] Two decades ago, the number of Chinese migrants in comparison to its total population was minuscule. In 1987, when a national population survey first included information on migration, only 15.2 million out of more than 1 billion, or about 1.5 percent, reported themselves to be migrants away from their place of household registration for more than six months.[9] By 1990, the size of the migrant population increased to 30 million, and by 1995, to 56 million. The 2000 census counted 80 million Chinese as members of the floating population. Including migrants who had arrived in their destination less than six months before would put the estimated number of temporary migrants in 2000 at 120 million, up from 88.5 million in 1995.[10] The annual population sample survey conducted by China's National Bureau of Statistics similarly reported that in 2002, one out of every ten Chinese was living in a place (town, township, or subdistrict) that was not the location of the person's household registration. Rapid increase in rural-to-urban migration was also the major force behind China's urbanization boom, which increased China's urban population by 157 million in the 1990s alone, an increase that almost equals the sum of the preceding four decades combined. Massive rural-to-urban migration accounted for 60 percent of all urban population growth during this period.[11]

Following nearly three decades of rapid economic expansion and increased flows of trade and labor between rural and urban China, the reintegration of China's two peoples has been painfully slow. At the same time that economic reforms have smashed the iron rice bowl in urban China and abolished the people's commune system in rural China, other institutional legacies remain powerful enough to separate the two peoples. In the poorest rural areas, government poverty relief policies together with economic growth have moved hundreds of millions of rural Chinese out of abject poverty.[12] In richer rural areas, businesses built largely on the basis of the collective economy, previously known as township and village enterprises, have turned a large number of rural laborers into factory workers and at the same time have made numerous enterprising millionaires and even billionaires. Yet, in spite of these profound changes, most government investment in economic growth and government-sponsored wage increases continues to target China's urban areas and disproportionately benefits urban Chinese. From 1991 through 2004, urban household income grew at an annual rate of 7.7 percent, whereas for rural households the pace was 4.9 percent.[13] In the first years of the twenty-first century, although urban Chinese no longer enjoyed full-scale, state-guaranteed welfare provisions as they did during the Socialist years, the urban-rural income gap enlarged to more than three to one, exceeding the pre-reform era level of the late 1970s.[14]

The persistent and increasing income gap between cities and the countryside is the most important source of overall income inequality and increase in inequality for China. As reported in a World Bank study, for China as a whole, "the rural-urban income gap explained one-third of total inequality in 1995 and one-half of the increase in inequality since 1985."[15] If urban public subsidies, which could augment urban incomes by as much as 80 percent, are included in the calculations, "rural-urban disparities accounted for more than half of total inequality in 1995 and explain even more of the increase since 1985."[16] Results from two multiprovincial surveys, one in 1988 and another in 1995, confirm this conclusion. As Azizur Rahman Khan and Carl Riskin, two principal scholars responsible for these surveys, concluded, "Inequality between urban and rural China dominates inequality within both populations in 1995, as it did in 1988. That is, the Gini ratio for China as a whole is higher than it is for either rural or urban China."[17] Due to rising urban-rural income gaps, China's overall income inequality level remained unchanged in the second half of the 1990s, despite an observed small decline in the level of inequality, both within rural and urban areas, especially within China's rural sector.[18]

Similarly, for the third group of Chinese, rural-to-urban migrants, integration into their destination cities has been slow and difficult. These rural-origin Chinese became effectively a group of second-class citizens in comparison with urban residents.[19] Studies of rural migrants in urban China have consistently portrayed a picture of migrant laborers working in a segmented labor market, earning less pay and fewer benefits compared with urban residents, and living in substandard housing with little social protection. In addition, the separation or segregation extends far beyond work and income and well into health, social networks, children's education, and, ultimately, citizenship rights.[20]

Two decades after opening the city gates to peasants, *hukou* status, an institutional legacy from the Socialist era, still carries an important symbolic as well as material value, as evidenced by a story reported in the

Chinese media in 2005. The story was about a Hubei Province family's efforts to change a member's *hukou* status from agricultural to nonagricultural. In this case, the person involved in status change happened to have died in a traffic accident. Why change *hukou* status when the person is no longer alive? A nonagricultural household registration status was important in this case because it carried a material consequence. According to insurance compensation rules, compensation for a death resulting from a traffic accident was set at twenty times the current average income level in the province where the person is registered. There were, however, two different averages, one for urban residents and another one for rural *hukou* holders (whether rural residents or migrants). In the year that the compensation was to be determined, urban average annual income in Hubei Province was 8,023 yuan, and the rural average was 2,890 yuan. The difference between the two, multiplied by twenty times, amounted to more than 100,000 yuan, a quite substantial sum for the family suffering from the loss of a member. *Hukou* in this case was the basis for determining a person's status for compensation. Chinese media questioned such differential pricing of an individual's life that is based not on the person's earning potential or other criteria, but solely on *hukou* status.[21]

To illustrate the coexistence of three different status groups of peoples in China today, I use data from the 2004 National Survey of Perceptions of Distributive Justice in China, hereafter referred to as the China Justice Survey.[22] The sample survey was designed to cover the entire national population aged eighteen to seventy, with a special effort to include migrants and with an oversampling of the urban population.[23] The Chinese Justice Survey was among the first surveys in China to benefit from using the global positioning system (GPS)/geographic information system (GIS)-assisted area sampling technology. In contrast to past Chinese social surveys that relied on existing household registration records as the sampling frame, GPS/GIS-assisted area sampling has a distinctive advantage in alleviating the problem of missing individuals in the sample frame due to their absence from their place of household registration. With increased migration between rural and urban areas and frequent reallocation within cities due to housing construction, household registration records have become increasingly incomplete and inadequate as the basis for survey sampling (for details on this phenomenon in Guangzhou city, see Chapter 9). Rural-to-urban migrants, who are away from their place of household registration, generally are not part of the urban household registration system. In cities, due to new housing construction and ownership of multiple housing units, in some neighborhoods as many as half of the registered residents cannot be found at their place of household registration. The GPS/GIS method bypasses the household registration system by first sampling geographic grids delineated by latitude and longitude coordinates from a population density map, followed by listing every household in the selected grids to provide the basis of sampling individual respondents.[24]

Migrants in this study are defined as those survey respondents whose household registration status was classified as "agricultural" and who were not living at their place of household registration but in an urban area at the time of the survey. In other words, these are rural-origin migrants who migrated from rural to urban areas. In regard to urban and rural respondents, I classify them by simply following their type of household registration. Out of the entire sample of 3,276 survey respondents, 1,295 are identified as urban, 203 as rural-to-urban migrants, and 1,748 as rural residents. Of the migrant subsample, about 80 percent migrated within the ten-year period before the survey. The small number of migrants in the survey sample imposes certain restrictions for statistical analyses, because any estimated statistics for this group will have larger standard errors than in the case of the larger categories of urban and rural residents. Accordingly, interpretation of the role of migrant status on perceptions of inequality and distributive justice needs to be made cautiously, in this case by examining the statistical significance of any group differences, as it is done later in this chapter. Identification of who is a migrant, however, is relatively straightforward, and such an identification can be used to differentiate them from the other two types of respondents.

There are clearly three types of Chinese today, and the differences among them are by no means simply geographical. As shown in Table 10.1, the three groups of Chinese vary markedly in their economic, social, and political characteristics. Urban Chinese on average have twice as many years of education as rural Chinese, are three times as likely to have ever used the Internet, and have three times higher Chinese Communist Party (CCP) membership prevalence. They work fewer days per week and fewer hours per day than the other two groups and are much more prominently represented in occupations such as government and Party officials, managers, and professionals. They are also much better paid and receive a much higher level of social benefits protection. The reported annual per capita household income in 2003 for urban respondents was more than twice that of the migrants and three times the rural respondents. More than half of urban respondents were covered by public pension and medical care plans, compared with only about one-tenth for the other two groups.[25] All three groups show a high percentage interested in media reports of social issues (60 to 75 percent), but urban residents again outrank the other two groups. In addition, with a half-century history of social separation, social and political differentiations between urban and rural Chinese have taken root, as shown by the intergenerational differences between these two groups. Parents of urban respondents have roughly the same if not a larger difference in educational and political attainment compared with parents of rural respondents than do the respondents themselves.

Table 10.1   Characteristics of three groups of respondents, China Justice Survey, 2004

	Urban	Migrant	Rural
Age (mean)	40.66	35.50	42.00
Gender (% female)	49.50	57.14	52.91
Education			
Mean years of schooling	10.72	6.92	5.53
Attainment (% over jr. high)	59.64	17.73	9.49
Father's education (% over jr. high)	24.14	7.78	4.80
Mother's education (% over jr. high)	14.40	2.09	1.07
Internet use (% ever used)	45.58	19.86	13.93
Political status			
CCP membership (%)	12.66	0.99	3.56
CCP membership among males (%)	16.51	1.15	6.24
Father CCP member	23.17	16.75	11.64
Mother CCP member	6.1	1.48	1.92
Work			
Days worked per week (mean)	5.77	6.21	6.32
Hours worked per day (mean)	8.77	9.21	9.33
Income (per capita, 2003 annual)			
Mean	10,588	4,889	4,033
S.D.	20,296	4,740	4,588

Table 10.1 (continued)

	Urban	Migrant	Rural
Median	6,250	3,600	3,333
Gini index	0.544	0.4496	0.4052
Social protection			
Have public health insurance (%)	50.78	9.9	15.31
Have public pension (%)	52.39	7.43	8
Occupation (%)			
Agriculture, herding, fishing	5.94	6.16	87.54
Commercial/service employee	13.40	23.97	1.84
Self-employed	11.19	19.86	2.59
Head of private business	1.93	2.05	0.2
Worker	29.14	34.25	5.24
Party/government cadre	4.28	—	0.34
Manager	12.02	2.74	0.68
Military/police	0.97	—	—
Professional/technical	15.75	4.11	1.16
Regular employee	5.39	6.85	0.41
Interested in media social report (%)			
Not at all interested	4.34	10.2	11.68
Not that interested	20.08	24.49	25.19
Somewhat interested	55.5	52.55	47.42
Very interested	20.08	12.76	15.71
N	1,295	203	1,769

Migrant respondents, though a small number in this survey, represent a group that is distinctive from the other two. The selectivity of migration is reflected in the characteristics of these migrants. Migrants on average are younger, and their educational level is higher than that of rural residents, but their political status is lower. They work longer hours than urban employees but earn less, and their level of social protection resembles more the population at (rural) origin than at (urban) destination. These migrants mostly engage in nonagricultural economic activities, but few are in high-status occupations. What is also interesting is that, even based on the small sample, migration selectivity appears to be familial or intergenerational. Migrants tend to come from families in which parents have higher educational and political attainment than the average rural population at their places of origin.

One System, Three Perceptions

These three groups of Chinese, separated by their objective characteristics, also form different groups in terms of perceptions of the Chinese social and political system. The differences in their perceptions of the current Chinese social system, however, are not always in the expected direction.

Migrants and rural respondents, though still lagging behind urban residents substantially in economic and political attainment, both reported more gains from the reform era and a greater degree of optimism toward the future. As shown by the numbers in Table 10.2, in contrast to 59 percent of urban respondents who reported that their lives at the time of the survey (2004) were better than five years before, 66 percent of rural respondents and 75 percent of migrants gave this response. The migrant group is also the most optimistic about the future among the three groups, with nearly two-thirds believing life will be better in five years (compared to 59–61 percent for the other two groups). The high level of positive endorsement of reform programs across the board and the higher support level among the lower strata of the society are consistent with findings from other studies based on surveys in China. China's rapid economic growth and increases in standards of living, together with the government's efforts to portray itself as a protector of the public well-being, have resulted in a high degree of optimism and confidence among the population.[26] The seemingly counterintuitive pattern that those in more disadvantaged positions reported greater improvement is not completely unexpected either. In any society, individuals often evaluate their current status by reference to their own pasts, rather than comparison with other social groups. For rural Chinese and rural-to-urban migrants, increased freedom to farm, to engage in nonagricultural production, and to move into cities all represented new economic and social opportunities, opportunities that were not part of the experience of urban residents. Instead, with the urban superrich in view on the one hand, and with the risk of downward mobility due to unemployment and income stagnation on the other, urban residents had more reasons than their rural counterparts to report a high level of anxiety and a lower level of satisfaction with living standards. The bottom line, however, is that for all three social groups, the overwhelming majority of the respondents had seen their standards of living improved, were optimistic about further increases, and were happy with their current economic situation.

A more positive and optimistic assessment of gains during China's reform era, however, does not translate readily into a more rosy evaluation of one's current social status. Rural residents and migrants reported a higher frequency of being treated unfairly by local government officials: 27 percent in the three years before the survey date, compared with 21

Table 10.2 Perceived social status, China Justice Survey, 2004

	Urban	Migrant	Rural
Life compared with five years ago			
Much worse	5.72	0.99	2.77
Worse	15.07	9.85	8.82
About the same	20.09	14.29	22.22
Better	48.69	64.53	55.62
Much better	10.43	10.34	10.57
Gained in reform era (11-point, mean)			
Mean	4.65	4.71	5.03
S.D	2.04	2.14	1.95
Life five years from now			
Much worse	2.32	0.49	1.13
Worse	6.26	1.97	6.33
About the same	30.29	31.03	33.52
Better	49.77	55.17	49.18
Much better	11.36	11.33	9.84
Satisfaction w/ living standards (scale 1–7, mean)	3.87	4.02	4.23
Living standards comparison			
Better than neighbors (%)	19.41	12.81	12.46
Better than others in the country (%)	12.76	5.91	4.73
Self-reported social position (scale 1–11, mean)			
Mean	4.78	4.09	4.21
S.D.	1.80	1.81	1.87
Treated unfairly by local officials (% yes)	20.82	26.6	27.36
N	1,295	203	1,769

percent among urban respondents. Members of the rural and the migrant groups are also aware of the fact that their social position is below that of the urban population. Migrants, despite their better economic circumstances than the rural population, reported the lowest social position among the three groups, a fact most likely related to their experience in urban areas. The difference among the three groups is statistically significant at 0.001 level.

The three groups also have different perceptions regarding the degree and types of inequalities in Chinese society and of the fairness versus unfairness of the system. As shown by results in Table 10.3, among the three groups, the urban population is the most critical group, with 81 percent believing income inequality is large or too large, 70 percent seeing China becoming more polarized, and only half of all respondents agreeing that hard work is always rewarded.[27] In answering a number of other questions intended to detect a respondent's trust or confidence in the current system, urban respondents also generally displayed less trust, with the highest proportion among three groups agreeing with statements such as "It is hard to say what is just or unjust" and "Officials do not care what common folks like me think."

Other, more complex, measures of perceived justice in the social system in China reveal similar differences among the three groups. To better gauge respondents' perception of the just nature of Chinese society today, I constructed a "System Distrust" factor based on a large number of other questions in the survey on what it actually takes in China to get ahead (see this chapter's Appendix for the list of questions used).[28] Urban respondents' average score on this factor is well above the other two groups, again confirming the finding in other studies that objective status is not always the best predictor of subjective attitudes and that urban and more educated people are the most critical of the system.[29] In contrast to urban respondents, migrants are less critical in most areas, and the rural population is the least critical. Such a higher level of distrust among urbanities is likely due in part to their reported lower level of satisfaction, as discussed above, and in part to their more frequent encounters with, and observations of, inequalities around them in cities, as well as through media reports that originate in cities.

Perceptions of inequality and the justice of the current system not only differ by the broad group boundaries dividing the three social groups; they also differ by other group boundaries. Specifically, the perceived

Table 10.3 Perceptions of inequality, China Justice Survey, 2004

	Urban	Migrant	Rural
Degree of income inequality (% "too large")			
Neighborhood	32.87	27.58	32.64
Own workplace	49.56	50.32	37.64
Whole country	80.99	78.17	63.87
More polarized? (% agree)	70.45	70.15	57.32
Trust in system (5-point, mean)			
Hard to say what is just or unjust	3.35	3.41	3.08
Discussing justice is meaningless	3.14	3.22	3.07
Officials do not care about common folks like me	3.64	3.62	3.03
Hard work rewarded? (% agree)	50.04	71.43	62.77
"System Distrust" factor			
Mean	0.2022	0.0422	−0.1530
S.D	0.8002	0.7842	0.7666
Conflicts between groups (% serious)			
Rich and poor	59.59	43.89	35.83
Hukou status	22.83	17.16	20.16
Old and young	24.92	14.74	18.21
Urban laid-off and migrants	31.42	19.5	19.78
Is it just ? (% strongly disagree)			
Give urban *hukou* more opportunity	12.44	15.15	9.99
Do not give migrant urban *hukou* easily	19.67	28.57	20.85
Do not allow migrant children to attend urban schools	35.19	42.86	36.34
Prohibit certain urban jobs for migrants	29.36	38.92	33.48
Do not allow migrants to receive urban benefits	28.58	37.44	31.14
"Status Discrimination" factor			
Mean	−0.0484	−0.1963	0.0579
S.D	0.8867	0.8616	0.9366
"Equal Rights" factor			
Mean	0.1133	0.2125	−0.1077
S.D	0.6998	0.6820	0.7329
N	1,295	203	1,769

degree of inequality becomes smaller when the reference group is closer to oneself (top panel, Table 10.3). For all three types of Chinese, in contrast to the perceived high degree of income inequality for China as a whole, the perceived degree of inequality within one's work organization and one's neighborhood is substantially smaller. In contrast to nearly three-quarters of all respondents who believed that income inequality in China was large or too large, less than half of that many thought so for their neighborhood and only slightly more than that thought so for their workplace. Such a difference in the perception of global versus local inequality may result from the lack of information on part of the survey respondents—namely, their view was not based on facts but exaggerated partly due to the media's influence. The difference, however, also reflects a social reality—namely, that the recent increase in income inequality is largely driven by enlarged inequality *between* different social categories and is coupled with a certain degree of persistent equality *within* each category.[30]

The three groups of Chinese differ not only in their perceptions of distributive justice for China as a whole, but also, to a greater degree, in recognizing and defending their own interests and rights in society. In particular, differences in perceptions of justice among the three groups are more pronounced when the question relates specifically to a particular social group. Urban residents reported more concerns with various kinds of social conflicts, such as those between rich and poor and between old and young, than the other groups, but the difference among the three groups is more noticeable when it relates to one's own group. Nearly a third (31 percent) of urban respondents believe that the conflict between urban laid-off workers and migrants is serious, compared with only about 20 percent for migrants and rural residents. Similarly, in a number of questions that were specifically targeted at measuring respondents' attitudes toward migrants, migrants as a social group clearly stand out ready to defend their rights of being treated as equals: in regard to *hukou* status, jobs, benefits, and their children's education. Nearly 30 percent of migrants strongly believe it unjust not to permit migrants to obtain urban *hukou* easily, whereas only about 20 percent of urban respondents agree. About 43 percent of migrants strongly believe that not allowing migrant children to attend urban schools is unjust, in contrast to only 35 percent of urban residents. Nearly 40 percent of migrant respondents believe that not allowing migrants to receive urban benefits is unjust, whereas only 28.6 percent of urban respondents hold the same view (see Table 10.3).

Other, more generalized measures of perceived social discrimination and unequal rights reveal the same pattern of differential perceptions among the three groups of Chinese. Based on a full battery of questions on migrants' rights and on equal rights among citizens in the China Justice Survey, I constructed two additional factors, one I named "Status Discrimination" and the other "Equal Rights." Questions used for constructing "Status Discrimination" include twelve items, seven of which specifically stated that it is fair for the rich and for urban people to be treated better and five about excluding migrants and people without non-agricultural *hukou* status from receiving equal treatment in jobs and social welfare. The "Status Discrimination" factor was created based on a factor with high loadings on items discriminating against migrants and rural residents. Questions used for constructing the "Equal Rights" factor include nine items asking respondents to evaluate statements about equal rights between men and women, between urban and rural residents, and between people of different social backgrounds. The survey questions used in constructing these two factors are listed in this chapter's Appendix. As shown at the bottom of Table 10.3, migrants' average score on "Status Discrimination" is well below that of the other two groups (-0.1963 versus -0.0484 and 0.0579), revealing that migrants are less likely to accept and to endorse discriminatory practices than either urban or rural residents. In addition, whereas both urban residents and migrants reported higher scores on the "Equal Rights" factor than rural residents, migrants as a group again have the highest score, revealing their strong desire for equal treatment. In these and almost all other comparisons, the differences among the three groups are highly statistically significant.

Group Membership and Boundaries of Perceptions

The three different status groups in China based on the *hukou* system have been shown here to have different perceptions of distributive justice concerns, especially regarding their own rights. These three types of Chinese also have clearly differing average personal characteristics, such as in educational attainment, in Communist Party membership prevalence, and in interest in, and access to, mass media. The question therefore becomes to what extent are the differences in perceptions described above due to personal characteristics instead of group membership status? In other words, to what extent are the differences in perceptions due to the mental boundaries that are shared by members in each of the three large social groups rather than to their individual characteristics?

One way to separate the roles of these two different dimensions, one at the individual and the other at the group level, is by carrying out statistical analyses using the multiple regression method. Individuals' scores on the three scales introduced above—"System Distrust," "Equal Rights," and "Status Discrimination"—are used in these analyses as dependent variables, with their variations predicted by both individual characteristics and status group membership. Individual characteristics used in this regression analysis include those differentiating the three groups, such as educational level and Communist Party membership. To control for the influence of other individual characteristics that may affect perceptions or the effect of other characteristics on perceptions, I have also included an individual's age and gender. Results of the multivariate statistical analyses are presented in Table 10.4.

The three groups of Chinese have clearly different views of the current Chinese economic and social system. Rural Chinese, who reported the most gain from reforms and highest level of satisfaction with current living standards (see Table 10.2), are also the ones who have the most faith in the system, as shown by the negative coefficient for "System Distrust" in column 1 of Table 10.4 (-0.2516 compared with the reference group, urban residents). In comparison to urban residents, migrants show a somewhat higher degree of distrust in the system, but the regression coefficient is not statistically significant. In addition, the faith in, and support for, the system among rural Chinese is not due to their lesser exposure to the mass media or lower educational levels, as these factors are controlled for in the regression analyses. When other factors are controlled for, Communist Party members also report a greater degree of support for the current system, as shown by the negative regression coefficient. Education and media exposure and interest, however, show an effect opposite to Communist Party membership. More educated Chinese hold more critical views toward the current system, as do those who follow media reports on social problems closely.

Different group membership also places Chinese citizens on different platforms in their preferences for equal rights. Here the pattern is differ-

Table 10.4 Group membership as a factor of perception, China Justice Survey, 2004 (multiple regression results)

	System distrust		Equal rights		Status discrimination	
	coefficient	p	coefficient	p	coefficient	p
Age (year)	0.0004	0.75	−0.0024	0.02	0.0046	0.00
Gender (male=1)	0.0116	0.69	−0.0343	0.19	−0.0478	0.16
Education (year)	0.0179	0.00	0.0161	0.00	−0.0041	0.41
Communist Party membership (yes=1)	−0.1680	0.00	0.0683	0.18	−0.0989	0.14
Group status (urban=1)						
Migrant	−0.0759	0.23	0.1907	0.00	−0.1850	0.01
Rural	−0.2516	0.00	−0.0794	0.01	0.0246	0.55
Media interest (not at all interested=1)						
Not very interested	0.0758	0.19	0.1568	0.00	−0.0707	0.28
Somewhat interested	0.1489	0.01	0.2697	0.00	−0.0962	0.13
Very interested	0.2928	0.00	0.4603	0.00	−0.3647	0.00
Constant	−0.1432	0.11	−0.2246	0.00	−0.0166	0.87
Adjusted R-squared	0.0629		0.0690		0.0250	
N	2960		3087		3041	

ent from the one above in assessing the fairness of the system. Of three groups, rural residents continue to be the most accommodating, as shown by the negative coefficient associated with their group membership in comparison to the reference group of urban residents. Migrants, who reported both the lowest satisfaction with life and the lowest social position among the three groups, sense the most need to achieve equal rights, as shown by the relatively large and positive regression coefficient in comparison to urban residents. Note that the "Equal Rights" factor is composed of nine different survey question items, most of which are not specifically about migrant rights (see this chapter's Appendix for the questions used). As a social group that has a rural origin and survives in an urban environment, migrants likely experience the consequences of unequal treatment most intensely and therefore express the strongest support for equal rights.

Migrants' awareness of their own predicament in today's Chinese society clearly sets them apart from the other two categories of Chinese citizens. This distinctiveness is shown by the results in the last column of Table 10.4. Here the "Status Discrimination" factor is composed of twelve questions, five of which relate specifically to discrimination against rural migrants (see this chapter's Appendix for the list of questions used). For this measure of distributive injustice perceptions, those in the migrant group clearly display a more disapproving attitude toward discrimination based on *hukou* or migrant status compared to urban and rural residents. Indeed, other than age (with older respondents being less sensitive to status discrimination) and the level of interest in media reports of social problems, migrant group membership is the only factor that makes a clear difference in attitudes toward discrimination based on status. Compared with urban residents, being in the migrant group produces an average reduction of 0.185 in our scale measuring endorsement of status discrimination (the mean score for all respondents is 0). Perceptions of justice, therefore, are not only affected by an individual's characteristics, such as education, Party membership, or exposure to the mass media, but also are clearly affected by one's status group membership. The three categories of Chinese citizens—urban residents, migrants, and rural residents—not only differ in their objective social and economic standing, but also in their perceptions of the justice or injustice of the social system, in their views on status group discrimination, and in their support for equal rights.

Three Peoples, One Destination?

China's Socialist experiment in the third quarter of the twentieth century created a society that is segmented following many different fault lines: residence, ownership sector, industrial sector, and work organizations.[31] Of all the cleavages, urban and rural separation is by far the largest and the most glaring. Three decades into a reform program that promised to close this gap by creating a nationwide market economy, significant differences persist between rural and urban Chinese. These differences are not only in standards of living, but also more importantly in life chances that are created and maintained by both old and new institutions. In addition, during the last three decades, and especially since the government relaxed its migration control policy in 1984, a third category of citizens has emerged composed of millions of Chinese migrants. In somewhat simplistic and broad terms, one can view contemporary Chinese society as made up now of three categories of citizens with distinct statuses.

Closing the urban and rural gap has been the single most challenging social reform in China in the last three decades. Whereas increased freedom of migration in the last two decades and more is a necessary step toward closing the urban-rural gap, in the process a third group of citizens—migrants who have left their rural origins and have moved into cities—has been created. The old urban-rural divide, easily identifiable by a geographic divide between cities and the countryside, has now turned into a more complex, three-way divide that is not so easy to categorize geographically, but clearly exists socially. The unique characteristics and status of rural-to-urban migrants have been documented extensively. What I have shown in this chapter only confirms and highlights the contrasts across the three groups. Citizens belonging to these three different groups have sharply differing educational, political, and economic statuses. Urban residents possess the highest levels of cultural as well as political capital, with a higher level of educational attainment and a larger proportion of Communist Party membership than either rural residents or migrants. They also enjoy a privileged economic status, with drastically higher income and benefit levels compared with either rural residents or migrants. In addition, what I have documented in this chapter is that these three status groups have also formed distinctively different perceptions of their own status in Chinese society and different views on distributive justice issues in Chinese society today. Such socially bounded perceptions of inequality have potentially important implications for the future of social integration in China.

The three groups' different perceptions of the same society are formed sometimes in reference to their past positions in the society and are also based on their current experiences. Chinese rural residents and migrants, although recognizing their lower status, also report more faith and optimism in the system. Their more positive evaluation of the current system is not caused by their lower educational level and being less informed, because their higher trust level persists even after taking into account the differences between them and urban residents in educational level, in Communist Party membership, and in exposure to media reports on social issues. Instead, these more positive attitudes are likely based on their perceived greater gains in standard of living in comparison with their even more disadvantaged past.

A more positive attitude toward the current system, however, does not translate readily into a blind acceptance of one's fate when it comes to unequal rights or, even worse, discrimination. Migrants, in particular, are very aware of their low status in urban society because of their rural origin, and they report openly their concern and disapproval of discrimination based on group membership status. They also have a stronger demand than the other two groups for equal rights and treatment. Perceptions of distributive justice in contemporary China, therefore, not only vary by an individual citizen's social and economic characteristics but are also bounded by the social category to which the person belongs.

These boundaries of perceptions suggest a long and hard road for making China an integrated society based on universal citizenship. The destination may well be the same for all three social groups—to undo the social injustices created under Socialism that differentiated the population by place of birth and to arrive at universal citizenship rights. However, the shift from two to three distinct categories of people in the last two decades in China reveals not only new divisions in a society, but also the tenacity of urban-rural inequality. The mental constructs among the three categories of the Chinese population reveal China's new social reality. These differing world views may also serve as an independent force contributing to the maintenance of the status categories that segment Chinese society today.

Appendix: Survey Questions Used in Constructing Factors of Discrimination and Rights

System Distrust

Question: "In today's society, there are many factors that decide a person's salary. In your opinion, how much influence does (item) actually have? Would you say most influence, large influence, some influence, little influence, or no influence at all?" (These questions were asked separately for each item below.)

Item: education, adverse work conditions, individual efforts, family size, job responsibilities, length of time at job, being male, contributions to work unit, relationship with superior, knowing people/having connections, city household registration status, age, specialized technical skill

Status Discrimination

Question: "Here are some opinions about social justice. Please indicate your attitudes about these opinions, showing whether you strongly agree, agree, feel neutral, disagree, or strongly disagree."

Items:

1. It is fair that some occupations receive more respect from society than others do.
2. It is fair for people of lower social classes to be given some additional help so they can have equal opportunities.
3. It is fair that those who are able to pay for it can give their children better educational opportunities.
4. It is fair that rich people can purchase better homes than other people.
5. It is fair that rich people can enjoy better health care than other people.
6. It is fair that people with household registrations in the city have more opportunities than those with household registrations in the countryside.
7. It is fair that those who hold power enjoy a certain degree of privileged treatment.

8. It is fair that the reforms in state enterprises have led to large numbers of people being laid off.
9. It is fair that rural migrants are not easily permitted to obtain household registration in the city.
10. It is fair that the children of rural migrants are not permitted to attend schools in the city.
11. It is fair that rural migrants are prohibited from performing certain occupations in the city.
12. It is fair that rural migrants are not allowed to obtain urban welfare benefits.

Equal Rights

Question: "Please express your opinion on each of the following statements. Explain if you strongly agree, agree, feel neutral, disagree, or strongly disagree with the statement."
Items:

1. People who work in production make a greater contribution to society than those who work in trade or sales.
2. City dwellers have benefited more from economic reforms than they should, while rural dwellers have benefited less.
3. City dwellers' standard of living is higher because they have made greater contributions to national development.
4. Rural and urban people should have equal rights to employment.
5. When they are few employment opportunities, men should work outside while women should stay at home to take care of the family.
6. The obvious gap between the rich and poor in our society violates the principle of Socialism.
7. In all lines of work, men and women should have the same employment and promotion opportunities.
8. People of different family backgrounds encounter different opportunities in society.
9. Men are more suited to leadership responsibilities than women.

LEI GUANG
FANMIN KONG

11 | Rural Prejudice and Gender Discrimination in China's Urban Job Market

The rural-urban divide and gender discrimination are enduring forms of social inequality in China today.[1] It is not surprising that both forms of discrimination manifest themselves in the urban job market.[2] Rural migrants in cities face discrimination that ranges from low wages and substandard working conditions to outright exclusion from particular jobs. Similarly, women workers tend to be crowded into particular occupations and face lower prospects for career advancement and wage increases.

This chapter studies China's urban job market discrimination that occurs at the point of recruitment or hiring. In the pre-reform period, employers did not make independent hiring decisions. It was up to labor bureau officials, who would assign individuals to what were mostly state- or collective-sector enterprises under a unified labor plan. Even in the case of out-of-plan hires, enterprise managers did not have full autonomy; they had to obtain approval from supervising labor bureaus. The urban labor system was geared to serving urban residents to the exclusion of rural laborers; at the same time the system worked to ensure that urban women could participate in the labor force and receive equal treatment in the workplace. The old system discriminated against rural residents but manifestly promoted equal treatment of female workers.

Reform has changed the labor system in at least two ways that impinge on hiring practices in Chinese cities. First, as the labor bureau extricated itself from the labor allocation process, enterprise managers turned increasingly to the labor market for new employees. A second change was that non-state companies generated more and more employment opportunities. These two changes have converged to make job hiring more of a market-based than an administrative process. However, these questions remain: How have these developments affected rural migrants and women seeking employment in the cities? Did an end to the administrative labor system bring about the end of hiring discrimination against these two groups?

The study discussed in this chapter was carried out against the backdrop of an emerging labor market in China. It aims to assess the extent of discrimination in the urban job market and the factors behind that discrimination, given the relative absence of direct government influence on recruitment decisions. In the following pages, we first review the current literature on labor market discrimination against women and rural migrants in the Chinese cities. We then describe data and methodology we implemented in a 2004 study of the job markets in Beijing. We present three kinds of data, including a hiring discrimination audit study of eighty-one companies, content analysis of job advertisements in a major newspaper, and phone interviews with human resource managers from seventeen Beijing companies. The final section presents our findings and gives our interpretation of urban job market discrimination in China today.

Rural Prejudice and Gender Discrimination in China's Urban Job Market

Job discrimination takes a variety of forms and occurs at different stages of the labor market process. Exclusionary employment practices may be sanctioned by explicit government policies, as was the case for decades under China's strict *hukou* regulation. At the height of *hukou* control in the 1960s and 1970s, urban employment was exclusively reserved for local city residents. There was little spontaneous rural-urban labor migration. Since the reform, even while the central government has tried to ease controls over population movement, municipal governments across China have enacted local regulations aimed at restricting migrant access to city jobs. *Hukou* thus remains a potent instrument of local control in urban job allocation, especially in the state sector and for credentialed occupations (such as accountants).

To this day, a local *hukou* is still typically required of all people applying for higher-end managerial or state-sector jobs in large cities. *Hukou* requirements for lower-end positions have been relaxed, leading to an influx of rural migrants into cities. As a result, in Chinese cities today there is an increasingly stark occupational segregation whereby migrants are relegated to the bottom of the job market. Urban citizens and rural migrants are, effectively, noncompeting groups with different job prospects in the urban job market.[3] One official survey showed that in 2002, 94 percent of rural migrants in Beijing worked in low-end jobs.[4] Another study in Wuhan in the 1990s showed that nonlocal, mostly rural workers tended to concentrate in the more "traditional" service sectors, such as the retail and catering industries, whereas local city residents and legal *hukou* migrants[5] were more evenly distributed across different occupations and "occupied more positions in the modern sectors."[6] Interestingly, if one were to examine the cluster of local and migrant labor in terms of the type of enterprise ownership, one would find a concentration of local workers in the state sector, whereas migrants were more evenly distributed across enterprise types.[7]

Hukou discrimination involves more than relegating temporary migrants to lower-end jobs or excluding them altogether from the urban job market. It also has an insidious effect on the workplace treatment of migrant workers *after* they obtain employment. Ching-Kwan Lee and others have documented the despotic conditions under which migrants, especially female migrants, worked in southern China in the 1980s and 1990s.[8] Such poor conditions still largely obtain today for the non-*hukou* workers as they typically receive lower pay compared to the local workers or migrants with proper *hukou* registration.[9] Worse, a significant number of temporary migrant workers do not receive payment, or they are not paid on time, sometimes months behind schedule. One researcher estimates that in 2003 at least half of the construction companies in China, many state-owned, owed migrants back wages. The private sector is not doing any better in this regard. A 2003 study found that workers at about 64 percent of the private and foreign-funded enterprises in Guangdong experienced one or more instances of late payment, illegal deduction, or nonpayment of wages.[10] Finally, temporary migrants are routinely denied work-related benefits, such as pension, housing allowance, unemployment insurance, and other amenities.

Insofar as gender discrimination is concerned, before the reform, China's official state policy was to promote women's employment in the formal economy. The Chinese Constitution also stipulates equal pay for men and women holding the same position. As a result, in the pre-reform period the rate of Chinese women's labor-force participation was among the highest in the world, and the gender gap in wages was kept to a low level. This is not to say that women had achieved equality with men before the 1980s. As an example, female workers faced a mandatory retirement age that was earlier than that of males. But reform did increase the overall level of gender discrimination in several ways.[11] Gender bias in the labor market today manifests itself in the disproportionately high layoff rate for female workers, the explicit stereotyping of women into certain occupations, and the generally lower wages women receive for the same positions.

Labor union investigations and other studies in the early 1990s showed even higher incidences of layoffs for female workers, sometimes at twice the rate of male workers.[12] According to official statistics, in 2002 women made up 37 percent of urban enterprise workers, but they accounted for 45 percent of the laid-off (xiagang) workers and 48 percent of the newly unemployed (registered) population.[13] Chinese researchers also found that female college graduates face much more difficulty in finding jobs than their male counterparts. In one recent survey of college graduates and their potential employers, as many as 80 percent of the female college graduates surveyed reported having experienced gender discrimination in their job search.[14]

In the pre-reform days of labor planning, there was evidence that women received systematically less advantageous job assignments than men, so women were underrepresented in the state sector and in high-wage or high-prestige occupations. Such gender-based sectoral bias has not changed much since the reform began. A survey of industrial enterprises in six major cities in 2000 found that, although state enterprises were biased toward men, the more inferior non-state sectors employed proportionally more female than male workers.[15] It was not uncommon, even early in the twenty-first century, to read newspaper job ads with discriminatory gender requirements. One study of two Shenzhen newspapers reported that 42 percent of the job ads sampled for one month stipulated gender as a requirement, and 64 percent of the advertised positions were open only to male applicants.[16] Many employers associated femaleness with broad occupational characteristics and steered women to positions they regarded as properly feminine. As Cindy Fan has observed, gender discrimination is especially prevalent among migrant workers who "are channeled into a narrow selection of gender-segregated jobs" because of sociocultural reasons and structural constraint on the migrants' access to job information and opportunities in the cities.[17]

The gender gap in China's urban labor market was not limited to occupational segregation. It was also reflected in the mobility that male and female workers experienced after employment A recent longitudinal study of six coastal cities showed a widening gender gap in mobility in the 1990s, as women were much more likely than men to change jobs because of family reasons or involuntary work termination and not for career considerations.[18] The study confirms a later analysis that found women to be less upwardly mobile beyond a certain rank than men, even if they all started at a similar rank and wage scale.[19]

Many studies also show female workers to be at a distinct disadvantage in terms of the wages. Analyzing the 1988 national household survey data, John Knight and Lina Song found that wage differences between men and women were most significant for the "older, less educated workers."[20] Another study of China's urban labor markets found that the gender wage gap increased during the period 1988–1994 so that disparity between men's and women's wages remained substantial well into the reform.[21] Even when researchers found no longitudinal change in the overall gender gap in earnings since the advent of reform, they concluded that persistent occupational segregation accounted for an increasingly large share of the gender gap in earnings as reform had progressed.[22]

The above discussion suggests that there was significant employment discrimination in China and that such discrimination may occur at different stages of the labor market process. Groups of individuals may be systematically excluded from certain occupations because of their rural origin or gender. This kind of discrimination is rooted deeply in the sociocultural milieu of Chinese society today. Then there was the on-the-job discrimination that occurred after employment. Jobs were segregated along gender or *hukou* lines, and individuals doing identical or similar jobs received vastly different pay or faced different prospects for promotion or termination because of certain group characteristics.

Nevertheless, the above-mentioned studies have paid relatively little attention to one important moment in the job-seeking process, namely the moment that hiring decisions are made. It is perhaps assumed that hiring decisions are a function of the existing structural discrimination in society. Such decisions are also so transient that we may assume they are unlikely to have any lasting impact on the overall pattern of discrimination in the labor market. Besides, there is usually little prior social interaction between the recruiter and job seeker that would justify claims of discrimination, as hiring decisions are typically made in a matter of days. A final reason for the lack of systematic studies of hiring discrimination might be, simply, the lack of data on hiring. Employers are reluctant to share information on what they regard as internal human resource matters, including decisions on hiring, promotion, and termination of employment. As a result, discrimination in hiring has received little analytical attention from scholars, a deficiency that has also been noted in the study of labor market discrimination in other contexts.[23]

We know from documentary evidence that many municipalities in the 1990s set aside jobs that excluded nonlocals, especially rural migrants. There were also many reports of female job seekers, especially recent college graduates, encountering great difficulties in finding jobs. But the evidence contained in such reports and analyses were generally textual, tangential, and anecdotal in nature.

The study outlined in this chapter was designed to remedy this situation by furnishing some direct evidence on the practice of hiring discrimination in China's urban job market today. It used an experimental design in the context of a real job market situation to pinpoint discrimination in hiring decisions. Specifically, it adopted an employment audit methodology by sending two pairs of job applicants, who were nearly identical in every other respect except their gender or rural/urban status, to apply for positions at job fairs. We were interested in knowing whether an applicant's gender and rural/urban status affect the likelihood of his or her receiving a positive response from potential employers. Assuming that two applicants were equally qualified for a job, what was the probability of only one receiving a job offer or an opportunity for a further interview? Was there any systematic bias against individuals because of gender or rural/urban status?

Audit Methodology and the Study of Hiring Discrimination in Beijing

Audit Methodology

An employment audit study involves training individuals as hypothetical job seekers (called testers or auditors) who are carefully matched on all but one characteristic (for example, race, gender, or in our case, rural-urban *hukou* status) and sent to apply for real job openings to see if they receive different treatment or responses from employers. To the extent that the two testers are equally qualified for a position, systematic bias in favor of one applicant over the other constitutes *clear* evidence of discrimination that is *directly* attributable to the varied characteristic in question.[24] In reality, there are so many intangibles to a job seeker's background that identical matching of testers with one, and only one, variation is extremely hard to achieve.[25] Selecting, training, and matching testers are thus crucial issues in the design of audit studies. A variant of audit studies that does not involve sending real people for interviews is done through "correspondence testing." This approach involves sending carefully matched resumes that are identical in all respects except the tested variable to potential employers. The probability of such resumes leading to follow-up interviews or jobs for the applicants can then be used as another gauge of measuring discrimination.

In spite of its limitation, the audit methodology has its obvious appeal. One such appeal, as we have just mentioned, is that the audit approach yields direct evidence of discrimination. This is because "auditing is usually based on close observation of individuals reacting spontaneously to a controlled choice between two or more candidates who are alike except for the presence of a protected trait."[26] It is an obvious improvement on indirect statistical inferences that typically involve regression models showing positive and statistically significant association between a selected independent variable (for example, race or gender) and disparities in the labor market outcome (that is, the dependent variable) while controlling for a host of other variables. As it were, the audit approach helps to reveal the "smoking gun" in discrimination practices.[27] Because of its directness, it is an especially good instrument for detecting more subtle forms of discrimination that are not easily detectable via other means.[28]

Another appeal of the audit approach "lies in its ability to combine experimental methods with real-life contexts." According to sociologist Devah Pager, "[T]his combination allows for greater generalizability than a lab experiment, and a better grasp of the causal mechanisms than what we can normally obtain from observational data."[29] In other words, any evidence of discrimination revealed by audit studies is "realistic" and convincing because of the real-life situation involved, and the method is especially helpful in pinpointing the cause of discrimination with a degree of exactness usually not obtainable in multivariate statistical models.

Owing to such appeals, audit methodology has been used by researchers since the mid-1960s in the study of labor market discrimination. In the late 1960s and early 1970s British researchers utilized both the method of paired-testers and correspondence testing to find out about the extent of racial discrimination in white-collar jobs.[30] In the United States the technique of audit studies was first used in the area of housing and then extended to employment in the late 1980s and 1990s.[31] The most influential studies on discrimination in both areas were conducted by Urban Institute researchers during this period.[32] More recent research has sought to overcome some of the common methodological problems associated with audit studies (for example, tester matching and the experimenter effect) and to expand the traditional focus on race and gender as the tested variables to include other social stigmas, such as a criminal record.[33]

The Beijing Audit Study Design

In the summer of 2004, we decided to apply this methodology in a pilot study of employment discrimination in urban China. As discussed above, discrimination against women and rural migrants was significant in Chinese cities, and much of it could be attributed to direct government action. But given subsequent labor market developments that seemed to mitigate the influence of government control over labor allocation—the relaxation of *hukou* regulations and the weakening of the official stance on female labor participation—we were interested to know if and how a job applicant's rural-urban status or gender might affect the likelihood of his or her receiving a positive response from the employer.

We hired four young students through our contacts at a local university: two female graduate students and two male college students (senior). They were chosen after phone and in-person interviews that screened out several other potential candidates. All four testers that we eventually hired were from outside of Beijing but had lived in the city for several years. One male-female pair came from nearby areas, so they sported an authentic Beijing accent and could easily pass as Beijing residents. The other two testers had slight accents, but neither was so strong that it might jeopardize their employment prospects at a first encounter. All four majored in humanities or social science disciplines as real-life students. After securing their consent and time commitment for the duration of the study, which would last for ten working days,[34] we conducted a full-day training session that included self-introduction, an explanation of our research objective, briefings on the audit methodology, research procedures, and logistics. We emphasized the need for them to assume different identities (while keeping their real names on the résumés in case an employer demanded to check their IDs) during the interview process, and we obtained their written consent for their participation in the research. In the afternoon, we worked with each tester to design a résumé that incorporated some of their real-life experiences. For example, for the two testers from rural areas, we decided to let them use their real birthplaces for their *hukou* registration. We used the remaining time to stage mock interviews and to go over a four-page questionnaire we asked each tester to fill out immediately after each interview.

We decided to incorporate the following elements in the résumés to make them as generic and identical as possible: all four testers were similar in age (twenty-four to twenty-six years of age) and had a junior (three-year) college education with majors in nontechnical fields of humanities, education, or administration. They all had comparable work experience in secretarial, clerical, sales, and junior-level administration, either in Beijing (for Beijing applicants) or in a rural town in Anhui or Jiangxi Province. To make them at least minimally appealing to as many employers as possible, we also included a section on special skills that included basic-level English proficiency expected of junior college graduates and rudimentary computer skills. All of the contents were fitted into a one-page resume that also included the applicant's *jiguan* (i.e. native place which also served as short-hand indication of one's rural or urban *hukou* status), gender, and contact information. The applicants' stated objectives were broadly similar: they were all interested in office jobs in sales, secretarial work, or administrative assistance, all jobs that fit their educational background and work experience. In short, the four applicants were ordinary junior college graduates, with some work experience but no special high-level skills, who were interested in entry-level positions in the service sector. They were substitutable workers insofar as work-related qualifications were concerned. What separated them from each other, then, was their gender and rural-urban status.

The decision to fit them with a junior college résumé interested in entry-level positions had to do with another decision we made about the venue of the field experiment and the sampling of job openings for interviews. With a limited budget and time constraint, we decided to focus on job fairs in the northwestern part of the city instead of sampling job ads and having our applicants respond directly to such ads, as is traditionally done in audit studies. Sampling employers at job fairs would limit the kind of jobs we could test, but we found that the variety of jobs available from job fairs was as much as the range of jobs advertised in newspapers. By the mid-2000s, in virtually all cities in China, job fairs were hosted at regular intervals by various labor market intermediary organizations such as "job introduction agencies" (generally affiliated with labor bureaus), "talent exchanges" (affiliated with government personnel departments), and other nongovernmental employment agencies. According to one survey done by the Development Research Center of the State Council in 2004, the job fair was the most utilized method of recruitment by urban enterprises. Some 60.4 percent of the enterprises surveyed mentioned hiring at job fairs, compared to the next two most frequently used methods: 46.3 percent of the enterprises used media advertisement and 42.8 percent relied on referrals from talent exchange centers.[35]

The job fairs we looked at were run by government personnel bureaus or their affiliated talent markets.[36] For our study such job fairs were not only convenient, but they had some advantages compared to other venues for sampling purposes. First of all, regular talent market fairs offered the kind of entry-level jobs that would potentially attract both migrants and local city residents. Because we were interested in comparing employers' attitudes toward local city residents and migrants from rural areas, we wanted to sample jobs that both groups of workers were likely to be in competition for. Talent market fairs typically targeted applicants with a junior (three-year) or regular college education. This was a key reason why we specified three-year college education for our testers. Higher educational credentials would have made them eligible for higher-end jobs which, even if they were advertised at the job fair, would have made it more difficult for us to detect hiring discrimination because more factors tended to come into play (for example, school reputation, specialization, etc.) in such cases. On the other hand, we did not want to go too low on the job ladder due to the relative absence of local city applicants in the low-end job market. Even for jobs at the junior college level, we found local residents were outnumbered by nonlocals.

Second, job fairs were usually supervised closely by the relevant government agencies (for example, the Personnel Department in the case of a talent market), so that employers recruiting at the fairs were less likely than in other venues to engage in overt discrimination. Thus, any discrimination we might detect under such circumstances would be equally, if not more, likely in other hiring venues. Finally, employers usually came to job fairs because there was some urgent need to fill positions. Given the urgency, they were more likely to make quick decisions about hiring than employers who placed "help wanted" ads in the newspaper all the time. A quick decision time ensured that we would not bias our analysis by failing to include favorable phone calls too far into the future. We could safely assume no decision or call for a second interview after two to three days of the interview constituted a negative response for the purpose of our analysis.

Audit Findings

Two teams of testers of the same sex, with each team made up of one Beijing resident and one rural townsperson from Anhui or Jiangxi Province, were sent to interview for jobs at eight job fairs variably named "human resource" or "talent" markets run by different levels of government agencies.[37] At each fair, on average, about forty employers set up interview booths, and the number of job seekers would usually peak in late morning with about 100 to 150 people at the fair.[38] Employers from all over Beijing were represented, and they were mostly private or joint-venture businesses trying to fill multiple positions (for example, sales, insurance, clerks, secretaries, junior managers, etc.). Job fair announcements were widely publicized in local newspapers, including *Beijing Talent Market News*.

Among the 81 employers whom our testers audited and interviewed with, 51 were interviewed by one tester, 23 by both members of the paired team, 4 by three testers and 3 by all four. A total of 121 interviews were recorded, with an average interview time of around 11 minutes. We must note that few employers explicitly stated local *hukou* or sex requirements in on-site job postings: less than 6 percent mentioned local *hukou* as a prerequisite, and about 12 percent specified a "male only" or "female only" requirement. In contrast, about 32 percent of the positions had some kind of age limit (for example, below 35), and, as one would expect from a talent market, more than 79 percent of the advertised positions required a high-school education or above.

We specified five possible outcomes to each interview: (1) an immediate job offer (which happened only once); (2) an offer of a subsequent interview at the company site; (3) an indication of interest with no firm commitment for further interviews; (4) the mere taking of résumés without any other response; and (5) refusal to take a résumé. We regarded (1) and (2) as positive responses, (4) and (5) as negative responses, and (3) as ambiguous and noncommittal, so we did not include it in either category, positive or negative responses.

All applicants received proportionally more positive responses than negative ones, but the difference between them was significantly larger for the urban testers (27.8 percent) than for the rural testers (5 percent); and for the male testers (22.7 percent) than the female testers (9.6 percent). The male urban applicant, whom we may regard as the baseline individual for whom little or no discrimination existed, had by far the largest positive over negative difference (42.5 percent) in employer response.

When we compared the outcome across male/female and rural-urban[39] groups, we obtained similar results. Figure 11.1 shows the percentage of negative responses all four testers received, first by rural-urban status and then by gender. It is clear that one's rural-urban status had considerable effect on the employers' attitude, with rural applicants receiving a far higher rate of negative responses (43.3 percent) compared to Beijing applicants. Rural *hukou* status thus increased one's chance of rejection by 15.4 percent.

Rural prejudice may take more subtle forms than overtly negative treatment by the employers. The recruiters' body language and hand gestures sometimes spoke volumes about the kind of receptions they meted out to different applicants. One general impression we got from reading our testers' descriptions of the interview scene was that the urban testers were much more prone to using expressions like "friendly" and "enthusiastic" to describe their encounter with the recruiters, whereas rural testers gener-

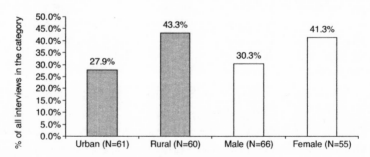

Figure 11.1 Negative employer responses to job applicants based on *hukou* status and gender. Source: 2004 Summer Audit Study.

ally refrained from such positive expressions and used "cool" or "courteous." Our male Beijing tester reported that one employer was so enthusiastic about him that "she fumbled in her handbag for a name card, then gave me one of only two brochures they have on display at the counter, and proceeded to mark a star on my resume . . ." (Audit transcript). In another situation, after a pleasant talk with a female recruiter, our male Beijing tester asked about the pay: "She whispered into my ear: young man, we will be colleagues after you join us, so why don't you make a request. I said it's got to be around 3,500. She said no problem. An ordinary associate makes that much, let alone an assistant manager [the position he applied for]. . . . She scribbled some notes on my c.v. and told me with a big smile: wait for our call tomorrow!" (Audit transcript). The situation with our rural female tester could be quite different. In one interview, she recorded that as soon as the employer read her résumé, he started querying her about related work experience and then even thought up two hypothetical scenarios to test her responses. She felt discouraged, and the rest of the interview did not go well (Audit transcript).

It is not immediately clear why employers, especially private-sector employers, would continue to discriminate against rural job-seekers, as most formal restrictions against hiring rural migrants had been lifted for the low-end job market by the early 2000s. The few state-owned enterprises our auditors approached were still quite adamant about the Beijing *hukou* requirement, but many private firms showed an eagerness to hire migrants. In one case, our Beijing female applicant was bluntly told that the job for which she was applying was not appropriate for her as "Beijing people lack motivations for hard work because they do not have livelihood pressure" (Audit transcript). Quite a few employers who were themselves from outside of Beijing showed preference for rural or non-Beijing hires for similar reasons.

A closer look at the recorded interviews revealed several possible considerations behind the employer's preference for local workers. One consideration was attributable to the classic "tastes for discrimination" by business customers.[40] Businesses discriminate against hiring outsiders because of their presumed clients' prejudices. For example, a recruiter from a media advertising agency assured our female Beijing tester that her local *hukou* was a big plus because "our clients would feel reassured and very comfortable knowing that they are negotiating with a local Beijing person" (Audit transcript). Another reason was that hiring local employees saves business expenses, such as housing subsidies. Two-thirds

(66.4 percent) of the employers in our sample did not provide housing, nor any housing allowance, which partly explains why local residence was an important consideration for many employers. For example, one employer from Haidian's Science Park decided to stick to locals because the Park "does not provide accommodation or other subsidy" to outsiders (Audit transcript). Yet a third reason was that many businesses simply did not want to deal with the outsiders' expectations regarding *hukou* transfer because they lacked the authority or quota to confer Beijing *hukou* on the non-Beijing employees. Under such circumstances the employer were willing to consider an outsider's application only after he or she indicated no expectations for *hukou* transfer.

The gender gap, measured by the difference in the rates of application rejection by male and female applicants, seemed equally significant. Figure 11.1 shows that, overall, female applicants received a higher rate of negative response than male applicants by a factor of 11 percent, only slightly lower than the rural-urban difference. Figure 11.2 presents the result of a cross-group comparison between the male pair of applicants and the female pair. This chart shows that the female tester from Beijing faced almost the same level of negative response as the rural male applicant did (39.3 percent vs. 42.4 percent). Interestingly, the finding confirmed the existence of a significant rural-urban gap (24.2 percent), but *only* among the male applicants. The magnitude of the effect of Beijing residency was minimal in the case of female applicants as *both* rural and urban women faced similarly high levels of negative treatment, with rural women having the highest rejection rate of all four testers (44.4

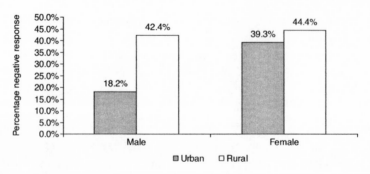

Figure 11.2 Negative employer responses to job applicants in different categories. Source: 2004 Summer Audit Study.

percent). In the case of women, the effect of gender seemed to override the difference in rural-urban residence, as female applicants faced high rejection rates regardless of whether they were from Beijing or rural provinces.

Besides the obvious bias, the audit was especially well designed for detecting less overt and hard-to-measure forms of discrimination. One such form involved "steering" or channeling job applicants toward positions that employers deemed to be more appropriate for them. According to Michael Fix, George Galster and Raymond Struyk, steering "is a process that makes available different, and typically inferior, opportunities" to the disadvantaged groups that sustains existing patterns of discrimination.[41]

Our testers' description of their encounter with employers was full of examples that illustrated subtle discrimination. In one case, our Beijing male tester applied for a clerk position, but was told that archival management was more appropriate for him because he was male (Audit transcript). Similarly, our rural male tester was told that he was not eligible for a secretarial position because it "involves taking care of chores in the company, for which even the best qualified male will not be considered" (Audit transcript). Another employer refused to consider women for technical positions in his company (Audit transcript).

Urban residency, exemplified by Beijing *hukou* in our case, can also become the basis of steering practices for some employers. Once, when a male recruiter overheard our Beijing tester expressing her wish to apply for a receptionist position, he burst out at her in disbelief: "You want to apply for a receptionist position! Aren't you a Beijing resident?!" (Audit transcript). Again, at another interview, she was duly urged to apply for a higher position than sales because she was a bona fide Beijing person (Audit transcript). One recruiter told her point-blank: "you need to raise your application threshold, because you are a Beijing native *and* have a college degree!" (Audit transcript).

Further Evidence on Hiring Discrimination: Job Ads and Human Resource Interviews

Newspaper Job Ads

Job advertisement was one area in which we expected a significant amount of discrimination in terms of explicit requirements about gender and rural-urban status. To investigate gender and residency bias in the written job ads in local Beijing newspapers, we conducted a content analysis of all of the ads carried by the *Beijing Talent Market News* (BTMN) for six months from January to June 2002. BTMN is the flagship paper published by the Beijing Talent Exchange Center under the Municipal Government's Personnel Department. It debuted in 1996 and was published twice a week at the time of our study. According to one official we interviewed at BTMN, it had the largest circulation among comparable employment information papers in Beijing. Its wide circulation, plus official affiliation with the Municipal Personnel Department, made the paper very attractive for both employers and job seekers interested in advertising hiring needs. According to the BTMN official, unsolicited ads generated about half of the overall volume in 2004. In the same year, the paper employed several dozens of ad solicitors and more than fifty distributors. Besides job ads, the paper also carries job-related news and stories as well as the latest regulations concerning the labor market and other employment-related matters.[42]

BTMN was one of twenty-five local newspapers that carried employment-related advertisements in 2003–2004. Each day, tens of thousands of "Help Wanted" or "For Hire" ads circulated in these papers, a testimony to how much things had changed from the days before the reform began, when the government monopolized the allocation of all jobs. Increasingly, one also found online ads making inroads into the lucrative job introduction business. Among the newspapers that carried job ads, BTMN tended to carry lower or entry-level positions, the kind of positions for which our testers interviewed in the audit study. Perhaps most significantly for our study, papers like BTMN and online job agencies helped to channel migrant workers to Beijing's job market. A self-analysis of the BTMN clientele by the paper's own staff in 1997–1998 already found that more than 60 percent of the job seekers advertising in the paper were from outside of Beijing. Most were under 35 years of age, and more women than men posted personal ads for hire during the period.[43]

From January to June 2002, a total of 2,368 companies advertised 6,553 positions in the pages of BTMN. Table 11.1 presents a breakdown of the occupational categories of the positions advertised in the paper.[44] We counted the number of positions that explicitly mentioned gender and Beijing residency requirements in the job ads. What we found confirmed the continuing existence of gender and *hukou* bias in the ads, but we were somewhat surprised that gender and *hukou*-based bias were much less significant in comparison with another variable we examined: age.

Figure 11.3 presents the proportion of jobs that listed explicit gender, *hukou,* or age requirement. It turns out that employers cared least about *hukou* in the job ads: merely 5 percent of the positions mentioned Beijing *hukou* as a requirement at all. A slightly higher percentage of the positions advertised (12 percent) had explicit gender requirements. Yet, 29 percent of the positions mentioned a specific age requirement (see Figure 11.3)! Other traits mentioned in the ads included experience, personality, height, appearance, veteran status, and so on, but age stood out as the most-often mentioned criterion in the job ads. When we broke down the occupations into various categories, we found that age requirements were pretty uniform across these categories, whereas gender requirements were most pronounced for clerical, sales, and service jobs (see Figure 11.4).

One reason we did not find high incidences of *hukou* discrimination may be due to the lower-level positions advertised in BTMN. Higher-level jobs generally had more stringent *hukou* requirements, and such jobs were usually not openly advertised in local papers. Instead, most such jobs were handled through special channels. For example, our auditors told us that new college graduates would not typically consult job ads in the local papers or visit the kind of regular job fairs included in this study; they relied on social networks and on specialized job fairs reserved for new college graduates. Universities and government agencies usually held college graduates-only job fairs in prestigious venues such as the International Exhibition Center. Beijing also established a permanent "job market

Table 11.1 Positions advertised in BTMN during January–June 2002

Job categories	Advertised positions
Administrative and managerial	1209
Professional and technical	2324
Clerical	952
Sales, service, and transportation	2060
Agricultural	8
TOTAL	6553

for the college graduates" in April 2002.[45] Jobs advertised at those fairs tended to have formal *hukou* requirements, and some employers obtained government quotas to hire a limited number of nonnative graduates to work in Beijing. In 2003, the Beijing Personnel Bureau stipulated that employers wanting to hire non-Beijing students needed to obtain prior approval from the Bureau. It further limited hiring criteria for non-Beijing graduates to those with special skills or from the country's top 281 universities.[46] In general, the dwindling but still significant number of state-sector employers retained strict *hukou* requirements for new hires.

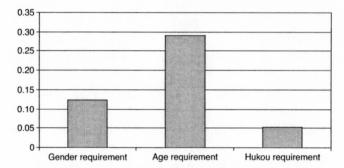

Figure 11.3   Advertised jobs with gender, age, and *hukou* requirements (NS = 6,545). Source: *Beijing rencai shichang bao*, January 2002–June 2002.

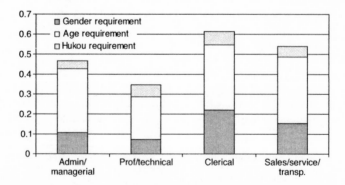

Figure 11.4   Gender, age, and *hukou* requirements by categories of advertised jobs (N = 6,545). Source: *Beijing rencai shichang bao*, January 2002–June 2002.

For those job ads that did display overt gender requirements, discrimination primarily took the form of gender-typing, as evidenced by the language of those ads. Many jobs were advertised as "female-only" and others as "male-only" positions. The former included maids, receptionists, secretaries, cashiers, karaoke bar hostesses, client relations clerks, cosmetic salespeople, waitresses, and so on, whereas the latter usually included such professions as security guards, custodians, technical designers, electricians, construction managers, and business developers. The following job ads that appeared in the BTMN was a good example:

> Beijing Youshi Brothers Trading Company, Ltd. The company sincerely wishes to hire in the following areas: 3 surveyors and designers: preference for people with experience in furniture or interior design and computer knowledge; 2 clerks, female, under 25, three-year college or above, computer skills; 6 workers: male, under 25, prefer workers with experience in carpentry and in handling aluminum/alloyed window frames; 2 business developers, male, three-year college or above, preference to those with experience in building materials sales; 2 drivers, under 30, familiar with Beijing roads.[47]

As we have already mentioned, local *hukou* was no longer a typical requirement for entry-level jobs by the early 2000s. This had to do with increasing urban demand for low-skilled workers in low-end jobs. Most urban residents continued to shun low-end jobs, except perhaps for some laid-off workers. But the latter were generally from an older age cohort with a different skill set, so they typically did not compete directly with young migrant workers in the same market.[48] Besides, many private companies were founded by outsiders who showed little antipathy toward hiring migrants.

This is not to say that *hukou* or Beijing residency was no longer important in the low-end job market at all. Most companies, for example, would only hire Beijing residents as accountants. This had to do with the city's certification requirements (e.g. only locally certified accountants were allowed to work in Beijing), but it also reflected the employers' distrust of employees without a permanent city address when it came to sensitive money-related matters. We also found that another area where companies tended to hire locals was in public relations or in jobs that required face-to-face interaction with clients. In such cases, Beijing residents were preferred because they were said to enhance the companies' image as "local" businesses and because they would know better than nonlocals on how to handle Beijing clients. One human resource manager we interviewed told us, "we ourselves are not from Beijing, but we want to hire a staff member from Beijing because Beijing *hukou* is necessary for many of our business dealings."[49]

The following ad is an illustration of why some businesses preferred local workers. Although Te'aite did not specify *hukou* requirement for the regular staff, it insisted on hiring Beijing residents as trainers and inspectors:

> Beijing Te'aite Domestic Service Company: Reputable domestic service company, registered with Beijing Industrial and Commerce Bureau, is seeking to fill the following positions: 1. Department I: 3 staff members, 25–40 years of age, responsible for the recruiting, dispatch and liaison of domestic service workers; 2. Department II: 2 training teachers, Beijing *hukou* required, 25–40 years of age, responsible for the training of domestic service workers; 3. Department III: 3 client service representatives, 25–30 years of age, articulate speaker; 4. Department IV: 2 inspectors, Beijing hukou required, 25–40 years of age, responsible for periodic inspection and visit in client households. All above positions are open to female applicants only, high-school education or above, bring cv. and other documents for interviews at company office between August 3–7.[50]

Human Resource Interviews

The relative non-importance of *hukou* in the entry-level job market was confirmed by a third set of data, telephone conversations with seventeen of the employers who had interviewed our auditors. Of the seventeen companies, two are state-owned and the rest are private or jointly owned businesses. In our telephone interviews, we asked human resource managers to rate the importance of various qualities associated with an applicant on a scale of 1 to 5. Table 11.2 presents the average score for the fourteen qualities we asked them to rate. Based on the numeric scores, we clustered these qualities into three broad groups in the order of their perceived importance to employers. It was a little surprising to us that having an "outgoing personality" should be the trait with the highest rating score, but the rest of the findings were consistent with what we had already detected in the audit studies. Among the most important qualities employers in this study looked for in a candidate were interview performance, age, relevant work experience, and education. Applicant's gender was ranked as of middling importance, along with party or youth league membership, veteran and marriage status, internal personnel reference, and experience working in the state sector. Least important for the HR managers in this study was the applicant's residence status or whether he or she was currently laid off or unemployed.[51]

This pattern suggests that employers at the low-end job market no longer considered city residency a significant factor in hiring. Even when Beijing *hukou was* required, it was not usually because of government regulation, but because the local workers had certain advantages over the nonlocals (for example, the locals generally did not need the business to provide housing).

Table 11.2   Degree of importance attached by HR managers to various qualities of candidate

Candidate qualities	Score (1 to 5)
C. Outgoing personality	4.11
K. Good interview performance	3.9
H. Young age (under 35 years old)	3.88
B. Relevant work experience	3.64
A. Good education	3.12
L. CCP or youth league membership	2.5
D. Male	2.47
M. Veteran	2.4
N. Currently an SOE employee	2.2
I. Unmarried	2.1
G. Recommendation by acquaintance or internal personnel	2
E. From Beijing	1.88
F. Not from Beijing, but from another city with urban *hukou*	1.58
J. Laid-off or unemployed workers from Beijing	1.4

Note: N=17. Interviewees were asked to rate each item on a scale of 1 to 5, with 5 representing most important and 1 representing least important. The English letter before each item represents the original order in which the fourteen items were asked.

How do we then account for the difference between what the advertisement and interview data show and the findings from our audit study that suggests *hukou*-based discrimination to be more prevalent? One possibility was that the positions advertised in the local papers belonged to an even lower job category than the ones presented at job fairs. This was possible because the type of job fairs we investigated were run by the personnel departments that tended to enforce strict minimum education credentials (junior college or above) at job fairs. Another possibility, which we think was more likely, was that employers did not bother to specify *hukou* in their ads or mention it as a formal requirement, but in practice, they tended to favor someone from Beijing over an outsider in a real interview situation. In other words, when they constructed an ad or answered hypothetical questions from the interviewers, employers were much less discriminatory toward migrants than when they faced a real decision about whom to hire.

Gender discrimination remained more pronounced than residence bias in the analysis of ads and human resource interviews. But even here, employers seemed willing to discount the gender factor in hiring decisions should they find a candidate who was young and well educated, had relevant experience and an attractive personality. This finding is corroborated in another part of our questionnaire where we gave human resource managers five choices and asked them to assign an exclusive number from 1 to 5 to each choice so as to rank them (with 5 representing most important and 1 least important). What we found was that the HR managers considered "experience" and "education" as far more important than "gender," "local residence," or "nonagricultural *hukou*," in the order of ranked importance (see Table 11.3).

Table 11.3 HR managers' ranking of selected factors influencing their hiring decisions

Hiring factors	Score (1 to 5)
Work experience	4.6
Level of education	4.2
Applicant gender	2.6
From Beijing	2.2
Urban *hukou*	1.7

Note: N = 17. Interviewees were first read the above five factors and then asked to rank them according to the importance attached to each factor on a scale of 1 to 5, with 5 representing most important and 1 least important. A number can be assigned once.

Conclusions

This study provides a variety of direct and indirect evidence, from an audit study to job ad analysis and a management survey, that confirms the continuing existence of significant discrimination against migrants and women in China's urban job market. Everything else being equal, being a migrant of rural origin reduces one's chances of being hired in Beijing by a factor of 15 percent relative to a Beijing city resident, whereas being a woman reduces one's chance by 11 percent relative to a male applicant. Indeed, being a woman, a rural migrant, or, in the worst case, a rural migrant woman, sharply diminishes an individual's chance of hiring by 21.1 percent to 26.2 percent compared to the odds enjoyed by a male job seeker from Beijing. The effect of rural origin, as indicated by their rural-town *hukou* status, seems to be greatest in the case of male applicants. But even the better-treated women from Beijing fare no better than the worse-treated male applicants.

Many analysts, especially those who are partial to market reforms, predict a significant decline of, and even an end to, rural prejudice with the formation of a unified national labor market.[52] In some ways, their prediction has been borne out. De jure discrimination—that is, explicit anti-migrant regulations sanctioned by the government—has either declined or is being ignored by the private-sector employers. Our findings show a significant decline in rural bias or *hukou* requirements in job ads and in management attitudes. But the audit study also confirms persistent discriminatory *practices* against rural migrants under market conditions. The difference is that practical considerations and biases against rural migrants now replace explicit government restrictions as the main factor behind urban employers' decision to favor the local city residents over rural migrants.

As was the case in the past, government policy now proscribes gender-based bias in employment matters. Although the government had much leverage in enforcing gender equity policy before the reform began, female job seekers are now largely left to their own devices as they negotiate the emerging urban labor market in China. Insofar as job market discrimination is concerned, rural and urban women are pretty much in the same boat as they face similarly high levels of negative treatment by employers compared to men.

Methodologically speaking, the present study contributes to the analysis of job market discrimination in China in two ways: one is that it provides fresh direct evidence of urban job market discrimination in China. In the past, researchers have tried to assess the extent of discrimination through qualitative research (for example, policy analysis, ethnographic fieldwork, participant observation, and interviews) or multivariate analyses of disparate treatment for men and women and rural-urban individuals. Such research is worthwhile, but it is often dogged by problems of inference, generalizability, and control. An audit study furnishes virtually incontrovertible proof of discriminatory behavior when similarly qualified applicants with differing rural-urban status or gender identities receive disparate treatment in the hands of employers.

Another contribution by the audit study is to identify hiring as a direct mechanism of discrimination that could lead to larger patterns of social inequality later on. Analysts have tried to explain rural-urban/male-female job segregation and wage disparity by a variety of factors such as human capital endowment, institutional barriers to mobility, or the relative abundance or scarcity of labor supply due to demographic reasons or market segmentation. Granted, employment is a long, drawn-out process. Our study only tested for discrimination in labor hiring at the point of *initial* job interviews. It provides evidence that the hiring process may bear some responsibility for sorting people into various employment groups with differential pay scales.[53] To the extent that our Beijing case is generalizable, this study provides an assessment of the extent of gender bias and rural prejudice inherent in the hiring practice in China's urban job market.

ARIANNE GAETANO

12 | Gender and Citizenship Inequality
The Story of Two Migrant Women

This chapter focuses on the migration of rural Chinese women to illustrate how attention to gender enhances understanding of the inequality that Wu Jieh-min calls "differential citizenship." As Wu argues in Chapter 3 in this volume, China's system of household registration, or *hukou,* is an institution that stratifies citizens through the imbalanced allocation of social as well as political rights. Such unequal citizenship is clearly evident in the situation of migrant workers.[1] This system of differential citizenship has enabled China's high economic growth through "easy and fast capital accumulation" by creating an "artificial reservoir of fresh workers" at zero cost to the state.[2] I will demonstrate that female migrant workers in Beijing are often doubly disadvantaged both as outsiders excluded from *hukou*-derived social resources and as women in a hierarchical gender system, even as they are the preferred labor force in specific employment sectors.

Since the launch of China's reform and opening program in 1978, rural women have been migrating to cities to work in industry and in the service sector in ever increasing numbers, constituting 33 to 50 percent of the total migrant labor population.[3] Initially overlooked by gender-blind scholarship both inside and outside of China or dismissed as purely non-economic population movement, female labor migration has since received a fair share of attention.[4] Importantly, literature on this topic has established that gender is implicated in the entire migration process, influencing migration motives, patterns, experiences, and outcomes, which can vary greatly between, as well as among, men and women due to different social positions and to asymmetrical relations of power.

Gendered social roles rooted in institutions of rural marriage, family, and household mutually reinforce gender ideology that constructs female workers as "naturally" temporary, flexible, nimble-fingered, patient, obedient, unskilled, and cheap.[5] Normative gender thus obfuscates inequalities rooted in the institution of *hukou* and the labor-capital relationship and naturalizes the subordinate status of young female rural migrant workers.[6] Consequently, it may be doubly hard for migrant women, compared to migrant men, to recognize and struggle against their disadvantaged position in the urban economy and society. Encouragingly, recent ethnographic research on single migrant women workers indicates that migration, in China as elsewhere in the world, complicates gender identity for women, due to tensions between conservative values and modern lifestyles or due to familial duties and autonomous desires.[7] Research among married migrant women likewise suggests that migration contributes to changes in household divisions of labor, intergenerational relations, and gender ideology in the family; alters women's views on marriage and women's reproductive knowledge and choices; and increases the difficulty of reintegration of returned migrant women into rural society.[8]

Detailed ethnographic fieldwork can help illuminate how differential citizenship and normative gender are interconnected and manifested in migrant women's everyday lives, as well as how they, as agents, accommodate or resist structures of inequality as gendered beings. I will focus my inquiry on the story of two key informants, sisters Zhou Lina and Zhou Lili, who migrated from an isolated hamlet in north China to Beijing in 1997 and with whom I have had sustained contact for nearly a decade. The longitudinal study sheds light on how time spent in the city, changes in the life course, as well as shifts in the external environment, including *hukou*-related policies, shaped their experiences and identities.

The sisters are typical of China's internal migrant women in that they were young, unmarried, and relatively uneducated (compared to urban peers) at the time of migration, although they had received less schooling than the average migrant.[9] Likewise, their migration from a poor rural area to a wealthier urban area, and from elsewhere in China to the eastern region, has long been the standard migratory pattern. However, as the first young women to venture so far from their home, and as members of the first cohort of migrants from relatively poor and remote northern China to Beijing, the sisters were very much pioneers.[10] In addition, their destination city of Beijing is somewhat atypical among cities. Although Beijing has long been a major destination for rural migrants, it exercises stricter control over them than do other megacities in China. The sisters are exceptional, too, in that they have remained in Beijing for a decade, whereas most rural women who were single at first migration terminated migration on marriage.[11] Nevertheless, their migratory trajectory and life experiences resonate with many of their peers, who share their ambivalence about migration as it calls into question established gender identity, relations, and roles.

The body of this chapter presents the sisters' migration story, followed by my thematic analysis of the broader context of gender and differential citizenship that it reflects. In conclusion I consider how their experiences can contribute to our theorizing about China's citizenship inequality, as well as female labor migration more generally.

The Migration Story of Two Sisters

Lina and Lili and their two younger brothers, Xun and Wei, were raised in a remote hamlet in an officially designated poverty region of mountainous northern China. Their father, Mr. Zhou, worked in coal mines from age sixteen until deteriorating health forced him to seek work elsewhere. In the early 1990s he became village head, and a few years later he joined the ranks of cadres by securing a post in the nearby township government; he thus became a person of some influence. Their father is self-taught in reading and some writing; their mother was illiterate, and she too had serious health problems. Lina, born in 1979, is the eldest; Lili was born two years later in 1981. Lina completed elementary school, but Lili dropped out. Xun completed two years of middle school and then quit to join the army. The youngest sibling, Wei, was not inclined toward school, but he did take courses in auto mechanics and earned his driver's license.

From an early age the sisters worked in their village weaving carpets by hand. In the early 1990s, the family rented out their village property and moved to the nearby township where Mr. Zhou was posted. Their father used his expanding social network to seek out better work opportunities for his children. Lina was hired for a monthly wage of 80 yuan as the assistant to the township Women's Federation cadre in charge of family planning. Lili was sent out to work sewing cloth sacks in a factory in the prefectural city. After six months of work, her father came to fetch her home because she still had not received any payment. Instead, he found her a job as a waitress in the county town, earning a monthly wage of 150 yuan. Lili disliked the job and fought with the chef, but when she tried to quit, her father scolded her and forced her to continue, for the sake of his "face" and his relationship with the restaurant owner.

In 1997, just after the Lunar New Year, sixteen-year-old Lili went to Beijing. Her father entrusted her to *laoxiang* (people from the same native place, also called *tongxiang*), a married couple who had lived in Beijing for twenty years. For ten months Lili worked as a hotel chambermaid until bankruptcy led management to lay off all the migrant employees without severance. The local Beijing staff kept their jobs as the hotel fought its battles in court. During these months, her father arrived in Beijing to work as a security guard for a compound that housed a small garment factory. He soon secured work for Lili operating a sewing machine making long underwear at the factory, which was run by a Beijing man and his wife. When he returned home in the winter of 1997 to tend to the girls' elderly grandparents, he sent Lina to Beijing to join her sister at the garment factory, where they worked until January 2000.

The garment factory paid low wages and offered no overtime compensation, though work hours often extended late into the night and there was no time off. The sisters' starting monthly salary was 260 yuan, including room and board; two years later their income was 400 yuan, excluding meals. The sisters each earned the praises of a more experienced migrant woman, whom they respectfully called *shifu* (master), who trained them on the sewing machine and with whom they would keep in touch over the years. During their time at the factory, the sisters spent little on themselves. Every other month, they pooled their savings of about 1,000 yuan and sent this amount home. Their parents in turn used the girls' remittances to finance the brothers' educations and later to pay for their mother's medical treatment.

Work at the sewing factory was tiring and unsafe, yet employees did not have any worker's compensation or health provisions. An accident with the sewing machine nearly severed Lili's finger and required stitches, which she paid for herself. In 1999 her appendix failed and rupture was imminent. Her desperate sister sought the boss's help, but he offered only one month's salary and would not allow the sisters to cash out their security deposits to use for the operation.[12] Lina spent a frantic few hours calling relatives and *tongxiang* throughout the city until she had raised 3,500 yuan, the cost of the appendectomy surgery that she had directly negotiated with a surgeon, whose asking fee was usually 5,000 yuan. Her sister came within an inch of losing her life. The sisters repaid their debts over the next eighteen months at the rate of 100 yuan each per month.

The sisters lived in a tiny and sparsely furnished room attached to the garment factory. A bunk bed made of planks of wood, a vanity table with a mirror that also served as a kitchen table, a coal burning stove, and a stool were all crammed into a mere $2\,m^2$ (21.5 ft^2). When the three of us sat together in the room, our knees touched. The factory shared a compound with an elementary school, and the sisters had use of the school's outside toilet and running water. They preferred their small hut to the dormitory that housed their coworkers because they could cook for themselves (although they had to pay for meals), they had a degree of privacy, and they felt it was safer. In their view, the co-ed setting of the dormitory encouraged improper fraternization between the sexes. They blamed that lax environment for the immoral behavior of a *laoxiang* who got involved with the boss's brother. The *laoxiang's* parents, apprised of the situation by Lili (unbeknownst to the young woman), ordered their daughter to return home.

At Chinese New Year in 2000, the sisters requested time off to go home to visit their family, which the boss refused to grant them. Indignant, Lina and Lili plotted to quit. After collecting their January paychecks, the sisters made a trip to the post office to send gifts of clothes to their parents (spending 50 yuan on the package) and to call their father to tell him of their decision. That night they moved their suitcases to their prospective new employer's dormitory across town. The next day they reported to a janitorial services *(baojie)* company contracted to a five-star hotel, where a former coworker from Henan had arranged tryouts for them.[13] The employment trial was successful and the sisters were hired.

In their new jobs the sisters' starting monthly salary was 390 yuan, which included the cost of two daily meals (including on a rest day) and lodging. Every ten days the workers received a day off, but only if their boss was satisfied with their work. The hotel laundry cleaned their work uniforms twice weekly, and they were provided hot showers daily. The cost of the uniform was deducted from the sisters' first paychecks, along with a deposit for the dormitory key and work ID, which amounted to a total deduction of 120 yuan. Their new employer also required that they have proper documentation, the charges for which were likewise incrementally deducted from their paychecks over several months. First the sisters were directed to have a health examination and were issued a certificate of clean health; 84 yuan was deducted from their first paycheck to cover this cost. A total of 208 yuan was deducted from the next paycheck to cover the cost of a temporary residence permit (180 yuan for nine months' validity) and for a marriage and family planning certificate (28 yuan), required only of female employees. An amount of 240 yuan was deducted from yet another paycheck for an employment permit. The validity periods of the certificates were not uniform, and the boss complained that paperwork processing was often delayed due to backlogs and quotas. (He was particularly anxious that workers would quit before he had recovered the costs of the permits.) The employees were subjected to strict discipline. If one employee was caught sleeping on a shift, the guilty party was fired, and the others on the shift were fined. If equipment was damaged, the cost was borne by the operator via paycheck deduction.

The sisters rose each morning at 5:30 A.M. and rode a bus for about forty minutes to get to the hotel by 6:30 for breakfast. Their daily shift ran from 7:00 A.M.–3:30 P.M., including a thirty-minute lunch break. They found the food at the staff cafeteria to be top quality and quickly got into a routine of eating as much as possible during the noon buffet lunch there so that they would not need to purchase much more than instant noodles or steamed buns for dinner. After their shift, they still had to attend an hour-long meeting chaired by their supervisors to review the day's errors or troubleshoot problems, plot out the upcoming tasks and schedules, and train on new equipment or procedures.

The janitor staff's dormitory was located far from the hotel, about thirty minutes by bicycle or forty-five minutes by bus. The sisters sometimes had use of a bicycle abandoned by a former coworker or one borrowed from coworkers on different shifts. Traveling between the dormitory and hotel was a tiring and risky undertaking, especially during the periodic police campaigns to "clean" the streets of vagrants, including migrants without proper documentation. As a result of their semi-legal status, many janitors were anxious about their commute from hotel to dormitory. In one week in the spring of 2000, three male employees were caught just outside their dormitory and detained for days until they had posted bail, which they borrowed from the boss and repaid through paycheck deductions.

Although meager, their lodging in the basement of an ordinary walk-up apartment was an improvement from that of their previous job. They shared a crowded room lined with bunk beds with eight to ten other female coworkers. The rooms were dank and dark, mosquito-infested in the hot season and clammy and cold in the winter, and smelled of the adjacent toilets. All fifty migrant employees were housed in this basement; girls and boys bunked in separate rooms and utilized separate washrooms and toilet facilities. Despite the rigid separation of sexes, dormitory life once again caused consternation for the sisters. They disapproved of coworkers who stayed in the men's dorm late at night or even overnight, which did occur. However, over time the sisters got used to socializing with the opposite sex and increasingly tolerated such behavior as the norm. Together, Lina and Lili toiled on the job for six months and then their paths diverged. Below I discuss each sister's story in turn.

Lina was employed at the cleaning company for more than a year. During that time her monthly wage increased to 450 yuan, until March 2001, when she fought with the boss over renewal of her work and temporary residence permits. In the past he had allowed the janitorial staff to avoid permit renewal fees by altering their permits such that they appeared to be newly issued. However, he put an end to this practice, saying Lina's altered permit was not convincing, and gave her an ultimatum: pay for the renewal through paycheck deduction, or resign. Angry and unwilling to pay the steep fees, Lina quit. However, she stayed on at the dormitory until she found a similar job at another hotel, which hired her on a trial basis. Lina explained that the second hotel was willing to try her because she had a certificate that verified her employment experience as a janitor at the five-star hotel. However, during the trial period, Lina heard disturbing reports of nonpayment of wages at her new hotel, and she started having second thoughts. When her new employer asked for an deposit of 210 yuan (rather than take a salary deduction over time), Lina decided to heed others' warnings and quit before she had truly begun that job.

Worn down by migrant working life and missing home after nearly five years away, Lina returned home for several months. Only after the Lunar New Year festival of 2002 did she return to Beijing to take a job assembling cassette tapes at a factory, an opportunity she learned about from her former *shifu* from the garment factory. She took the job because it offered up to 1,000 yuan per month, depending on her productivity. Food and lodging were not included, so she had to pocket as much of that salary as possible by skimping on essentials. She rented a room for 180 yuan monthly rent on the outskirts of the city and commuted by bus for up to 1.5 hours each way to and from work. Her abode was a small and Spartan makeshift room on the rooftop of a one-story brick house (*ping-fang*) rented from former farmers with urban residency. Lina fetched water from a tap on the bottom floor and hauled it up a ladder in a bucket to wash herself and clothes; she cut her hair short so it did not need frequent shampooing, and she paid 3 yuan for a hot public shower only once a week. She ate little, subsisting on steamed buns, raw vegetables, and instant noodles that she prepared herself.

Lina worked an entire month without any break before receiving her first paycheck. The boss did not offer time off, and the piece-rate wage motivated Lina to work constantly. Although the job and living conditions took a toll on her health, Lina continued in this manner for almost two years, until severe swelling in her kneecap caused by arthritis forced her to quit. Lina's parents came to Beijing during her hospitalization for surgery that set her back 3,000 yuan plus lost wages during several months of recovery. Fortunately, she was able to live with her sister during that time, helping Lili through pregnancy and childbirth. In retrospect, Lina expressed anger toward the *shifu* who found the cassette assembly job for her, accusing the woman of misleading her about the job from the start. Once Lina had started working at the factory, she could not demand more time off or a lighter workload because doing so would lose "face" for her *shifu*.

After recovering from the surgery, Lina returned to hotel housekeeping, finding it less of a strain on her joints than doing factory work. She worked until the Chinese New Year of 2005, when she returned home to be introduced to the man she would marry that summer. Yet just weeks after the wedding, the discovery of her husband's infidelity propelled Lina back to Beijing, leaving behind her husband and a newly furnished home. She took refuge with her married sister, until she again found work as a hotel housekeeper. Early in 2006, Lina quit her job, returned home to file for divorce, and then returned to Beijing and a new hotel housekeeping post. When we reconnected in the summer of 2006, she was working in an unrated private hotel that catered mainly to out-of-town businessmen on company trips. Although her monthly salary was low, only 700 yuan, Lina was content because of the light workload (that is, not so many rooms to clean daily), the regular 8:00 AM to 6:00 PM work hours, and two rest days each week. Six months later, she had switched to a two-star hotel near a major tourist site that catered to international budget travelers. This hotel paid slightly higher wages than the previous one, gave bonuses for overtime and holiday hours, provided a clean and safe dormitory (in the attic of the hotel itself), and had a lighter workload than at the previous hotel. She planned to stay in the job for the foreseeable future, yet she also expressed a longing to go "to some other place" (except any town or city in her home province) because she felt sick of Beijing. She bemoaned how little she had to show financially for ten years of migrant life and worried about her future.

Meanwhile her sister Lili, after working at the janitorial company contracted to the five-star hotel for half a year, was transferred by the parent company to another location, an office building, under a new supervisor, a Beijing native. Over the next year, a romance gradually blossomed between twenty-year old Lili and her thirty-six-year-old new boss, and in June 2001 the couple applied for a marriage license. They moved into their newly renovated bridal suite in his family's three-bedroom apartment, which they shared with his retired and widowed mother, his divorced and temporarily out-of-work sister, and the sister's son.

Just before the marriage became official, Lili quit the janitorial company to join a friend, a former coworker from her initial (1997) hotel job, selling shoes at a market stall, pocketing about 1,000 yuan/month. When a developer purchased the property a few months later, the stall closed, and Lili was out of work again. She waited until after her wedding ceremony, which took place at the Lunar New Year of 2002, to search for a new job. On her own she applied for a variety of jobs, responding to posted vacancy announcements, until she found a hotel that would hire her at a monthly rate of 600 yuan without requiring her to pay the costs of permits up front. The hotel was a state-run guesthouse whose clients were mainly Party members on official business in the capital. In this hotel she worked as chambermaid alongside a dozen middle-aged Beijing women, educated women (for example, high school and college graduates) who had been laid off from other state sector jobs. Like Lili, they were contract employees (*linshigong*) and therefore not entitled to any benefits. Four other chambermaids with Beijing *hukou* were formal (*zhengshi*) contract workers, and they were entitled to paid vacation, health-care subsidy, and occasional bonuses. Only one chambermaid, a Beijing native who had been hired before 1982, was still employed under the "iron rice bowl" set of benefits, and she alone would eventually receive a pension. Among these women, Lili had the advantage of youth, which surely led to her promotion a year later to shift supervisor. She stayed at this hotel for more than two years, until she became pregnant. During this time, Lili was the major breadwinner for her family while her husband upgraded his knowledge by taking adult technical training courses.

After celebrating her child's first birthday in September 2005, Lili reentered the workforce and was hired at the rank of shift supervisor at a three-star hotel in Beijing's central shopping and tourist district. There she earned 1,200 yuan per month, working regular 8:00 AM to 5:00 PM work hours with one day off each week. She was able to maintain her position at the hotel until early 2007, when a crisis in childcare forced her to give up the hotel job to stay home with her child. Up to this point, Lili's child had been enrolled in a subsidized day care affiliated with her mother- and sister-in-law's work unit. When that day-care facility closed during summer months and holidays, Lili usually could work out ad hoc child care by involving her mother-in-law, sister-in-law, husband, and even Lina. But as no kin were available to provide child care during the 2007 Chinese Lunar New Year holiday period, Lili had no choice but to quit her job. However, Lili expressed dissatisfaction with her role as fulltime caregiver and resolved to find a solution so that she could continue with paid work outside the home.

During the decade in which the sisters worked in Beijing, their brothers grew up and found their own paths to employment. The eldest brother, Xun, followed his sisters to Beijing in 2000 and joined them at the janitorial company, working the night shift cleaning the floors of the five-star hotel. Soon after, a *tongxiang* found him work at a wholesale market selling seafood. Xun did well in retail and was soon promoted to the position of supervisor. In 2001 his retail boss dispatched him to Shenzhen to open a branch for the wholesaler, and his monthly earnings surpassed 1,000 yuan. Eventually, Xun was able to use his cumulative experience to secure a position as a manager of a facilities and security firm contracted to a large state-owned company. By 2007, his monthly salary was a stable 3,000 yuan per month.

In 2004, Xun invested his savings in an apartment in the county-town (which had been newly designated a "small city") nearest to the siblings' natal village. His sister Lina contributed a loan of 10,000 yuan toward the 180,000-yuan purchase; Lili did not contribute. The Zhou parents moved into the apartment along with their youngest child, Wei. The move and purchase of property enabled the sisters to transfer their *hukou* location to the county-town and change its type to "urban." Mr. Zhou and Wei together purchased a van and began a small-scale transport business, shuttling goods and people between the county town and townships and villages. By 2007 the business was quite lucrative, generating a monthly profit of up to 3,000 yuan. Later that year, Xun returned from Shenzhen with his fiancée, a coworker and *tongxiang*. After their wedding, the newlyweds moved into the apartment shared by Xun's parents and younger brother. Xun invested in the family transport business. Today, he runs the business jointly with Wei. Mr. and Mrs. Zhou have retired.

Gendered Expectations of Migrant Daughters

Although young Chinese rural women often migrate independently, even without parental consent,[14] most make that decision in the social and cultural context of the family and household as well as local social networks.[15] The Zhou sisters' migration was very much dictated by their places in kinship and gender hierarchy. Lili's position as second daughter made her available for migration while her elder sister remained at home to help their mother with housework and her younger brothers attended school. The very fact that she has younger brothers speaks to her parents' desire to have sons, even in violation of family planning regulations. According to China's family planning policy, rural couples are allowed to have a second child if their first child is a girl, and the ideal family includes a son. It is not unusual for couples to defy the birth limit until they succeed in bearing a son. In China's largely patrilineal tradition, sons are especially valued because they carry the family name and in turn have a filial duty to care for their parents in old age, an important role given rural China's insufficient social security system.

As daughters eventually marry out of their natal households and into another family, parents may invest less in their development when household resources are scarce, preferring to invest in sons. Although the Zhou sisters appear to have left school of their own will, which in turn freed them to take up wage work, statistics reveal that rural Chinese girls received less education than boys in the 1990s, and this gap has been attributed to gender discrimination.[16] However, new research by Emily Hannum, Meiyan Wang, and Jennifer Adams (see Chapter 6 in this volume) suggests this gender gap in rural compulsory education may be closing, in large part due to recent state initiatives to improve access to education. Yet other scholarship reports that when rural parents migrate with their children, they are more likely to take with them their sons, who can benefit from superior educational facilities of urban areas, and leave their daughters behind.[17]

Most migrants leave their villages with the primary intention of earning money.[18] As fathers and husbands are expected to be the primary wage earners in a family, they shoulder the greatest responsibility for generating income through migration and remittances. Most migrants remit a portion of earnings to families, and much evidence shows that, in keeping with this gender role, male migrants remit more than do female migrants.[19] However, C. Cindy Fan has argued that migrant women remit as much as men as a *proportion of their earnings*.[20] A daughter may be encouraged to set aside some of her earnings for her future marriage.[21] At the same time, a daughter effectively contributes to her household's economy by becoming self-supporting through migration.

Unmarried male migrants usually use remittances for home renovation or construction to prepare for their future family, as was the case with Xun. Indeed, rising standards of living and young people's modern desires for a postmarital residence that is independent of parents and in-laws, combined with an increasingly competitive marriage market, have put great pressure on bachelors to earn incomes in order to meet traditional expectations of "marrying in a bride" to the native place.[22] As dutiful Chinese working daughters of earlier decades have done, the two sisters sent home their remittances from their first few years of work in Beijing to finance their brothers' educations.[23] This use of remittances reinforces traditional gender ideology and contributes to gender inequality in the household and family. Yet when publicly acknowledged, remittances can raise daughters' status and authority in the household.[24] For example, among Thai Buddhists, remitting wages is seen as a selfless act that increases daughters' spiritual merit.[25]

Two years out, the Zhou sisters stopped turning over their earnings to their parents and began spending money on themselves, particularly on clothes and cosmetics, as well as high-tech consumer goods, all of which enhanced the self-image of each as fashionable and up-to-date women.[26] As they matured, they became more concerned about their individual futures, and they each opened a savings account. They used some savings for dowries, mainly buying furniture and home decor. (Unfortunately, Lina lost much of her investment with her divorce.) After marriage, both sisters continued to help out their parents with small gifts of money, particularly at New Year's or on visits home. Lina indirectly contributed to her parents' retirement by loaning money to her brother for the purchase of an apartment. Lili's remittances provided for her own family's financial needs.

A rural-urban economic divide contributed to the conditions of poverty and underdevelopment in the Zhous' native place that in turn necessitated their migration for the sake of the household economy. The Zhou sisters exemplify rural migrant women's relative disadvantages, including their younger ages and lower education levels at migration, compared to male migrants. Their father's authority in their migration decisions and the use of their remittances to finance their brothers' educations reflected and reinforced their subordinate position in the household. Much research confirms the tendency of female migrants to identify with the family and place others' needs above their own personal desires, using remittances for siblings' and then children's educational needs in particular, thus fulfilling normative gender role expectations.[27]

Yet the very act of migration empowered the sisters as they took up a masculine role of migrating out to work and supporting their families. Although Lili was at first a reluctant migrant worker, she later expressed pride to be the first woman in her village to have migrated. As a young girl she had eagerly awaited the New Year holiday when her father and his fellow miners had returned home, their pockets stuffed with sweets for children. Now she envisions herself part of this celebrated tradition of migration and return. In addition, as she and her sister came to crave the "sweets" associated with urban consumption, they held onto their remittances in order to indulge such desires. In this regard, migration fosters expansion of gender roles and identities, as dependent daughters (or wives) also become independent wage earners and financial decision makers.

Gendered Networks, Occupations, and the Labor Process

Like the Zhou sisters, most migrants locate work opportunities through informal social networks of kin and co-villagers, which arguably lower the costs and potential risks associated with migration.[28] This tendency is especially so for young single rural women because they may be subjected to rumors about sexual promiscuity.[29] Such stereotypes only compound the very real possibility of gender violence facing migrant women in the city. As defense against damage to reputation and as protection from perceived threats, migrant women seek the protective care of their social network members, even as this may further subordinate them to paternal authority. For example, when Lili protested to her father about having to work as a waitress, his authority and appeal to "face" trumped her resistance.

Over time the Zhou sisters actively forged their own social networks, bringing *tongxiang* out to work. Coworkers, especially those from the same native place, can be an important source of emotional support and companionship, financial support, and a conduit for future job opportunities. The sisters also recognized that the more *tongxiang* they could convince their bosses to hire, the less chance that they themselves would be let go, for in such a scenario their *tongxiang* would be compelled by loyalty to quit too, leaving the boss without any workers. However, management can also exploit native place differences to keep workers from recognizing their collective interests.[30] Social networks can also serve as extensions of the rural community, using surveillance and gossip to bind migrant women to entrenched gender and sexual norms. Such conservative social mores are also in the best interest of managers, who prefer to maintain a workforce of single female workers, thereby keeping labor costs low and productivity high.[31] For example, Lili informed on a wayward *laoxiang*, reporting her behavior to her parents. Intervening in order to save the young woman from a potentially worse fate such as pregnancy and abandonment, Lili nonetheless enforced an entrenched patriarchal code that punishes women's displays of sexuality outside of marriage.

Tongxiang networks tend to be strongest among same-sex peers, and thus they reinforce the status quo of a sex-segregated job market, channeling rural women into a narrow range of jobs.[32] The Zhou sisters' initial employment options were further limited to those open to nonlocal *hukou* holders and shunned by urban workers, those requiring no previous experience or training, and those deemed to be gender-appropriate categories of work. Together, such factors have been shown to limit migrant women's earning potential, even when compared with their male peers.[33] In China, as elsewhere in the world today, female migrants overwhelmingly concentrate in labor-intensive industrial assembly work of the apparel industry, which pays relatively high wages but discriminates against women workers in promotion and training.[34] Migrant women also predominate in domestic service and hotel housekeeping, which are low-wage and low-status jobs. These tendencies demonstrate the feminization, and hence devaluation, of certain occupations associated with women's domestic roles (for example, housework) and are hence considered "unproductive" chores rather than (paid) "work." The feminization of such jobs is at once a global phenomenon and one that in China is reinforced by a Confucian tradition that ascribed gendered meanings to activities according to spatial location (that is, inside and outside).[35] In such occupations, it may be difficult for women to identify primarily as workers deserving of rights. In the "global factory," management invests in the image of the "maiden worker" as a means to exert control over the labor process and labor power in the interest of maximizing profit.[36] Similarly, in domestic work and small enterprises, the family model subjects young female migrant workers to a soft form of paternal authority with a similar result.[37]

Gendered assumptions about certain categories of work as being morally and sexually indecent further narrow migrant women's job choices. For example, Lili's father strongly objected to her working at a hotel and intervened to find her a different job. As Lili explained, back in the countryside people associate women and hotel work with prostitution, mainly because that is where it takes place. "Working in a garment factory" sounded more reputable than working in a hotel because of more positive meanings that are ascribed to the factory as work*place*. Indeed, the sisters took care to hide their identities as hotel housekeepers from people back at home in order to protect their own and their family's reputation. The necessity of doing so demonstrates that female migration and employment challenges patriarchal authority by transgressing against conservative social and sexual mores.

Prospects for Economic and Social Mobility

The Zhou sisters each accumulated several years' experience working in the apparel industry and in hotels, and Lili had a brief foray into retail. After nearly a decade in Beijing, however, neither woman had managed to move into more lucrative employment, nor had either accrued much savings or social security benefits. Their intertwined statuses both as women and as rural migrants in numerous ways thwarted their upward economic mobility.

Although the Zhou sisters' wages rose slightly over the years, their earnings remained low by Beijing standards, at the level of the working poor, largely due to their "unskilled" jobs. Discrimination tied to the *hukou* system meant the sisters were denied employment benefits and subsidized housing and health care yet were vulnerable to fines and regulations. Although in 2001 the government decreed it illegal to bar outsiders from particular occupations,[38] subtle discrimination in hiring against migrants, and women, has persisted.[39] The Beijing women who worked alongside the sisters at the five-star hotel doing identical tasks made more money and received better benefits. This situation had changed a bit by 2002, such that a majority of Lili's Beijing coworkers at the state-run guesthouse had labor contracts similar to hers.

Up until recently, the sisters were confronted with numerous pay deductions, including permit fees, security deposits, and lodging and meal costs, not to mention any fines that put them in debt to employers from the start of a contract period. Once hired, they had little incentive to quit until these debts were paid off, increasing their vulnerability to exploitation. In addition, residence and work permits were nontransferable, so a new job meant another round of fee deductions, discouraging them from changing jobs. On the upside, most of their bosses simply disregarded the permit system altogether; only at the janitorial services company were they required to have documentation, and even there document forging was often condoned. Also, by 2006 the sisters needed only a temporary residence permit, which was then affordable (5 yuan to cover the cost of the photo ID) and convenient to obtain.

When they faced nonpayment of wages or excessively harsh work conditions, the sisters would either endure or quit. Legislation to protect migrants' rights is relatively new and enforcement is imperfect.[40] Investigations have revealed a host of violations of migrant women workers' legal rights, including earnings below the minimum wage set for the locality, improper withholding of wages, extended work days, excessive and inadequately compensated overtime, inadequate rest time, unsafe work conditions, inadequate social security benefits, and violation of women's "special rights," such as guaranteed maternity leave. Employers often illegally "safe keep" migrant workers' official documents, such as their national identity cards; require security deposits up front or through paycheck deductions; and delay salary payment to prevent frequent labor turnover.[41] Migrants are often hired without a legitimate labor contract, which is the precondition for any sort of legal recognition and access to social security.[42] Domestic work in particular falls into a legal gray area and is not recognized to be "work" as defined by the Labor Law.[43]

Migrant women workers' "low quality"—their lack of knowledge and understanding of the law—is often cited as the main obstacle to their legal protection.[44] But another impediment is their status as "outsiders" in the localities where they are employed. As nonlocals, they do not have rights to participate in local elections, nor do they have any social connections to local officials, who in turn have no obligation to represent their interests. Indeed, local officials are more likely concerned about protecting industries in their vicinity, because these contribute to the local economy and these depend on a steady supply of cheap (migrant and female) labor.[45] Yet these local officials sit on arbitration boards to which migrant workers are required to turn when labor disputes arise.[46] Migrant workers have recently been invited to join worker's trade unions; however, unions in China are not independent of the state, and regulations on organizing prevent the formation of alternate unions or labor associations.

Migrant women can fall prey to sexual harassment in their workplace and public space, although to date little attention has focused on this issue.[47] At the garment factory where the sisters worked, the boss's son periodically caused trouble for the women workers; the sisters said they always locked their door when he tried to visit. In her years working as a hotel chambermaid, Lina became adept at sidestepping propositions by traveling businessmen. Living away from their families and rightfully distrustful of authorities, rural migrant women have few resources to resist advances of predatory men. Irregular and extended work hours and long commutes from living quarters in city outskirts to employment sites in city centers exacerbate the dangers for migrant women in public space.

Cycling home late one night after a housekeeping night shift, Lili was attacked by a man but managed to flee unhurt. The sisters' mobility in public space was further constrained by anti-vagrant policing, at least until the policy of custody and deportation of migrants lacking proper documentation was declared illegal in 2003.[48] "Street sweeps" like the one that led to the detention of several of the sisters' coworkers at the five-star hotel reportedly reappeared in Beijing as the city prepared for the 2008 Olympics.[49]

Migration and work may negatively impact on a migrant's health and well-being. Migrant women workers in China's export apparel, toy, and electronics industries are especially at risk for occupational health risks and safety hazards, as has been documented by the domestic and international media. Migrant women often complain of neurasthenia and fatigue from mental stress of the migrant lifestyle.[50] They have higher rates of gynecological infections and diseases than their local (urban) counterparts, have more and riskier abortions than do their nonmigrant peers and urban counterparts alike,[51] and have greater rates of stillbirth and maternal death at pregnancy.[52]

The Zhou sisters suffered both immediate and long-term health consequences as a result of their work. Lili endured an industrial accident. Lina's arthritis in her knees was likely caused or exacerbated by the repetitive motions of assembly work. Medical expenses created debts for the sisters that forced them to continue working, a phenomenon referred to as the "migration trap."[53] Although factory work paid higher wages, the sisters ultimately chose hotel housekeeping to better protect their well-being. As they aged, the sisters sought jobs that offered lighter workloads and more rest days, even when this meant accepting lower wages. Today, Lili has chronic lower back pain. Her sister suffers painful toothaches. Since 2006, the sisters have been paying into a citywide worker's compensation and pension scheme, but neither has any health insurance.

The sisters aspired to learn more marketable skills and find more lucrative work, but numerous obstacles prevented them from doing so. They felt insecure about their ability to study new subjects, given their low level of education in a society that increasingly emphasized educational achievement as an index of culture (wenhua). They internalized their outsider status and felt inferior among others, including more educated migrants. Perhaps a middle school diploma would have raised their confidence. Then again, their jobs allowed them little free time to pursue a course of study. They also lacked information about, and access to, technical training programs, such as those run by neighborhood or resident associations, which mainly conducted outreach to urban residents. The sisters recognized that they had only their youth to rely on to make a living. They were well aware that older women, including laid-off urban workers, had fewer job options. Taking gender differences for granted, the sisters did not attribute their present or future choices to gendered cultural practices or structural inequities. But they did feel injustice as migrants who would have no social safety net on which to rely after retirement.

The lack of alternatives meant that each sister's future security would derive primarily from marriage, as is the case with most rural Chinese women. Nearly universal in rural China, marriage is the primary means by which rural women come into property, as their inheritance rights are commonly disregarded by their own parents. Some young women migrate with the hope of changing their "fate" by making a better match that what otherwise would be possible, either through raising a larger dowry or marrying into a wealthier household. Certainly migration raises their expectations for their future mate and makes them reluctant to marry an ordinary peasant. Most hope to find a partner who has migration experience and a marketable skill, such as a fellow migrant. Few rural women succeed in marrying an urban spouse, for reasons of cultural prejudice against such matches as well as a long-standing regulation (in force until 1998, when it was abolished; see Chapter 15 in this volume) that children inherit their mother's *hukou*, making it difficult for the offspring of such unions to obtain the benefits of an urban childhood, especially schooling. Migration and work keep rural women unmarried longer than normal, yet with age their marriage prospects decline (unlike for men). Not only do rural men desire slightly younger brides, they also prefer never-migrated ones, as they associate migrant women with sexual promiscuity. For these reasons, migrant women's raised expectations for marriage are not easily met.[54]

Lili's migration trajectory led to marriage into an urban household, so she did not need to return to the countryside and the poor life of a farmer's wife. But what appears a successful conclusion to her migration story is colored by the reality of her household's relative poverty, which necessitates that she continue working for the family's survival. Desiring the respect and acceptance of her husband's kin as well as neighbors, some of whom she feels look down on her because of her rural origins, Lili has been at times frustrated by the low status of her menial job and her working-class lifestyle. Ironically, a truly urban identity is out of her reach because she cannot attain the bourgeois family ideal, in which the wife has the luxury of being a full-time mother. Although Lili increasingly identifies as "urban," she is unable to fully embrace it. Since returning to work (outside the home) after the birth of her child, Lili has also had to balance dual identities and roles as both mother and worker, unable to properly or fully occupy either. This double burden is common to many of the world's working mothers but is particularly hard for an economically disadvantaged migrant mother and is compounded by the exclusivity of affordable child care (and education) in Beijing.

Lina's migration experience was barely interrupted by her marriage because it ended so soon in divorce, prompting her to continue life as a migrant worker. Her future is very precarious because she is aging out of the marriage market and yet faces social and economic pressure to remarry. Should she remain single, she will be hard-pressed to be self-supporting. Patrilineal customs and her parents' exodus from the village make her landless; in addition, she is unwilling to live in a rural area. Although she accepts remarriage as inevitable, her previous experience has made her wary. For the moment, then, she remains an independent working girl in the city.

Conclusions: Gender, Migration, and Differential Citizenship

In this chapter I have explored how cultural constructions of gender and social roles intertwine with unequal citizenship accorded rural labor migrants in China's cities, particularly Beijing, to shape the lives of two female rural labor migrants in complex ways. Their dual statuses as women and migrant outsiders have in many ways compounded their economic vulnerability and social subordination. But this is not the whole story, and I have also endeavored to explain how migration invariably challenges normative gender by expanding possibilities for identity—encompassing those of migrant, waged worker, financier, consumer, breadwinner, and urban (house-)wife (Lili) and divorcée (Lina)—and by shaking up entrenched social roles and sexual mores.

Certainly the increased range of options resulting from migration brings rural Chinese women's lives closer to those of their urban counterparts, who, for example, have higher rates of (paid) workforce participation. However, urban Chinese women still receive more government (as well as nongovernment) support for their economic and social aspirations.[55] The Zhou sisters' narrative shows identity is continually negotiated, as when the sisters strove to balance their familial duty to remit wages and autonomous desires, to apply traditional values in new settings, to utilize *tongxiang* social networks to forge urban pathways, and to juggle their roles as mothers and workers. Their story may be added to the increasingly complex picture of how women migrant workers exercise agency by making everyday choices and life decisions in ways that may either challenge or reinforce existing gender ideologies and power relations.[56]

The differential citizenship maintained largely through the *hukou* institution is a unique contributor to Chinese rural migrant women's sense of ambiguity about identity. Yet such feelings are common enough among transnational female migrants who cross national, ethnic/racial, linguistic, and cultural borders as well as among rural-urban migrant women workers in Indonesia, Thailand, and the Mekong region and among working daughters in Taiwan.[57] This pattern implies that for women, the impact of migration on gender identity, roles, and relations may be as important to subjectivity formation as one's position as a migrant worker and outsider.[58]

Significantly, the Zhou sisters' migration trajectory defies a dominant trend in China whereby a combination of low education and lack of marketable skills, gender discrimination in the labor market, and pressure to marry pushes young migrant women back to the countryside after just a few years, ending their initial migration episode. The sisters' tenacity evidences a strong resistance to powerful institutions of state and market, which collude to maintain a temporary, flexible, obedient, feminine, and cheap labor force. The longer they stay in Beijing, the more likely they are to make demands of employers and government for those same citizenship rights accorded to others. At the same time, their ability to continue working in the city will depend on a steady demand for their labor.

Migration has been personally empowering for the sisters. They are confident of their mastery of hotel housekeeping skills and have résumés to prove that. They say that migrant work has given them confidence in their "greater ability to survive hardship" (*sheng ji nengli bi bieren qiang*). Although the language of feminism is not a part of their vocabulary, their activities bespeak a questioning of some foundational beliefs about gender identity, roles, and relations in their own lives and personal relationships. Recently in China the state and nongovernmental organizations have begun to address China's unequal citizenship by acknowledging that migrant workers (among others) have rights that deserve legal protection (see Fei-Ling Wang, Chapter 15 of this volume). This chapter emphasizes the need to further address gender inequality and rights. Meanwhile, I take hope from the Zhou sisters and other migrant women, who in their daily struggles for survival and a better life have unintentionally spearheaded this process.

XIAOJIANG HU
MIGUEL A. SALAZAR

13 | Ethnicity, Rurality, and Status

Hukou and the Institutional and Cultural Determinants of Social Status in Tibet

In contemporary China, the rural-urban divide is the most salient dimension of social stratification. The role of ethnicity, regarded as the most important dividing line in many countries, is less clear. China regards itself as a multiethnic nation, and, indeed, 7 percent of the population formally belongs to an ethnic minority. Especially in the western regions of China, where there is a large proportion of the population comprises ethnic minorities, a better understanding of the relation between ethnicity and rural-urban status is needed to understand processes of social stratification and the sources of social tension and conflict.

This chapter addresses two questions: what is the interrelationship of rural-urban status and ethnicity in determining status hierarchies? How do the two dimensions operate simultaneously to form a system of social distinction? We will investigate the relationship of ethnicity and rural-urban status not only as *cultural* dimensions of distinction and discrimination but also as *institutionalized* forms of distinction in contemporary China in general.

We focus on the case of Tibet.[1] Tibet highlights the complexity of status determination mechanisms in China. With its political situation that can be expected to maximize ethnic identification, Tibet is also the region with the largest rural-urban gap in terms of economic development within China. In addition, a large number of migrants—who mostly belong to the ethnic Han majority but who are also overwhelmingly of rural origin—have entered the region since the reforms of the 1980s. These Han migrants and their status have since become the focus of a heated debate on the social stratification of Tibet.

The status of rural Han migrants in Tibet is perceived differently by outside observers and by Lhasa residents with urban household registrations. At the time that we were leaving for fieldwork, Westerners who learned that our research focused on migrants in Tibet often asked questions such as the following: "Did the Chinese government allow you to study this 'sensitive' topic?"[2] In contrast, when government officials in Tibet (mostly ethnic Tibetans, but also Han) learned about our research, their reaction was often the following: "Is there anything to study about these people? Why don't you do research on something more important?" They did little to hide their contempt for our research subjects. This experience brought into sharp relief the different ways in which a social space can be parsed out into strata of honor and contempt: while Westerners' first reaction was to see Han migrants as factors in an ethnic conflict, urban elites in Tibet saw them as, at best, nuisances.

The assumption that social stratification falls primordially along ethnic lines informs much of the debate in the West about the role of migration in Tibet. That debate assumes that Han migrants will be treated by the authorities as "a privileged race" and be given exclusive preference and benefits; that their presence will be considered desirable by government officials; and that their ethnic status will afford them a consistent advantage in competition with Tibetans.

The empirical data, however, do not mesh well with that assumption. For many urban Han, rural migrants, fellow Han or not, are hardly in their sphere, and there is very little expectation of mutual ethnic solidarity. Urban Tibetans do not perceive rural Han as a status threat or as unfair competitors. Similarly, rural Han migrants in Lhasa do not perceive themselves to be in any way part of a dominant ethnic supra-stratum or expect to be entitled to the "benefits of their race." Instead, when discussing social distinction and hierarchy, both Tibetan and Han Lhasaites tend to focus on the rural-urban dimension.

This chapter focuses on these perceptions of status among Lhasa dwellers and maps the relative prestige and prejudice associated with certain social categories. We propose that those perceptions have been shaped by three interlocking factors. The first is the institutionalized

rural-urban discrimination system based on *hukou* and the related segmentation of market positions and occupational opportunities. The second
is the co-optation of "ethnic policies" by the state, which aligns certain
privileges with both an ethnic category and urban status. The third are
the categories of the traditional Tibetan system of distinction with its
strong stereotypes about rural cultural inferiority. These two latter stig-
matizing sets of cultural stereotypes resonate with each other and reinforce the low-prestige associations of the roles assigned to Han migrants
in Lhasa.

The rest of the chapter is organized as follows: The next section lays out
the multiple dimensions of boundary-making in Tibet. The third section
examines how the *hukou* system underlined social hierarchy in Tibet before the economic reform. The fourth analyzes how ethnic policy, as implemented in Tibet, actually reinforces the rural-urban divide. The fifth
looks at how the new ethnic Han migrants are positioned in the social hierarchy by urban Tibetans. The sixth looks at how the rural Han migrants
position themselves in the social hierarchy of Tibet. The final section concludes the three dimensions of the rural-urban divide in Tibet.

Multiple Dimensions of Boundary-making in Tibet

As in most societies, the boundaries between social groups in contemporary Tibet are drawn across multiple dimensions. Using a Weberian framework, these dimensions can be divided conceptually into three groups:
institutionalized distinctions, cultural distinctions (that is, distinctions
constructed as a consequence of status differentiation or cultural sche-
mas, rather than institutionally established) and economic distinctions.
Table 13.1 presents institutional and cultural dimensions of distinction in
contemporary Tibet.

Rural-Urban Divide

The rural-urban divide in China has become both the principal mode of
institutional differentiation and the most culturally prominent dimension
of status distinction. In terms of institutional differentiation, the *hukou*
(household registration) system as a factor in social stratification is one of
the most striking phenomena in contemporary China and has become an
active area of scholarly exploration.[3] Urbanites have access to formal

Table 13.1   Multiple dimensions of boundaries in contemporary Tibet

	Institutionalized and formal	Cultural and informal
Rural-urban divide	*Hukou* system (enforced by PRC state; weakened after reform, but still effective)	Social distinctions based on family origin and cultural traits
Ethnicity	Official fifty-six ethnic groups and "ethnic policies" (institutionalized by PRC state)	Conventional ethnic markers: ancestry, language, "culture," etc.
"Class" Traditional	Traditional class system (enforced by pre-PRC Tibetan government; dismantled by the PRC state)	Legacy, memory and knowledge of the traditional system of distinctions based on family origin and occupation
Maoist	Political class system (Enforced by the Maoist state, discarded after reform)	Political power, *guanxi*, etc.

avenues of advancement and public services that are either blocked to or restricted for the rural population. Urban *hukou* holders also enjoy a higher degree of official recognition of their rights and increased protection of their interests as citizens. In essence, the *hukou* system encodes a system of split citizenship, with rural *hukou* holders relegated to second-rate citizenship.[4]

In the cultural dimension, which corresponds to the status/prestige level of stratification, rural-urban status is also the dominant marker of distinction. Markers of rural identity—in clothes, speech, and conduct—are considered undesirable traits by urban dwellers. Rural identity is often managed as a spoiled identity by people of rural extraction worldwide.[5] Similarly, rural culture has been regarded as inferior throughout Chinese history.

The institutional *hukou* system and the cultural prejudice against rural culture overlap in contemporary China. The *hukou* system has reinforced the stigmatization of rural cultural traits and makes rural provenance a tainted identity. Rural status has come to index caste-like associations of cultural inferiority.

The loosening of the *hukou* system after reform occurred in stages: first, geographic mobility increased, and later controls of institutional mobility started to weaken. Nowadays, Chinese have gained full freedom of *geographic* mobility, but most do not have freedom of *institutional* mobility. Therefore, though people from the countryside can now geographically travel to, and physically work and live in, cities, they are unable to access full rights as citizens, including education, employment, social welfare, and regular status for their children. This fact has significant consequences for the status of rural Han migrants in the Tibetan city of Lhasa.

Ethnicity

In contrast to the common perception of China as an ethnically homogeneous society, the Chinese state often emphasizes the multiethnic nature of the country, consistently remarking on the presence of fifty-six ethnic groups officially designated within its national boundaries. Ethnicity in China has, naturally, both an institutional and a cultural dimension. The cultural dimension is reflected in such conventional ethnic markers as ancestry, language, clothing, and customs. The strength of these markers and the stereotypes of ethnicity vary across different groups and depend on predominant models of cultural distinction: how ethnic categories have been constructed and what markers have been deemed to be salient. The traits associated with an ethnic category may be positive, negative, or neutral, and the stereotypes associated with a given ethnic group will be deployed in different ways in different contexts.

At the institutional level, starting in the 1950s China's system of ethnicity was built on the Soviet model of nationalities.[6] China identified fifty-six ethnic groups and gave them formal status. The state then set up a whole set of institutional arrangements to give preferential treatment to ethnic minorities with regard to access to economic, cultural, and political resources. These preferential treatments are often grouped together and called "ethnic policy" (*minzu zhengce*).

These ethnic preferences have resulted in a partial split in the status value of ethnicity. Regardless of the cultural prejudices of Han toward minorities, formal status as an ethnic minority is desirable at an institutional level, especially in the areas of education, family planning, and political representation.[7] This template of ethnic minority preferences has provided the Chinese state with an ancillary strategy to deal with political unrest in Tibet.

"Class"

Class division was the dominant stratification system, both in traditional Tibet and during the Maoist period. This legacy affects current stratification by providing a conceptual substratum on which models of distinctions have been constructed.

Qualifications are needed when using the term "class" to define these two hierarchical systems. While both systems were originally closely connected to economic class, both were in practice closer to caste systems: membership was largely defined by birth and distinction was largely interpreted in terms of ritual pollution, inherited taints of blood, and inherent negative traits associated with low-caste status.

The "class" categorization in traditional Tibet—defined as the society before the "1959 Socialist Transformation"—divided the population strictly into "upper and lower classes, nobles and ordinary men, by a clearly defined gradation in which everyone knew his or her proper place."[8] In practice, there were three main classes: nobles, commoners, and "low people." These categories defined every aspect of people's lives. There was no chance for lower-class people to move up the social ladder (unless, with extreme rarity, the lower-class family gave birth to a boy later recognized as the reincarnation of a high lama, in which case the family could become noble). Marriage was also strictly within one's own social class,[9] and these categories were hereditary.

This traditional "class" system of extreme inequality stood in clear opposition to the egalitarian Communist ideology. By "transferring Tibet into a socialist society," the state of People's Republic of China (PRC) dismantled this caste system and imposed a political class system based on Marxist ideology.[10] Surprisingly, the Maoist system, which was supposedly based on a definition of class in terms of ownership of the means of production, soon took on overtones of caste separation all over China, including Tibet. In the new system, the "class extraction" of a family was ranked on a "red to black" scale of class purity determined on the basis of economic status in the "old society." This "redness" scale, in turn, determined to a large degree a family's status in the new society. Former serfs and outcasts gained privilege. Former aristocrats found themselves in a precarious position *vis-à-vis* the Communist state. Class extraction was treated as an inherited condition, and the descendents of former "black" strata were overtly discriminated against in the new order.[11]

After the end of the Cultural Revolution and the beginning of economic reform, the government rapidly discarded the black-red political class system in China. Nevertheless, the political class system did naturalize the use of formal state treatment as the main source of information regarding a group's status: state privileges signaled high status overall during the Maoist era, and the tendency to read state privileges as a marker of overall distinction remained (compare, for example, the perception of welfare and affirmative action in the United States).

On the other hand, consciousness of the traditional Tibetan caste system, along with various religious and cultural practices, has experienced a revitalization since the start of the reform. The traditional class system, even though it lacks institutional support from the state, has again started to affect people's behavior. The ex-noble class has regained some of its cultural prestige, and former low-caste people are again encountering interpersonal discrimination. When choosing a marriage partner, for example, ex-noble families are widely accepted as more desirable, and nowadays many people refuse to marry into the former "unclean" class.[12] One of the consequences of economic reform that is unique to Tibet is this reawakening of consciousness of traditional classification.

As will be seen later, this traditional system has informed Tibetan reactions to the "new kind of Han" who started to come into Tibet as the *hukou* system loosened its geographic barriers. These revived traditions have given Tibetans a meaningful model to account for the new system of distinction imported from Chinese inland regions.

Social Hierarchy in Tibet before the 1980s

During the Maoist era, the *hukou* system formed a strong barrier to physical or geographic mobility for the general population. This system had the side effect of structuring contact between ethnic groups. Ethnic contact in a meaningful sense between ethnic Han and Tibetans started from the 1950s when Tibet was formally incorporated into the PRC. The increasing political and economic links between Tibet and China inland areas resulted from the construction of three highways (the Qinghai–Tibet highway and the Sichuan–Tibet highway in 1954 and the Yunnan–Tibet highway in 1973), which shortened travel to and from Tibet from several months to several weeks and later to several days.

Various studies have estimated the total number of Han cadres in pre-reform Tibet, mostly remarking on their rather modest numbers.[13] From the 1950s to the 1970s, the central government sent about 100,000 ethnic Han public administrators to Tibet.[14] Most of them served for limited periods and were not all present simultaneously. This is a small number compared to 2 million ethnic Tibetans. However, the social positions held by these Han were not low. All ethnic Han shared the same occupational status—they were government personnel sent to Tibet by the government on work assignments.

The assignment of cadres to Tibet started from the initial stage of military cadres (1950s) to a later influx of administrative personnel, doctors, teachers, and the like (1960–1970s) and later other technical personnel (1980s). Though there were various policy changes from the 1950s to the 1980s (most significantly, in the 1980s, from long-term assignments into fixed-term [five-year or three-year] rotations)[15], the overall spectrum of cadres remained the same: they were all government personnel working for the state.[16]

The pre-reform *hukou* system ensured that there were no Han peasants in Tibet before the early 1980s. Therefore, there were no exemplars of the intercept between the categories of "rural" and "Han": for Tibetans of this period, ethnic Han were synonymous with the government elite. The ethnosocial hierarchy was simple and clear: Han were the ruling elite, and Han stereotypes reflected the perceived cultural (rather than economic) traits of that elite.

The concentration of ethnic Han in some work-units instead of others also caused residential segregation from the local Tibetan residents. As a result, Tibetans living in the traditional urban center in Lhasa almost never saw any Han in their daily life.[17] This lack of regular contact highlighted the occupational and cultural markers of the Han as a ruling, official elite. Han concentration among those of the highest social status also made ethnicity irrelevant for status hierarchies at any but the highest level.

Ethnicity as an Institution in Tibet since the 1980s

As part of its effort to suppress separatism, the central government's macro Tibet strategy is to provide massive financial subsidies. This strategy, sometimes criticized as an attempt to "win the stomachs" of Tibetan elites, has succeeded in creating a new urban Tibetan middle class with significant financial and local political power. While this policy does not necessarily buy their loyalty, it does entangle their prosperity with China's and creates a newly entitled stratum whose social position is superior to that of the ethnic Han rural population in all respects.

The policy of "oversubsidizing" Tibet has a critical feature: it is in practice a highly urbanized policy. Despite the negligible productivity of most economic sectors in Tibet, salaries for state employees are set very high and are fully subsidized by the central government.[18] The policy has brought urban Tibetans a significant increase of income. In fact, the wages and level of consumption of TAR state employees have for years remained among the highest in the country, easily on a par with the most prosperous regions in the country—Shanghai, Guangdong, and Beijing (see Table 13.2).

The high income of state-owned unit employees in the TAR is more striking when compared with the low living standards in the rural areas of Tibet (see Table 13.3). Tibet's rural incomes, which are unsubsidized

Table 13.2 Average wage of staff and workers in state-owned units

Year	TAR (yuan)	National average (yuan)	TAR's ranking (of 31)
1985	1,996	1,213	1 (of 30)
1990	3,225	2,284	1
1995	7,572	5,625	4
2000	15,566	9,552	3
2001	20,112	11,178	2
2002	25,675	12,869	1
2003	27,611	14,577	3
2004	30,165	16,729	4
2005	28,644	19,313	4
2006	32,355	22,112	4

Source: *Statistical Year Book of China* (Beijing: China Statistical Press, 1989–2007).

and therefore reflect the level of local productivity, have been among the lowest and slowest-growing in the country. A low level of state investment, coupled with the difficulties associated with the low population density in Tibet's rural areas, have also led to rural Tibetans having levels of education and training lower than those in impoverished Han areas. This makes the divide between the urban and rural populations in the TAR the steepest among all regions in China.

The heavily urban-centered subsidization policy and the striking rural-urban gap within Tibet reinforce the hierarchy of urban over rural areas. This strategy is a localized reiteration of the large-scale model of preferences that underlie the *hukou* system. The *hukou* system amounts to a program of affirmative action for a powerful subgroup (urban residents) at the expense of a disadvantaged majority. The attempted co-optation of the Tibetan urban elites by oversubsidizing their consumption makes the preferential treatment of urban populations even clearer. The process of "Tibetanization" of cadres and local officers has also meant that urban Tibetans have now been guaranteed the jobs and privileges of state employment.[19]

The newly rich in Tibet, backed by the power of the state, do not feel discriminated against, at least within the Lhasa social order. Because the state provides positive discrimination for ethnic minorities—to be precise, for urban ethnic minorities—the individual ethnic prejudice on the part of the Han can easily be ignored.[20]

Table 13.3 Per capita net income of rural households

Year	TAR (yuan)	National average (yuan)	TAR's ranking (of 31)
1985	352.97	397.60	20 (of 30)
1990	649.71	686.31	17
1995	1,200.31	1,577.74	22
2000	1,330.81	2,253.42	31
2001	1,404.01	2,366.40	31
2002	1,462.27	2,475.63	31
2003	1,690.76	2,622.24	28
2004	1,861.31	2,936.40	30
2005	2,077.90	3,255.93	27
2006	2,435.02	3,587.04	26

Source: *Statistical Year Book of China* (Beijing: China Statistical Press, 1986–2007).

Situating the New Ethnic Han in Tibet since Reform

Economic reform in Tibet witnessed the withdrawal of a large number of Han cadres and almost simultaneously an influx of Han migrant workers. Since the 1980s, the net transfer of cadres and net migration of "permanent" residents to Tibet has been negative. The permanent ethnic Han population in the TAR has fallen, from the highest level of 120,000 in 1980 (6.6 percent of total TAR population) to about 70,000 in the 1990s (3.1 percent of total TAR population).[21] From 1981 to 1983, during the peak of ethnic Han cadre withdrawal, 20,000 Han cadres and technicians and 25,000 Han skilled workers were ordered to leave Tibet. Including their family members, 80,000 ethnic Han with TAR *hukou* left Tibet permanently during this three-year period.[22] The remainder of the permanent urban Han population in Tibet is concentrated in the Lhasa area and in the state sector. In 2005 some 21,000 cadres of TAR were ethnic Han, which represents 30 percent of total cadres in TAR.[23]

At the same time, a large number of ethnic Han migrant workers entered Tibet and started to work in "low-class" jobs as manual laborers and to run small businesses in the retail and service sectors.[24] In general, migrants in Lhasa share the characteristics of their counterparts in other places in China. They form part of the enormous rural *hukou* population of laborers and small business owners that can be found in every Chinese city. The main difference is that they concentrate overwhelmingly in the tertiary sector, due to the lack of manufacturing jobs in Lhasa, and so most are employed as shop assistants or own their own small businesses (ranging from street market stalls to more formal shops).

Most of the migrants in Lhasa worked in other Chinese cities before they went to the TAR. Most of them will move to another city within a few years, a "spiral" pattern of migration in which migrants search for opportunities, accumulate capital, and develop skills by trying their hand at new businesses and trades. As a result, their stays are short and their businesses have a very high turnover rate (according to data from the 1990s, only 10 to 15 percent stay in Lhasa for more than five years; 70 percent leave within a couple of years). These migrants rely heavily on their hometown-based and kin-based social networks rather than on institutional channels for support and protection, and they make use of those networks to obtain resources, capital, access to suppliers, and so on. Like many other migrant groups around the world, there is a clear tendency for migrants of a given region to focus on a particular economic niche; for example, cell phone sales are dominated by Anhui natives, silver jewelry by ethnic Bai and so on.[25]

In the 1980s this influx of Han migrant workers presented to urban Tibetans a whole new group of people carrying the label of ethnic Han. "Ragged peasants" new to the city—to any city—were a familiar scene in most Chinese cities in the 1980s. Like rural migrants everywhere in China, Han rural migrants in Tibet are subject to systematic institutional discrimination in terms of social status, housing, education for their children, health care, and other social welfare rights, and they are clearly disadvantaged in matters of access to power, legal recourse, and protection of their interests. This new influx of migrants formed a cohort of Han outsiders with a set of characteristics entirely different from those Han with whom Tibetans were familiar.

At the start the new group caused quite a stir among Lhasa Tibetans. Their lowly structural position was a clear signal of their marginal position in the social hierarchy, and urban Tibetans needed to account for this distinction by redefining the meaning of the category "Han" and absorbing the significance of the *hukou*-enforced rural-urban distinction. How could Lhasa Tibetans make sense of the sudden appearance of a whole new group of ethnic Han? They certainly belonged to the dominant ethnic group, but they were clearly not upper-class elites. A Tibetan writer remembered how this happened in the 1980s:

> We were used to certain kinds of Han people, like school teachers, doctors, my colleagues, and all that. So when the Han peasants first arrived, I didn't give them much thought. But one day I was in the street and saw a few Han standing by a street crossing, looking around as if looking for somebody. They were hesitating and looked so intimidated. Suddenly I realized that they were unable to cross the street! There weren't that many cars in the street at that time, but they were still so afraid. They didn't know traffic lights! And I was like, Aha! They were just uneducated peasants like our nomads!

The earlier "ethnic Han = elite" stereotype was spectacularly denaturalized by the influx of Han rural migrants. This contradiction made the pre-reform ethnic hierarchy questionable and forced local urban residents to revise their understanding of the status hierarchy to accommodate new tokens that did not fit existing categories. The above quote illustrates a number of features of this transition. First, it shows the "Aha!" moment of realization that the hitherto valid system of categorization was no longer so. Second, it reveals that the cultural markers that urban Tibetans used to diagnose distinction—such as the ability to navigate traffic lights—are a quintessential form of *urban* cultural capital. Third, it makes an explicit comparison to a low-prestige group already well defined: Tibetan nomads, a group on whose status inferiority both urban Tibetans and urban Han could agree.

To the Tibetans, not only did the new Han look and act differently, they also engaged in totally different activities. Unlike the familiar Han officials who worked in the walled government agencies and lived in the compounds of state owned work units, the new migrants settled on street corners to conduct a wide variety of small businesses. Like their counterparts in other Chinese cities and abroad, the Han migrants in Lhasa were the main labor source for low-end jobs that Tibetan urban dwellers disdained.[26] Also, as was the case in most Chinese cities of the time, many types of services were not available in Lhasa before rural migrants arrived. The reaction of urban Tibetans to the newcomers' providing some of these services is instructive. A Tibetan official remembers:

> There were no pedicabs in Lhasa before Han migrants started them. Having a man pedaling, sweating and panting like crazy in front of a cart, it's like . . . it's like an animal pulling a cart and you can almost use a whip on him. Only animals would do that. Only those Han men would do that. Tibetan young men refused to do it.

Similarly, he continued:

> We Tibetans don't shine shoes on the street. Holding other people's stinky feet with your hands and putting them right in front of your face? How gross is that?! I would never do that even if you gave me ten thousand yuan.

The dirty jobs that migrants undertook had a considerable effect on Tibetans' perceptions because these jobs combined elite negative attitudes toward hard and dirty jobs with specifically Tibetan cultural prejudices. To Han, running a pedicab or shining shoes are simply undesirable but potentially profitable low-skilled jobs. For Tibetans, however, "dirty jobs" had strong cultural connotations because of the traditional associa-tion of "dirty work" with "low-caste people." This association of dirt with ritual pollution and therefore with lower caste is in turn a survival from traditional Tibetan social rankings.

In traditional Tibet, the "lowest rank," also called the "unclean peo-ple," consisted of families of specialized workers such as butchers, black-smiths, leather-workers, carpenters, and corpse-cutters (for sky burial preparation).[27] When Han migrants took up "dirty work," they were im-mediately classified as "low caste." Because only low-caste people would do "dirty work," whoever was doing the "dirty work" must be "low caste," and they could be safely looked down on regardless of their ethnicity. This coincidence of dimensions of distinction—traditional distinctions and the new system of *hukou* status—reinforced each other and helped urban Tibetans denaturalize the association of Han with "government official." Thus, the influx of Han rural migrants recast the identity land-scape in Tibet.

At the same time as the cultural stereotypes of ethnicity changed, the early reform brought about new modes of interaction between urban Tibetan dwellers and rural Han migrants. These are still the dominant modes of interaction in Lhasa. Either as market interactions (as buyers and sellers, landlords and tenants, employers and hired laborers), as insti-tutional interactions (as city patrols and illegal street vendors, as tax col-lectors and tax payers), or as other informal interactions (as receivers and givers of bribes, as someone who bestows a favor and someone who needs a favor, etc.), these new modes of interaction all reproduce a hierarchical relationship between a privileged urban class and an unprivileged rural migrant class. In essence, the relation is between urbanites and peasants, between first-class citizens with urban *hukou* and second-class citizens with rural *hukou*.

The arrival of a large number of "low-status" ethnic Han in Tibet dur-ing the reform era has defused the ethnic hierarchical order formed in the pre-reform period, instead of strengthening the ethnic hierarchy in Tibet in favor of the Han, as some people expected. Rather than activate defensive Tibetan identity boundaries, the low-status Han migrants reas-sured Tibetan urban elites of their privileged status position in the sys-tem. In this process, ethnicity as the main marker of distinction became more complicated.

Han Migrants' Perception of the Status Hierarchy in Tibet

The other side of this redrawing of the identity landscape by urban Tibetans is the perception by Han rural migrants of their position in the pecking order. To rural Han migrants, the Tibetan traditional system is not meaningful, but the *hukou*-enforced division between rural and urban is highly so. The rural Han migrants in Tibet find it natural to fit Tibetans into the "rural-urban" cleavage rather than to read ethnic Tibetans as inferior to Han.

In fact, Han migrants judge their potential customers first by their urban status and only secondarily by the traits associated with their ethnicity. For the Han migrant petty business owners in Tibet, the division is clear. Tibetans from the countryside are considered "dirty, and they won't buy things. I am afraid to let them touch the product. If they break a thing, you can't make them pay." Urban Tibetans, on the other hand, are the most coveted customers. The same vendor who dismissed rural Tibetans as nuisances described his urban Tibetan customers using a comparison to the putative traits of other Chinese urban centers:

> Urban Tibetans are rich, fashionable and like to spend. They follow new trends, want to buy new models, new fashions. They are like Shanghainese, they like to spend on clothing and gadgets. They are like Hong Kong people, they like to spend on jewelry. So if you can keep a step ahead of competitors to get a new model, you will make money from urban Tibetans.

The most common word used by Han migrant businesspeople to describe urban Tibetans is *shimao* (trendy)—a word ubiquitous among the upwardly mobile urban elites throughout China. Class, urban status, and ethnicity are conflated into a single image of urban Tibetans as desirable customers, imbued with the flair of other urban elites. Urban Han customers are classed similarly to urban Tibetans, except that they are considered slightly less fashion-conscious. In contrast, fellow Han rural migrants are considered "utilitarian shoppers. They want cheap things. There is little money to be made from them."

In other spheres of interaction, Han migrants also classify and treat urban Tibetans as social superiors who are both targets of resentment and desirable partners, if a relationship can be established. In terms of the critical task of creating *guanxi*, Tibetan officials are well understood to be as useful and desirable as Han officials of the same rank. It is often remarked, with some chagrin, that linguistic barriers make it harder to sweeten up those officials. On the one hand, this attitude shows that certain ethnic markers are more than just symbolic. Language and cultural differences do matter at a practical level in creating distinctions between the ethnic groups. On the other hand, for many migrants, even strong and blatant ethnic boundaries such as language are considered nondecisive obstacles, not insurmountable barriers.

There is a further clear reversal in the perception of the inequalities of the marriage market. In the pre-reform era, it was not uncommon for Han cadres (often single men who were sent for extended periods of service) to marry Tibetan women, and that was understood by Tibetans as hypergamy (marrying a man of higher caste). In present-day Lhasa, a rural Han migrant woman dating an urban Tibetan man would be understood to be "marrying up," and her migrant peers would probably both resent her as a gold digger and envy her for her lucky break.

Han rural migrants know that the local urban Tibetans look down on them. Using a parallel to Western categories, they accept their ranking as "Han trash"—except that the emphasis falls squarely on the "trash" (that is, rural) part of that construction, not the "Han." There is some amusement in the fact that Han status once conferred automatic respect regardless of rural status. In the words of one respondent,

> I heard that in the past the Tibetans treated Han people really well. They would call all Han females "Aunt" and all Han males "Uncle," regardless of their age. Like a 40-year-old Tibetan man would call a Han teenage girl "Aunt." It was so funny. Now they don't. They think they are your daddy.[28]

Among rural Han, there is a strong perception that their second-rate status cannot be overcome merely by economic success. Middle-class levels of wealth do not alter the stigma of being slotted into second-class citizenship status. This resistance of the status system to economic considerations is clearly shown by the migrants' aspirations for their children. The "proper career path" is to attend university and land an urban job working for the state. Of all the rural Han interviewees in Lhasa, a perfect 100 percent wanted their children to "go to university so s/he can get a job." By "job" they exclusively meant government jobs with an urban *hukou*. In the words of one interviewee:

We eat all this bitterness so our son can go to school and get a job. No, what we are doing is not a "job," it's just "making a living." No matter how much money this business makes, people still look down on you because you are from the village. A "job" is to sit in an office, get paid every month and be respected.

In sum, rural Han migrants recognize the institutional disadvantage that they suffer due to their *hukou* status. They also recognize the lowly status assigned to their rurality by mainstream cultural stereotypes. They know that those disadvantages and discriminatory stereotypes prevail in the context of Lhasa, despite any putative claims of status superiority based on their ethnicity. They hope to help their offspring escape from the institutional and status trap of their rural status, but they rarely express doubts about their own lowly position in the system.

The Three Dimensions of the Rural-Urban Divide

In this chapter, we argue that the formation of actual status categories in Tibet involves three dimensions: (1) The rural-urban divide includes an institutional context and a cultural context. The institutional context gives preference to urban dwellers and ultimately results in a segmentation of the Lhasa market into separate niches favoring unequal exchange relationships (both economic and informal) between urban locals and rural migrants. The nationwide cultural context is marked by cultural constructs that are severely derogatory toward people of rural origin and their traits. (2) Ethnicity and ethnic policies provide an institutional context that gives urban Tibetans subsidized standards of living, institutional privileges, and protection against certain market pressures. Ethnicity, while affecting people's sense of prejudice, is not strong enough to overcome the institutional arrangement. (3) "Class" gives a local context influenced by traditional class constructs and equates lower caste with certain occupations and traits.

Before the reform, the rural-urban system and accompanying population immobility allowed the state to structure the contact between people of different ethnic groups. Ethnic contact was limited to state-sponsored arrangements, mostly in the form of sending high-status Han into minority regions. Han people from other social strata, especially Han rural *hukou* holders as a whole, were absent from any contact. In

Tibet, that meant that social status (cadre status) and ethnicity (ethnic Han) were one and the same.

After the reform, the *hukou* system still affected the social distinction in ethnically complex regions but through different mechanisms. On the one hand, when the reform allowed massive migration of "under-class" peasants into Tibet, Han rural migrants provided a contrast to Han officials and stimulated a reinterpretation of ethnicity and class. Although Han migrants are of the same ethnicity as Han government officials, they are outside the state's protection. Concentrated in the low-prestige manual labor and service sectors, they fit into the "low caste" category according to both the dominant *hukou*-status system and the reemerging consciousness of the traditional Tibetan caste system. The difference between urban Han and rural Han allows Tibetans to recast the categorization parameters of Han ethnicity and with it the landscape of ethnic classification.

As a result, in the context of contemporary China, and in Lhasa in particular, the institutional factors predominate in the domain of daily status. With the *hukou* system being the dominant, state-enforced classifier of social distinction, the issue of ethnicity in China is heavily "cross-classified." To a degree, cultural prejudice based on ethnicity is decoupled from institutional discrimination based on "rurality." This weakens the impact of ethnicity in the actual outcome of social distinction and transfers discriminatory biases onto the institutionalized category of *hukou* status.

The institutionalized discrimination of urban against rural is stronger (or more continuously present) than the noninstitutionalized prejudice between different ethnic groups. Urban Tibetans are aware of the prejudices held by Han, but in the context of the institutional structures of Lhasa, these prejudices have no "bite," because they have limited consequences for urban Tibetans' daily status. Instead, urban Tibetans can focus on an institutional system that gives them a desirable status and provides them with visible privileges. Rural Tibetans, of course, have no such privileges to fall back on.

This does not mean, of course, that ethnicity is erased from the consciousness and prejudices of social actors, or that *hukou* "trumps" ethnicity. However, the combined effects of *hukou* and cultural discrimination against rural residents produce consequences so strong that, even in a region where ethnic conflict is active, ethnicity cannot trump *hukou*.

Because a "master identity" is important for political mobilization, there is a tendency for people to define a group with only one identity and to deny others. However, individuals simply do not have a single identity. The banal truth is that the importance of levels of identity is contextual. In the case of Lhasa, rural-urban status has a persistent, quotidian presence that sometimes obscures and sometimes reinforces the political strength of the ethnic identification (as seen in the recent Lhasa riots; see this chapter's appendix).

When and where balancing institutional conditions fail to provide equilibrium, ethnic prejudices are likely to retake a front seat in determining social status. The long-lasting conflict between Tibetan separatism and the PRC state means that the ethnic fissure will not disappear. Lastly, the "protective" effect of the institutional pattern does not apply to rural Tibetans. They must face the double discrimination of their ethnicity and their rural status, and it is the burden of their double identity that conditions their opportunities and presents them with barriers.

Appendix: The Rural-Urban Divide and the March 2008 Lhasa Riots

On March 14, 2008, a series of riots erupted in Lhasa, the first serious explosion of public violence there since 1989. There is not enough available data to analyze the causes and nature of the unrest and the process by which participants were mobilized and targets selected. However, from the limited information, we can still see that, even in the context of intercommunity violence—the single most intense expression of ethnic differentiation—the structural effect of the rural-urban divide is evident and important.

The riots took the form of attacks on property and persons—in particular, looting and arson attacks on shops owned by non-Tibetan migrants, mostly ethnic Han and Hui. Some of these attacks were fatal. Reports of casualties from the riots included 18 civilians with 382 injured, plus 1 policeman killed and 241 injured. The property losses reported included 848 shops, 7 schools, 120 houses, 6 hospitals, and 84 vehicles. Direct losses amounted to 300 million yuan (US$43 million).

Details about the participants and victims of the riots are scarce.[29] The only relatively concrete and systematic information available is for the 18 civilians killed and for some perpetrators who were arrested. Though these people cannot be viewed as strictly "representative" of the victims and rioters as a whole,[30] the information does provide a glimpse into the identity of those involved, and through them, the nature of the social tension in Tibet. We have disaggregated data of these victims and the identities of the alleged perpetrators in Tables 13.4 through 13.8. A blank table cell indicates no information is available.

On the basis of these fragmentary data, we can see that the events in Lhasa represented more than a simple, clear-cut racial or ethnic riot. The attacks were directed against a subset of an ethnic group by a subset of another ethnic group. Most attackers were young Tibetans from rural areas. Most victims were rural migrants from other provinces who were either small business owners or employees of small businesses in Lhasa.

Furthermore, many witnesses remarked on the surprising slowness of the police reaction to the riots. The only foreign journalist present at the

Table 13.4 First fatal arson incident: Yichun Garment Store (in Lhasa Urban District), owned by Han. All victims were shop assistants who were hiding inside the shop.

Victims	Ethnicity	Age	Sex	From	Status
Cirenzhuoga	Tibetan	21	Female	Shigatse Prefecture, TAR	Rural
He Xinxin	Han	19	Female	Baoling County, Henan Province	Rural
Yang Dongmei	Han	24	Female	Yuechi County, Sichuan Province	Rural
Liu Yan	Han	22	Female	Suining County, Sichuan Province	Rural
Chen Jia	Han	18	Female	Suining County, Sichuan Province	Rural

Arsonists	Ethnicity	Age	Sex	From	Status
Qimeilazong	Tibetan	20	Female	Nanmulin County, Shigatse Prefecture, TAR	Rural
Bianji	Tibetan	21	Female	Sajia County, Shigatse Prefecture, TAR	Rural
Bianji	Tibetan	23	Female	Nimu County, Lhasa Municipality, TAR	Rural

Note: Lhasa Municipality includes one urban district ("Lhasa Urban District") and seven rural counties.

Table 13.5 Second fatal arson incident: Playboy Garment Store (in Lhasa Urban District), owned by Han. The victim was the owner's daughter, who was hiding inside the shop.

Victim	Ethnicity	Age	Sex	From	Status
Liu Juan	Han	20	Female	Shaodong County, Hunan Province	Rural

Arsonist	Ethnicity	Age	Sex	From	Status
Danzeng	Tibetan	27	Male	Chaya County, Changdu Prefecture, TAR	Rural

Table 13.6 Third fatal arson incident: Hongyu Trousers Store (in Lhasa Urban District), owned by Han. The victim was a shop assistant who was hiding inside the shop.

Victim	Ethnicity	Age	Sex	From	Status
Zuo Rencun	Han	45	Male	Shaodong County, Hunan Province	Rural

Arsonist	Ethnicity	Age	Sex	From	Status
Luosangjiancai	Tibetan	27	Male	Lhasa Urban District, TAR	Urban?

Table 13.7 Fourth fatal arson incident: Motorcycle shop (in Dazi County, Lhasa municipality), owned by Han. The victims were the shop owner, his wife, son, and two repairmen. All were hiding inside the shop.

Victims	Ethnicity	Age	Sex	From	Status
Liang Zhiwei	Han	33	Male	Henan Province	Rural
Wu Hongxia	Han	31	Female	Henan Province	Rural
Liang Chaofan	Han	8 months	Male	Henan Province	Rural
Zhang Yongtao	Han	17	Male	Henan Province	Rural
Ru Jinliang	Han	19	Male	Henan Province	Rural

Arsonists	Ethnicity	Age	Sex	From	Status
Luoya	Tibetan	25	Male	Dazi County, Lhasa	Rural
Gangzu	Tibetan	22	Male	Dazi County, Lhasa	Rural

Table 13.8 Other victims: manner of death undisclosed. Perpetrator unknown.

Victims	Ethnicity	Age	Sex	From	Status
Wangduidajie	Tibetan	24	Male	Dangxiong County, Lhasa Municipality	Rural
Labaciren	Tibetan	30	Male	Lhasa Urban District	Urban?
He Jianshu	Han	60	Male	Qionglai City, Sichuan	
Gao XX (given name unknown)	Han	30	Male	Yongdeng County, Gansu Province	Rural
Unidentified			Male		
Unidentified			Male		

riots—James Miles of *The Economist*—speculates that the authorities intended to give the rioters free rein until the initial spasm ran its course, allowing them to destroy property that belonged mostly to rural migrants.[31] It is quite likely that the police response would have been swifter if the attacks had focused on residential areas where urban Han and urban Tibetans live. (Note that the majority of migrants live where they work. Arson attacks on shops were in essence attacks on migrants' residences.)

Whatever the factors involved in creating the tensions, it is obvious that, in mobilizing the rioters and defining their targets, the combination of ethnicity and rural status was predictive of both perpetration and victimization. Therefore, to gain a better understanding of the social and political tensions in present-day Lhasa, or the social stratification of China's ethnic regions in general, both dimensions should be considered and studied further.

V | Evolving Policy toward Rural Migrants and the Rural-Urban Gap

14 | Bringing the City Back In
The Chinese Debate on Rural Problems

On March 8, 2000, Li Changping, a Party secretary from a rural township in Jianli County, Hubei Province, sent a letter entitled "Heartfelt Words from a Township Party Secretary" to then Chinese premier Zhu Rongji. In the letter he related his personal experience of disintegration in a rural township and wrote the now famous three lines: "peasants are really poor; rural life is exceedingly hard; and agriculture is in deep crisis." His simple but powerful formulation of a deepening rural crisis confronting China today struck a chord with the public in China. His statements summed up three interrelated aspects of a generalized rural crisis, namely, decreasing peasant income is leading to an agricultural decline and social disintegration in rural areas. This came to be known as the "three-rural crisis," or, in short in Chinese, *sannong* problems.

Li's book, which expanded on the themes he mentioned in the letter, was published in 2002 and became a national bestseller.[1] Media reporting on *sannong* issues also increased dramatically after 2000, as can be seen from the number of articles on the very topic published in the *People's Daily*. After 2002, a majority of the articles in the *People's Daily* associated *sannong* with the word *problem* (see Figure 14.1). Similarly, the number of scholarly and popular articles in Chinese journals and magazines on the rural crisis shot up after 2000. A search of the Chinese Academic Journals database (published by East View Online Services) that contains more than two thousand Chinese serial publications turned up 1,087 articles with the word *sannong* in the title in 2004, whereas it listed only 34 such articles in 1999.

The *sannong* problem has also evidently caught the attention of Chinese policy makers at the highest level. Zhu Rongji reportedly referred Li's case twice to lower-level officials for investigation. Several officials in Li's county were removed on corruption charges. In March 2001 the formulaic expression "three rural issues" found its way into Zhu Rongji's report on the Tenth Five-year Plan to the National People's Congress, in which he declared that "the problem of agriculture, rural society, and peasants is a most important one concerning the overall situation of reform, opening up, and modernization."[2] Significantly, the Chinese Communist Party issued three consecutive No. 1 Directive Documents on rural issues in 2004, 2005, and 2006, emphasizing the need to reduce the peasant burden, increase rural income and augment state investment in rural areas. The Party clearly wanted to use these No. 1 Documents as a way to signal the importance of rural issues, hoping perhaps to replicate the success it had with the earlier rural reforms in the early 1980s, when five consecutive No. 1 Documents focusing on agricultural, land, and other rural issues helped to bring about fundamental changes in the Chinese countryside.

The rise of *sannong* discourse reflects overlapping concerns among the Chinese public, academics, and officials about the state of rural China,

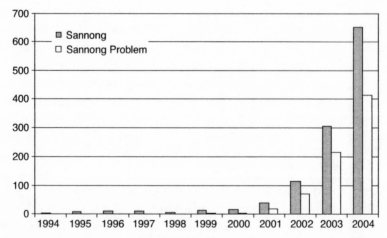

Figure 14.1   Rise of *sannong* discourse in China. Author calculations based on a content analysis of *Renmin ribao* (*People's Daily*).

and especially about rural poverty, social instability, and the growing income gap in the countryside. *Sannong* is a polyvocal discourse, as the nature of the crisis is being debated from different ideological perspectives, and as various participants in the debate try to redefine rural people's relations with the state, the market, and the urban population from different intellectual positions. Under the circumstances, differing definitions of the crisis would lead to different diagnoses of its causes and solutions. At a policy level, the *sannong* discourse seems to underlie a new, although still halfhearted, push in recent years by the Chinese government to tackle the so-called three rural issues.

In this chapter, I first discuss several elements in the official *sannong* discourse that seem to portend a new orientation in the Chinese state's approach to rural problems. In particular, there is a new awareness that the present-day rural crisis is intertwined with the government's urban policies. Many analysts of China's current rural crisis thus call for a realignment of rural-urban relations. Exactly how this should be done is a subject of controversy. In the second and third parts of the chapter, I discuss two dominant ways of understanding the rural-urban problems in China and associated approaches to solving them. Each emphasizes a different institutional locus and envisions a distinctive rural-urban relationship. In the fourth part of the chapter, I provide a sketch of the state's attempts at reforming rural-urban relations during the reform period. Finally, I critique both the official policy and the two representative views on troubled rural-urban relations in China. I argue that addressing China's rural organizational deficit is key to solving the rural crisis.

What Is New about the Official Rural Discourse?

The official *sannong* discourse dates back to the late 1990s and early 2000s. However, academic interests in the linked nature of three rural issues precede this period. Sociologist Lu Xueyi has suggested that "sannong was proposed as an analytical framework, as well as the theoretical lens" through which one studies China's rural issues, in the late 1980s.[3] Early *sannong* studies generally meant going beyond viewing the countryside as a base of agricultural production. But it was not until the mid-1990s that one detected a discernible policy shift from a productionist focus to emphasis on sociological and redistributive issues (for example, rural disorder and peasant income). What is more, all of these issues are now viewed as interconnected, and they in turn are linked to broader issues of social harmony and rural-urban relations. The new *sannong* discourse is manifested in the latest policy on "the construction of a new countryside" (*xin nongcun jianshe*) contained in the CCP's No. 1 Document in 2006.[4] It also finds expression in Hu Jintao's effort to forge a "harmonious society" and a new reform consensus about the need for social equity.[5]

Three changes are worth noting about the *sannong* discourse. First is the shift from a traditional emphasis on food security to a concern with distribution focusing on the plight of rural population, especially that of the grain-producing peasants. Since the 1950s, agricultural production has been at the core of the state's interest in rural areas. This is because the Chinese state regarded the self-sufficiency of food grain as an issue of paramount importance. Chinese officials often cite a statistic that China has about 7 percent of the world's arable land but must feed one-fifth of the world's population. From the 1950s till the mid-1980s, the state maintained a nationwide granary system and placed the purchase and marketing of food grain under strict government monopoly. This was done to ensure an adequate grain supply and to keep down food prices for the urban nonagricultural population. Even when much of the rural economy was marketized after the reform, concerns with food security have led the state to reverse course on its grain procurement policy several times. For example, the central government announced a lifting of controls over grain prices in 1992–1993, but it soon retracted that policy and reinstated a fixed price and mandatory procurement system in the next few years. In 1994 the Central Rural Work Conference again declared agriculture as the Party's top priority, so agriculture came to drive the government's rural policy agenda once more.[6] To ensure local compliance, the central government also charged the provincial governors with the responsibility of ensuring grain self-sufficiency in their regions, under a so-called "grain-bag responsibility system."[7]

After the mid-1990s, however, the traditional emphasis on domestic grain production began to shift, along with changes in the climate of opinion that started earlier in the decade about China's grain storage, market conditions, and the prospect for continual agricultural growth. Since the early 1990s, influential economists had been pointing out that China's food stock had been growing and that price hikes in food grain had been typically caused by temporary regional rather than national shortages.[8] According to these economists, an appropriate solution should focus on removing the trade barrier between regions so as to build a unified national market for grain. In 1995, Lester Brown from the Worldwatch Institute published a disturbing analysis of China's impending food crisis, but many experts on China were quite optimistic about the prospect of a sustainable increase in grain production in years to come.[9] Perhaps most importantly for the confidence of Chinese policy makers, China successfully weathered sharp fluctuations in grain prices in the early 1990s, and from 1994 to 1996, the national grain stock was augmented by three consecutive years of bumper harvests. In 1998, four years after the 1994 Central Rural Work Conference that sounded the alarm on food security, the Party Central Committee declared chronic grain shortage to be in the past, asserting that the country had reached a general equilibrium in the domestic grain supply and demand, with supply slightly outstripping demand in bumper harvest years.[10] Whether or not domestic grain supply will indeed keep up with demand is beside the point. This statement, coming from the highest political authority, marked more of a change of perspective than an actual turning point in domestic grain supply. From this point on, the debate on the "problem" of agriculture would be less about the stock of food grain in the country than about the quality, variety, degree of value-added, and global competitiveness of China's agricultural products.

Indeed, surplus grain has led to a different problem of declining peasant income in the 1990s. Bumper harvests, it turns out, have not improved the villagers' welfare, but they have lowered the living standard for a large number of rural people whose main income comes from cultivating grain. Chinese analysts suggest that declining peasant income amid bumper harvests will lead to the exodus of more rural population, which could eventually cause the social disintegration of China's countryside.[11] Government officials who watch the national food grain stock worry that further decline in agricultural income will make villagers even more reluctant to farm than is already the case. Declining peasant income thus loops back to the problem of inadequate grain production. It is in this context that peasant livelihood or income has replaced agriculture as the government's core concern. For example, Chen Xiwen, associate director of the State Council's Development Research Center and a key player in the rural policy process, considers the declining rate of peasant income growth as the most serious rural problem since the mid-1990s.[12]

A second shift in the *sannong* discourse is from a compartmentalized to a comprehensive approach to the perceived rural crisis. This change stems from the realization that the rural crisis is multidimensional and that different aspects of the crisis are interrelated in complex ways. Seemingly distinct problems about rural income, agriculture, or rural social disorder are not separate, so they must be submitted to policies that provide comprehensive solutions. To ensure agricultural growth, for example, rural producers must be paid adequately so they have an incentive to stay in the rural areas and in farming. In turn, prosperous peasants are not only productive producers but form the basis of a stable rural society.

There is always a danger in emphasizing the interlinkage of the three issues so that ruralness is overidentified with agriculture. Indeed, one of the criticisms about the *sannong* discourse is that it conjures up the image of farmers from traditional agricultural villages, thus leaving aside a wide swathe of rural life not connected to farming. Official emphasis on the plight of grain-cultivating peasants reflects this view of rural life as still tightly bound up with agriculture. But rural life in China has never been fully defined by agriculture, and this is even truer today than it was before the reforms. There is tremendous occupational diversity in rural areas. Most rural households utilize a mixture of livelihood strategies, as family members combine farming with wage labor in nearby industries, migrant work, petty trade, rural handicrafts, and small business. Official statistics show that after 2000 more than half of the net annual income of rural households comes from wages, industries, transfer payments, and other nonagricultural sources.[13] According to a national survey in 2001, about 30 percent of the rural population engages in nonagricultural activities, which include trade, industry, government, and civil service. Among those whose main income comes from agriculture, another one-third engages in specialty agriculture (that is, they are not grain cultivators) or has significant income from nonagricultural sources.[14] In view of the significance of nonagricultural aspects of rural life, the stagnation of rural income in China goes beyond the decline of farming.

Finally, a third important shift in the new *sannong* discourse is the attempt to bring the city into the equation on rural problems and their solutions. A widening rural-urban income gap has been identified as a main source of the rural crisis (see Chapters 4 and 5 in this volume). Figure 14.2 presents information on the decline in rural per capita income, living expenditure, and savings rate relative to the same urban indicators from 1978 to 2003 based on official statistics. As the rural-urban income gap widens, the rural population has less and less to save or spend compared to their urban compatriots. Official statistics show that although overall rural savings were between 22 and 35 percent of urban savings after 1990 (see Figure 14.2), *per capita* rural savings hovered around 10 to 14 percent of comparable urban figures during the same period. The plight of rural people is thus magnified when it is viewed against the backdrop of a widening gap between rural and urban areas in terms of any welfare indicator that includes savings and consumption.

Chinese analysts and policy makers now agree on the importance of understanding the urban connection of China's rural problems. As Wen Tiejun puts it, "the root cause of the problems of peasants, agriculture, and rural society is in the city."[15] Rural disorder, poverty, and stagnation may be felt or experienced in the countryside, but their causes, and cure, lie outside of rural households and villages. For example, residual control over rural-urban migration is believed to lead continuingly to excess labor in rural areas, which in turn leads to low agricultural productivity and rural poverty. Urban discrimination against rural migrants is now regarded as another contributing factor to rural-urban inequity. Hu Angang, an influential policy analyst in China, has reportedly labeled the plight of

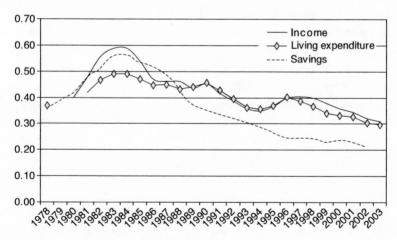

Figure 14.2   Rural-urban ratio in per capita income and living expenses and in overall savings (1978–2003). *Zhongguo tongji nianjian*, various years, published by the National Statistical Bureau.

rural migrant workers as the "fourth" rural problem. His statement thus highlights the fact that China's new urban order is deeply implicated in the country's rural crisis.[16]

In the next two sections, I distinguish two general approaches to re-aligning rural-urban relations in the Chinese debate on rural problems. The two approaches are unified in their position that reforming rural-urban relations holds the key to solving the present-day rural crisis, but they emphasize, respectively, market forces and autonomous rural communities as solutions. To the extent that proponents of both approaches call on the Chinese state to play an important role in helping to resolve the crisis, government policies in the 1990s have privileged state inter-vention. What is missing from both the mainstream *sannong* debate and recent government policies, however, is a frank discussion of the rural-urban power imbalance and ways of addressing this structural problem.

Connecting the Rural and the Urban Via the Market

Justin Yifu Lin, the founding director of Beijing University's China Cen-ter for Economic Research, is an influential voice on Chinese agriculture and rural development.[17] He is credited with having coined the term "new socialist countryside," which has been adopted by the government in framing its latest rural policies. Over the years, he has been a consis-tent advocate of using the market to break administrative barriers to labor and investment flows between rural and urban areas. As early as 1994 he identified declining peasant income as China's main rural prob-lem and proposed developing a national labor market and liberalizing rural financial institutions as solutions.[18] According to him, labor migra-tion not only helps to solve the labor shortage problem in coastal areas, but it also allows investment to flow back to rural areas through remit-tances. A rural financial market that is separate from the state banking system would help channel rural savings to local industries, because state banks are biased toward urban enterprises.

Lin was not alarmed by the sharp increase in grain prices in the early 1990s. He attributes the cause to state procurement and local protection-ism rather than to a decline in grain output, let alone a general agricul-tural crisis.[19] To him, mandatory state procurement favors regional grain self-sufficiency, prevents agricultural specialization in the inland provinces, and raises the cost of producing grain in coastal areas. Once grain is in the government's hands, local protection further impedes the flow of surplus grain from one region to another, thus creating pockets of temporary shortage and a society-wide psychology of food scarcity. For this reason he advocates abolishing the state's grain procurement system. His insistence on letting the market work also leads him to argue against using agricultural subsidies to raise rural income.[20]

Lin is not against all state intervention, however. After all, the labor market itself does not create jobs. It merely channels labor to where jobs are. Lin envisions a large role for the government in the area of job creation. But he is against the idea of expanding the payroll of state enterprises in cities even though he realizes that most of the industrial jobs are going to be located in urban areas. His proposal is for the state to invest in *rural* infrastructural projects, such as in a piped water supply, electricity, and roads, to both create jobs in rural areas and to generate demand for urban industrial and consumer products.

In a series of articles going back to the early 2000s, Lin describes how a relatively small amount of investment in rural infrastructure goes a long way to expand the domestic market for such urban consumer durable goods as color TV sets, refrigerators, and washing machines. According to a report Lin wrote for Party officials in 2001, rural residents had an average net income in 2000 that was above the comparable income urban residents had in the early 1990s. But rural people only owned a fraction of the durable goods in 2000 that urban consumers owned a decade earlier, even though the prices of these products had dropped by more than half in the intervening years.[21] To him, the rural lag in consumption indicated a huge potential demand in rural areas for urban manufactured products. What has prevented this potential from being actualized is the underdevelopment of rural infrastructure. After all, one cannot use a refrigerator in a village without a reliable supply of electricity! So the key to generating rural demand is to build rural roads, power lines, and water supply systems.

Lin may be talking about the rural problem, but his eyes are firmly on urban industries. In the early 2000s, the urban manufacturing sector was hobbled by the problem of surplus production. Domestic demand was weak. Urban employment was down, while rural income was sliding. It was in this context of urban contraction that Lin has proposed a rural modernization strategy that he believes will create a virtuous cycle of rural-urban interaction: the state jump-starts the process by investing in rural infrastructure; improved rural roads, water, and electricity supply lead to an increase in the demand for urban products; strong rural demand for urban products leads to expanded production and thus more jobs in the cities; rural excess labor then migrates to cities to fill such jobs; and finally, rural income rises as a consequence of initial state investment and subsequent migratory employment in the cities.

Lin foresees gradual reduction in the number of farmers through labor-intensive industrialization and rural-urban migration. But he stops short of calling for an end to the family farm system, emphasizing regional specialization, not economies of scale, as a way to bring about more efficient resource allocation. He warns against another Great Leap Forward in urbanization in which government officials stipulate the size, location, and population composition of new urban centers.[22] His critics, though, charge that the logic of rural modernization and urbanization would lead to the eventual demise of family farms. All things considered, Lin's proposal amounts to a kinder and gentler form of developmentalism than the present pattern that privileges urban-centered industrialization and the transfer of rural labor to urban areas. His is a rural modernization strategy premised on the free flow of rural labor (to the city) and urban commodities (to rural areas). Although Lin believes strongly in government involvement and investment in the beginning stages, he ultimately stresses the market stimulus rather than extensive state intervention as a catalyst to desired changes in rural areas. He envisions a virtuous cycle of rural-urban interaction based on labor/commodity exchange. He believes that his modernization strategy will not only lead to some parity in rural and urban infrastructure but bring about long-term growth and income increase in rural areas.

But is the unleashing of market forces going to narrow the gap between rural and urban areas, even while we assume that it will lead to closer economic ties between them? The answer to this question is by no means certain. Two scenarios, both of which are real possibilities given recent developments, would point to a negative answer to the above question. One is that closer rural-urban ties could intensify the exploitation of rural labor by metropolitan-based employers. The other is that rural modernization projects could widen the rural-urban gap when they are introduced into an already inequitable rural environment.

In the first scenario, we can look at some of the malevolent development in the labor market in recent years. China's labor market has grown tremendously during the reform: the state labor bureaus have given up control over labor allocation; villagers experience unprecedented mobility, especially after the 1990s; and a mushrooming of intermediary labor market organizations brings rural workers directly to urban employers. However, massive rural-urban migration has not led to any significant overall improvement of the rural migrants' economic position. Although most migrants have found employment in the cities, their wages have remained more or less stagnant for more than a decade. A recent Labor Ministry report cited studies that show that, in the most marketized Pearl River Delta region, migrants' monthly wage increased by a paltry 68 yuan in the twelve years between 1992 and 2004.[23]

What is worse is that a majority of the rural migrant workers (72.5 percent, according to one official survey) are not paid the wages they are promised or have experienced serious wage arrears.[24] One Chinese analyst estimates that in 2003 at least half of the construction companies owed migrants back wages. The employees at about 64 percent of the private and foreign-funded enterprises in Guangdong have experienced one or more instances of late payment, illegal deduction, or nonpayment of wages.[25] Sociologist Ching Kwan Lee calls the nonpayment crisis "the most explosive labor grievance" in China today.[26] So far, it seems that a functioning labor market has not only failed to improve migrants' income situation significantly but has created new sources of rural-urban conflict.

A second scenario has to do with growing rural inequality that could contribute to widening the gap between the rural poor and urban society. Rural families now increasingly rely on remittances and other kinds of nonagricultural income for their livelihood, but the blessing of higher nonagricultural income is mixed for the rural population. Official statistics show that the Gini coefficient for rural income distribution has increased from .21 in 1978 to .34 in 1995 and .37 in 2003.[27] Other researchers have found that the level of rural inequality is higher than what the official statistics suggest. A study by Keith Griffin, Azizur Rahman Khan, and Amy Ickowitz noted the creeping up of the Gini ratio for rural per capita income, from .34 in 1988 to .42 in 1995, before declining slightly to .38 in 2002.[28] Experts also agree that nonagricultural income is the main culprit for growing inequality, while farm-derived income actually mitigates the situation owing to the relatively equal land distribution.[29]

The market-based *sannong* discourse recognizes the general decline of rural income as a problem, but it neglects the fact that the urban labor market has become a force enlarging inequality within the rural society. Consider then introducing infrastructural projects into such an increasingly inequitable environment in order to create demand for the urban-produced consumer goods. These projects will almost certainly benefit some segments of the rural population, but it is hard to imagine they will help narrow the gap between one end of a stratified rural society and the other, urban areas. In this sense, closer market ties between rural and urban areas present at best a partial solution to the identified rural crisis by channeling more goods and income to the better-off in rural areas. But marketizing rural-urban relations is unlikely to narrow the gap between the two sides.

(Un)Bridging the Rural and Urban: Family Farm and Rural Autonomy as Solutions

Similar concerns about the effect of the market are behind a different and distinctly anti-market response to rural problems. Specifically, the anti-market response is motivated by a fear that marketized rural-urban exchange is not only inadequate but could cause harm because it would lead to the erosion of household economy, the socioeconomic and political basis of present-day rural order. For more than two decades, the household responsibility system has served as an anchor for rural stability. It has generated adequate food grain while releasing large numbers of cheap laborers for urban industries. But the system rests on a delicate bargain between peasants and the state: the state gave up control over rural production decisions in exchange for a fixed amount of grain from the peasants; the peasants accepted the state's withdrawal in social service provision in exchange for the guarantee of access to land. Although the state has eased control over agricultural production in recent years, it is not holding up its part of the bargain on assuring land to peasants. Local state agencies have turned to farm land as an untapped resource for development projects or to make up fiscal shortfalls. Stories abound of zealous local officials who requisition land from the villagers at a low price and turn around to sell or lease it to the highest bidders. Chinese researchers have estimated in 2004 that about 20 million peasants lost their land to various urban development schemes in the previous decade.[30]

Each year in the 2000s, more people have joined the landless ranks in the countryside. In the meantime, rural local bureaucracies have grown so bloated that they impose a severe and increasing financial burden on the villagers even when formal state taxes were scaled back. Rural fee hikes were once the main causes of frequent peasant protests in the 1990s.[31]

Rural land taking and increased local fees strike at the heart of the implicit bargain between the state and peasants. These factors have led to a dramatic rise in peasant grievances and protests.[32] The number of petitions by rural people surpassed those by urban residents for the first time in 2000. In 2001 and 2002 a majority of the "letters and visits" handled by the Ministry of Agriculture concerned rural land taking.[33] In this context, proponents of the anti-market *sannong* discourse have taken up the cause of preserving the family farm as key to resolving the rural crisis. As Wen Tiejun, one of the most vocal defenders of the small farm system, puts it, "preserving small peasant economy is a long-term and necessary project in the countryside . . . It is impossible to fix the increasingly serious rural problems in the short term."[34]

Wen begins his analysis of the rural economy by noting the uniqueness of the peasant household as a conjoined unit of production *and* consumption. He argues that the peasant household is not only a productive entity, but it also serves vital social reproductive functions.[35] Similarly, agricultural land is more than a factor of production in the economic sense, because it serves as a social safety net for all villagers in the absence of state-provided social insurance for the rural population. Historically specific conditions in rural China, that is an extremely high population/land ratio, further constrain the workings of market forces. For all of these reasons, Wen dismisses the market as the solution to China's rural crisis. He opposes the privatization of agricultural land and advocates returning industrial land from state monopoly to community control. He wants to keep the present system of household economy intact while permitting land rental or subleasing at the margin. To sum up, he regards the market approach as "inappropriate in the context of peasant marginalization, declining rural economy, and unsustainable agriculture."[36]

Wen further argues that the principles of the market have limited applicability in other areas of the rural economy besides land. According to him, it is unrealistic to count on the market mechanism alone to transfer all surplus labor from agriculture to nonagricultural sectors. The market is unlikely to be the conduit for investment to flow to rural areas. In fact, established investors tend to avoid the rural sector because there is little profit to be made in small family farms with fragmented land holdings.[37] Indeed, in recent years state-owned financial institutions have seemed to exhibit this kind of behavior. As they adapt to the market, they too are abandoning the rural sector. He points out that fewer than one-quarter of rural households are now eligible to obtain loans from state-owned commercial banks.[38] As a result, usurious private lenders have emerged to fill the vacuum in rural finance.

Distrustful of the market, Wen is equally suspicious of the efficacy of state projects that are aimed at modernizing the rural economy. In his view, direct government transfers will not amount to much because of their relatively paltry amount and the enormous number of rural households in need of help.[39] On the other hand, state investment in the new technology does not usually improve the life of direct producers. Instead, it usually benefits the bureaucratic offices handling the money or the state industrial-commercial complex distributing or utilizing such technology. Indeed, he claims that some of the newer services and technologies pushed by the government end up being a new burden to the producers (for example. marketing of new hybrid seeds to farmers). Ordinary peasants are usually excluded from the more profitable rural sectors, such as the processing and marketing of agricultural products. State agencies and their commercial affiliates reap most of the benefit in the rural commercial sector by virtue of their monopoly on the marketing of modern inputs (for example, fertilizer, pesticides, seeds, and investment).

So what is to be done when neither the market nor the state can be trusted to address China's rural problems? On one hand, Wen calls for the strengthening of family farms as a subsistence guarantee for the rural producers. He opposes drastic changes to the household responsibility system, labeled by the Party as the "basic rural economic system." On the other hand, Wen advocates reforming rural governance, which for him means thinning down rural bureaucracy, ending state monopoly in rural services, and opening up profitable sectors to rural producers. In particular, he proposes cutting out the township-level administration and replacing it with county representative offices. He also advocates an end to the state monopoly on rural trading, finance, and marketing so that rural people may form their own cooperatives in these areas.[40] Compared with urban-based state agencies, Wen believes that rural co-ops are more likely to plow back their profit into agriculture or agricultural services.[41]

He goes so far as to propose an end to the system of "city governing county" or "town governing village" to end the urban exploitation of rural areas.[42]

In Wen's view, then, the state has precious little to contribute directly to rural revival beyond guaranteeing the "rural basic economic system." One area in which Wen thinks the state can make an impact is to help generate jobs for the rural population. "If China's problem was about the peasants, and the peasant problem was about land in the twentieth century," Wen wrote, "China's problem in the twenty-first century is still about peasants, but the peasant problem now is about employment."[43] Wen thus favors massive public works projects in western China to absorb labor from densely populated rural areas.[44]

Unlike Justin Lin's strategy of using the market (and a pro-market state) to narrow the rural-urban gap and perhaps to draw down the rural population, Wen advocates a form of rural reconstruction that does not envision urbanization as its goal but that aims to strengthen rural communities. To him, rural-urban integration has only harmed the rural interests in the past, as evidenced by the ill-fated "city governing county" system. Even though Wen has proposed large infrastructure projects similar to those proposed by Lin, Wen differs on the purpose and locational choice of such projects. Whereas Lin's purpose is to raise rural income and increase effective demand for urban goods by modernizing rural infrastructure in the densely populated rural regions, such as central China, Wen is more interested in generating low-wage employment in the remote western region for rural workers from all over China. In other words, Wen wants to use the public works projects to bring about a trans-regional rural-to-rural population shift instead of rural-to-urban migration.

"Coordinated Development": An Evolution of State Policy on Rural-Urban Relations

There is plenty of irony in the positions held by Justin Lin and Wen Tiejun, two of the most vocal participants in the *sannong* debate in China. Although Lin embraces the market, he calls on the state to be proactive and use public investment to spearhead rural development. In rejecting the state, Wen is ultimately motivated by considerations of state preservation. Wen may not believe in the modernization/market paradigm within which Justin Lin has proposed his solution, but he shares with Lin the concern with political stability in the countryside. It is thus not surprising that the government's rural policies in recent years seem to have incorporated elements from both proposals and envision a significant role for the Chinese state. These policies identify the lack of rural-urban connectedness as the problem and anticipate a narrowing of the gap with closer rural-urban interaction. At the same time, they stress the importance of preserving family farms and strengthening rural communities, a theme emphasized by Wen and his colleagues. In this context, "coordinated rural-urban development" emerged as a central policy concept that links the two different aspects in the Chinese state's rural policies. It presumes a development model in which the state is the linchpin institution that is capable of safeguarding the rural community and achieving rural-urban integration at the same time.

Coordinated development emerged as the Chinese state's rural-urban policy at the Sixteenth Party Congress in 2002.[45] But the state has grappled with the rural-urban issue since at least the mid-1950s. One symbolic moment was in 1956 when Mao published his treatise on the Ten Major Relationships, in which he expounded on the need for the gradual elimination of differences between the rural and the urban, between peasants and workers, and between laborers and intellectuals. Arguably, some of the Maoist policies, including sending urban youths to the village and rural industrialization, were partly motivated by such considerations. After the reforms began, the Chinese state's commitment to balancing rural-urban development was behind two earlier policies aimed at the rural-urban integration: one was to encourage village and township enterprises and small town development; the other was to reorganize rural-urban administration. In recent years, the state has emphasized two additional measures: increased fiscal transfers in support of rural infrastructure and agriculture and the removal of administrative barriers to the flow of commodities, labor, and capital between the rural and urban areas.

The rural small town received the earliest attention as a viable institution bridging the rural and the urban during the reforms. Historically, small towns had served essential support functions to the surrounding villages in commerce, culture, industry, administration, and marketing.[46] During the Maoist period, rural small towns (except those serving as administrative centers) withered because the state outlawed commodity trade and took over other functions traditionally performed by small towns. The rural-urban gap appeared to have widened against the backdrop of small town atrophy. After onset of the reforms, flourishing rural industries and commerce have led to a rapid development of rural towns in the 1980s and 1990s. To ease the population pressure on big cities, the state also lifted control over rural town settlement. More importantly, it began to view small-town development as part of a grand strategy to bridge the rural and the urban.[47]

Besides small-town development, the state has tried to bring rural and urban areas closer together through the so-called city-governing-the-county system. Under this system, either rural counties are placed under adjacent urban administration or entire rural prefectures are converted into cities, with the counties as constituent units. The policy of city conversion resulted in the proliferation of urban units in China in the 1980s and 1990s. By the end of 2000, 78 percent of China's once rural prefectures were designated cities and 19 percent of county-level units were so designated by 2001.[48] Similar reorganization has been carried out at lower levels, subjecting rural townships to the control of county-level cities. As a result, large numbers of rural counties and townships are now subordinated to urban authority, some directly as urban districts. At the current rate of geographical expansion, officially designated urban areas are projected to reach 45 percent of Chinese territory by 2010.[49]

Insofar as its effect on rural-urban relations is concerned, the city-governing-the-county system has proven to be more of a problem than a solution. The system has achieved a measure of rural-urban integration, but it has done so at the price of subordination of rural interests to urban authorities. Rural residents may obtain urban *hukou* after their counties convert to cities, but the newly conferred urban status does not amount to anything substantial in terms of jobs and retirement pensions. On the contrary, city conversion gives officials new power to requisition rural land, which many have used to deprive the villagers of their land contracts.[50] In the end this policy may have led to increased urbanization, but it has not produced rural-urban equity or balance, a professed goal of the integration. This may be one reason why the central government intervened in the late 1990s to slow down the conversion of rural counties into cities.

The latest initiative, under the banner of Socialist New Countryside, continues to view the present-day rural crisis as a transient problem in the course of industrialization and urbanization. But for now, the state's policy focus has shifted to rural reconstruction itself, particularly to job creation, rural infrastructure, and the raising of rural income. Instead of treating the town or city as an ideal organizational form (for example, small-town development) or as a governing mechanism (for example, the city-governing-the-county system) for rural areas, the central government now wants to enlist the "help" of the city as a source of budgetary transfer and raising rural income. As a corollary, it now calls for the removal of the remaining barriers to rural-urban migration and for an end to urban discrimination against rural workers.

The latest Party policy is that China "has entered a developmental stage whereby industry [should] serve agriculture and cities [should] support the countryside."[51] This is reminiscent of similar slogans about industry serving agriculture in the Mao era, but this time around the Chinese state is less motivated by ideological reasons than by practical socioeconomic and political problems. The state is also resorting to fiscal and pro-market policies rather than planning measures in an effort to narrow the rural-urban development gap. Recent repeal of agricultural tax and continuing *hukou* reform are well-publicized examples. In the last few years, these policies have brought tangible improvements to the rural economy and society in the form of reduced tax burdens and increased agricultural support. But it is hard to see how policies alone could address the deep structural problems of China's rural-urban schism. For sure, past state policies such as *hukou* control have contributed to China's rural-urban disparity, and new policies may be enacted to counter their negative effect. At a fundamental level, the urban domination over rural society stems from a structural cleavage that reflects rural-urban power imbalance. I argue in the next section that the power imbalance is most fundamentally caused by a dearth of organizational resource in rural areas. Simply put, a disorganized rural society lacks the capacity to press its interests both within and outside of the political system.

Organizational Deficit and Rural-Urban Power Imbalance

Urban bias is a pervasive problem in virtually all developing societies. In his classic study of the phenomenon, Michael Lipton pointed out thirty years ago that the rural-urban dichotomy was the moving force underlying the slow and inequitable growth in developing countries.[52] On the surface, China's case seemed a little different, at least in the Maoist era when the state espoused an anti-urbanism ideology and when distinct urban-rural interests were hard to specify. But it is now well established that, *in spite of* its anti-urbanism ideology, China under Mao had followed a set of urban-biased policies.[53] Even policies that were manifestly designed to balance rural-urban relations ended up paradoxically widening the gap between the town and countryside.[54] Some analysts had used "state bias" to characterize China's manifestly urban-biased policy, especially in the Maoist era. These analyses focused on the state's development strategy, which favored industry over agriculture in the pre-reform period and tended to attribute continued rural-urban disparity during the reform to institutional inertia and the state's muddled approach to market reform.[55]

Some scholars have advanced explicitly political explanations as to why urban-biased policies have continued to exist during the reform era, especially after 1989. Jean Oi argues that "urban biased policies are the insurance policies the regime buys to ensure that those in the urban areas . . . will refrain from political activity that will endanger the stability of the regime."[56] Cai Fang and Yang Tao attribute post-reform urban bias to political pressures that urban interest groups brought to bear on the government.[57] But these are all generalized observations. None of the scholars attempted to specify the nature of urban interest groups or to explain the causes of rural weakness. In fact, Oi doubts that urban-biased policies in China reflect the political activities by any organized groups. "Unlike Africa and other developing countries," she writes, "there is no identifiable group of urban elites that has shaped policy. Likewise, there is no rural elite that has been bought off in order to pass policies detrimental to the mass of the rural population."[58]

Today it is debatable whether a recognizable urban elite has emerged in China that is capable of exerting influence on the government policy process. In answering this question, one may need to distinguish between ordinary urban citizens and the urban-based bureaucratic class.[59] The latter is the most organized group in Chinese politics and wields tremendous power.

Turning to the countryside, however, one may agree with Jean Oi about the lack of identifiable groups of power and influence comparable to the urban bureaucratic interests. Indeed, China has been suffering from a gradual organizational decline manifest in all areas, from the decline of Party organizations to a lack of civic associations to the emaciation of grassroots administration. As a result, rural people are left with little formal or informal organizational resources on which they can draw to assert their power or balance out the urban influence in the policy process. This is not to say that organization is the only way for China's peasants to assert their power. Given the right circumstances and political support from the above, disorganized peasants are capable of moving national policy in a direction that favors them, as Daniel Kelliher and others have shown in the case of rural reform in the 1980s.[60] Under normal circumstances, however, organizational resources are critical to asserting group influence on the policy process.

First, China's rural population is severely underrepresented in formal political organizations, from the People's Congress to the Communist Party to the Youth League. China's election rules stipulate a much higher voter/representative ratio in the People's Congress elections for rural areas than for urban areas. Under the current Election Law, for example, as many as four times the votes are needed to elect a representative from a rural district compared with those needed for an urban district.[61] Though this is an improvement over the previous election law that stipulated an even higher voter/representative ratio for rural areas, the proportion of rural representatives remains very low. For example, Anhui Province is allotted 115 represenatives for the Tenth National People's Congress (NPC) with a population of 59.9 million, as compared to a total of 114 representatives for Beijing and Tianjin with a combined population of 23.8 million in 2000.[62] The pattern of rural underrepresentation is repeated at the provincial level and below. In the case of Anhui Province, 45 percent of its NPC representatives currently live and work in the capital city Hefei, whereas only 13 percent come from the sixty-five or so rural counties or county-level cities.[63] Many of the so-called "rural" representatives to the NPC are the leading cadres in rural counties. If one were to adopt the stricter category of the "peasant" (that is, an ordinary rural resident with agricultural *hukou*, or a low-level office holder who is not on the government payroll), the proportion of "peasant" representatives has declined even more dramatically during the reforms. The NPC's peasant membership fell from 20.6 percent in 1977 to 8.1 percent in 1999. For the provincial People's Congresses, membership fell from 20.2 percent in 1977 to 10.5 percent in 1998.[64]

Similarly, as in the case of NPC representation, the Chinese Communist Party and its affiliated Youth League have moved away from their traditionally strong organizational base in rural areas. Rural shares of both the Party and Youth League membership have declined steadily since the reform era started. In 2004 the agricultural sector (including forestry, animal husbandry, and fishery) accounted for less than 30 percent of the Youth League membership and 25 percent of the local-level Youth League organizations.[65] As for the Communist Party, peasant members made up 59.6 percent of the Party in 1949, a historical high point that reflected the Party's strong presence in the countryside during the Revolution. Since then, the proportion of peasant members declined to about 46.9 percent in the CCP on the eve of reform in 1978. The relative decline of rural Party membership has been even more precipitous during the reform as the Party has sought to broaden its social base in urban areas. By 2000 the proportion of peasant Party members had dropped to 32.5 percent.[66] For ordinary rural members, their loss of influence on the local and national policies is even more pronounced than their dwindling membership share suggests. This is because rural Party members are usually excluded from the formal political process. Office holding, rather than party activism, has become a prerequisite for selection into the Party Congresses at all levels. As an example, leading cadres made up about 75.7 percent of the representatives at the Sixteenth Party Congress in 2002, and this was an improvement over the previous two Party Congresses, when leading party cadres made up 78 percent and 75.9 percent of all representatives, respectively.[67]

Party organizations that still operate in the rural areas face chronic recruitment problems and a grave legitimacy crisis. The Chinese press is filled with discussions about the problem of an aging Party membership base in rural areas. Officials have disclosed that during the period from 1994 to 2000, about half (48.8 percent) of all village Party branches were considered weak, backward, paralyzed, or otherwise not functional at one point or another.[68] Recently, two investigations of Fujian and Hunan Provinces revealed widespread Party paralysis and criminal infiltration of rural local governments, such that local strongmen often hijack rural administration for private gains.[69]

The point of the above discussion is not to suggest that an invigorated Party and state presence will necessarily bring about positive changes in the countryside. Much also depends on how the rural state and Party apparatuses relate to rural people and assert their influence in the national policy-making and implementation process. A repressive rural local government that is at the same time subservient to urban authorities is the worst possible combination for the rural population. To avert this outcome, one must simultaneously build up formal rural organizations (including rural government agencies) *and* subject them to countervailing influence by more independent rural organizations. This brings me to a second observation about the organizational deficit in rural areas today: that is the underdevelopment of voluntary associations and civic groups that are wholly or partially independent of the Party-state apparatus. Although urban China seems to have experienced a renaissance of civic groups and associational activities since the reform,[70] rural China continues to suffer from an all-around organizational malaise that goes back to pre-reform days.

In a study of Chinese civic associations in the mid-1990s, Minxin Pei found that there were far fewer grassroots civic associations in rural than in urban areas. Besides, average rural civic associations tended to have smaller membership sizes than urban ones, and a much smaller proportion of the rural associations than urban ones directly catered to local needs.[71] A recent survey of the farmer's professional associations in China found that only 7.5 percent of China's villages (even though the absolute number seems impressive at about 55,000 villages) had functioning associations of any kind in 2003, and that a very small fraction (about 2.08 percent) of the farm households participated in them.[72] In addition, the authors of the study point out that a vast majority of these associations (84 percent) were established under the sponsorship of government officials, so it is difficult to judge if they will be able to function as independent pro-farmer organizations. One encouraging sign is that rural professional associations seem to have expanded at an accelerated pace in recent years. And the latest "new socialist countryside" policy seems to have put some emphasis on the development of rural cooperatives and non-state legal-financial institutions in rural areas.

However, there is still very little diversity in rural non-state associations, as most of them are based on economic, or industry, trade and professional relations. The Chinese government is still quite wary about creating horizontal associations based on noneconomic ties. Rural religious and lineage groups are viewed with suspicion, as are multifunctional peasant associations. As a result, rural people in China remain politically "a sack of potatoes," perhaps with the exception of sometimes well-organized protesters,[73] Scholars have variably attributed this state of affairs to the erosion of traditional lineage-based institutions such as guilds, charities, ancestral halls, and education academies after 1949 or to a historical lack of corporate identity or solidary institutions in most rural areas in China.[74] Whatever the explanation, today rural China remains very much a one-dimensional space organizationally, because it lacks crisscrossing noneconomic associations that could press rural demands from both within and outside of the Chinese political system. The rise and fall of peasant associations in the PRC's history demonstrate how difficult it is for politically inclined organizations, even ones that were allied with the Party, to survive modern state penetration.[75] Recent calls by Chinese scholars to restore general-purpose peasant associations seem to have gone unheeded by government officials.[76] For the foreseeable future there does not seem to be any strong push for organizing peasants outside of the realm of economics and state-sanctioned institutions.

Conclusions

In China urban-biased policies seem to have followed the decimation of autonomous rural organizations in the 1950s. Over time, these policies have undermined the ability of China's rural population to reconstitute its organizational capacity. The reforms have only reinforced the rural organizational decline through the demolition of rural collective institutions. Under such circumstances, tilting certain policies in favor of the countryside is unlikely to produce any lasting change in rural-urban relations. For sure, the Chinese government has taken unprecedented measures in recent years to reduce peasant tax burdens, waive rural school fees, redesign a rural health insurance system, and, most recently, implement a rural minimum livelihood guarantee system (nongcun dibao zhi). All of these policies have ameliorated rural poverty, but they have not fundamentally addressed the structural power imbalance between rural and urban interests. To borrow the language of Chu Chengya, a rural scholar from China, favorable rural policies "may improve peasant conditions within the system of urban bias, but they are unlikely to lead to an overhaul of the system itself."[77]

Redressing the rural-urban balance requires more than reducing rural taxation, redirecting fiscal resources to rural areas, or creating a unified rural-urban labor market. It also requires going beyond the family farm or village community to create associational ties among the rural population. Above all, a fundamental change in the rural-urban relations hinges on strengthening the capacity of existing rural organizations and forging new solidary associations (for example, peasant associations) that empower rural citizens vis-à-vis urban interests. In the long run, the encouragement of new rural organizational forms would help provide an effective way for rural society to move out of conditions of atrophy under the existing system. As Yu Jianrong has argued, rural organizations could also serve to aggregate rural interests, channel grievances, defuse extremist action, and thus ensure stability in the countryside. But as I have shown in this chapter, both the mainstream debate on China's rural problems and recent government policies have not paid sufficient attention to the issue of rural organizational deficit, in spite of renewed emphasis on rural-urban relations. Until the Chinese policy community grapples with the organizational issue, there will not be any substantial reversal of the bias against rural areas, much less a softening of the caste-like rural-urban cleavage plaguing China since the 1950s. Sooner or later, the Chinese government's current pro-rural policies are going to run up against powerful urban-based interests, against which rural areas have no countervailing influence.

15 | Renovating the Great Floodgate
The Reform of China's *Hukou* System

The hukou system is a water pump. . . . How much wealth it has pumped out of the rural area!
> —Li Changping, longtime local official in rural Hubei and later a
> Beijing-based freelance reporter and writer, 2005[1]

Fearing flood, people constructed a grand dam to regulate water. Later, it is discovered that the dam has blocked the smooth flow of the river and hurt the environment upstream and downstream. Some say, let's dynamite the dam. But the water level is so high now and, if the dam is blown away recklessly, can the downstream handle the consequences?
> —The chief of the Civil Affairs Bureau in a large city in western China,
> commenting on *hukou* reform, 2005[2]

Functioning as a legal Great Wall, a great floodgate, China's *hukou* (household registration) system has divided people and regulated internal migration for more than a half century in the People's Republic of China (PRC). Much of China's profound gap between the rural and urban sectors, and among the different regions, is either directly created by or essentially maintained by the *hukou* system. Despite repeated efforts at reforming it since the 1980s, the *hukou* system remains a fundamental institution that helps to define politics, social life, and economic development in the PRC today.[3]

The *hukou* system defies a clear-cut normative assessment about its role and functions. It undoubtedly creates and perpetuates some of the most rigid and unfair sociopolitical and economic discrimination and injustice in the world through administratively excluding the majority of the Chinese people from vibrant and prosperous urban centers. It also seems to have contributed to rapid, albeit uneven, economic growth and minimized the development of urban slums. The *hukou* system powerfully brews social tensions and political grievances and significantly exacerbates ethical problems of inequality and inequity for a Chinese government that now aims to create a "harmonious society" and achieve a "peaceful rise," while crucially serving Beijing's fundamental interests of political stability, population control, and regime survival. Solidifying and reinforcing the rural-urban and interregional gaps for generations, the *hukou* system has been a key floodgate that is now under increasing strain, and its renovation has given reasons for hopes and hypes about narrowing and even erasing China's rural-urban gap. A removal or crumbling of this legal Great Wall would certainly reshape China's political landscape and the nation's future but could also lead to the drowning of thriving Chinese cities and the dream of China's quick, peaceful rise.[4] Despite being an easy target of criticisms, the *hukou* system remains an indispensable pillar of sociopolitical stability and economic development, which are the central objectives for the PRC at the national and local levels these days.

After a brief description of the basics of the *hukou* system, especially its restrictions of internal migration as a key to China's rural-urban gap, I will report on recent efforts at reforming the system and discuss the prospects for this peculiar and profound Chinese institution. There are great needs and tremendous pressure for renovating the *hukou* system so as to preserve this extremely important instrument of social control for Beijing while reducing its political costs through pacifying the increasingly mobile and still largely excluded rural population. There are powerful reasons for urban centers, especially privileged major cities, to resist the real changes that would be needed to genuinely narrow the Chinese rural-urban gap. And the excluded rural population still has very few resources and almost no political power, other than unorganized violent protests, to really change the *hukou* system (see the discussion in Chapter 14 in this volume).

Therefore, thus far the reform of the *hukou* system has been slow, heavily localized and regionalized, frequently cosmetic, utterly incomplete, and often distorted and reversed, reflecting both the enormity and the complexity of the task itself and the overall reality of the Chinese political system, which, under the authoritarian regime of the Chinese Communist Party (CCP), has structurally favored the minority of the population living in urban areas. Some of the changes may have actually further enlarged the rural-urban gap by creating powerful internal brain drains and capital drains. Localized barriers of "entry conditions" may have actually made "permanent migration of the peasants to the cities harder than before."[5] Beijing still retains the final say about the system, and there is tight control over words and acts involving *hukou* reforms. Barring major, tectonic shifts of political power inside the CCP and real political reforms, the PRC *hukou* system is likely to remain as a great floodgate, crumbling while being renovated, separating and dividing the Chinese people, chiefly along the fault line of rural versus urban.

The Basics

Created in the centrally planned economy of the 1950s, the *hukou* system has its long historical roots in imperial China and can be traced back to the fifth century BCE, during the Warring States period. It was institutionalized and adopted with varied degrees of effectiveness and extensiveness as an important part of the Chinese imperial political system by dynasties from the Qin (third century BCE) to the Qing (1644–1911). The Republic of China (ROC) and the People's Republic of China (PRC) both established a national *hukou* system. However, only in the PRC did the *hukou* system achieve an unprecedented level of uniformity, extensiveness, rural-urban duality, effectiveness, and rigidity.

On January 9, 1958, Mao Zedong promulgated *The Regulation on Hukou Registration of the People's Republic of China* and finalized the creation of the PRC national *hukou* system. Twenty-seven years later, on September 6, 1985, Beijing adopted its *Regulation on Resident's Personal Identification Card in the People's Republic of China* (it was amended to be *The Law on Resident's Personal Identification Card in the People's Republic of China* on June 29, 2003). These two regulations and their implementation procedures are the main legal basis for the *hukou* system.

The PRC State Council and its ministries have issued numerous, often ad hoc, regulations, provisional regulations, directives, decrees, and documents that have substantiated and fine-tuned the *hukou* system. The majority of those "State Documents," estimated to be more than six hundred from 1958 to 2005, have concerned the ever-changing criteria and mechanisms of control of internal migration, especially *qianyi* (permanent migration with *hukou* relocation). The Ministry of Public Security (MPS) and the local public security bureaus and police stations are the administrators of the *hukou* system. Specialized *hukou* police officers are assigned to be in charge of *hukou* matters in each *hukou* zone: a neighborhood, street, *danwei* (work unit), or a township. With the authorization of the central government, provincial and municipal governments can make and have made marginal changes and experimental modifications of the *hukou* system in their respective jurisdictions.

The *hukou* system requires every Chinese citizen to be officially and constantly registered with the *hukou* authority (the *hukou* police) from birth. This registration is the legal basis for personal identification. The categories of nonagricultural (urban) or agricultural (rural), the legal address and location, the unit affiliation (employment), and a host of other personal and family information, including religious belief and physical features, are documented and verified and become incorporated into the person's permanent *hukou* record. Until 1998, a person's *hukou* location and categorization or type were determined by his mother's *hukou* location and type rather than his birthplace; at that time a reform went into effect that allows a child to inherit the father's *or* mother's *hukou* location and categorization. (The police only started to enforce this much-cheered reform, however, five years later in 2003, and it was still three more years later, in 2006, before it was enforced in Beijing.)[6]

One cannot acquire a legal permanent residency and numerous community-based rights, opportunities, benefits, and privileges in places other than the place of his or her *hukou*. Only through proper government authorization can one permanently change *hukou* location and *hukou* categorization from rural to urban. Travelers, visitors, and temporary migrants must be registered with the *hukou* police for extended (longer than three days) stays in a locality, usually through local innkeepers. For longer than a one-month stay and especially when seeking local employment, one must apply and be approved for a temporary residential permit. Violators, if caught, are subject to fines, detention, forced repatriation, criminal prosecution, and even jail sentences. *Hukou* files are routinely used by the police for investigation, social control, and crime fighting.

Four Functions

In general, the semi-secretive PRC *hukou* system has been used to perform four functions, three of them uniquely Chinese.[7] First, it registers residents, collects and stores information about the populace, and provides personal identification and certifies relations and residence. This is a routine function of government commonly found in other countries as well.

Second, the PRC *hukou* system is the basis for resource allocation and subsidization for selected groups of the population (mainly urban *hukou* holders, who are a clear minority). This function has shaped much of Chinese economic development in the past half-century by politically affecting the movement of capital, goods, and human resources, heavily favoring urban centers with investment and subsidies. In the years from 1959 to 1962, among the estimated 36 million people who died due to the great famine caused by the disastrous "Great Leap Forward," almost all were rural residents excluded from urban-*hukou*-based food rations.[8] In 2009, Beijing announced a comprehensive and ambitious health care program, calling for the creation of four different medical insurance and health care systems based on the *hukou* system for the urban employed, urban residents, rural residents, and the poor respectively with sharply differentiated benefits and coverage.[9]

Third, the *hukou* system allows the government to control and regulate internal migration, especially rural-to-urban migration. The basic principles of PRC migration control have been to restrict rural-to-urban and small-city-to-large-city migration but to encourage migration in the reverse direction. China's urbanization, as a consequence, has been relatively slow compared to its economic development level. China's urban slums are also relatively small and less serious, compared to those in many other developing nations, such as Brazil or India.

Fourth, the *hukou* system has a less well-known but very powerful role of social control involving the management of so-called targeted people (*zhongdian renkou*). Based on *hukou* files, the police maintain a confidential list of the targeted people in each community (usually less than 5 percent of the community's total population) to be specially monitored and controlled. Such focused monitoring and control of selected segments of the population have contributed significantly and effectively to China's political stability.

The PRC *hukou* system has been enjoying a strong institutional legitimacy, unlike the similar but now disgraced and disintegrated *propiska* (residential permit) system in the former Soviet Union, certainly a result of the power of the authoritarian PRC state. Today, the *hukou* system continues to perform those crucial functions, fundamentally contributing to the seemingly puzzling coexistence of China's rapidly developing market economy and the remarkable stability of the CCP political monopoly.

Adaptations, Legalization, and Modernization

As with many other aspects of Chinese society, the *hukou* system went through changes and adjustments during the Chinese economic reform of the past three decades,[10] although the overall system remains intact, demonstrating a remarkable resilience. The system's much-examined function of resource allocation and subsidization to urbanites has now been reduced by advancing market forces, as urban rations of food and many other supplies have either disappeared or become insignificant. But urban *hukou* holders in major cities now still enjoy significant (monetarily even increased) state subsidies in housing, health care, employment, and especially education (see the analysis in Chapter 5 of this volume). A Beijing resident, for example, can get into college with a minimum admission score that is significantly (a quarter or more) lower than a resident in the nearby Shandong Province.[11] The administration of the function of internal migration control is now reformed, relaxed, and localized, giving rise to increased mobility of the population in general and rural laborers in particular.[12] Yet both the governing principles and the enforcing mechanisms of internal migration regulation essentially are unchanged.

The much less known but highly crucial function of the *hukou* system, management of targeted people, remains highly centralized, rigid, and forceful, although its effectiveness has been declining steadily. In addition to technical improvement, there has been effort to enhance this sociopolitical control function in the 2000s, such as the creation of a secret police force of "domestic security protection force," heavily relying on use of the archives and the management of targeted people.[13] In 2006 major cities like Shanghai and Shenzhen adopted a new *juzhuzheng* (residential permit) card to replace the previously used *zhanzhuzheng* (temporary residential permit) card as the required ID card for any migrant staying longer than one month. The new credit card-sized ID card now stores in its chip much more extensive information, including the holder's "job status, credit history, criminal record, and birth-planning record," that was not recorded on the old card.[14]

Run by the MPS and local police stations *(paichusuo)*, the *hukou* system has seen a localization of its administration in the reform era, as exemplified by schemes of so-called blue-seal *hukou* (transitional local urban *hukou*) that have various qualifications, "entry conditions," and implementation procedures in different localities to allow the migration of selected groups of people.[15] In April 2002, Shanghai suspended the granting of the blue-seal *hukou* to those who have purchased a "commercial" housing unit in the city, citing "too many new residents." But neighboring cities like Nanjing continue to lure the rich to buy their apartments by offering blue-seal *hukou* quotas. Other cities have simply replaced the blue-seal *hukou* with entry-condition-based permanent *hukou*.[16]

For generations, every Chinese citizen has known the ubiquity and power of the *hukou* system, yet it has remained just an "administrative" system with sketchy legal foundations. It has been highly nontransparent and is never mentioned in *The PRC Constitution* or *The PRC Civil Code*. Other than the 1958 *Regulation on Hukou Registration* and the 2003 *Law on Resident's Personal Identification Card*, the system has been governed and regulated by mostly "internal" decrees and directives. In the spirit of developing a rule of law (or more appropriately, rule by law) in the PRC, there have been many talks in Beijing since the 1980s about making a PRC *Hukou* Law to firmly ground this important system in "modern legal language." Yet, as of mid-2009, this effort still seemed stuck at an early stage, with no date for completion in sight.[17] The main reason behind the delay in promulgating a *hukou* law seems to be Beijing's political dilemma of how to preserve this highly important tool of social control without legally documenting its inherently discriminatory and unethical nature.

To manage the massive files of the *hukou* system, the MPS started to establish an electronic *hukou* database in 1986 and received special funding for national computerization of the *hukou* system in 1992. By 2002, almost all (more than thirty thousand) police stations nationwide had computerized their *hukou* management. Some 1,180 cities and counties joined regional computer networks for file-sharing of the *hukou* records of a total of 1.07 billion people (about 83 percent of the total population), and 250 cities joined in one single national *hukou* computer network to allow for instantaneous verification of *hukou* information covering 650 million people (about half of the total population).[18] In 2002 the MPS further required all hotels with fifty beds or more to have computer links to instantaneously transmit the photos of all guests to local police stations so as to effectively register most, if not all, visitors.[19] In February 2005, after years of effort, some major cities like Xiamen completed the computerization of all of their *hukou* files from before 1987, when they started to process and store *hukou* files electronically, all the way back to 1957, when cities first created their citywide *hukou* databases.[20]

The "Deep Reforms" Since 2001

On June 10, 1997, the PRC State Council approved the MPS's *Experimental Plan on Reforming the Hukou System in Small Cities and Towns* and *Suggestions on Improving Rural Hukou Management*. The experimental stage was replaced with a national implementation of the reform on March 30, 2001, ushering in a round of "deep reform" of the *hukou* system that has four major components. First, there is a general relaxation of internal migration restrictions for certain selected groups of people, such as elderly parents, children, and highly educated "talents" and skilled workers. A streamlining of internal migration procedures for temporary or permanent migration has also taken place nationwide.[21]

Second, on October 1, 2001, the government began to abolish the decades-old rural-to-urban migration quota system in all small cities and towns (defined as county-level cities, county seats, and established towns).[22] Anyone who has a stable nonagricultural income and has had a permanent residence in a small city or town for at least two years will automatically qualify to have an urban *hukou* and become a permanent local resident, but "all the migration registration procedures are still to be followed strictly."[23] Some medium and even large cities are also authorized to do the same, with a higher and more specific income, employment, and residence requirement as the "entry conditions."[24] The government planned to use five years, until 2006, to complete this reform to "establish an integrated labor market for urban and rural residents in Eastern China . . . in order to eliminate market segmentation there."[25] As I will report below, this deadline passed three years ago, and the plan seems to have been postponed nationwide and put on hold indefinitely in almost all major urban centers.

Third, the localized practice of selective migration to major cities, nicknamed "*hukou* in exchange for talents and investments," has been further polished, repackaged, and nationally adopted. Under the new regulations, major urban centers openly set up high prices for their much sought-after *hukou*.[26] Highly educated workers with at least a college degree who are hired by local employers can now get local temporary *hukou* or even permanent hukou in most Chinese cities with greater ease.[27] The going rate for a set of three Beijing urban *hukou* (self, spouse, and one child) is no less than for a multimillionaire investor or a foreign-educated "talent." According to one calculation, to live in Beijing and own a business to qualify for Beijing *hukou* under the new regulations (employing 100 workers and paying 800,000 RMB tax a year), one must have a net worth of at least 8 to 16 million RMB.[28] However, in the late 1990s the average asset size of private businesses in China was only 530,000 RMB.[29] Alternatively, one can purchase a high-end "commercial" unit of apartments to qualify to be a local *hukou* applicant—by a one-time expenditure of at least 500,000 RMB in cash, twenty to thirty times the average annual wage in Beijing.[30] Similar schemes exist in Shanghai, with a slightly lower price tag.[31] To "purchase" a major city's urban *hukou* this way is still subject to the available moving-in quota. In Beijing, a city that in 1999 had at least 2.37 million temporary *hukou* holders, only 715 families acquired local urban *hukou* through housing purchases.[32] Other than the needed skilled labor and the super-rich, China's major urban centers still want few "outsiders" to be their new citizens.

Finally, in line with China's entry into the World Trade Organization (WTO) and Beijing's pursuit of improving its international image, a national wave of "erasing" the unsightly rural-urban distinction in the *hukou* system started to take place in 2001–2002. Many localities, mostly small cities and towns, experimented with various measures to replace the names of rural (agricultural) versus urban (nonagricultural) *hukou* with a uniform "residential *hukou*" that still has the distinction between "permanent *hukou*" and "temporary *hukou*," so as to claim having "abolished agricultural *hukou*."[33] To relocate one's *hukou* so as to acquire a local residency and become a full member of a new community, however, still requires that the applicant meet various locally set "entry conditions" that usually include having a stable and officially sanctioned local job (with specific minimum income) and a local legal residence for at least two years.[34] Some provinces have ventured further. Guizhou, one of the poorest provinces, decided to give a small city/town urban *hukou* to anyone who meets the income and residence requirements immediately, waiving the usual two-year waiting period. Shanxi, another less-developed province, used urban *hukou* in nearby small cities and towns to reward migrant rural residents who moved to remote regions to reclaim desert land through tree planting.[35]

Forced Repatriation: Changes and Continuity

A major mechanism of the *hukou* system's regulation of internal migration, especially rural-to-urban migration, has been police random checks of residential papers and the forced repatriation of unapproved and undocumented migrants.[36] The often brutal process of repatriation was halted after a well-publicized tragedy in 2003. On March 17, the police in Guangzhou arrested a young migrant from Wuhan named Sun Zhigang for having no identification papers, although he was actually lawfully employed there. He was brutally beaten to death three days later by police and fellow inmates during the repatriation process. The case was rather unnewsworthy except for the fact that Sun was a college graduate with an urban *hukou* (albeit not a local Guangzhou *hukou*). His fellow migrants, who were educated urban (but nonlocal) residents publicized the story via the Internet and cell-phone messaging. The case was eventually picked up by some brave reporters and editors at an influential local newspaper, *Nanfang Dushi Bao* (Southern Metropolis News). The spread of the Sun story led directly to a public outcry against the irrationality and injustice generated by the *hukou* system, especially the practice of forced repatriation that had now evidently victimized a migrant who was otherwise a privileged urban resident with a college education, a "talent" rather than a simple "floater."

Reacting to try to maintain sociopolitical stability and create "social harmony," Beijing ordered a dozen perpetrators, including several police officers, executed or sent to jail for many years. The PRC State Council canceled the 1982 "Measures of Detaining and Repatriating Floating and Begging People in the Cities." In its place they issued "Measures on Repatriation of Urban Homeless Beggars" on June 18 and "Measures on Managing and Assisting Urban Homeless Beggars without Income" on June 20, establishing new rules governing the handling and assisting of destitute migrants. Many cities—including the most controlled, Beijing—decided soon after that *hukou*-less migrants must be treated with more care. They are no longer automatically subject to detention and forced repatriation, unless they have become homeless, paupers, or criminals.[37]

This change of repatriation policy was a much-needed reform and has been widely praised as a humane move by the Hu Jintao–Wen Jiabao leadership. However, as an interesting twist that vividly reveals political reality in the PRC, soon after, in 2004, three editors and reporters who broke the Sun Zhigang story were fired, arrested, and sentenced under trumped-up charges of bribery and corruption. One was released after eight months in prison and another was paroled in February 2007, while the third is still serving his eight-year sentence at the time of this writing. Furthermore, the relaxation of repatriation policy has suddenly increased the population of street people, beggars, and other "undesirables" in places like Shanghai's Nanjing Road and Beijing's Tiananmen Square, prompting the quiet restoration of repatriation by 2006 in many places and open calls for tougher restrictions against migrants from the outside, especially from rural areas. Discussion of the danger of "Latin-Americanization" and concern about decay of the Chinese urban business environment in general soon emerged.[38]

According to the revised law on personal identification cards, also adopted in June 2003, the random check of personal identification cards and residential papers without a proper reason was restricted somewhat, amid many complaints and criticisms. Official media even openly showcased two events as examples to urge local police to be more careful in dealing with migrants or suspected migrants: On January 18, 2003, a young businesswoman, Hao Yanhong, an urban resident of another major city, Shenyang, was detained in Shanghai's Xuhui District by the police just four days after her arrival in the city on a legitimate business trip. After spending twenty-four days in a repatriation center as a suspected permit-less migrant, Hao was released on bail, for an astronomical amount of 1.5 million RMB (about US$183,000). Some eleven months after her release, however, she was "surprisingly" granted an apology and compensation of 1,187 RMB (about US$144) from the Shanghai police, who made a special gesture by paying her a visit in Shenyang, more than a thousand miles away.[39]

About the same time in the same district of Shanghai, a Dr. Jia Fang-jun (a postdoctoral fellow employed by a state-owned elite biology and cell research institute studying the reproduction of seahorses), was randomly checked on the street while biking home at 11 PM on February 17, detained overnight, and roughened up by the police for not carrying proper identification. His "outsider" appearance (nonlocal accent and casual clothing) made the police mistake a much lured "talent" for an unwanted permit-less migrant. Jia academically and futilely argued with the police, "Why does a Chinese citizen need a permit to live in his own country?" Much luckier than Mr. Sun, Dr. Jia was released the next day when his employer went to the police to report him "missing." He then went to court repeatedly to clear his name and record. After eleven months, he obtained an injunction from the Xuhui Court that exonerated him and fined the police 100 RMB (US$12). He was reported later to be pleased and "undaunted," but he remembered to "go home earlier and carry IDs all the time."[40]

The relaxation of random ID checks of suspected migrants, however, appears to have been limited and short-lived. The few cases reported by the media in which the police were forced to apologize or were fined because of their sloppy and mistaken checks and detentions all involved outside but urban *hukou* holders. Many more cases involving rural migrants could be seen only rarely in Web postings. Furthermore, after just a few months, by the end of 2004, the police quickly and quietly restored and even enhanced the random checks, deemed very useful in fighting crime and maintaining social control. Anecdotal evidence suggests that police harassment of migrants, especially those from rural areas, was about the same in 2006–2008 as before 2003. The infamous detention and repatriation centers and stations (*shourong zhan*) are now renamed "assistance stations" (*jiuzhu zhan*), and the police are instructed to enforce the *hukou* system with "voluntary repatriation first" before using force.[41]

Mandatory registration and required temporary residential permits; random and humiliating checks of ID papers on the street, especially in or near train stations; surprise checks by storming into migrant housing units after midnight; and detention and forced repatriation of the permit-less appear to be continuing routinely, albeit quietly, now in major cities like Beijing, Guangzhou, Shanghai, and Wuhan, and even in small cities in the Pearl River Delta.[42] To polish China's image for the 2008 Olympic Games in Beijing, the city government proposed to keep away almost all non-Beijing *hukou* holders during the games by sending home at least 1 million migrant workers and small business owners and prohibiting outsiders from visiting the city without the written approval of the government "above the county level."[43] Critical foreign reporters have reported some of those ongoing detention and repatriation activities as "Beijing black jails" and "China's Olympic lies."[44]

Suspension and Rollbacks

Merely eight months into the reform of 2001, in mid-2002, the national wave to rename the rural-urban distinction was ordered stopped by Beijing pending "further instructions." The "deep" reform was put on hold nationally to ensure a smooth CCP leadership change in 2002–2004. Officially, the suspension became necessary because of the government's inability to accommodate the massive number of new urban residents.[45] The story of Zhengzhou, a large, interior city, illustrates this quite well. On August 20, 2004, the *hukou* police in that city, the capital of Henan Province (which has one of the largest rural populations in China), suspended the "new deal on *hukou*" (started in 2001 but accelerated only in 2003) that allowed nonlocal *hukou*-holders easier chances to become Zhengzhou *hukou*-holders. The reason for the abrupt suspension was:

> Rapid increase of (urban) population has caused traffic jams and acute drain of educational resources, led to new depletion of social welfare provision, exerted great pressure on medical facilities, and greatly increased criminal cases, threatening public security.[46]

Zhengzhou, with 2.5 million residents, took in a total of 250,000 new residents under the three-year reform. This 10-percent increase was decried by old residents and was vividly reported by the local media to be significantly beyond the city's absorption ability. Due to the inflow of too many "ordinary migrants" with school-aged children (as opposed to those desired investors and "talents" or skilled workers), the schools in the privileged provincial capital city were suddenly packed, with routinely 80 to 90 pupils per class, and the streets were jammed with no relief in sight. The city quickly decided to stop its ambitious plan of becoming a place of 5 million permanent residents and returned to its old "entry-permission" policy that was designed to trade local *hukou* "for talents and investment." Many other cities in Henan and elsewhere quickly did the same.[47]

The Zhengzhou-style *hukou* reform, dubbed by some critics as a "Great-Leap Forward of urbanization" (referring to the fiasco under Mao Zedong in 1958–1961) failed rather quickly.

Of course, it was a matter of political power and vested interest rather than a simple issue of resource shortage. While the city of Zhengzhou had no money to improve its appalling deficiencies in transportation, education, and environmental protection, the government of a relatively poor district of the city, Huiji District, spent massive amounts (more than 700 million RMB or US$87 million) in 2003–2004 to build itself an office and residential complex that rivals the White House or Disneyland in size and appearance.[48]

More fundamentally, hasty opening of the floodgate, like the Zhengzhou-style leap forward, threatens the key political utility of the *hukou* system. Granting local *hukou* status easily and "automatically" to those who may qualify (such as those joining their urban relatives) seemed to negate the long-used "temporary residential permit" system and the compulsory registration of visitors, taking away the tool the police use to monitor, control, and regulate the mobile population in the politically sensitive urban centers. The change of repatriation policy and the limit of random ID checks further reduced the incentives for migrants, especially those yet to qualify for local "entry conditions," to get registered and hence controlled by the local police. The management of targeted people and the overall task of keeping the urban centers orderly had thus become hugely difficult and much less effective, directly threatening sociopolitical stability, for which the *hukou* system is of special and crucial value.[49] In some places, like Guangzhou, the rate of registration of "outsiders," mainly migrant rural residents, went down to as low as only a quarter of the previous rate by 2006.

Therefore, not only was there an abrupt suspension of the *hukou* reform; there were also clear rollback moves as many cities reinstituted and strengthened the temporary residential permit system that had been "abolished" only a year or two earlier. Such a required permit restored the basis for control and harassment of migrants, supposedly for the purpose of fighting rising crime caused by the surge of migrants. Two years after the Zhengzhou halt, in the fall of 2006, the city decided to bring back the infamous temporary residential permits and resume random checks of suspected outsiders, a reversal of *hukou* reforms that nonetheless won the support of more than 60 percent of the city's polled residents.[50]

Many other major cities, such as Wuhan, Shanghai, and Guangzhou, had similar rollbacks even earlier, in 2004 and 2005.[51]

The "deep" reform clearly got stuck. By mid-2009, three years after the originally planned year of completing the reform, the PRC *hukou* system appeared to have changed little in its role of separating the rural from the urban and regulating internal migration. In 2006–2009, the reports, stories, and comments in the Chinese media about the "unfairness," "irrationality" and lack of "genuine" reform of the *hukou* system, mainly its rural-urban dichotomy, were as numerous and identical as those that appeared seven to eight years earlier. Even on the East Coast, in some of the most open areas such as the Pearl River Delta, *hukou*-based local versus outsider and rural versus urban distinctions and separations were as rigid and important as ever.[52]

Further But Cosmetic Reforms in 2005

Intended to be localized and controlled, the reform of the *hukou* system started with high fanfare in 2001. It was quickly suspended nationwide in 2002–2004 and had some rollbacks in many places. But the rising tide behind the *hukou* floodgate continued to generate new forces to bend the system to suit the growing mobility of the Chinese population, especially rural laborers. A further relaxation of migration control, if not an erasing of the rural-urban distinction, became increasingly hard to avoid. Increased sociopolitical pressure caused by decaying rural communities and the ever-enlarging rural-urban income gap[53] resulted in skyrocketing mass riots and violent protests (from 8,700 in 1993 to 74,000 in 2004 and then 84,000 in 2005[54], and over 100,000 in 2008), prompting Beijing to seek pacification in the countryside. Some reform-minded public intellectuals such as Hu Xingdou, a professor based in Beijing, have helped to push for further changes of the *hukou* system, especially its obvious discrimination against the majority rural population. Since 2004, Hu openly and repeatedly has criticized the *hukou* system as "unconstitutional," contending that it ought to be completely overhauled if not abolished right away so as to give every Chinese "the freedom of relocation *(qianyi ziyou)*" he or she rightfully deserves under WTO-membership-implied international standards or simple "socialist" ethics.[55]

After President Hu Jintao consolidated his grip on power inside the CCP and as a major effort to address the accumulating grievances among the peasants—especially the crucial need to control the politically more potent migrant laborers, who are generally young, restless, and somewhat educated—*hukou* reform picked up some momentum again in the fall of 2005. This was quickly and flatteringly dubbed by official media as "the fourth reform" of the *hukou* system. More accurately, however, it was an attempt to resume the suspended "deep" reform of 2001.

In October 2005, the MPS announced that it would soon propose a new, broad, "grand and deep *hukou* reform" to be adopted by the State Council nationwide. The objective was to create a "nationally uniform *hukou* system" and a uniform *hukou* category that erases the distinctive categories of rural and urban *hukou* and further relaxes migration control in medium and major cities, beyond the small cities and towns where such relaxations had occurred earlier.[56] It appeared that the *hukou* system's unsightly distinction and the ever-enlarging income gap between the rural and urban populations were perceived as major political liabilities threatening Hu Jintao's plan for a "harmonious society." Beijing started to call again for taking away some rough edges.

On cue from the top, local officials of almost every major urban center, always anxious to have an impressive political report card *(zhengji)* to show Beijing, started to launch various campaigns to do away with the rural-urban duality of the *hukou* system. The main thrust was still the suspended measures of replacing the rural (agricultural) versus urban (nonagricultural) *hukou* duality with "permanent *hukou*" versus "temporary *hukou*" duality under a uniform category of "residential *hukou*" so to quickly "do away with agricultural *hukou*" and the "discriminatory legacy of the *hukou* system." Active resumption of the reform was reported in eleven provincial regions ranging from Zhejiang to Inner Mongolia (out of a total of thirty-one).[57] As before, however, the various locally set "entry conditions" of housing and income were still in place everywhere for the now recategorized outsiders to acquire a local permanent *hukou* in the cities where they want to settle.

The latest *hukou* reforms, however, seem to be largely cosmetic and marginal in nature and are essentially empty for the majority of the rural population. In fact, rural residents may actually be worse off after the nominal change of their *hukou* category. Under the pretence of getting rid of their "agricultural" *hukou*, many villagers near expanding cities have quickly lost their user's rights (or "collective ownership") of land to local governments (in alliance with local developers), who have simply declared a completion of urbanization and nationalized the land (*shougui guoyou*). With often grossly inadequate compensation, the land has been quickly taken away—in a process resembling simple robbery—from the villagers (now nominally urban residents) and then auctioned off, often with a hundredfold and even a thousandfold profit for the local officials and the well-connected developers in just one transaction.[58]

In addition, the former peasants stand to lose a host of land-associated rural subsidies that have been dispensed by the central government since 2003; yet they have no prospect of competing for scarce nonagricultural jobs with the massive numbers of unemployed and underemployed laborers already in the cities while having basically no access to the already restrictive provision of social welfare benefits that are earmarked only for local, permanent (that is, the "genuine") urban *hukou* holders. As a result, as one influential critic pointed out in 2007, the real consequence of such a Great Leap Forward style of urbanization and cosmetic reform of the *hukou* system has been that, increasingly, many peasants have seen "three-nos"—no land, no jobs, and no social welfare protection.[59] By the end of 2005, such "three-no" former peasants may have totaled as many as 40 million.[60]

Jobs and Death Benefits

More substantively perhaps, after 2006 some state jobs were decreed to be available to selected people with nonlocal *hukou;* "qualified" (at the minimum, this means holding a college degree) rural *hukou*-holders began to be allowed to take part in civil service examinations for some state jobs.[61] Private employers, whether Chinese or foreign firms, have been hiring workers since the late 1990s with little concern for their *hukou* status or types. But they are still required to make sure that their employees all have either a local permanent *hukou* or a valid temporary residential permit. Some cities like Shanghai started in 2005 to allow nonpermanent residents with legitimate local employment to participate in some local insurance programs, health-care schemes, and even pension plans.[62]

Legally, a highly discriminatory and inflammatory use of the *hukou* system started to fade in 2006. Until then, victims with different *hukou* types suffering the same wrongful injury or death were always compensated very differently, no matter how long they might have lived and worked together in the same location (see the example discussed in Chapter 10 in this volume). The cap of such accidental death benefits was legally set as the equivalent of twenty years' per capita net income in the victim's *hukou* zone.[63] The vast economic gap between urban and rural areas, therefore, created a legal double standard for human life in the PRC: in death, the family of a victim with a rural *hukou* generally gets about a quarter to one-third of that awarded to a victim with an urban *hukou*.[64] Despite many outcries, mostly in some local media and on the Internet, calling for "same life, same value," the government started to address this glaring discrimination only in 2006.

In March 2006, the PRC Supreme Court hinted at its willingness to modify the old rules. In June, Beijing issued a new state-compensation law and a new regulation governing air-transportation-related compensation. The two new decrees ruled for the first time that all Chinese victims of airline-related or government-caused wrongful injuries or deaths will be compensated at the same rate based on the average annual wages of urban state employees. In July 2006 in Chengdu there was the first-ever PRC court injunction ordering private parties to pay compensation at the urban rate to the family of a wrongfully killed wealthy rural *hukou* holder who had lived in the city for more than a decade.[65] At about the same time, governments in Chongqing, Henan, and Shandong adopted similar new policies setting compensation rates based on the average income of where the victim was employed, rather than where his or her *hukou* was located.[66] In July 2008, Shenzhen Municipal Court finally issued a new guideline requiring insurance companies to compensate the victims of traffic accidents who are rural *hukou* holders at the same rate as local urban *hukou* holders. However, a rural victim must have lived in Shenzhen for at least one year and have "a stable income" at the time of the accident to be treated "equally."[67]

Resistances and Hindrances

Cosmetic or substantive, the 2005 resumption of *hukou* reform ran out of steam soon after its start. Only a few days after the previously mentioned MPS announcement in October 2005 of the new reform plans, the official Xinhua New Agency itself reported that the MPS had "clearly changed its attitude" and decided to no longer talk about major overhauls anymore. Perhaps as an authorized gesture to send signals, Xinhua's flagship news weekly, *Outlook,* reported in November that "authoritative insiders of the MPS" leaked that "actually, the MPS made its new reform plans two years ago," but its national implementation "has been slow and obstructed by the relevant ministries and some local governments."[68]

It is interesting and profound to see that the MPS, the chief enforcer of the *hukou* system, appears to be interested in further relaxing the system's role of regulating internal migration and erasing the rural-urban dual categories, while the "other" ministries and local governments will resist such "deep" reforms. It seems that the MPS (and likely the top leadership of the CCP too) has desires, as illustrated by the argument long held by MPS *hukou* officials and experts, to enhance the value and effectiveness of the *hukou* system's role in sociopolitical control by "shedding" its "add-on" role of regulating internal migration and allocating resources and erasing the politically contentious rural-urban dual designation.[69] Yet, without massive new resources and new jobs to accompany the removal of the floodgate between rural and urban, other ministries (who may be more concerned about resources) and corporatist local leaders (who rely on good report cards, mainly derived from GDP growth figures and images of glittering and tranquil urban centers, to get promoted) will necessarily resist. Local officials in Guangdong believed that even controlled rural-to-urban migration in 2006–2010 would force a 10 percent annual increase in local welfare spending, way beyond the financial ability of even this rich province.[70]

Therefore, not only have major cities like Zhengzhou, Guangzhou, and Nanjing repeatedly watered down and even halted their *hukou* reforms, but smaller interior cities like Hohhot "and many other cities" in Inner Mongolia have daringly defied the order of doing away with the dual rural-urban categorization by January 1, 2006. They have refused to even grant local urban *hukou* to "qualified" rural migrants as instructed by Beijing and the provincial government and have openly declared so with "little repercussion."[71] Liu He, a senior cadre of the Central Commission on Financial and Economic Affairs, openly declared in March 2006 that "China's *hukou* reform must be a gradual process and the system can't be abolished." He insisted that a "green card"-style of temporary residential permit would be enough to address the legal status of migrant workers.[72]

More than two years after their resumption, in late 2008, the official media reported that *hukou* reforms were once again "stuck in deep water" due to complicated vested interests involving the necessary real-location of resources. The national reform plan and the draft of the *hukou* law were both still hidden in drawers somewhere inside the MPS. The eleven provinces that experimented with various measures of *hukou* reform, as authorized by Beijing since 2001 and especially since 2005, mainly in the area of relaxing rural-to-urban migration and erasing the dual rural-urban categorization, "all are experiencing difficulties and lo-cal resistance."[73] In the localities where the "uniform" *hukou* was put into place to replace the agricultural and nonagricultural *hukou*, "many real barriers have emerged to still keep the rural and urban populations apart." Chief among those long-lived, real but now more apparent, barri-ers are the distinctions and discriminations against former "outsiders" in employment, social status, education, medical care, wage levels, social security, and job-training.[74] In 2008, Deputy Minister of the MPS Bai Jingfu openly declared that *hukou* reform would continue to be carried out in a localized, piecemeal fashion.[75] The Xinhua News Agency con-cluded at the end of 2008 that the "main obstacles to *hukou* reform are from the vested-interest groups" and the complicated involvement of more than 14 agencies of the central government; hence the *hukou* reform has become a major test of the CCP's leadership and governing capacity as serious as the creation of the PRC in 1949 and the starting of the reform and opening in 1978."[76]

Perhaps seeing through the emptiness of the new "uniform" *hukou* or deeply distrusting government officials, many peasants have now become reluctant to accept the "change" of their *hukou* type and simply refuse to give up their agricultural *hukou* and their land. Some started to view the latest *hukou* reform as just new schemes designed to extract more re-sources from peasants. It remains to be seen how this battle over land and *hukou* between peasants and local governments will eventually play out.[77] So far it seems quite clear that without well-defined and protected property rights and private land ownership and free media, and with weak political rights and no independent legal system, the long-excluded Chinese peasants have little means other than desperate and violent pro-tests to protect their land and other interests, let alone to improve their life chances, with or without the proposed *hukou* reforms. Renowned PRC economist Li Yining of Peking University listed openly "the user's right of land" with the *hukou* system as the "two core issues in the reform of the rural-urban duality."[78]

Assessing *Hukou* Reforms: Hype, Doubts, and Critics

There has been in the PRC an interestingly diverse assessment of the *hukou* reforms so far. Each spring has become literally the time for talking about the subject, especially right around March when the Chinese National People's Congress is in session. Usually, the Chinese media catch up with the latest reform moves, real or proposed, and describe the latest decrees with strong, mostly unwarranted, adjectives like "brand new," "breakthrough," and "complete." Most articles simply cheered the PRC government for "treating the rural compatriots the same as city dwellers" from now on. The usual role of the carefully controlled and censored Chinese media in illustrating, promoting, and justifying state polices and mobilizing the public remains the same. The unmistaken repetitiveness of the media coverage, including the nationwide recycling of exactly the same official lines and quotes and exactly the same few stories and cases, suggests that the government still exercises a careful and tight control over the discourse on *hukou* reform.[79] Foreign media seem to be also frequently misled by those unwarranted enthusiasm about a possible "abolition" of the *hukou* system.[80] The reporting and public discussion are still clearly limited to the *hukou* system's role of blocking internal migration and creating rural-urban discrimination. Many important aspects of the system, such as the politically highly sensitive but crucial management of targeted people, are still taboo issues.

Doubts and Critics

Somewhat different from six years ago, there are now clear and quick reactions noticeable in the Chinese media and especially in cyberspace and in private conversations that raise doubt about the sincerity and effectiveness of *hukou* reforms. Even some of the official media have started to reveal the cosmetic nature and limited scope of the reforms. Some called the reform simply "a show game."[81] A demographer concluded that the reform of simply "unifying" the rural and urban *hukou* is likely to fail.[82] Many more Chinese readers, mainly on the Internet, simply mocked and ridiculed the shameless media hypes.[83]

Wang Taiyuan, a leading PRC *hukou* authority and a former senior *hukou* officer of the MPS (now a professor at the Chinese Public Security University), quickly commented in late 2005 that the "new" ideas and

actions of the so-called "fourth reform" were "nothing more than repeat-
ing" those already proposed first in 1998 and then pronounced again in
2001. As a true insider, Wang concluded his observation of China's *hukou*
reform in the past five years this way:

> The declared (reform measure) may not be really implemented; the
> implemented (measures) may not be really completed; the completed
> may not be really well accompanied (with necessary changes to give the
> new local/urban residents equal rights and benefits).[84]

Wang's candid statement was perhaps based on his personal experience. As a senior cadre/scholar, a top *hukou* specialist, and a former
senior *hukou* officer of the MPS, Wang is a Beijing *hukou*-holder. His
own father is an urban *hukou*-holder but of a small county-seat town in
Sichuan Province. When the elder Wang had a stroke, he could not get
medical treatment in the "better, large" hospitals in Beijing because his
hukou location required that he be treated locally or lose his medical insurance that was only valid in the city where his *hukou* was located.[85]
This is indeed strong, albeit a bit ironic, testimony about the power and
relevance of the *hukou* system in governing the Chinese political economy and Chinese life chances.

There are now also more penetrating criticisms and thoughtful ideas
about the *hukou* system and the reform of it. One voice is the outspoken
Professor Hu Xingdou mentioned previously. Hu, an idealist with some
"neo-left" populist coloring, has labeled the *hukou* system "unconstitutional" and has openly appealed for its abolition. He also criticized the
so-called "deep" reform since 2001 as meaningless and even counterpro-
ductive. Echoing many others, Hu believes the cosmetic reform has actually hurt the rural population more by giving local officials a perfect
pretense to take away land from rural residents in an "urbanization by
recategorization" that offers the ruralites little more than an empty title
of "urban resident" and next to nothing for their land. The latest *hukou*
reform may have been simply motivated by the sinister desire of local officials to exploit the peasants, rather than by any sincere and effective
efforts to help the rural population that is increasingly falling behind in
China's national dash to get rich.[86]

Other thoughtful and penetrating critics include Yu Jianrong, a senior
and influential expert on the Chinese rural economy and China's *xinfang*

(appealing or complaining to higher levels) system. Yu has appeared in public speeches together with Hu, sharing many views and being equally outspoken. But he appears to be more of a pragmatic insider. Yu has argued for a long time that the key to addressing the rural-urban gap and the rising tide of social unrest in general and rural unrest in particular is to allow people and especially peasants to organize themselves for local self-governance and to develop an independent and effective judiciary.[87] His overall disappointment about the CCP's lack of political reform in the direction of democracy and rule of law, widely shared by many Chinese intellectuals these days, is very apparent, although people like him still appear to be for peaceful reform rather revolution. About the *hukou* reform so far, Yu bluntly called it a "mistake" and just another exploitation of the Chinese peasants through taking away their land for an empty title of "urban residents." Contrary to the calls for abolishing the *hukou* system, Yu actually insists that the rural-urban duality of the *hukou* system should be maintained to protect the peasants from corrupt and out-of-control local officials and developers. What should be done is to give the peasants more political rights and power to organize independent trade unions and farmer's associations and better access to an independent judicial system and to more state financial subsidies (see the discussion in Chapter 14 in this volume).[88]

Some noted experts and influential scholars like Ge Jianxiong, He Weifang, and Qin Hui seem to share Yu's views to various degrees.[89] Some major members of the ruling elite have also openly expressed similar ideas of empowering the peasants through organizing and educating them.[90] It is becoming increasingly common for critics now to view the necessity for *hukou* reform more from the perspective of human rights and citizen rights, unlike in the late 1990s when most of the critiques were of the system's economic irrationalities. A less scholarly but extensive critique of the *hukou* system filled with anecdotes is simply titled "China's Biggest Human Rights Case: The Current *Hukou* System."[91] In March 2008, more than thirty leading Chinese dissident intellectuals wrote an open letter to the PRC National People's Congress, calling for "an immediate abolition of the rural-urban dual *hukou* system." Perhaps attempting to preempt any independent union/farmers association movement that has long been deemed by the CCP as a fatal threat, the state-run trade union, the 151-million-member-strong All-China Federation of Trade Unions, finally declared in 2007 that it would start to recruit

"10 million new members" from the previously unrecognized rural migrant workers.[92]

Money Talks, Leaks Develop

Clear localization and strong commercialization of the *hukou*-based regulation of internal migration have developed considerably since the 1980s.[93] As a direct result, the rural-urban distinction and the social separation under the system are now routinely bridged with monetary transactions, even in the most tightly controlled urban centers like Beijing. Other than the officially sanctioned sale of local *hukou* in the form of "trading *hukou* for investment and talents" and for proven political loyalty,[94] there has been a widespread black market in individual transactions in *hukou* of desired location and type. Powerful retail-style commercialization has effectively provided many ad hoc leaks or flood-discharging tunnels to save the overall stability of the floodgate. Expedient arrangements like the temporary residential permit and its evolved version of "green card"-style, quasi-permanent *hukou* have also effectively neutralized the most potent opponents to the *hukou* system: educated youth and the rich. The great floodgate of the *hukou* system hence also functions as a giant water pump, facilitating a massive internal brain drain and capital drain to enlarge China's rural-urban gap and regional disparities.

Beijing is a good example of how money and cosmetic changes have helped to compromise and preserve the *hukou* system as a floodgate and a pump. The national capital city has the tightest migration control of any city and is already severely short of space, water, and clean air. But political decisions by the central government to shower the city with resources, opportunity, and prestige have made it a top destination for educated and ambitious young Chinese. In 2006, for example, more than forty thousand "talents" with master's or doctorate degrees jammed one job fair that offered four thousand jobs with Beijing *hukou*.[95] By 2005, Beijing city already had 15 million residents (11 million were local permanent *hukou* holders), far more than the population size of 12.5 million the state had planned for the city by 2010. Some local officials have hence openly called for more flood control.[96] But money still allows many to effectively penetrate this forbidden city. One interesting leak, based on a monetary mechanism, has been the sale of *hukou* quotas to "qualified" talents, such as college graduates.

Every year, hundreds of thousands of college graduates with non-Beijing *hukou* (many originally from rural areas) face a tough choice: they could go back to their home city/town as an urban *hukou* holder there; or they could become *"jingpiao yizu"* (floating people in Beijing) under a Beijing temporary residential permit for an unknown, often indefinite period of time if they can secure legitimate local employment and local housing, enduring de facto second-class citizen status and all the pain and disadvantage associated with it.[97] But they could also buy some of the very limited (only fifteen thousand per year) Beijing *hukou* quotas that are allocated to politically favored employers and *danweis* (units), who in turn decide to sell them for cash. "Ninety percent of the (qualified) students say that they would purchase a quota if the price is right." Indeed, the illegal but "very reliable" market for *hukou* quota has been very active, with the going price of 25,000 RMB in 2005, roughly one year's total income of a white-collar worker just out of college.[98]

To comfort and pacify those second-class outsiders who nonetheless bring in much-needed capital and labor, in 2005 the Beijing city government issued new ethics textbooks to students in grades K–12 that required students to learn how "not to show discrimination against outsiders *(waidi ren)*" in addition to how to count money and eat Western food.[99] However, it seems to be money, more than gestures of cosmetic reforms, that keeps the massive army of second-class citizens relatively content so far. Many well-educated migrants with a good local job simply choose to ignore the required registration for a temporary residential permit for as long as they can and prefer to forget about their second-class citizenship. Asked by the author in early 2007, a well-educated "outsider" who had held a good white-collar job in a major foreign-invested company in Beijing for many years commented:

> *Hukou* is of course still useful, and even important if you really want to be a genuine Beijing person *(Beijing ren)* or raise a family here. But I'm OK (without a permanent Beijing *hukou*) as long as I make good money.[100]

Money talks loudly indeed. As long as the Chinese economy, especially in the major urban centers, hums along well, the great floodgate of the *hukou* system, with all of its unintended leaks and renovated flood-discharging tunnels, will keep the massive body of relatively still water, the unorganized, uneducated, and unwanted rural population, at bay.

What Is in a Name?

At least nominally, the latest *hukou* reform has started to do away with the discriminatory legal labeling of rural *hukou* holders. This is a major, albeit highly symbolic, victory of the advancing market institutions and new norms of citizenship and human rights in China. Of course, the *hukou* system is not abolished as universal residential registration; the basic principles of internal migration control, and the unique sociopolitical control through the management of targeted people, still remain. But the change of a name, if fully implemented by overcoming resistances and hindrances, may still give rise to a profound sociopolitical transformation. A uniform category of "resident *hukou*" (versus being an outsider, whether of rural or urban origin) could indeed empower the long-excluded rural population to substantively demand their fair rights as equal citizens in China's urban centers, creating new momentum, reasons, and energy for more real reform of the Chinese political system that has created the unbalanced allocation of resources favoring the minority of the population in urban centers. Much can be in a name in China. In the name of equal citizenship under a uniform *hukou* category, the CCP's total monopoly of political power could lose a time-tested tool to "divide and rule." The great floodgate of the *hukou* system may be only gradually renovated with largely cosmetic measures. But once the gate is opened, the flow would likely take its own course, with plenty of uncertainties and unknowns. Only time will tell if the massive rural population will stream in ever so peacefully, or whether the flood will overwhelm the dam, leading to a sudden and total collapse of the *hukou* system and the authoritarian political system that rests on it.

Conclusions

Five years ago, I wrote the following about the future of the *hukou* system:

> Historically speaking, for the PRC *hukou* system to be abolished or cease to be an effective institutional exclusion, many great changes have to take place in China's politics, economy, society, and culture. . . . Further development of the Chinese political economy and China's external relations may reduce the intensity and extent of the *hukou*-based

institutional exclusion. . . . A more democratic and liberal polity in China may further decrease the utility and increase the cost of *hukou*-based sociopolitical control. The PRC *hukou* system may then possibly have a genuine transformation from an institutional exclusion and administrative social control to merely a system of simple residential registration and identification. . . . The increasingly combining and merging evolution of the *hukou*-based institutional exclusion with the money-based institutional exclusion appears to be forming a two-dimensional structure as the new basis for dividing and organizing the Chinese in the years ahead.[101]

The latest developments have shown little to contradict this assessment.[102] For more than two decades, gradual and incremental reforms have relaxed and decentralized internal migration control under the *hukou* system, especially in small cities and towns. With that change, the system's life has been extended by accommodating the growing needs of the labor market for population mobility. Some of the system's old rigidity has been smoothed out by a fast-growing economy and the new resources generated outside of state allocation. Some of the unsightly features and categorizations are being removed by controlled reforms. While China has experienced explosive economic growth and massive movement of laborers in the past three decades, urban slums and social unrest so far are still manageable, thanks largely to the adapting and continuing functioning of the *hukou* system.[103]

The *hukou* reforms in the PRC so far have been chiefly motivated by political concerns rather than by ethical considerations. The reforms have not even mentioned, let alone altered, the sociopolitical control functions of the system. In fact, in order to strengthen the increasingly useful but gradually ineffective "original role" of the *hukou* system to control the Chinese people in an era of great changes and uncertainties, Beijing has attempted to reform the *hukou* system almost exclusively by reducing and eventually "shedding" its expensive add-on functions of internal migration control and resource allocation. There has also been a clear development of localizing the function of the *hukou* system as floodgates to keep the rural majority out. Variations in entry conditions and in effectiveness of migration control across the regions have allowed local governments substantial power to exclude peasants and other "outsiders" while extracting as much as possible from them in the form of land, cheap labor, and savings and investment. The effectiveness of the latest *hukou* reforms is yet to be fully seen. But it is already clear that the renovation of China's great floodgate has been tightly controlled, localized, gradual, and incomplete. The actual enforcement of reform proposals varies greatly across regions.

Hukou Reform and the Rural-Urban Gap

The *hukou* system has been historically responsible for the creation and maintenance of China's rural-urban gap. Yet it seems clear that a removal of the system now may do little to bridge that gap without comprehensive reforms of many other aspects of the Chinese political economy. So far, other than relaxing some internal migration controls to give mobility to the rich and the educated as well as manual labor as needed, the main thrust of the *hukou* reform has been to rename the contentious rural versus urban categorization. However, it is the location, rather than categorization, of one's *hukou* that matters more now. The key distinction between permanent local (*changzhu*) *hukou* and temporary (*zhanzhu*) or outside (*wailai*) *hukou* now determines the vastly varied social status, rights, and benefits of the divided Chinese, rural or urban alike.

The majority of Chinese still have *hukou* located outside the prosperous urban centers, including the now-estimated 140 to 160 million migrants, or "floating population," who currently reside in cities.[104] They may soon be all recategorized as "residents" in their *hukou* files and on their personal identification cards but still be unable to change the location of their *hukou* permanently without official approval, now increasingly based on the migrant's net worth, education, and job prospects. In Ningbo of Zhejiang Province, a national model of *hukou* reform, only about 30,000 migrants, less than 2 percent of the 2 million migrants from the countryside (who constitute one-third of the city's total population) were expected to qualify for local *hukou* in the 2001 reform.[105] In Shijiazhuang of Hebei Province, only 11,000 migrant workers (out of 300,000 in the city) were qualified to apply for local *hukou* in 2001. By 2003 fewer than 20,000 qualified.[106] No matter how much hype is put out about how deeply the reforms are developing, as long as the sociopolitical control function of the *hukou* system is valued and maintained so that the change of one's permanent location must still be approved by the government, China's rural-urban gap will at most be affected only marginally.

A general scarcity of resources and a historical monopoly of political power by the CCP elite living in major urban centers have rendered officially launched *hukou* reform simply incapable of seriously addressing the rural-urban gap in the PRC. In 2005 a typical Chinese migrant worker from a rural area was required to pay about 10 percent of his or her annual income to obtain and carry all the *hukou*-related papers (a total of a dozen cards in most cities) so as not to be caught as an illegal. Nearly half of the migrant workers worked twelve to sixteen hours every day with no weekends off. In the prosperous Pearl River Delta, migrants only had about a 10 percent increase in average wages in the past twelve years, while the local economy had grown by nearly 20 percent every year in that same period.[107]

In addition, *hukou* reforms have actually brought new problems to exacerbate the Chinese rural-urban gap. A clear internal brain drain and capital drain have developed, as massive funds and talents are lured to the cities and become even more unevenly concentrated in just a few major urban centers. In Guangzhou in 2006, "286 graduates and postgraduates vied for 11 positions as street cleaners. In the end, one PhD, four master's degree, and six bachelor degree holders were recruited after heated competition."[108] The various "entry conditions" that have now become the main barriers to internal migration, sanctioned by the "reformed" *hukou* system, have created localized, regionalized, but uniformly enforced discrimination against the poor, uneducated, and rural migrants. The reforming *hukou* system has become a giant pump that ceaselessly sucks talents and resources away from the excluded rural areas and smaller, more remote cities.[109] The *hukou* reform has thus created different fault lines between the rural and urban populations at different places as the great floodgate's water level now varies across the country. While this may extend the life of the *hukou* system for sociopolitical control purposes, it simply hides the rural-urban divide in the divisions and discriminations along the numerous fault lines among regions, cities, and villages.

China's rural-urban gap will not go away by decreed changes in the name of a *hukou* category. What is needed is a new politics of flood control that will allow a dual economy to grow fast, mainly in the privileged urban sector, while effectively and reliably narrowing the rural-urban gap, something the CCP-dominated, urban-based PRC ruling elite appears to be uninterested and unable to do. The much-criticized and hated rural-urban categorization is likely to fade away. But all indications are that the increasingly localized discrimination against the rural population will continue. This is indeed a major indicator and result of China's stuck political reform that is still accumulating mounting governance deficits.[110]

To manage China's rural-urban gap without drowning the prosperous urban centers or causing uncontrollable social disorder calls for good renovation and utilization of the *hukou* system, the crumbling but still highly crucial great floodgate. Yet this will require a great deal more to change than what has been decreed or promised.[111] Unless and until the Chinese people, especially those in the rural areas and in the excluded small or remote cities, can genuinely empower themselves with sufficient information, self-organization, and political participation—things that are possible only under a rule of law with free media—the official reforms of the *hukou* system are unlikely to narrow China's ever-enlarging rural-urban gap. This is a high-stakes political game, but the Chinese rural population is systematically and utterly suppressed and remains politically powerless. The *hukou* system, therefore, is likely to continue to organize the Chinese people through division and exclusion, functioning as a great floodgate and a powerful pump to perpetuate and expand rural-urban disparities.

Notes

Contributors

Notes

1. The Paradoxes of Rural-Urban Inequality in Contemporary China

1. Past studies of note on these topics include Rhoads Murphey, *The Fading of the Maoist Vision: City and Country in China's Development* (New York: Methuen, 1980); Sulamith Potter, "The Position of Peasants in Modern China's Social Order," *Modern China* 9 (1993): 465–499; Mark Selden, "City versus Countryside? The Social Consequences of Development Choices in China," in Mark Selden, ed., *The Political Economy of Chinese Socialism* (Armonk, NY: M. E. Sharpe, 1988); Kam Wing Chan, *Cities with Invisible Walls* (New York: Oxford University Press, 1994); Dorothy Solinger, *Contesting Citizenship in Urban China: Peasant Migrants, the State, and the Logic of the Market* (Berkeley: Univ. of California Press, 1999); and Fei-ling Wang, *Organizing through Division and Exclusion: China's Hukou System* (Stanford, CA: Stanford Univ. Press, 2005).

2. Although the Chinese Communist Party gained national political power in 1949, they preserved a mixed and predominantly petty capitalist economy until the socialist transformation campaign was launched in 1955, so that a centrally planned socialist system was not fully in place until 1956. By the same token, although the launching of market reforms and the dismantling of the institutions of centrally planned socialism began in 1978, this second social revolution was implemented in gradual stages, so that China did not achieve a primarily market-oriented and therefore de facto capitalist economy until the latter half of the 1990s. Note that the Cultural Revolution launched in 1966 is not treated here as a comparable, third social revolution, because for all of its disruption and tumult, the institutional changes introduced were much more limited and temporary than either the changes of 1955–1956 or those after 1978.

3. Revisionism—that is, revising Marxism—was the political epithet used by Chinese polemicists in the 1960s and 1970s to claim that the USSR was only nominally socialist but under the surface little different from a capitalist society; they

based this claim on the fact that patterns of income distribution, inequalities, and incentives in the USSR were similar to those found in the United States and other advanced capitalist societies. Western scholarship generally agrees with Mao on this point, arguing that the imperatives of industrialization created similar patterns of inequality in advanced socialist and capitalist societies. See, for example, Walter Connor, *Socialism, Politics, and Equality* (New York: Columbia Univ. Press, 1979); Gerhard Lenski, "New Light on Old Issues: The Relevance of 'Really Existing Socialist Societies' for Stratification Theory," in David Grusky, ed., *Social Stratification: Class, Race, and Gender in Sociological Perspective* (Boulder, CO: Westview, 1994). (Of course, Western analysts do not share Mao's faith that there could be a modern industrial society with much less social inequality.)

4. China's critics in the Soviet Union and Eastern Europe contended that it was China rather than they that was being "revisionist," because socialism is supposed to involve distribution of wages and other rewards according to contributions to society, rather than equally or according to need. Indeed, one team of Polish sociologists contended that a socialist society was and should be more genuinely meritocratic than a capitalist society. See W. Weselowski and T. Krauze, "Socialist Society and the Meritocratic Principle of Remuneration," in G. Berreman, ed., *Social Inequality: Comparative and Developmental Approaches* (New York: Academic Press, 1981).

5. The leadership team of Hu Jintao and Wen Jiabao that took over in 2002–2003 has voiced much more concern about inequality than that of its predecessors, Deng Xiaoping and Jiang Zemin, and it has begun implementing a number of new policy initiatives to address the problem, some of which are described later in this chapter and in subsequent chapters.

6. See Azizur Khan and Carl Riskin, *Inequality and Poverty in China in the Age of Globalization* (New York: Oxford Univ. Press, 2001); Azizur Khan and Carl Riskin, "China's Household Income Distribution, 1995 and 2002," *China Quarterly* 192 (2005): 356–384; and Björn Gustafsson, Li Shi, and Terry Sicular, eds., *Inequality and Public Policy in China* (New York: Cambridge Univ. Press, 2008).

7. The terms "state socialism" and "centrally planned socialism" refer to the USSR and its Eastern European satellites, China under Mao, and other societies that eliminated all private ownership of productive resources and enterprises. Other societies that are sometimes referred to as socialist, such as Tanzania or India in the 1970s, Scandinavia, and even Great Britain, still possess substantial and even dominant private ownership and market distribution and do not fit the patterns described here.

8. For theoretical statements of how socialism in practice promotes inequality rather than equality, see Milovan Djilas, *The New Class* (New York: Praeger, 1957); Ivan Szelenyi, *Urban Inequalities under State Socialism* (New York: Oxford Univ. Press, 1983). Given the jaundiced views that Marx had about peasants and rural life and the strong urban-industrial bias of planners in socialist societies generally, it should come as no surprise that, whatever is said about rural residents in regime slogans, in practice they have been exploited and neglected in socialist societies.

9. It would make a more appealing and even more paradoxical story if we could report that China's shift to market distribution since 1978 has led to a systematic *reduction* of rural-urban inequality in China, contrary to the conventional account, which associates markets with inequality. However, the reality is too complex to support such a simple generalization. See the discussion in Martin Whyte, "Social Trends in China: The Triumph of Inequality?" in A. Barnett and R. Clough, eds., *Modernizing China* (Boulder, CO: Westview, 1986); and Ivan Szelenyi and Eric Kostello, "The Market Transition Debate: Toward a Synthesis?" *American Journal of Sociology* 101 (1996): 1082–1096.

10. See, for example, the discussion in Victor Nee, "A Theory of Market Transition: From Redistribution to Markets in State Socialism," *American Sociological Review* 54 (1989): 663–681; and Victor Nee, "The Emergence of a Market Society: Changing Mechanisms of Stratification in China," *American Journal of Sociology* 101 (1996): 908–949.

11. See the discussion of the workings of the class label system in the Mao era in Richard Kraus, *Class Conflict in Chinese Socialism* (New York: Columbia Univ. Press, 1981); Elisabeth Croll, *The Politics of Marriage in Contemporary China* (New York: Cambridge Univ. Press, 1981).

12. The claim here is only that class labels of the past no longer play an important role in influencing individual opportunities. However, the legacy of that system in the Mao era, involving pervasive discrimination for two decades against those with "bad class" labels, produced educational, occupational, and even marriage deficits for the targeted groups and individuals that many have not been able to overcome to this day. I thank Ralph Thaxton for pointing out to me the important distinction between the labels no longer mattering versus those who bore the labels in many ways still being disadvantaged.

13. There is an abundance of literature on a strong cultural tradition of native-place psychology among Chinese migrants and the continuing role of native places and native-place associations in organizing social life in pre-1949 Chinese cities, characteristics some claim inhibited the development of a general sense of urban citizenship or class identification in China compared with Western societies. See, for example, G. William Skinner, "Mobility Strategies in Late Imperial China," in C. Smith, ed., *Regional Analysis*, vol. I (New York: Academic Press, 1976); Sybille van der Sprenkel, "Urban Social Control," in G. W. Skinner, ed., *The City in Late Imperial China* (Stanford, CA: Stanford Univ. Press, 1977); William Rowe, *Hankow: Conflict and Community in a Chinese City, 1796–1895* (Stanford, CA: Stanford Univ. Press, 1989); and David Strand, *Rickshaw Beijing: City People and Politics in the 1920s* (Berkeley: Univ. of California Press, 1989).

14. T. Cheng and M. Selden, "The Origins and Social Consequences of China's *Hukou* System," *China Quarterly* 139 (1994): 646–668.

15. The "invisible wall" phrase comes from Chan, *Cities with Invisible Walls*. For evidence on the sharp reductions over time in the rural origins of residents of one large city during the Mao era (Chengdu, Sichuan), see Martin Whyte, "Adaptation of Rural Family Patterns to Urban Life in Chengdu," in G. Guldin and A. Southall, eds., *Urban Anthropology in China* (Leiden: E. J. Brill, 1993).

16. To be sure, urban bias is a pervasive phenomenon in developing societies in which political elites—who reside and raise their children in the cities—tend to systematically favor cities and urban development over the countryside. On the general phenomenon, see Michael Lipton, *Why Poor People Stay Poor* (Cambridge, MA: Harvard Univ. Press, 1977). However, it could be argued that state socialist societies are even more biased toward urban areas than developing capitalist societies and that China in the Mao era displayed especially extreme forms of urban bias, despite official slogans such as "agriculture first" and "industry should serve agriculture."

17. Urban China differed from the Soviet Union in having more total bureaucratic allocation of labor and inability of individuals to change jobs. See the discussion and comparative figures in Barry Naughton, "*Danwei:* The Economic Foundations of a Unique Institution," in Xiaobo Lu and Elizabeth Perry, eds., *Danwei: The Changing Chinese Workplace in Historical and Comparative Perspective* (Armonk, NY: M. E. Sharpe, 1997). During the Mao era, there was a major effort to redistribute resources and funds from already developed to less-developed parts of the economy, typified by withdrawal of resources from China's largest and richest city, Shanghai (see Nicholas Lardy, *Economic Growth and Distribution in China* [New York: Cambridge Univ. Press, 1978]). However, the redistributed resources were used overwhelmingly to invest in industrial growth in smaller and newer cities in China's interior and even in industrial complexes located in remote mountain areas (as in the "third" front campaign of the 1960s—see Barry Naughton, "The Third Front: Defence Industrialization in the Chinese Interior," *China Quarterly* 115 [1988]: 351–386), rather than in agriculture or rural development (see the discussion in Nicholas Lardy, "State Intervention and Peasant Opportunities," in William Parish, ed., *Chinese Rural Development* [Armonk, NY: M. E. Sharpe, 1985]).

18. What other developing society has seen its largest city shrink in population over time? That is what happened to Shanghai, which had more than 7 million people in 1957 and only about 6 million in 1973. See Christopher Howe, *Shanghai: Revolution and Development in an Asian Metropolis* (New York: Cambridge Univ. Press, 1981).

19. See Solinger, *Contesting Citizenship in Urban China*. Access to these benefits was not equal within the urban population, however. Some of these public goods were available only to the roughly four out of five adults employed in state-owned (rather than urban collective) enterprises, and even within the state sector, those employed in or connected with high-priority firms managed at high levels of the

bureaucratic system generally received better treatment than others. See the discussion in Andrew Walder, "The Remaking of the Chinese Working Class, 1949–1981," *Modern China* 10 (1984): 3–48; and Yanjie Bian, *Work and Inequality in Urban China* (Albany: SUNY Press, 1994).

20. However, certain categories of rural residents—those employed on China's limited number of state farms, as well as certain local officials, teachers, and medical personnel—were classified as state employees and/or nonagricultural population, and they were thus entitled to treatment more comparable to the urban population.

21. Bureaucratic control over prices and the use of price differentials were also the primary means of extracting low-cost agricultural products to feed urban residents in the Soviet Union. When China's agriculture was collectivized in 1955–1956, the resulting collective farms were termed "agricultural producers' cooperatives" (APCs). In 1958, as part of the Great Leap Forward, the APCs were merged into much larger units called "rural people's communes." After the collapse of the Leap, communes were reorganized into somewhat smaller units, but the commune was retained as China's form of collectivization until the decollectivization that was carried out in the early 1980s.

22. On China's green revolution, see Benedict Stavis, *Making Green Revolution: The Politics of Agricultural Development in China* (Ithaca, NY: Cornell University Development Committee, 1974). For state restrictions on crop diversification in the 1970s, see Lardy, "State Intervention and Peasant Opportunities." On the Great Leap famine and its aftermath, see Dali Yang, *Calamity and Reform in China: State, Rural Society and Institutional Change since the Great Leap Famine* (Stanford, CA: Stanford Univ. Press, 1996). On the general difficulties of agricultural development in the Mao era, see Nicholas Lardy, *Agriculture in China's Modern Economic Development* (New York: Cambridge Univ. Press, 1983); and Robert Ash, "Squeezing the Peasants: Grain Extraction, Food Consumption, and Rural Living Standards in Mao's China," *China Quarterly* 188 (2006): 959–998.

23. See the discussion of how the *hukou* system worked at the grass roots in Potter, "The Position of Peasants." After 1998, new regulations allowed an individual to claim the registration status of either his or her father or mother. See the discussion in Chapter 15 later in this volume.

24. Over the years the People's Liberation Army relied heavily on rural recruitment. Unlike officers, enlisted personnel were supposed to return to their original residences and *hukou* when their service was completed, even if they had been serving in an urban location. However, the additional training and skills acquired in the military often led to leadership or other specialized roles back in the village, rather than a return to life as an ordinary farmer.

25. There are some exceptions to these generalizations. The unpopularity of the program that sent between 17 and 18 million urban educated youths to settle in

the countryside in the decade after 1968 led to a change in the rules, so that youths sent down after about 1973 were promised a return to their cities of origin and a recovery of their registration status in that city if they had spent a designated number of years (often three) laboring in agriculture. See the account of this program in Thomas Bernstein, *Up to the Mountains and Down to the Villages: The Transfer of Youth from Urban to Rural China* (New Haven, CT: Yale Univ. Press, 1977).

26. When urban educated youths were forcibly resettled in rural villages, the state provide a one-time "settling down fee" that was supposed to ease the financial burden on the receiving villages. It was assumed that over time the rusticated youths would acquire farming skills and become contributors to, rather than drains on, village economies. However, given the poor preparation of most urban youths and the substantial morale problems involved in rural resettlement, it is questionable how often this optimistic scenario was fulfilled.

27. One exception to this generalization is that some urban employers, particularly factories, could request permission to hire temporary, contract laborers to meet short-term fluctuations in production activity. In some cases they could recruit such temporary workers from rural locales (see Solinger, *Contesting Citizenship in Urban China*, 39–40). For accounts of the systems of urban rationing and controls of other essentials during the Mao period, see Lynn White, *Careers in Shanghai* (Berkeley: Univ. of California Press, 1978), Chap. 4; and Martin Whyte and William Parish, *Urban Life in Contemporary China* (Chicago: The Univ. of Chicago Press, 1984), Chap. 4.

28. Short-term visits were possible, such as on business assignments or to visit relatives, with the proper travel papers and after converting grain or local grain-ration coupons to the provincial or national grain-ration coupons required to purchase food in the destination city. People who managed to stay in a place where they were not registered were referred to as "black people, black households" *(heiren heihu)*. The main instance of this occurring on any scale involved urban youths who had been sent down to the countryside in the mass campaign after 1968 who sneaked back and stayed with family or friends. In these cases they might prevail on their hosts to share ration coupons and food in order to evade the system, but even so, the black market, theft, and other shady activities to which some youths resorted in order to survive contributed to a sense of declining urban social order in the 1970s (see Martin Whyte, "Social Control and Rehabilitation in Urban China," in S. Martin et al., eds., *New Directions in the Rehabilitation of Criminal Offenders* [Washington, DC: National Academy Press, 1981]).

29. A long-overdue increase in the state procurement prices paid to farmers for their obligatory grain deliveries in 1979 also contributed to the shrinking of the rural-urban income gap in the early 1980s.

30. See the evidence presented in Martin Whyte, "City versus Countryside in China's Development," *Problems of Post-Communism* 43 (1996): 9–22. For data on more

recent trends in the rural-urban gap in schooling and in health care, see Chapters 6 and 7 below.

31. Important studies of the situation of migrants in China's cities include Li Zhang, *Strangers in the City* (Stanford, CA: Stanford Univ. Press, 2001); Daniel Wright, "Hey, Coolie!" in Daniel Wright, *The Promise of the Revolution* (Lanham, MD: Rowman & Littlefield, 2003); Arianne Gaetano and Tamara Jacka, eds., *On the Move: Women and Rural-to-Urban Migration in Contemporary China* (New York: Columbia Univ. Press, 2004); and Pun Ngai, *Made in China: Subject, Power, and Resistance in the Global Workplace* (Durham, NC: Duke Univ. Press, 2005).

32. A sociologist in China, Li Qiang, has arrived at a similar formulation, viewing China's population as divided into three distinct castes: rural residents, migrants, and urban residents. See Li Qiang, *Nongmin Gong yu Zhongguo Shehui Fenceng* [Migrant workers and China's social stratification] (Beijing: Social Science Academy Press, 2004). (My thanks to Yang Yu, who alerted me to this source.)

33. After a widely publicized incident in 2003 involving the death of a migrant in detention, new regulations were passed designed to minimize such abuses, although in this volume's Chapter 15 Fei-ling Wang raises questions about how effective these changes have been. Migrants are supposed to register with a local police station if they are staying for more than three days in their destination city, and they must apply for temporary household registration if they are staying longer than a month, but these requirements are unevenly enforced, and it has been estimated that fewer than half of the migrants present in the city are officially registered in this manner. On the working-condition abuses suffered by many migrants, see Anita Chan, *China's Workers under Assault* (Armonk, NY: M. E. Sharpe, 2001). For an account of the bulldozing of one well-known migrant settlement ("Zhejiang Village" on the outskirts of Beijing), see Li Zhang, *Strangers in the City*.

34. One study states, "even the impoverished, academically unsuccessful urban Chinese [youths] . . . tended not to think about themselves as part of a lower class because they, like most urban Chinese citizens, saw themselves as united with urban citizens of all classes in a superior urban citizenship category defined by its opposition to an inferior rural citizenship category." Vanessa Fong, "Morality, Cosmopolitanism, or Academic Attainment? Discourse on 'Quality' and Urban Chinese-Only-Children's Claims to Ideal Personhood," *City and Society* 19 (2007): 87.

35. China's institutionalized discrimination against migrants has been criticized as a major human rights abuse. See Human Rights in China, *Institutionalized Exclusion: The Tenuous Legal Status of Internal Migrants in China's Major Cities* (New York: Human Rights in China, 2002). For comparisons with undocumented aliens in the United States, see Kenneth Roberts, "China's 'Tidal Wave' of Migrant Labor: What Can We Learn from Mexican Undocumented Migration to

the United States?", *International Migration Review* 31 (1997): 249–293. For comparisons with the apartheid regime in South Africa, see Peter Alexander and Anita Chan, "Does China Have an Apartheid Pass System?", *Journal of Ethnic and Migration Studies* 30 (2004): 609–629.

36. In recent years authorities in many cities have experimented with abolishing the distinction between agricultural and nonagricultural *hukou*. However, they maintain the legal distinction between local resident *hukou* and outsiders. This change does not help rural migrants, because they remain consigned to the inferior caste position as outsiders and cannot readily obtain local resident *hukou* status even if they have lived in the city for many years.

37. See the figures in Barry Naughton, *The Chinese Economy: Transitions and Growth* (Cambridge, MA: MIT Press, 2007), 182. Urban population statistics in China involve multiple complexities and puzzles—particularly the fact that official city size statistics are affected by administrative boundary changes and the variable inclusion of large rural areas within city administrative jurisdictions and not solely by the natural increase of the existing urban population and rural-urban migration. Because experts engage in heated debates about what constitutes the most meaningful figures for the urban population proportion at any point in time, we will be content here with these "ballpark" urban population estimates.

38. Rachel Murphy, *How Migrant Labor Is Changing Rural China* (New York: Cambridge Univ. Press, 2002).

39. Villages that had successful business enterprises could tax the profits of such businesses to meet these local expenses, thus reducing the need to dun village families with extra fees. Because such enterprises were concentrated in China's coastal provinces, the burden problem seems to have been most severe in interior provinces (see the discussion in Thomas Bernstein and Xiaobo Lu, *Taxation without Representation in Rural China* [New York: Cambridge Univ. Press, 2003]).

40. During the Mao era, there was some emphasis on the development of rural industry. However, the goal of such village factories was to meet rural needs for cement, farm tools, fertilizer, and other agriculture-related products, not to produce for the domestic or foreign market or to augment village incomes. As such, the employment and other impacts of the village factories were limited before the reform era (see American Rural Small-Scale Industry Delegation, *Rural Small-Scale Industry in the People's Republic of China* [Berkeley: Univ. of California Press, 1977]). The recent estimates of TVE employment come from Naughton, *The Chinese Economy*, 286.

41. Deng did not hold the top formal position in the CCP during this period (with the successive incumbents in that post being Hua Guofeng, Hu Yaobang, and then Zhao Ziyang), but nonetheless he was in effective command of the Chinese political system (even as late as 1992, when his "Southern tour" of Shenzhen and

other growth centers set off a new round of market reforms and economic growth).

42. On the campaign to open up the West, see David Goodman, *China's Campaign to 'Open up the West': National, Provincial, and Local Perspectives* (New York: Cambridge Univ. Press, 2004). For initial steps to tackle the "burden problem," see Bernstein and Lu, *Taxation without Representation*. The effort to reduce the rural tax and fee burden already has had considerable impact, according to the data in a national survey I directed in China in 2004. About 70 percent of the rural respondents in that survey replied that there had been some or substantial reduction in the taxes and fees they paid compared with three years earlier.

43. The *dibao* system is a very modest minimum income program in which the urban poor receive cash subsidies from local governments. See Wang Meiyan, "Emerging Urban Poverty and the Effects of the *Dibao* Program on Alleviating Poverty in China," *China and the World Economy* 15 (2007): 74–88.

44. In one of the most recent examples of these efforts, in August 2008 the Ministry of Education proclaimed that central government funds would be provided to urban schools to pay for the expenses of enrolling and educating migrant children in an effort to advance the long-proclaimed but frequently thwarted goal of giving children of urban migrant workers the same educational opportunities that urban children have. See "Free Schooling for Migrant Kids," *China Daily*, August 27, 2008.

45. Wang, *Organizing through Division and Exclusion*.

2. Small-Town China

1. The idea of a rural-urban continuum was first applied to Chinese history in the monumental volume edited by G. William Skinner, *The City in Late Imperial China* (Stanford, CA: Stanford University Press, 1977); see the chapters by F. W. Mote, "The Transformation of Nanking," 102–103, G. William Skinner, "Introduction: Urban and Rural in Chinese Society," 258–261, and Sybille van Der Sprenkel, "Urban Social Control," 609. As a related piece of evidence, a demographic study by Liu Ts'ui-jung (Liu Cuirong) on the lower Yangzi River valley during the Ming-Qing period finds that except for slightly higher remarriage and polygamy rates among urban males, there were few differences between urban and rural societies in terms of marital fertility, mortality, and contraceptive behavior; see Liu Cuirong, *Mingqing shiqi Changjiang xiayou diqu dushihua zhi fazhan yu renkou tezheng* [Urban development and demographic characters in the lower Yangzi River valley during the Ming-Qing period], in Liang Gengyao and Liu Shufen, eds., *Chengshi yu xiangcun* [City and countryside] (Beijing: Zhongguo dabaike quanshu chubanshe, 2005), 247–285 (reprint of a 1986 article).

2. See Wilt Idema, "Putting Peasants in Their Place," paper presented at the international conference on "Rethinking the Rural-Urban Cleavage in Contemporary China," Harvard University, October 6–8, 2006.

3. Historian Mark Elvin once summarized the situation: "The city was in some respects feared by peasants. One Ch'ing [Qing] official wrote that 'country-folks are terrified to enter their county capital, dreading the officials as if they were tigers.' The city was a place where taxes and rents were often paid, and where lawsuits were tried. It was the haunt of criminals such as the 'market bullies' who were experts at victimizing peasants. In times of famine, it was in the city that farmers sold starving children whom they could no longer feed." See Mark Elvin, "Chinese Cities since the Sung Dynasty," in Philip Abrams and E. A. Wrigley, eds., *Towns in Societies: Essays in Economic History and Historical Sociology* (Cambridge: Cambridge University Press, 1978), 79–89. One may also add that Chinese literature was full of praise for the pastoral lifestyle and both Confucian statecraft and Taoist idealism were essentially rural oriented.

4. Following are a few major works in Chinese on small towns in the Jiangnan or Yangzi delta region in late imperial times: Fu Yiling, *Mingdai Jiangnan shimin jingji shitan* [A preliminary study on the economy of the townspeople in Jiangnan during the Ming dynasty] (Shanghai: Shanghai renmin, 1957); Liu Shiji, *Ming Qing shidai Jiangnan shizhen yanjiu* [A study of market towns in Jiangnan during the Ming-Qing period] (Beijing: Zhongguo shehui kexue chubanshe, 1987); Zhao Gang, *Zhongguo chengshi fazhan shi lunji* [A collection of essays on the history of urban development in China] (Taipei: Lianjing, 1995); Fan Shuzhi, *Ming Qing Jiangnan shizhen tanwei* [Research on market towns in the Ming-Qing period] (Shanghai: Fudan Unversity Press, 1990) and *Jiangnan shizhen: chuantong de bianqe* [Market towns in Jiangnan: Changing tradition] (Shanghai: Fudan University Press, 2005), which is an enlarged version of Fan's 1990 book; Chen Xuewen, *Ming Qing shiqi Hang Jia Hu shizhen shi yanjiu* [Research on the history of market towns in the Hang-Jia-Hu region during the Ming-Qing period] (Beijing: Qunyan chubanshe, 1993); Fan Jinmin, *Ming Qing Jiangnan shangye de fazhan* [Commercial development in Jiangnan during the Ming-Qing period] (Nanjing: Nanjing University Press); Bao Weimin, *Jiangnan shizhen jiqi jindai mingyun* [Jiangnian small towns and their modern fate] (Beijing: Zhishi chubanshe, 1998); and Li Bozhong, *Jiangnan de zaoqi gongyehua, 1550–1850* [Early industrialization in Jiangnan, 1550–1850] (Beijing: Shehui kexue wenxian chubanshe, 2000). For an informative study on Japanese scholarship related to small towns in late imperial China, see Linda Grove and Christian Daniels, eds., *State and Society in China: Japanese Perspectives on Ming-Qing Social and Economic History* (Tokyo: University of Tokyo Press, 1984).

5. Mary Clabaugh Wright, *The Last Stand of Chinese Conservatism: The T'ung-Chih Restoration, 1862–1874* (Stanford, CA: Stanford University Press, 1957).

6. Gilbert Rozman, *Urban Networks in Ch'ing China and Tokugawa Japan* (Princeton, NJ: Princeton University Press, 1974), 31.

7. G. William Skinner, "Cities and the Hierarchy of Local Systems," in *The City in Late Imperial China* (Stanford, CA: Stanford University Press, 1977), 287.

8. For a discussion on population and urban communities in pre-1949 China, see Hsiao-tung Fei, *China's Gentry: Essays on Rural-Urban Relations* (Chicago: University of Chicago Press, 1968), 91–107.

9. Zhang Yungao, comp., *Baoshan xian xu zhi* [Supplementary county gazetteer of Baoshan] (1921), vol. 1: 178.

10. Liu Dajun, *Wuxing nongchun jingji* [Rural economy of Wuxing] (N.p.: Zhongguo jingji tongji yanjiusuo, 1928), 122.

11. Fan Shuzhi, *Jiangnan shizhen* [Market towns in Jiangnan] (Shanghai: Fudan University Press, 2005), 512.

12. Zhao Gang, *Zhongguo chengshi fazhan shi lunji* [Essays on urban development in China] (Taipei: Lianjing chubanshe, 1995), 140–142.

13. Fei Xiaotong, *Lun xiaochengzhen ji qita* [Essays on small towns and other issues] (Tianjin: Tianjin renmin chubanshe, 1986), 18.

14. http://www.chinanews.com.cn/2003-10-19/358685.html.

15. *Nanxun zhenzhi* bianzuan weiyuanhui, comp., *Nanxun zhenzhi* [Gazetteer of Nanxun] (Shanghai: Shanghai kexue jishu chubanshe, 1995), 85–86.

16. Liu Dajun, *Wuxing nongchun jingji.*

17. *Nanxun zhenzhi*, 33.

18. *Nanxun zhenzhi*, 283.

19. Philip C. C. Huang, *The Peasant Family and Rural Development in the Yangzi Delta, 1350–1988* (Stanford, CA: Stanford University Press, 1990), 48.

20. Among the most prosperous towns in the Yangzi delta region were the "cotton towns" (for example, Zhujin, Fengjin, Qibao, Zhujiajiao, Nanxiang, Luodian, Waigang, and Zhouzhuang), "silk towns" (for example, Shengze, Puyuan, Wang Jiangjing, Wangdian, and Shuanglin), and "rice towns" (for example, Pingwang, Chang'an, Xiashi, and Hushu). See Fan Shuzhi, *Jiangnan shizhen,* Chaps. 3–5.

21. See, for example, the recent debate on Kenneth Pomeranz's *The Great Divergence: China, Europe, and the Making of the Modern World Economy* (Princeton, NJ: Princeton University Press, 1999) regarding development and underdevelopment in the lower Yangzi region in *Journal of Asian Studies* 61, no. 2 (May 2002): 501–662.

22. See for example, Hanchao Lu, "Arrested Development: Cotton and Cotton Markets in Shanghai, 1350–1843," *Modern China* 18 (1992): 468–499.

23. The proportion of small-town residents in China's total urban population was considerably larger than that in Japan and England. In the nineteenth century, 74 percent of the British urban population lived in large or medium-sized cities, as did 71 percent in Japan, compared with 49 percent in China; see Zhao Gang, *Zhongguo chengshi fazhan shilun,* 140–142.

24. Fei Xiaotong, *Lun xiao chengzhen ji qita,* 20–21.

25. Bao Weimin, *Jiangnan shizhen jiqi jindai mingyun,* 240.

26. Among the best-known groups in this category were the Anhui (Hui) merchants in the salt business and the Shanxi (Jin) merchants in the credit or money exchange business.

27. Chung-li Chang, *The Chinese Gentry: Studies on Their Role in Nineteenth-century Chinese Society* (Seattle: University of Washington Press, 1955), 51.

28. Duara, Prasenjit. *Culture, Power, and the State: Rural North China, 1900–1942* (Stanford, CA: Stanford University Press, 1988), 15–16.

29. Yang Xiaomin, *Huishang* [The Anhui merchants] (Beijing: Remin wenxue chubanshe, 2006), 115. The saying, which has a couple of versions, originally appeared in volume 129 of Sima Qian's classic, *Shiji* [Historical records] (Hangzhou: Zhejiang guji chubanshe, 2000), 987.

30. Lien-sheng Yang, "Economic Justification for Spending: An Uncommon Idea in Traditional China," *Harvard Journal of Asiatic Studies* 20 (1957): 36–52.

31. Fan Shuzhi, *Jiangnan shizhen*, 29, quoting Gu, *Xiaoxia xianji zaichao.*

32. Antonia Finnane, *Speaking of Yangzhou: A Chinese City, 1550–1850* (Cambridge, MA: Harvard University East Asia Center, 2004), 239.

33. For a glimpse of a Huizhou-style house, see Nancy Berliner, *Yin Yu Tang: The Architecture and Daily Life of a Chinese House* (Boston: Tuttle Publishing, 2003), Chap. 3, and Yang Xiaomin, *Huishang*, 103–126.

34. *Jinshang* [The Jin Merchants] (A pamphlet published by Zhongguo qingshaonian yinxiang chubanshe, n.d.), 28, 39. The Qian Courtyard was the site where a 1991 movie, *Raise the Red Lantern* directed by Zhang Yimou, was shot.

35. Zhang Jianzhi, *Jiaye Nanxun* [Hometown Nanxun] (Nanjing: Jiangsu jiaoyu chubanshe, 2003), 130.

36. For example, a recent book series on China's surviving ancient towns *(guzhen)* lists 190 popular small towns that currently attract tourists for their fine preservation of traditional houses and urban layout. See Zhongguo guzhen you bianjibu, comp., *Zhongguo guzhen you* [Tourism in Chinese ancient towns] (Xian: Shaanxi Normal University Press, 2003).

37. Tobie Meyer-Fong, *Building Culture in Early Qing Yangzhou* (Stanford, CA: Stanford University Press, 2003), 2, 182–183.

38. Zhou Qingyun, comp., *Nanxun zhi* [Gazetteer of Nanxun] (1922), vols. 9–11.

39. *Nanxun Liushi zhipu* [A genealogy of the Liu lineage in Nanxun], vol. 5: 40–42.

40. Lu Xu, *Lu Xun zawen shuxin xuan* [A selected collection of Lu Xun's essays and letters] (Fuzhou: Fujian renmin chubanshe, 1972), 255; and Lu Xun, *Lu Xun quanji* [A completed collection of the works of Lu Xun] (Beijing: Renmin wenxue chubanshe, 1981), vol. 6: 168.

41. *Nanxun zhenzhi*, 244–247.

42. The fieldwork of Fan Shuzhi, see Fan, *Jiangnan shizhen*, 185.

43. Kawakatsu Mamoru, *Min Shin Kōnan shichin shakai shi kenkyū* [Social history of market towns in the lower Yangzi Delta during the Ming and Qing periods] (Tokyo: Kyuko Shoin, 1999), 203–216.

44. Xu Chi, *Jiangnan xiaozhen* [A Jiangnan small town] (Beijing: Zuojia chubanshe, 1993), 606.

45. The line is from a Yuan dynasty poem titled "Autumn Musings" *(Qiusi)*, written by poet and dramatist Ma Zhiyuan (ca. 1250–1324). The translation is mine.

46. Yu Dafu, *Yu Dafa wenji* [Collection of the works of Yu Dafu] (Guangzhou: Huacheng chubanshe, 1982), vol. 4: 27.

47. Feng Zikai, *Yuanyuan Tang suibi ji* [Essays from the Yuanyuan Studies] (Hangzhou: Zhejiang wenyi chubanshe, 1983), 492–497.

48. Feng Zikai, *Yuanyuan Tang suibi ji*, 409.

49. Feng Zikai, *Feng Zikai wenji* [Collection of the works of Feng Zikai] (Hangzhou: Zhejiang wenyi chubanshe, 1990), vol. 6: 122.

50. Ibid., 125–126.

51. See Hanchao Lu, *Beyond the Neon Lights* (Berkeley: University of California Press, 1999), Chaps. 4–6; and Hanchao Lu, "Away from Nanking Road: Small Stores and Neighborhood Life in Modern Shanghai," *Journal of Asian Studies* 54 (1995): 92–123.

52. Feng Zikai, *Yuanyuan Tang suibi ji*, 139.

53. Geremie Barmé, *An Artistic Exile* (Berkeley: University of California Press, 2002), 9.

54. Xia Mianzun, *Ruan Lingyu de si* [The death of Ruan Lingyu] (Beijing: Huawen chubanshe, 1998), 222–225.

55. Ibid., 10.

56. Xu Chi, *Jiangnan xiaozhen*, 614.

57. Hu Shi, *Sishi zishu* [Memoirs at age 40] (Beijing: Zhongguo wenlian chuban gongsi, 1993).

58. Zhang Fuling, *Caotang changchun: Zhu Qizhan* [Lasting spring in a thatched cottage: Zhu Qizhan] (Jinan: Shandong huabao chubanshe), 19.

59. Liang Shiqiu, *Liang Shiqiu sanwen xuanji* [Selected essays of Liang Shiqiu] (Tianjin: Baihua wenyi chubanshe, 1988), 4.

60. Lin Yutang, *With Love and Irony* (New York: The John Day Company, 1940), 53–54.

61. Lin Yutang, *Lin Yutang zizhuan* [Autobiography of Lin Yutang] (Nanjing: Jiangsu wenyi chubanshe, 1995), 5–6.

62. For the photograph, see Jonathan Spence and Anniping Chin, *The Chinese Century: A Photographic History* (London: HarperCollins Publishers, 1996), 54.

63. Yuan Jingxue, "Wo de fuqin Yuan Shikai" [My father Yuan Shikai], in *Wenshi ziliao xuanji* [Selected historical reference materials], no. 47.

64. Zhang was first put under house arrest in Xikou's Confucian temple called "the Pavilion of the Supreme Educator" *(Wenchang ge)*, which survives to this day.

65. Jonathan Fenby, *Chiang Kai-shek: China's Generalissimo and the Nation He Lost* (New York: Carroll & Graf, 2003), 489.

66. Weng Yuan, *Wo zai Jiang Jieshi fuzi shenbian sishisan nian* [My forty-three years' service for Chiang Kai-shek and his son] (Beijing: Huawen chubanshe, 2003), 22.

67. *Zhenming* [Contend], Hong Kong, May 2006, p. 11, based on Deng Yingchao's diary.

68. *Renmin ribao* [People's Daily], July 19, 2006, p. 4.

69. The number of administrative towns decreased from 5,403 in 1953 to 3,672 in 1955; see Wang Chunwang, *Zhongguo chengshihua zhi lu* [The road of Chinese urbanization] (Kunming: Yunnan renmin chubanshe, 1997), 100.

70. Gu Shengzu, *Dangdai Zhongguo renkou liudong yu chengzhenhua* [Population mobility and urbanization in contemporary China] (Wuhan: Wuhan University Press, 1994), 297; and Fu Chonglan, *Xiao chengzhen lun* [On small towns] (Taiyuan: Shanxi jingji chubanshe, 2003), 344.

71. See Gu Chaolin, *Zhongguo Chengzhen tixi: lishi, xianzhuang, zhanwang* [Chinese urban system: history, current situation, and prospect] (Beijing: Shangwu chubanshe, 1996), 192 and Tables 7–12.

72. For example, during that period village women who married men who had "commercial food grain" status were unquestionably considered to be seeking upward social mobility; there were many sagas related to such marriages. See also William L. Parish and Martin King Whyte, *Village and Family in Contemporary China* (Chicago: University of Chicago Press, 1978), 190, 389n53.

73. Linda Grove, *A Chinese Economic Revolution: Rural Entrepreneurship in the Twentieth Century* (Lanham, MD: Rowman & Littlefield, 2006).

74. Wang Mengkui et al., eds., *Zhongguo tece chengzhen hua daolu* [The road to urbanization with Chinese characteristics] (Beijing: Zhongguo fazhan chubanshe, 2004), 2, 97.

75. Zou Bing, *Xiao chengzhen de zhidu bianqian yu zhengce fenxi* [The changes of small town system and related policy analyses] (Beijing: Zhongguo jianzhu gongye chubanshe, 2003), 3–4.

76. The quote is from the English *People's Daily Online*, May 12, 2005; see also Wang Mengkui, et al., *Zhongguo tese de chengzhen hua daolu*, 163.

77. In Chinese, "Cuncun ru chengzhen, zhenzhen ru nongcun"; see Zou Bing, *Xiao chengzhen de zhidu bianqian yu zhengce fenxi*, 148.

78. Charles J. Galpin, *Rural Life* (New York: The Century Co., 1918), 64. Although the notion "rurbanism" or "rurban" was originally introduced by Galpin to depict the nature of rural society in the American Midwest, it has also been applied to developing countries such as India; see, for example, Richard G. Fox, "Rajput 'Clans' and Rurban Settlements in Northern India," in Richard G. Fox, ed., *Urban India: Society, Space, and Image* (Durham, NC: Duke University Program in Comparative Studies on Southern Asia, 1970), 167–185.

79. Andrew G. Walder, *Zouping in Transition: The Process of Reform in Rural North China* (Cambridge, MA: Harvard University Press, 1998), 11.

80. She Xiaoye, *Cunzhuang de zaizao: yi ge "chaoji cunzhuang" de shehui bianqian* [The transformation of a village: social changes in a "super village"] (Beijing: Zhongguo shehui kexue chubanshe, 1997), 38–39, 113, 332–333. Linda Grove has observed similar patterns in Gaoyang in central Hebei Province, where almost

all of "new factories and trading firms were private enterprises, and almost all of the capital invested in industry came from local sources." See Grove, *A Chinese Economic Revolution*, 4.

81. Zou Bing, *Xiao chengzhen de zhidu bianqian yu zhengce fenxi*, 164.
82. Ibid.
83. Bozhong Li, *Agricultural Development in Jiangnan, 1620–1850* (New York: St. Martin's Press, 1998), 171–172.
84. Hanchao Lu, *Beyond the Neon Lights*, 3–8.
85. One may note that the nostalgia for old Shanghai that held sway in the city at the turn of the twenty-first century was not only about Shanghai's celebrated cosmopolitism in the Republican era but also about the city's ability to care for certain small-town lifestyle; see Hanchao Lu, "Nostalgia for the Future: The Resurgence of an Alienated Culture in China," *Pacific Affairs* 75 (2002): 169–186.
86. Ebenezer Howard, *Garden Cities of To-Morrow* (London: Faber and Faber, 1946), 46–47.
87. Ibid., 67–68.
88. See Norton Ginsburg, Bruce Koppel, and T. G. McGee, eds., *The Extended Metropolis: Settlement Transition in Asia* (Honolulu: University of Hawaii Press, 1991).
89. Fu Chonglan, *Xiao chengzhen lun*, 15.
90. See, for example, a sociological study of three towns located in north China, central China, and the Yangzi River Delta, respectively, found a resurgence of traditional festivals and leisure activities in each of the towns; see Richard J. R. Kirkby, Ian K. Bradbury, and Guanbao Shen, eds., *Small Town China: Governance, Economy, Environment and Lifestyle in Three Zhen* (Surrey, England: Ashgate Pub. Ltd., 2001), 57–58, 99–103, 138–142.
91. *Shijie zhoukan* [Supplement to World Journal], no. 1191 (Jan. 14–Jan. 20, 2007; New York): 54–56.
92. See Peter Hall and Colin Ward, *Sociable Cities: The Legacy of Ebenezer Howard* (Seattle: Academy Press, 1999), especially Chap. 2.

3. Rural Migrant Workers and China's Differential Citizenship

The author would like to express sincerest gratitude to many anonymous friends and interviewees in the field, with special thanks to Martin Whyte and Mark Selden for their revision suggestions. Thanks also to Elizabeth Perry, Arthur Kleinman, Lan Pei-chia, Tseng Yen-fen, Huang Teh-bei, Deborah Davis, Phillip Hsu, and participants at various conferences for their comments on earlier versions; to Chang Kuei-min and Chiou Ming-je for their brilliant research assistance; and to David Boraks for editing assistance.

1. This decree was put into effect by the State Council in 1982.
2. See Teng Biao, "Constitutional Review that should not be circumvented," http://www.huayilawyers.com/Website/index.php?ChannelID=9&NewsID=270 (accessed February 10, 2006).

3. "Rules for Relief and Management of Vagrants and Beggars in the Urban Area," put into effect in August 2003. See, however, the discussion in this volume's Chapter 15 by Fei-Ling Wang of the case of Sun Zhigang and the subsequent tightening of controls over migrants in the years after 2003. See http://www1.people.com.cn/GB/shizheng/1026/1923232.html (accessed January 18, 2006).

4. See Mervyn Matthews, *The Passport Society: Controlling Movement in Russia and the USSR* (Boulder, CO: Westview, 1993).

5. See Dorothy Solinger, *Contesting Citizenship in Urban China: Peasant Migrants, the State, and the Logic of the Market* (Berkeley: University of California Press, 1999), 33–34.

6. For studies on the interrelationships between *hukou* and migration control in China, see Lincoln Day and Ma Xia, eds., *Migration and Urbanization in China* (Armonk, NY: M. E. Sharpe, 1994); Alice Goldstein, Michael White, and Sidney Goldstein, "Migration, Fertility, and State Policy in Hubei Province, China," *Demography* 34, no. 4 (1997): 481–491; Kam Wing Chan and Li Zhang, "The *Hukou* System and Rural-Urban Migration in China: Processes and Changes," *China Quarterly* 160 (December 1999): 818–855; Delia Davin, *Internal Migration in Contemporary China* (New York: St. Martin's Press, 1999); Tyrene White, "Domination, Resistance and Accommodation in China's One-Child Campaign," in Elizabeth J. Perry and Mark Selden, eds., *Chinese Society: Change, Conflict and Resistance* (London: RoutledgeCurzon, 2003), 183–203; Fei-Ling Wang, "Reformed Migration Control and New Targeted People: China's *Hukou* System in the 2000s," *China Quarterly* 177 (2004); and Fei-Ling Wang, *Organizing through Division and Exclusion: China's Hukou System* (Stanford, CA: Stanford University Press, 2005).

7. For reports and studies on the *propiska* regime's persistence, see Susan Brazier, "Propiska," http://www.nelegal.net/articles/propiska.htm (accessed February 16, 2006); Cynthia Buckley, "The Myth of Managed Migration: Migration Control and Market in the Soviet Period," *Slavic Review* 54, 4 (1995): 896–916; Human Rights Watch, Europe and Central Asia Division, 1998, "The Residence Permit System (Propiska)," http://www.hrw.org/reports98/russia/srusstest-04.htm#P284_66713 (1998, accessed February 16, 2006); Noah Rubins, "The Demise and Resurrection of the Propiska: Freedom of Movement in the Russian Federation," *Harvard International Law Journal* 39, no. 2 (1998): 545–566; Roman Woronowycz, "Constitutional Court strikes down internal passport system," *Ukrainian Weekly* 69, no. 47 (November 25, 2001); Damian S. Schaible, "Life in Russia's Closed City: Moscow's Movement Restrictions and the Rule of Law," *New York University Law Review* 76 (2001): 344–373; and WLSP (Westerner Living in St. Petersburg), "Propiska system" (July 5, 2005), http://www.cdi.org/russia/johnson/9193-8.cfm (accessed February 16, 2006).

8. See Solinger, *Contesting Citizenship in Urban China*.

9. The extrabudgetary fees include "living expenses in the detention station," "deportation fees," and "fees for increasing urban accommodation," and so on. This is strikingly similar to the post-Soviet Union states, as reported by Human Rights Watch, where the residency permit system provides ample opportunities for police corruption. See Human Rights Watch, Europe and Central Asia Division, 1998, "The Residence Permit System (Propiska)."

10. This is according to the "Labor Law" enacted in 1994. For another instance, the Ministry of Labor promulgated "Temporary Regulations for the Management of Transprovincial Movement of Rural Laborers" in the same year. See Tan Shen, "Wailaigong de Zhuyao Wenti" [Major issues of the migrant workers], *Zhongguo Shehuixue Wang* [Chinese Sociological Net], 2004, http://www.sociology.cass.net .cn/shxw/shld/t20040913_2704.htm (accessed January 15, 2008). See also Fei-Ling Wang's chapter, in this volume, Chapter 15.

11. Solinger, *Contesting Citizenship in Urban China,* 3; cf. also Lei Guang, "Reconstituting the Rural-Urban Divide: Peasant Migration and the Rise of 'Orderly Migration' in Contemporary China," *Journal of Contemporary China* 10, no. 28 (2001): 471–493.

12. Quoted from *Southern Metropolis News,* June 25, 2003.

13. Quoted from *Southern Metropolis News,* June 25, 2003.

14. Reported by Joseph Kahn in the *New York Times,* November 3, 2005.

15. For another example, the *Wall Street Journal* reported in 1994 that the central government would soon tear down the two-tier *hukou* system. See Li Zhang, *Strangers in the City: Reconfigurations of Space, Power, and Social Networks within China's Floating Population* (Stanford, CA: Stanford University Press, 2001), 219.

16. See T. H. Marshall, "Citizenship and Social Class" (originally published in 1939), in Bryan S. Turner and Peter Hamilton, ed., *Citizenship: Critical Concepts* (London: Routledge, 1994).

17. Marshall, "Citizenship and Social Class," 9.

18. See Albert O. Hirschman, *The Rhetoric of Reaction: Perversity, Futility, Jeopardy* (Cambridge, MA: The Belknap Press of Harvard University Press, 1991), Chap. 1.

19. Solinger, *Contesting Citizenship in Urban China,* 1, 278.

20. For the concept of "devaluation of citizenship," see Peter Schuck, "Membership in the Liberal Polity: The Devaluation of American Citizenship," in Rogers Brubaker, ed., *Immigration and the Politics of Citizenship in Europe and North America* (Lanham, MD: University Press of America, 1999), 51–65; and Rogers Brubaker, "Membership without Citizenship: The Economic and Social Rights of Noncitizens," in Rogers Brubaker, ed., *Immigration and the Politics of Citizenship in Europe and North America* (Lanham, MD: University Press of America, 1999), 145–162. For the concept of "denizen," see Tomas Hammar, "State, Nation, and Dual Citizenship," in Rogers Brubaker, ed., *Immigration and Politics of Citizenship in Europe and North America* (Lanham, MD: University Press of America, 1999), 81–96.

21. Karl Polanyi, *The Great Transformation: The Political and Economic Origins of Our Time* (Boston: Beacon Press, 1975), 77–102.

22. Polanyi, *The Great Transformation*, 77–78. Cf. Zhou Hung, "Cong 'Shudiguanli' dao 'Pujixing Tizhi'" [From "Territorial Jurisdiction" to "Universalism Principle"], *Zhongguo Shehui Baozhang* [Chinese Social Security], 8 (2003).

23. Cf. Marshall's explication, "Citizenship and Social Class," 14–15, 19–20.

24. The Speenhamland Law was formally replaced by the new Poor Law in 1834. The new law required that all poor relief should be nationally administered. See Polanyi, *The Great Transformation*, 101–102.

25. Cf. Tiejun Cheng and Mark Selden "The Origins and Social Consequences of China's *Hukou* System," *China Quarterly* 139 (1994): 646–668.

26. Andrew Walder, *Communist Neo-Traditionalism: Work and Authority in Chinese Industry* (Berkeley: University of California Press, 1986).

27. For the concept of *chaxu geju*, see Fei Xiao-tong, *Xiangtu Zhongguo* [Peasant China] (Hong Kong: Sanlian Chubanshe, 1991 [1947]). I took the translation from Gary Hamilton and Wang Zheng, "Introduction," in Hamilton and Zheng, *From the Soil: The Foundations of Chinese Society: A Translation of Fei Xiaotong's Xiangtu Zhongguo* (Berkeley: University of California Press, 1992), 19–20. This translation is paired with another term of Fei's, that is, *tuanti geju* (organizational mode of association), which is regarded as the organizing principle of Western societies.

28. Cf. Jeffrey Sachs, Wing Thye Woo, and Xiaokai Yang's interpretation of my earlier fieldwork: the Chinese way of industrial development has carried a style of feudal institutional legacies. See Sachs, Woo, and Yang, "Economic Reforms and Constitutional Transition," Social Science Research Network Electronic Paper Collection (October 2000), http://papers.ssrn.com/sol3/papers.cfm?abstract_id=254110 (accessed August 8, 2008).

29. For example, the rural-urban divide and industrial-agricultural dualism helped the state to extract surplus for industrialization and to control the society. See Chih-Ming Ka and Mark Selden, "Original Accumulation, Equity and Late Industrialization: The Cases of Socialist China and Capitalist Taiwan," *World Development* 14, no. 10–11 (1986): 1293–1310.

30. For the concept of infrastructural power, see Michael Mann, "The Autonomous Power of the State: Its Origins, Mechanisms and Results," *Archives europeennes de sociologie* 25 (1984): 185–213. For the "statist choices" aimed at controlling population movement, see also Dorothy Solinger, "Citizenship Issues in China's Internal Migration: Comparisons with Germany and Japan," *Political Science Quarterly* 144, no. 3 (1999): 455–478.

31. Will Kymlicka and Wayne Norman, "Citizenship in Culturally Diverse Societies: Issues, Contexts, Concepts," in Will Kymlicka and Wayne Norman, eds., *Citizenship in Diverse Societies* (Oxford: Oxford University Press, 2000), 1–41.

32. Marshall, "Citizenship and Social Class," 20. Emphasis added.

33. Actually, the term *"mingong* workers" was already used in Mao's time to refer to those urbanites who were employed in the industrial sector without fully state-sanctioned industrial citizenship—that is, to refer to "temporary workers" who lacked state benefits such as pensions and health care. Cf. Martin King Whyte, *Small Groups and Political Rituals in China* (Berkeley: University of California Press, 1974).

34. See also Wang Feng's chapter, Chapter 10, in this volume.

35. At the end of 1993, Shewei had a local population of 1,860 people in 495 households, while hosting more than 20,000 migrants working and living in 115 foreign-invested factories. See Wu Jieh-min, "Yazha Renxing Kongjian: Shenfen Chaxu yu Zhongguoshi Duochong Boxue" [Human Space Squeezed: Differential Status and Chinese Style of Multiple Exploitation], *Taiwan Shehui Yanjiu Jikan* [Taiwan: A Radical Quarterly in Social Studies], no. 39 (2000): 1–44.

36. The village assets, including lands, belong to all villagers as a collectivity, and non-villagers are naturally excluded from the collective benefits. According to The Constitution of the People's Republic of China, Article 10, Item 2, "The land of rural and suburban area . . . belongs to the collective; the land used for housing and individual farming . . . also belongs to the collective." The Land Administration Law of the PRC, Article 8, states, "Collectively-owned land . . . should be managed and regulated by collective agricultural organizations such as the village producer's cooperatives or villagers committee." These set up a system of rural ownership at the level of administrative village. In addition, according to The Township and Village Enterprises Law, Article 10, "the property rights of the rural enterprises belong to the entire laborers of the rural community."

37. For instance, I found a foreign-invested factory in a Guangdong village that employed 1,700 workers but only registered 1,100 migrant workers with the public security bureau in order to save the "head taxes." This practice has remained widespread, based on my field interviews in East and South China over the last several years. For the negotiable "head tax" and its institutional basis, see Wu Jieh-min, "Strange Bedfellows: Dynamics of Government-Business Relations between Chinese Local Authorities and Taiwanese Investors," *Journal of Contemporary China* 6, no. 15 (1997): 319–346.

38. See also Anita Chan, *China's Workers under Assault: The Exploitation of Labor in Globalizing Economy* (Armonk, NY: M. E. Sharpe, 2001).

39. Cf. Bin Wong, "Citizenship in Chinese History," in Michael Hanagan and Charles Tilly, eds., *Extending Citizenship, Reconfiguring States* (Lanham, MD: Rowman and Littlefield, 1999), 97–122.

40. According to the earlier laws, children should inherit their rural or urban *hukou* status through the maternal line. Cf. Sulamith Potter, "The Position of Peasants in Modern China's Social Order," *Modern China* 9 (1983): 465–499. This rule effectively prevented the enormous number of "returnees" from going back to their fathers' home cities. It was abolished in 1988 and the children born since then

have been allowed to claim their own *hukou* status through either the maternal or the paternal line.

41. One of the earliest national policy announcements about the blue seal can be found in "Notice regarding implementing city and township residents *hukou* effective within the local jurisdiction," issued by the Ministry of Public Security in 1992. See Cao Jingchun, "Guanyu Lanyin Hukou Wenti de Sikao" [Thoughts about the Blue-seal *Hukou*], *Renkou yu Jingji* [Population and Economy], no. 6 (2001): 15–21. Cf. also L. Wong and W. P. Huen, "Reforming the Household Registration System: A Preliminary Glimpse of the Blue Chip Household Registration System in Shanghai and Shenzhen," *International Migration Review*, no. 32 (1998): 974–994. Municipal cities such as Shanghai promulgated "Shanghai Municipality temporary provisions for the management of blue-seal *hukou*" in February 1994. These provisions were modified in 1998 to further encourage investment-type migration and stimulate the real estate market. See http://www.shanghai.gov.cn/shanghai/node2314/node2316/node2341/node2577/userobject6ai496.html (accessed January 2, 2006).

42. Cao Jingchun, ""Guanyu Lanyin Hukou Wenti de Sikao."

43. Liu Yingfeng, "Zhongguo Lanyin Huji Zhidu de Qiyuan yu Bianqian" [Origins and Changes of the Blue-seal Hukou System], Master's thesis, Institute of Sociology, National Tsing Hua University, Taiwan (2008), 32, Table 3-3.

44. Liu Yingfeng, ""Zhongguo Lanyin Huji Zhidu de Qiyuan yu Bianqian," 14–20.

45. For example, the Shanghai Municipal Government ceased issuing blue-seal *hukou* in April 2002 and stated that "the existing preconditions and number of applicants for the blue seal do not correspond with the total amount control target of the permanent residents, and thus have caused a series of negative effects on the city's economic and social development." Notice that Shanghai ceases to admit blue-seal *hukou* issued by Shanghai Public Security Bureau, March 2002), see http://www.shanghai.gov.cn/shanghai/node2314/node2316/node2329/node2487/userobject6ai1094.html (accessed January 2, 2006).

46. "Temporary provisions for 'Shanghai Municipality residence permit system' for introducing talented persons," 2002, see http://www.shanghai.gov.cn/shanghai/node2314/node3124/node3125/node3130/userobject6ai1122.html (accessed June 21, 2009); and "Temporary provisions for Shanghai Municipality residence permit system," 2004, see http://www.chinacourt.org/flwk/show1.php?file_id=96219 (accessed June 21, 2009).

47. Chen Yingfang, "'Nongmingong': Zhidu Anpai yu Shenfen Rentong" ["Peasant Workers": Institutional Arrangements and Identity], *Shehuixue Yanjiu* [Sociological Research], no. 3 (2005): 119–132.

48. Data collected from field interviews in August 2005.

49. According to Rogers Brubaker, in the European context, legal immigrants—denizens—as such are not inclined to obtain citizenship, because they are almost fully covered by the welfare programs offered to the citizens, except in the

"political sphere" (voting rights) and getting jobs in public service. See Brubaker, "Membership without Citizenship: The Economic and Social Rights of Nonciti- zens." See also Hammar, "State, Nation, and Dual Citizenship"; and Christian Joppke, "How Immigration is Changing Citizenship: A Comparative View," *Eth- nic and Racial Studies* 22, no. 4 (1999): 629–652.

50. Field interview in August 2005. According to Article 4 of Temporary provisions for Shanghai Municipality residence permit system, 2004, the residence permit is valid for one, three, or five years, respectively.

51. *Shanghai Tongji Nianjian* 2005 [Shanghai Statistical Yearbook 2005], 68, 74.

52. *Kunshan Tongji Nianjian* 2006 [Kunshan Statistical Yearbook 2006], 47, 49.

53. *Dongguan Shehuijingji he Shehuifazhan Tongji Gonbao,* 2005 [Bulletin of National Economy and Social Development of Dongguan, 2005].

54. *Shenzhen Shi Shehuijingji he Shehuifazhan Tongji Gonbao,* 2006 [Bulletin of National Economy and Social Development of Shenzhen City, 2006].

55. Kymlicka and Norman, "Citizenship in Culturally Diverse Societies."

56. Solinger, "Citizenship Issues in China's Internal Migration: Comparisons with Germany and Japan," 456.

57. For the case of Zhejiangcun, see Li Zhang, *Strangers in the City: Reconfigura- tions of Space, Power, and Social Networks within China's Floating Population* (Stanford, CA: Stanford University Press, 2001).

58. See the discussion of these reforms in Chapter 15 of this volume by Fei-Ling Wang.

59. In October 2001, the State Planning Council and Ministry of Finance sent down a document in curbing the corruptive and rent-seeking behavior through issuing various certificates. In March 2005, the Ministry of Labor and Social Security further abolished several outdated rules and provisions about controlling the free flow of migrants.

60. Article 17, Management of Floating Population Statute in Guangdong Province. See http://dangan.jianghai.gov.cn/Article_Show.asp?ArticleID=12226 (accessed June 21, 2009).

61. See a report on *Yangcheng Wanbao* [Yangcheng Evening News] by Zhou Min, "Zhanzhuzheng Jiujing Gaixiang Hechuqu?" [Whither the Temporary Residence Card?], October 17, 2002, in http://www.chinanews.com.cn/2002-12-17/26/254459 .html (accessed March 30, 2006).

62. "Opinion regarding the further improvement of peasant workers' children com- pulsory education," document forwarded by the State Council, October 1, 2003.

63. Field interviews in Shanghai, August 2005.

64. Reported on Xinhua Wang [Xinhua Net], July 30, 2008, http://news.xinhuanet .com/edu/2008–07/30/content_8858472.htm (accessed August 30, 2008).

65. Chen Yingfang, "'Nongmingong': Zhidu Anpai yu Shenfen Rentong."

66. *Shanghai Statistical Yearbook* 2005, 68.

67. Zhou Min, "Wither the Temporary Residence Card?"

68. According to *Guangdong Statistical Yearbook* (2005: 114), the *hukou* population was 1.8 million and documented migrants numbered 6.5 million, but the government "actually managed a total population of 12 millions" (*Xinjingbao*, August 8, 2005), which means there were more than 10 million migrants, including the documented and undocumented; see http://big5.xinhuanet.com/gate/big5/news .xinhuanet.com/zhengfu/2005–08/08/content_3324664.htm (accessed April 8, 2007).

69. See also Solinger, *Contesting Citizenship in Urban China*, 66–71.

70. According to the laws, participants in the social insurance can transfer their personal accounts at will. Our interviews with local officials confirmed it. However, migrant workers widely perceived that local governments often set up obstacles to transferring accounts.

71. Joppke, "How Immigration is Changing Citizenship: A Comparative View," 629.

72. Marshall, "Citizenship and Social Class," 38.

73. Ibid., 20.

74. For this interpretation, see Hirschman, *The Rhetoric of Reaction*.

75. Marshall, "Citizenship and Social Class," 20. Emphasis added.

76. During the Mao era, the concept of people *(renmin)* appeared to be better received than that of citizen *(gongmin)* for political reasons. See Xingzhong Yu, "Citizenship, Ideology, and the PRC Constitution," in Merle Goldman and Elizabeth J. Perry, eds., *Changing Meanings of Citizenship in Modern China* (Cambridge, MA: Harvard University Press, 2002), 288–307.

77. Solinger, *Contesting Citizenship in Urban China*, 241.

78. The phenomenon of urban citizenship devaluation occurs because denizens are offered more or less comprehensive social welfare except political rights in the Western European context. Cf. Yasemin Soysal, *Limits of Citizenship: Migrants and Postnational Membership in Europe* (Chicago: University of Chicago Press, 1994); and Joppke, "How Immigration Is Changing Citizenship."

79. Chen Yingfang, "'Nongmingong': Zhidu Anpai yu Shenfen Rentong" 130.

80. Cf. Chen Yingfang, "'Nongmingong': Zhidu Anpai yu Shenfen Rentong," 131.

81. Cf. Charles Tilly, *Durable Inequality* (Berkeley: University of California Press, 1998).

82. Quoted from a policy restatement by the State Council, "Several opinions regarding solving the problems of migrant peasant workers," passed on January 18, 2006.

83. In the commune system the collective was supposed to provide minimal funds to the childless elderly to cover food, clothing, housing, medical care, and burial expenses.

84. For the concept of authoritarian resilience, see Andrew Nathan, "China's Changing of the Guard: Authoritarian Resilience," *Journal of Democracy* 14, no. 1 (January 2003): 6–17.

85. Figures generated from http://reference.allrefer.com/country-guide-study/soviet -union/ (accessed March 1, 2006).

86. Figures compiled from *China Statistics Yearbook* 2004; Third National Population Census in 1982, http://www.stats.gov.cn/tjgb/rkpcgb/qgrkpcgb/t20020404_16769.htm (accessed March 1, 2006); and Sixth National Population Census in 2005, http://www.stats.gov.cn/tjgb/rkpcgb/qgrkpcgb/t20020404_16769.htm (accessed March 1, 2006).

87. For the notion of "socialist serfdom," see Martin Whyte's introduction to this volume in Chapter 1.

88. Cf. Stephen Castles, "Nation and Empire: Hierarchies of Citizenship in the New Global Order," *International Politics* 42, no. 2 (June, 2005): 203–224.

89. See the State Council, "Several opinions regarding solving the problems of migrant peasant workers" [Guowuyuan Guanyu Jiejue Nongmingong Wenti de Ruogan Yijian], approved by the Standing Committee of the State Council, January 18, 2006. http://big5.xinhuanet.com/gate/big5/news.xinhuanet.com/politics/2006-03/27/content_4351076.htm (accessed January 12, 2009).

4. How Large Is China's Rural-Urban Income Gap?

We are grateful to Anthony Shorrocks, Martin K. Whyte, and participants at the Fairbank Center Conference, "Rethinking the Rural-Urban Cleavage in Contemporary China," held at Harvard University on October 6–8, 2006, for their comments and suggestions. We thank the Swedish International Development Cooperation Agency, Ford Foundation, Centre for International Governance Innovation, and University of Western Ontario for funding that facilitated this work.

1. For estimates of China's rural-urban income gap, see Dwayne Benjamin, Loren Brandt, John Giles, and Wang Sangui, "Income Inequality during China's Economic Transition," in Loren Brandt and Thomas G. Rawski, eds., *China's Great Economic Transformation* (New York: Cambridge University Press, 2008), 729–775; John Knight and Lina Song, *The Urban-Rural Divide: Economic Disparities and Interactions in China* (New York: Oxford University Press, 1999); Shi Xinzheng, "Urban-Rural Income Differentials Decomposition in China 1990s," M.A. Thesis, China Center for Economic Research, Peking University, Beijing, 2004; Dennis Tao Yang and Zhou Hao, "Rural-Urban Disparity and Sectoral Labor Allocation in China," *Journal of Development Studies* 35, no. 3 (1999): 105–133; and X. B. Zhao and S. P. Tong, "Unequal Economic Development in China: Spatial Disparities and Regional Policy Reconsideration, 1985–1995," *Regional Studies* 34, no. 6 (2000): 549–561.

2. For a discussion of income components and the measurement of income in China, see Azizur R. Khan and Carl Riskin, "Growth and Distribution of Household Income in China between 1995 and 2002," in Björn Gustafsson, Li Shi, and Terry Sicular, eds., *Inequality and Public Policy in China* (New York: Cambridge University Press, 2008), 61–87.

3. See Khan and Riskin, "Growth and Distribution of Household Income in China between 1995 and 2002," and Chapter 5 of this volume.

4. A recent study fills this information gap. See Loren Brandt and Carsten A. Holz, "Spatial Price Differences in China: Estimates and Implications," *Economic Development and Cultural Change* 55, no. 1 (2006): 43–86.

5. Spatial price indices are from Brandt and Holz, "Spatial Price Differences in China." For discussion of international best practice in the measurement of household income, see Timothy M. Smeeding and Daniel H. Weinberg, "Toward a Uniform Definition of Household Income," *Review of Income and Wealth* 47, no. 1 (2001): 1–24; and Expert Group on Household Income Statistics, *The Canberra Group: Final Report and Recommendations*, Ottawa (2001).

6. International guidelines on the measurement of household disposable income counsel against including employer and employee contributions to social programs, because including both the ex ante contributions and the ex post benefits can lead to double counting. Also, employer and mandatory employee contributions to pension and health insurance programs can be viewed as forms of payroll tax, in which case they should be subtracted from disposable income, which is the measure of income used here. See Expert Group on Household Income Statistics, *The Canberra Group: Final Report and Recommendations*. By our rough calculation, removing employer and mandatory employee contributions from Chapter 5's income estimates would lower the urban-to-rural income ratio from above 3 to around 2.6 or 2.7. Including migrants would further lower the gap, perhaps to 2.5 or less.

7. For a description of the survey and data, see Li Shi, Luo Chuliang, Wei Zhong, and Yue Ximing, "Appendix: The 1995 and 2002 Household Surveys: Sampling Methods and Data Description," in Gustafsson, Li, and Sicular, eds., *Inequality and Public Policy in China*, 337–353. The CHIP dataset also includes a survey for 1988. We do not include 1988 in our analysis because some of the information required to recalculate the gap is not readily available for that year and because our focus is on more recent trends.

8. The sample also includes Chongqing, which was formerly part of Sichuan province but became a separate province in 1997. For consistency, Chongqing observations are treated as part of the Sichuan sample in both 1995 and 2002.

9. For discussion of NBS statistics on urban versus rural populations, see Kam Wing Chan, "Misconceptions and Complexities in the Study of China's Cities: Definitions, Statistics, and Implications," *Eurasian Geography and Economics* 48, no. 4 (2007): 383–412; and Kam Wing Chan and Man Wang, "Remapping China's Regional Inequalities, 1990–2006: A New Assessment of *de Facto* and *de Jure* Population Data," *Eurasian Geography and Economics* 49, no. 1 (2008): 21–56.

10. Other target variables—for example, household per capita consumption—are sometimes used for the analysis of inequality. A discussion of the advantages and

disadvantages of using household per capita income to study China's inequality is available in Terry Sicular, Yue Ximing, Björn Gustafsson, and Li Shi, "The Urban-Rural Income Gap and Inequality in China," *Review of Income and Wealth* 53, no. 1 (2007): 93–126.

11. The rental value of owner-occupied housing is not always recognized as a part of income because it takes the form of services rather than cash. The value of these services, however, could be converted to cash by renting out the property or by selling the property and investing the proceeds in cash-yielding assets. For example, suppose two households are identical except that the first household lives in its house and the second household rents out its house (perhaps renting an apartment for its own residence). Obviously, rental income should be counted in the second household's income. But, this would make the second household's measured income higher than that of the first household, even though in fact the two households have the same income. For consistency, then, the first household's income should include the imputed rent that it would have received if it had rented out its house. For discussion of this issue and of household income measurement more generally, see Congressional Budget Office of the U.S. Congress, *Tax Treatment of Homeownership: Issues and Options* (Washington, DC: U.S. Government Printing Office, September 1981); and Expert Group on Household Income Statistics, *The Canberra Group: Final Report and Recommendations.*

12. Some analyses of inequality use equivalence scales to adjust for differences in household composition and size. Unfortunately, no recent estimates of equivalence scales for urban and rural China are available, and we do not have the information required to estimate them.

13. The absolute difference is equal to urban income minus rural income. In constant 1995 prices, the absolute difference between urban and rural incomes in 1995 was 2,360 yuan and in 2002 was 3,867 yuan.

14. See Sicular, Yue, Gustafsson, and Li, "The Urban-Rural Income Gap and Inequality in China." Other studies that control for urban-rural differences in household characteristics are Knight and Song, *The Urban-Rural Divide;* and Shi, "Urban-Rural Income Differentials Decomposition in China 1990s."

15. For more detail on the findings discussed in this section, as well as an explanation of the empirical methods, see Sicular, Yue, Gustafsson, and Li, "The Urban-Rural Income Gap and Inequality in China."

16. For further discussion, see Sicular, Yue, Gustafsson and Li, "The Urban-Rural Income Gap and Inequality in China."

17. See Kam Wing Chan and Hu Ying, "Urbanization in China in the 1990s: New Definition, Different Series, and Revised Trends," *China Review* 3, no. 2 (Fall 2003): 49–71. Reclassification can also occur if the definition of urban places changes, which in fact has happened in China. The NBS adopted a new definition of urban places for the 2000 census that replaced the definition that was adopted

for the 1990 census and used during the 1990s. The change in definition was fairly complex; interested readers should see, for example, Zhou Yixing and Laurence J. C. Ma, "China's Urbanization Levels: Reconstructing a Baseline from the Fifth Population Census," *China Quarterly* 173 [2003]: 176–196). The NBS now publishes data for the 1990s that are adjusted to conform to the new definition of urban places. Some recent studies—for example, Chan and Hu—criticize the NBS's adjustments. We recalculated inequality levels and the contribution of the rural-urban gap to inequality using Chan and Hu's alternative population estimates. Our results change very little, so we simply use the NBS population statistics for our calculations. For an estimate of the effect of keeping place definitions constant, see Benjamin, Brandt, Giles, and Wang, "Income Inequality during China's Economic Transition." That paper concludes that reclassification causes overstatement of the rural-urban income gap, because reclassified rural areas tend to be the ones that have experienced the fastest income growth. Residents of the now richer, once-rural places are counted as urban, and residents of those places that grow more slowly and remain relatively poor continue to be counted as rural.

18. NBS coverage of migrants has improved in recent years. In 2000 the NBS revised its urban sampling framework so that selection of households within neighborhood committees (*jumin weiyuanhui*) was no longer restricted to households with urban registration. Since 2000, then, the NBS urban household survey has included some unregistered migrants, but they continue to be underrepresented.

19. For more details about the migrant subsample, see Li Shi, Luo Chuliang, Wei Zhong, and Yue Ximing, "Appendix: The 1995 and 2002 Household Surveys: Sampling Methods and Data Description."

20. Liang Zai and Ma Zhongdong, "China's Floating Population: New Evidence from the 2000 Census," *Population and Development Review* 20, no. 3 (2004): 467–488. Their estimate includes all inter-county migrants in cities and towns who have resided in their destination for six or more months and who do not have local household registration status.

21. See Mo Rong, *2003–2004 nian Zhongguo jiuye baogao* [2003–2004 China Employment Report] (Beijing: Ministry of Labour and Public Security Press, 2004). In Mo's analysis migrants are defined as workers employed outside their township of residence for more than six months; movements for marriage, study, and to join the army are excluded. The 16 percent figure includes only rural migrants employed in urban areas.

22. Note that the gap in income between registered urban residents and rural-to-urban migrants does not fully capture the gap in their economic welfare, as migrants have little access to urban social services and on average work longer hours than do registered urban residents.

23. The Theil T gives an increase in inequality when migrants are included, but by 2 percent. The fact that different inequality measures disagree on whether

including migrants increases or decreases inequality reflects the fact that the Lorenz curves of the two income distributions cross.

24. Note also that our calculations hold constant the incomes of other groups. That is, these calculations do not take into account the possibility that migration could affect the incomes of those remaining behind in rural areas as well as of the registered urban population. One would expect that migration would cause incomes to increase for those remaining in rural areas and to decrease for the urban population.

25. The Gini coefficient places more weight on the middle of the income distribution than the Theil indexes, but even so including migrants has little impact on measured overall inequality in China in 2002. Using the same CHIP survey data as we use here, Azizur R. Khan and Carl Riskin, in "Growth and Distribution of Household Income in China Between 1995 and 2002," report a Gini coefficient of 0.450 excluding migrants and 0.448 including migrants.

26. Robert Eastwood and Michael Lipton, "Rural and Urban Income Inequality and Poverty: Does Convergence between Sectors Offset Divergence within Them?" in Giovanni Andrea Cornia, ed., *Inequality, Growth and Poverty in an Era of Liberalization and Globalization* (Oxford: Oxford University Press, 2004) 112–141; and Knight and Song, *The Urban-Rural Divide*, 338.

27. Fan Shenggen, Zhang Linxiu, and Zhang Xiaobo, "Reforms, Investment and Poverty in Rural China," *Economic Development and Cultural Change* 52, no. 2 (January 2004): 395–421; and Zhang Xiaobo and Fan Shenggen, "Public Investment and Regional Inequality in Rural China," *Agricultural Economics* 30, no. 2 (2004): 89–100.

28. In 1995 nonlabor earnings accounted for 47 percent of the difference between mean urban and rural per capita household incomes. In 2002 the percentage of nonlabor income was 43 percent. Note that labor earnings per capita include wages and net income from self-employment, including agricultural self-employment. Nonlabor earnings include all other forms of income. See Sicular, Yue, Gustafsson, and Li, "The Urban-Rural Income Gap and Inequality in China," Table 9.

5. Reestimating the Income Gap between Urban and Rural Households in China

An earlier version of this paper was presented in the conference on the rural-urban gap in the PRC, held at Harvard University on October 6–8, 2006. The authors thank Albert Park, Martin Whyte, and other participants for their comments on the paper.

1. The numbers have been calculated by the authors using the data in *China Statistical Abstract 2005*, 102.

2. John Knight and Lina Song, *The Rural-Urban Divide: Economic Disparities and Interactions in China* (Oxford: Oxford University Press, 1999).

3. Li Shi and Yue Ximing, "Investigation of Income Gap between Urban and Rural China" (in Chinese), *Caijing*, February–March 2004.

4. Li and Yue, "Investigation of Income Gap between Urban and Rural China."

5. Qiu Xiaohua, the former director of the National Bureau of Statistics, made an assertion in 2003 that the income gap between urban and rural China is about 6:1. This figure has been widely cited in media and research reports. See, for example, http://www.ifg.org/pdf/ChinaReality.pdf.

6. Li Shi, Chuliang Luo, Zhong Wei, and Ximing Yue, "Appendix: The 1995 and 2002 Household Surveys: Sampling Methods and Data Description," in Björn Gustafsson, Li Shi, Terry Sicular, eds., *Income Inequality and Public Policy in China* (Cambridge: Cambridge University Press, 2008).

7. An earlier version of Chapter 4 was published as Terry Sicular, Yue Ximing, Björn Gustafsson, and Li Shi, "The Urban-Rural Income Gap and Inequality in China," *Review of Income and Wealth* 53 (2007): 93–126.

8. A. R. Khan and Carl Riskin, "Income and Inequality in China: Composition, Distribution and Growth of Household Income, 1988 to 1995," *China Quarterly* 154 (1998): 221–253.

9. See Sicular et al., "The Urban-Rural Income Gap"; and Sylvie Démurger, Martin Fournier, and Li Shi, "Urban Income Inequality in China Revisited (1988–2002)," *Economics Letters* 93 (2006): 354–359.

10. See Khan and Riskin, "Income and Inequality in China"; Khan and Riskin, "China's Household Income and Its Distribution, 1995 and 2002," *China Quarterly* 192 (2005): 356–384; Irma Adelman and David Sunding, "Economic Policy and Income Distribution in China," *Journal of Comparative Economics* 11 (1987): 444–461; Sicular et al., "The Urban-Rural Income Gap"; Démurger et al., "Urban Income Inequality in China Revisited"; and Martin Ravallion and Shaohua Chen, "China's (uneven) Progress against Poverty," *Journal of Development Economics* 82 (2007): 1–42. The estimates of regional cost of living variations for China are presented in Loren Brandt and Carston A. Holz, "Spatial Price Differences in China: Estimates and Implications," *Economic Development and Cultural Change* 55 (2006): 43–86.

11. Björn Gustafsson, Li Shi, Terry Sicular, and Yue Ximing, "Income Inequality and Spatial Differences in China, 1988, 1995, and 2002," in Gustafsson et al., *Income Inequality and Public Policy in China*.

12. Adelman and Sunding, "Economic Policy and Income Distribution in China."

13. World Bank, *Sharing Rising Incomes: Disparities in China* (Washington, DC: The World Bank, 1997).

14. The justification is based on a stipulation of the State Council on housing reform in 1988, which proposed an explicit housing subsidy calculated as 25 percent of the wage of urban employees if the rent of public housing was fully evaluated in market value.

15. Cai Fang and Yang Tao, "Political Economy of the Income Gap between Urban and Rural Areas," *Social Sciences in China*, Issue 4, 2000.

16. The restrictions on rural residents migrating to urban areas were loosened during the economic transition, and rural residents were able to seek jobs in the cities. However, today they cannot register as permanent urban citizens and cannot generally be employed in the formal sector. Usually they can only obtain informal jobs, and social security programs for the most part do not cover the informal sector or informal employees. See the discussion in Chapter 3 of this volume.

17. Wang Lina and Zhong Wei, "Housing Welfare and Income Distribution in China's Cities," in Zhao Renwei, Li Shi, and Carl Riskin, eds., Re-study on Income Distribution in China (Beijing: China Finance and Economic Press, 1999).

18. The survey included the following question: What would the rent be if your apartment was rented out in the housing market?

19. Details on the regression model used are not reported here but are available from the authors on request.

20. Before the New Cooperative Medical Scheme was introduced experimentally in some counties beginning in 2003, rural people took full responsibility for their own medical care and medical expenses out of pocket.

21. The educational subsidy obtained by urban households is much more than that obtained by rural households, which results from the different educational finance systems implemented in the two parts of China. In rural areas, households pay not only school fees but also additional fees called Auxiliary Education Fee (jiaoyu fujia fei). The Auxiliary Education Fee is a type of quasi-tax. However, urban households only pay school fees that are set at lower levels compared to those paid by rural households. Given the fact that more educational opportunities and higher-quality education is provided for urban children, city governments have to subsidize education to a greater extent.

22. We can obtain the annual total educational expenditure, but not the amount spent per student, from the Chinese Statistical Yearbook of Educational Expenditure. We divided the total of educational fees for every educational level by the total students at that level to get the educational fee paid per student.

23. Once again, details on the regression model are available from the authors on request.

24. Adopting the income definition of NBS, the Gini coefficient of personal income is 0.32 in urban China in 2002, as shown in Table 5.6.

25. Brandt and Holz, "Spatial Price Differences in China."

26. Khan and Riskin, "China's Household Income and Its Distribution"; Li Shi and Yaohui Zhao, "The Decline of In-kind Wage Payment in Urban China," Journal of Chinese Economic and Business Studies 1, no. 2 (2003).

6. Rural-Urban Disparities in Access to Primary and Secondary Education under Market Reforms

1. Dennis Tao Yang, "Determinants of Schooling Returns during Transition: Evidence from Chinese Cities," *Journal of Comparative Economics* 33 (2005): 244–264; Junsen Zhang, Yaohui Zhao, Albert Park, and Xiaoqing Song, "Economic Returns to Schooling in Urban China, 1988 to 2001," *Journal of Comparative Economics* 33 (2005): 730–752.

2. Wei Zhao and Xueguang Zhou, "Returns to Education in China's Transitional Economy: Reassessment and Reconceptualization," in Emily Hannum and Albert Park, *Education and Reform in China* (London: Routledge, 2007); and Junsen Zhang and Yaohui Zhao, "Rising Schooling Returns in Urban China," in Hannum and Park, *Education and Reform in China*.

3. Alan de Brauw, Jikun Huang, Scott Rozelle, Linxiu Zhang, and Yigang Zhang, "The Evolution of China's Rural Labor Markets during the Reforms," *Journal of Comparative Economics* 30 (2002): 329–353; Alan de Brauw and Scott Rozelle, "Returns to Education in Rural China," in Hannum and Park, *Education and Reform in China;* Yaohui Zhao, "Labor Migration and Returns to Rural Education in China," *American Journal of Agricultural Economics* 79 (1997): 1278.

4. We thank the Carolina Population Center and the China Centers for Disease Control for providing access to the China Health and Nutrition Survey, which is funded by NIH (R01-HD30880, DK056350, and R01-HD38700).

5. A detailed description of these additions and replacements can be found at on the Web site documenting the CHNS: http://www.cpc.unc.edu/projects/china/design/sample.html#920.

6. This description draws directly from the official sample description for the project, available at http://www.cpc.unc.edu/projects/china/design/survey.html.

7. We had initially planned to compare the 1990 and 2000 censuses but have found that a readily comparable definition of rural residence is not currently available.

8. In many of the years of the CHNS, minority status appears to be available only for household heads and spouses of household heads.

9. In the CHNS, if a family member is away, whether long-term or short-term, but will come back, that person is still counted with the family of origin. If the family member establishes a new household, that person is counted in the new household. According to census counting procedures, some of the children of rural residents who migrate to cities would be counted at their place of *hukou* registration, while others would be counted in the cities. If they have lived in the city for more than half a year or have lived in their place of current residence for less than half a year, but had left their registered household for more than half a year, they would be counted where they lived (in the city). If they have been in their place of current residence for more than half a year, then they would be counted at their place of current residence. If they have been in their place of current resi-

dence less than half a year and had left their place of household registration for less than half a year, then they would be registered in their place of origin.

10. Cheng Kaiming, "Education, Decentralization, and Regional Disparity in China," in Gerard A. Postiglione and Wing On Lee, eds., *Social Change and Educational Development: Mainland, China, Taiwan, and Hong Kong* (Hong Kong: Centre for Asian Studies, University of Hong Kong, 1995).

11. John N. Hawkins, "Centralization, Decentralization, Recentralization: Educational Reform in China," *Journal of Educational Administration* 38 (2000): 442–455; Mun C. Tsang, "Education and National Development in China since 1949: Oscillating Policies and Enduring Dilemmas," *China Review 2000* (2000): 579–618.

12. Ministry of Education, People's Republic of China Law on Compulsory Education (Beijing: Ministry of Education, 1986).

13. Ministry of Education, Article 9, People's Republic of China Education Law, 1995.

14. Ministry of Education, Article 10, People's Republic of China Education Law, 1995.

15. Heidi Ross, *Where and Who Are the World's Illiterates: China* (UNESCO Global Monitoring Report China Country Study) (Paris: UNESCO, 2006), 39.

16. Ministry of Education, *Action Plan for Revitalizing Education for the 21st Century*, 1999. Electronic version posted to http://www.moe.edu.cn/.

17. Gerard A. Postiglione, "School Access and Equity in Rural Tibet," in Hannum and Park, *Education and Reform in China.*

18. State Council, *2003–2007 Action Plan for Revitalizing Education*, March 2004.

19. CERNET, "China to Spend 218 Bln Yuan Promoting Rural Education," 2005. Retrieved July 7, 2006, http://www.edu.cn/20051227/3167788.shtml.

20. CERNET, "China to Spend 218 Bln Yuan Promoting Rural Education," 2005. Retrieved July 7, 2006, http://www.edu.cn/20051227/3167788.shtml; for a different timeline for eliminating fees, see CERNET, "Rich-Poor Education Gap to be Addressed," 2005. Retrieved July 7, 2006, http://www.edu.cn/20051130/3163495 .shtml.

21. These were calculated as fifth-grade enrollments/grade one enrollments five years before.

22. Ministry of Education, *2003 Nian Xiaoxue Xuesheng he Chuzhong Xuesheng Boliulü* (2003 Retention Rates for Primary and Junior Secondary Students) (Beijing: Ministry of Education, n.d.) Retrieved September 9, 2006, http://www.moe .edu.cn/edoas/website18/info14306.htm.

23. United States Agency for International Development (USAID). *Global Education Database (GED Version 6)* (Washington, DC: Office of Education of the US Agency for International Development, 2005). Retrieved July 14, 2006, http:// qesdb.cdie.org/ged/index.html.

24. Calculated as third-grade [*chuzhong sannianji*] enrollments/first-grade [*chuzhong yinianji*] enrollments three years before; see Ministry of Education, *2003*

Nian Xiaoxue Xuesheng he Chuzhong Xuesheng Boliulü. (2003 Retention Rates for Primary and Junior Secondary Students)

25. Rachel Connelly and Zhenzhen Zheng, "Educational Access for China's Post-Cultural Revolution Generation: Patterns of School Enrollment in China in 1990," in Hannum and Park, *Education and Reform in China;* Rachel Connelly and Zhenzhen Zheng, "Enrollment and Graduation Patterns as China's Reforms Deepen, 1990–2000," Hannum and Park, *Education and Reform in China.*

26. Connelly and Zheng, "Enrollment and Graduation Patterns as China's Reforms Deepen."

27. The difference between the two years was significant at P < .0001 by a Fischer's exact test on the two-by-two contingency table of exclusion by year (1989, 2004).

28. These issues are interrelated.

29. Rachel Connelly and Zhenzhen Zheng have drawn similar conclusions from analyses of 1990 and 2000 census data. See Connelly and Zheng, "Educational Access for China's Post-Cultural Revolution Generation"; Connelly and Zheng, "Enrollment and Graduation Patterns as China's Reforms Deepen"; Rachel Connelly and Zhenzhen Zhang, "School Enrollment and Graduation Rates in Western China Based on the 2000 Census," *Journal of Chinese Economic and Business Studies* 5 (2007): 147–161.

30. People's Daily, "China Pledges Elimination of Rural Compulsory Education Charges in Two Years," *People's Daily Online* 2006 (March 5). Reports on the timeline for eliminating tuition charges vary; see also CERNET, "China to Spend 218 Bln Yuan Promoting Rural Education," 2005. Retrieved July 7, 2006, http://www.edu.cn/20051227/3167788.shtml.

31. Xinhua News Service, "China Adopts Amendment to Compulsory Education Law," *Xinhua Online 2006* (June 29).

32. People's Daily, "Draft Amendment to Compulsory Education Law under 1st Review of China's Legislature," *People's Daily Online* 2006 (February 25); Xinhua, "China Adopts Amendment to Compulsory Education Law."

33. Barry Sautman, "Ethnic Law and Minority Rights in China: Progress and Constraints," *Law and Policy* 21 (1999): 284–314.

34. Ross, *Where and Who Are the World's Illiterates: China,* 25; B. Sautman, "Ethnic Law and Minority Rights in China," 289; and J. Lin, "Policies and Practices of Bilingual Education for the Minorities in China," *Journal of Multilingual and Multicultural Development* 18 (1997): 193–205; Postiglione, "School Access and Equity in Rural Tibet."

35. Postiglione, "School Access and Equity in Rural Tibet."

36. Xinhua, "China Adopts Amendment to Compulsory Education Law."

37. For a review, see Yiu-Por Chen and Zai Liang, "Educational Attainment among Migrant Children: The Forgotten Story of Urbanization in China," in Hannum and Park, *Education and Reform in China.*

38. Li Wenli, "The Role of Higher Education Financing Policy for Providing Equal Enrollment Opportunity and Resource Distribution," *Peking University Education Review* 2 (2006): 34–46.

39. Liu Jingming, "The Expansion of Higher Education and Uneven Access to Opportunities for Participation in It, 1978–2003," *Chinese Education and Society* 40 (2007): 36–59.

40. Li, "The Role of Higher Education Financing Policy for Providing Equal Enrollment"; and Liu, "The Expansion of Higher Education."

41. Liu, "The Expansion of Higher Education."

42. In their report on a multi-country project on spatial inequality in human development, economists Ravi Kanbur and Anthony Venables note that despite a "sense" in the policy community that spatial inequality is rising in most developing and transition economies, there is "remarkably little" systematic documentation about spatial and regional inequality. Ravi Kanbur and A. J. Venables, "Rising Spatial Disparities and Development," *United Nations University Policy Brief* 3 (2005): 1–8.

43. See Zhang's 2006 review of comparative research and analysis of school systems in southern and western Africa: Zhang Yanhong, "Urban-Rural Literacy Gaps in Sub-Saharan Africa: The Roles of Socioeconomic Status and School Quality," *Comparative Education Review* 50 [2006]: 581–602.

7. Disparities in Health Care and Health Status

1. William Hsiao, "Transformation of Health Care in China," *New England Journal of Medicine* 310, no. 14 (1984): 932–936.

2. Therese Hesketh and Wei Xing Zhu, "Health in China: From Mao to Market Reform," *British Medical Journal* 314, no. 7093 (May 1997): 1543–1545; Therese Hesketh and Wei Xing Zhu, "Health in China: The Healthcare Market," *British Medical Journal* 314, no. 7094 (May 1997): 1616–1618; Magnus Lindelow and Adam Wagstaff, *China's Health Sector—Why Reform Is Needed,* Prepared for China Rural Health AAA (Washington, DC: World Bank, April 2005); Jonathan Watts, "China's Rural Health Reforms Tackle Entrenched Inequalities," *Lancet* 367, no. 9522 (2006): 1564–1565; and Jonathan Watts, "Protests in China over Suspicions of a Pay-or-die Policy," *Lancet* 369, no. 9556 (2007): 93–94.

3. Watts, "China's Rural Health Reforms."

4. Local governments resorted to other sources of revenue, such as increased licensing and service fees. Although these extra-budgetary revenues increased, they only amounted to 4 percent of GDP in 1994. See also the discussion in Christine Wong and Richard Bird, "China's Fiscal System: A Work in Progress," *ITP Paper,* no. 0515 (Ontario: International Tax Program, October 2005).

5. The drop in the share of government subsidies is partly due to rapidly rising total health expenditures and inflation.

6. R. Zhou, "Responsible utilization of antibiotics should be a societal responsibility," Sanmenxia Central Hospital, Paper No. 223.

7. David Blumenthal and William Hsiao, "Privatization and Its Discontents—The Evolving Chinese Health Care System," *New England Journal of Medicine*, 353, no. 11 (2005): 1165–1170.

8. Peter Smith, Christine Wong, and Yuxin Zhao, *Public Expenditure and the Role of Government in the Chinese Health Sector,* Prepared for China Rural Health AAA (Washington, DC: World Bank, May 2005).

9. Center for Health Statistics and Information, Ministry of Health, *An Analysis Report of the National Health Survey in 2003* (Beijing: Ministry of Health, 2004).

10. Richard Steckel, "Stature and the Standard of Living," *Journal of Economic Literature* 33, no. 4 (December 1995): 1903–1940; T. Paul Schultz, "Wage Gains Associated with Height as a Form of Health Human Capital," *AEA Papers and Proceedings* 92, no. 2 (2002): 349–353; John Strauss and Duncan Thomas, "Health, Nutrition, and Economic Development," *Journal of Economic Literature* 36, no. 2 (1998): 766–817.

11. J. Geng, "Six Main Causes for Expensive and Inaccessible Health Care," *Xinhua*, February 20, 2006.

12. L. Zhu, "Communique of the Sixth Plenum of the 16th CPC Central Committee," *Xinhua*, October 11, 2006.

13. C. Feng, "President Hu Promises Bigger Government Role in Public Health," *Xinhua*, October 24, 2006.

14. Central Committee of CPC, *Decisions of the Central Committee of the Communist Party of China and the State Council on Further Strengthening Rural Health Work* (Beijing: Central Committee of the Communist Party of China, 2002).

15. Liang Wannian and Daniel K. Y. Chan, "Community Health Care Reform and General Practice Training in China—Lessons Learned," *Medical Education Online* [serial online] 9, no. 10 (2004).

16. Zhao Y., Wan Q., Tao S., et al., "Analysis and Result on China Health Account Assessment for the Year of 2002," (in Chinese) *Chinese Health Economics* 23 (2004): 5–10.

8. The Narrowing Digital Divide

I wish to thank Dr. Ran Tao of the Centre for Chinese Agricultural Policy, Chinese Academy of Sciences, and Yu Senqing, Yin Shihong, Wu Xiaorong, Fan bin, Kuang Xiaoqian and Song Jianping at the Jiangxi Academy of Social Sciences for generously enabling and supporting the fieldwork for this research. I am also grateful to the people and officials in Rivercounty in Jiangxi for their good nature and help. Further, I wish to thank Vanessa L. Fong, Mark Selden, Martin K. Whyte, and the two anonymous reviewers at Harvard University Press for their helpful comments on this chapter. Finally, I acknowledge the invaluable funding support for the 2004 fieldwork from the Leverhulme Contemporary China Studies Programme at Oxford, funding support for the 2006 fieldwork from the Nuffield Foundation, and funding support for the 2007 and 2008 fieldwork from the British Inter-University China Centre at Oxford.

1. Jack Linchuan Qiu, "The Internet in China: Data and Issues" (working paper, Annenberg Research Centre, October 1, 2003); Yuezhi Zhao, "Caught in the Web: The Public Interest and the Battle for Control of China's Information Superhighway," *Info* 2, no. 1 (2000): 42–66; Yuezhi Zhao, "The State, the Market and Media Control in China," in Thomas Pradip and Zahoram Nain, eds., *Who Owns the Media: Global Trends and Local Resistance* (London: Zed Books, 2004), 179–212.

2. Karsten Giese, "Internet Growth and the Digital Divide: Implications for Spatial Development," in Christopher R. Hughes and Gudrun Wacker, eds., *China and the Internet: Politics of the Digital Leap Forward* (London: Routledge, 2003), 30–57; Eric Harwit, "Spreading Telecommunications to Developing Areas in China: Telephones, the Internet and the Digital Divide," *China Quarterly*, no. 180 (December 2004): 1000–1030; Wensheng Wang, "Bridging the Digital Divide Inside China," in the Annual Conference of the Association of the Internet, Centre for the Scietech Documentation Information (CITYBeijing : Chinese Academy of Social Sciences, 2002), http://www.jsai.or.jp/afita/afita-conf/2002/part7/p533.pdf; Xiangdong Wang, "Mobile Communication and Mobile Internet in China," Stockholm School of Economics (October 2001); Zhao, "The State, the Market and Media Control in China"; and Jun Zhang, "Market Transition, State Connections and the Internet Geography in China," *China Review* 6, no. 1 (2006): 93–123.

3. Giese, "Internet Growth and the Digital Divide"; Harwit, "Spreading Telecommunications to Developing Areas in China"; and Zhang, "Market Transition, State Connections and the Internet Geography in China."

4. Carolyn Cartier, Manuel Castells, and Jack Linchuan Qiu, "The Information Have-Less: Inequality, Mobility and Translocal Networks in Chinese Cities," *Studies in Comparative International Development* 40, no. 2 (2005): 9–34.

5. Zhuangqun Hu and Chuanwu Huang, *Analysis of China Telecom Development* (Beijing: Social Science Academic Press, 2006).

6. Hu and Huang, *Analysis of China Telecom Development*, 207.

7. Kenneth Lynch, *Rural-Urban Interaction in the Developing World* (London: Routledge, 2005), 151.

8. *Jiangxi ribao* [Jiangxi Daily], March 31, 2006, b1, b4.

9. Xiangdong Wang, "Mobile Communication and Mobile Internet in China," Stockholm School of Economics (October 2001), 52.

10. Hu and Huang, *Analysis of China Telecom Development*, 146.

11. In 2000 Rivercounty began relocating the county seat from one side of a river to another. This involved clearing land, constructing a whole new town, and moving all government offices and functionaries from one to the other.

12. *Yichun ribao* [Yichun Daily], April 3, 2006.

13. The authors of the report define "internet user" as a "Chinese citizen aged 6 and over who averagely uses the internet at least one hour per week."

14. China Internet Network Information Centre/CINIC, *Statistical Survey Report on Internet Development in China,*(Beijing: CINIC, January, 2007).

15. Cartier, Castells, and Qiu, "The Information Have-Less."

16. Ibid.

17. Yuezhi Zhao, "Caught in the Web: the Public Interest and the Battle for Control of China's Information Superhighway," *Info* 2, no. 1 (2000): 42–66.

18. Wang, "Bridging the Digital Divide Inside China."

19. Zhao, "Caught in the Web."

20. Interview, Branch Manager, Rivercounty branch of China Telecom, July 24, 2006.

21. Changzhu Huang, "China's Experience in Leapfrogging Technical Development," http://orbicom.uquam.ca; file name asia2.pdf (accessed August 10, 2006), 18; and Gordon A. Gow and Richard K. Smith, *Mobile and Wireless Communications* (Berkshire: Open University Press, 2006).

22. Interview, Rivercounty branch, China Telecom, July 25, 2006; *Jingganshan bao* [Jingganshan Daily], July 2, 2006.

23. China Mobile's monthly revenue per user decreased from 91 yuan in December 2006 to 82 yuan at the end of March 2007. See "Budget Users Rein in China Mobile," *BBC News*, Tuesday, April 22, 2008, http://news.bbc.co.uk/2/hi/7360782.stm.

24. Interviews, Rivercounty branches of China Mobile and Unicom, July 24, 2006.

25. Ibid.

26. Interview, manager, China Post, Wanzai County, Jiangxi, May 30, 2006.

27. Interview with Internet cafe owner, age 26, July 25, 2006.

28. Interview with Internet cafe owner, age 22, July 25, 2006.

29. Cartier, Castells, and Qiu, "The Information Have-Less."

30. Beatriz Carrillo Garcia, *New Urban Space in China: Towns, Rural Labour and Social Inclusion* (PhD diss., University of Technology, Sydney, 2007); G. William Skinner, "Differential Development in Lingnan," in Thomas P. Lyons and Victor Nee, eds., *The Economic Transformation of South China: Reform and Development in the Post-Mao Era* (Ithaca: Cornell University Press, 1994), 17–54.

31. Cartier, Castells, and Qiu, "The Information Have-Less," 24.

32. Interview, Rivercounty branch of China Mobile, July 24, 2006.

33. Rachel Murphy, *How Migrant Labor Is Changing Rural China* (New York: Cambridge University Press, 2002).

34. Raymond Ngan and Stephen Ma, "The Relationship of Mobile Telephony to Job Mobility in China's Pearl River Delta," *Knowledge, Technology and Policy* 21, no. 2 (June 2008): 55–63.

35. Heather A. Horst and Daniel Miller, "From Kinship to Link-up: Cell Phones and Social Networking in Jamaica," *Current Anthropology* 46 (2005): 755–778.

36. Ye Jingzhong, James Murray, and Wang Yihuan, *Left-Behind Children in Rural China* (Beijing: Social Sciences Academic Press, 2005).

37. Visit to the premises of a pig farmer entrepreneur accompanied by officials from Siguqiao Township, Shangrao, Jiangxi, December 2007.

38. See, for example, Hu Jinxing, "Farmers of Liaoxi: Going Online to Prepare for the Busy Farming Season," *Yichun ribao* [Yichun Daily], March 7, 2006.

39. Qu Hongbin, *The Great Migration: How China's 200 Million Surplus Workers Will Change the Economy Forever* (London: HSBC Global Research, October 14, 2005).

40. Interview, Mr Nie, poultry farmer, WX village, Rivercounty, December 16, 2007.

41. Interview, post office manager, Rivercounty, July 24, 2006.

42. Interview, Village post-office agent, Rivercounty, Jiangxi, July 25, 2006.

43. Eszter Hargittai, "Second-Level Digital Divide: Differences in People's Online Skills," *First Monday* 7 (2002), http://firstmonday.org/issues/issue7_4/hargittai/index.html, cited in Soraj Hongladarom and Achara Endz, "Turning Digital Divide into Digital Dividend: Anticipating Thailand's Demographic Dividend" (paper presented at the Conference on the Demographic Dividend, College of Population Studies, Chulalongkorn University, November 6, 2003).

44. This example to illustrate the quality of an informational society is adapted from Felix Stalder, *Key Contemporary Thinkers: Manuel Castells* (Cambridge: Polity Press, 2006).

45. Dai, Xiudian, "ICTs in China's Development Strategy," in Christopher R. Hughes and Gudrun Wacker, eds., *China and the Internet* (London: Routledge, 2003), 8–29, (9–10).

46. Yongling Zhong, *Information Services in Rural China* (Bangkok: Food and Agriculture Organisation, 2004); and Scott Waldron, Colin Brown and John Longworth, "State Sector Reform and Agriculture in China," *The China Quarterly*, no. 186 (June 2006): 277–294.

47. Shaohui Zhang and Chunhui Guo, "Jiaqiang nongye xinxihua, cujin xin nongcun jingji jianshe" [Strengthen agricultural informationalization, promote the economic construction of the new countryside], *Hebei keji shifan xueyuan xuebao* [Hebei Normal University of Science and Technology] 6, no. 4 (December 2007): 63–65, 76.

48. Victor Shih and Zhang Qi, "Who Receives Subsidies?", in Vivienne Shue and Christine Wong, eds., *Paying for Progress in China* (London: Routledge, 2007), 145–165.

49. Björn Alpermann, "The Post-Election Administration of Chinese Villages," *China Journal*, no. 46 (2001): 45–67.

50. Kathleen Hartford, "Cyberspace with Chinese Characteristics," *Current History* (September 2000), http://china-wired.com/pubs/ch/home.htm; Zhao, "Caught in the Web."

51. Governments use these Web sites to publicize locally relevant policies and economic opportunities; to offer services such as online applications for replacement identity cards; and to enhance the transparency of government procedures.

52. *Jiangxi Ribao* [Jiangxi Daily], July 27, 2006.

53. Interview, Rivercounty Government Information Centre, July 25, 2006.

54. Interview, Rivercounty Organisation Department, August 9, 2004.

55. Scott Waldron, Colin Brown, and John Longworth, "State Sector Reform and Agriculture in China," *China Quarterly,* no. 186 (June 2006): 277–294.

56. Waldron, Brown, and Longworth, "State Sector Reform and Agriculture in China."

57. Interview with the Director of the Agricultural Information Centre, Rivercounty, Jiangxi, July 30, 2004; Interview with the Head of the Rivercounty Bureau of Agriculture, Jiangxi, July 24, 2006.

58. Zhong Yongling, *Information Services in Rural China: Field Surveys and Findings* (Bangkok: Food and Agriculture Organization of the United Nations, Regional Office for Asia and the Pacific, 2004).

59. *Jiangxi ribao* [Jiangxi Daily], April 1, 2006; and *Yichun ribao* [Yichun Daily], April 24, 2006.

60. Figures provided by the Rivercounty Bureau of Agriculture, December 2008.

61. Interview with the Director of the Agricultural Information Centre, Rivercounty, Jiangxi, July 30, 2004.

62. Ran Zhang, "Changing Legal Constructions of the Right to Education in China" (paper presented at the Annual Meeting of the American Educational Research Association, Chicago, April 9–13, 2007).

63. Zhang, "Changing Legal Constructions."

64. Xuehui An, Emily Hannum, and Tanja Sargent, "Teacher Qualifications, Teaching Quality and Student Educational Outcomes," *China: An International Journal* 5, no. 2 (2007): 309–334.

65. The Sunshine project also allows parents to contact teachers online and to view their child's grades online—a function that is likely to benefit the children of computer-literate and connected county seat parents over those of their classmates from rural families. Sunshine project is also the most established in county seat schools where most students have urban backgrounds and least established in township middle and high schools in which most students are from rural backgrounds. *Jiangxi Ribao* [Jiangxi Daily], May 18, 2006; *Yichun ribao* [Yichun Daily], April 27, 2006; Interview, Rivercounty China Telecom, July 25, 2006; and interview, Wanzai China Telecom, May 29, 2006.

66. Recorded interview, Headmaster, PB village primary school, Rivercounty, December 14, 2007.

67. Emily Hannum and Albert Park, "Educating China's Rural Children in the 21st Century," *Harvard China Review* 3, no. 2 (2002): 8–14. This article discusses the problems of teacher retention in poor rural areas.

68. Pranab Cafedhan and Dilip Mookherjee, "Decentralizing Antipoverty Program Delivery in Developing Countries," *Journal of Public Economics* 89, no. 4 (2005): 675–704; Phil Brown and Albert Park, "Education and Poverty in Rural China," *Economics of Education Review* 21, no. 6 (December 2002): 523–541; and Ravi Kanbur and Xiaobo Zhang, *Spatial Inequality in Education and Health Care in China*, Discussion Paper no. 4136 (London: The Centre for Economic Policy Research, December 2003).

69. Yuanli Liu, Keqin Rao, and William C. Hsiao, "Medical Expenditure and Rural Impoverishment in China," *Journal of Health, Population and Nutrition* 21, no. 3 (September 2003): 216–222; Simone Brant, Michael Garris, Edward Okeke, and Josh Rosenfeld, "Access to Care in Rural China: A Policy Discussion," Working Paper, (International Economic Development Program, Gerald R. Ford School of Public Policy, University of Michigan, April 2006); and Rachel Murphy, "Paying for Education in Rural China," in Shue and Wong, *Paying for Progress in China*, 69–95.

70. M. Torero and J. von Braum, *Information and Communication Technologies for Development and Poverty Reduction* (Washington DC: International Food Policy Research Institute, 2006); and S. Chowdhury and M. Torero, *Rural Urban Linkages in Bangladesh: Impact of Infrastructure and the Food Value Chain on Livelihoods and Migration of Landless Households* (Washington, DC: International Food Policy Research Institute, 2006), cited in Joachim von Braun, *Rural-Urban Linkages for Growth, Employment and Poverty Reduction* (Washington DC: International Food Policy Research Institute, 2006). While statistical studies indicate that interaction effects between electricity, roads, and phones promote income increases, it is not well understood how these occur. It is thought that the interaction effects propel income increases through their influence on time/labor allocation, improved purchasing power, reduced transaction costs, and so on. Since the early 2000s rural China has experienced a major increase in infrastructure investment, including in roads. See Linxiu Zhang, Renfu Luo, Chengfang Liu, and Scott Rozelle, "Investing in Rural China: Tracking China's Commitment to Modernization," in Shue and Wong, *Paying for Progress in China*, 117–144. It is likely the interaction effects will also exert a positive impact on incomes in rural China.

71. C. E. Cragg, N. Edwards, Z. Yue, S. L. Xin, and Z. D. Hui, "Integrating Web-Based Technology into Distance Education for Nurses in China: Computer and Internet Access and Attitudes," *CIN: Computers, Informatics, Nursing*, no. 21 (2003): 265–274; J. Tucker, C. Jia, G. Henderson, M. Cohen, J. Davis, and X. Wang, "Online HIV/STI Chinese Clinician Training," *Sexually Transmitted Infection* 80, no. 2 (April 2004): 154; S. Q. Yu and Minjuan J. Wang, "Modern Distance Education Project for the Rural Schools of China: Recent Developments and Problems," *Journal of Computer Assisted Learning* 22, no. 4 (2006): 273–283; and Bernadette Robinson, "Using Distance Education and ICT to

Improve Access, Equity and the Quality in Rural Teachers' Professional Development in Western China," *International Review of Research in Open and Distance Learning* 9, no. 1 (2008), http://www.irrodl.org/index.php/irrodl/article/viewArticle/486/1015.

72. China Internet Network Information Centre/CINIC, *Statistical Survey Report on Internet Development in China* (Beijing: CINIC, January 2007).

9. The Impact of Variations in Urban Registration within Cities

We thank the Hong Kong Research Grant Council (Grant No. HKBU2135/04H and HKBU24907) and Hong Kong Baptist University for financial support. We are grateful to Professor Martin King Whyte, Professor Mark Selden, and anonymous reviewers for valuable comments on an earlier draft of this chapter.

1. T. J. Cheng and M. Selden, "The Origins and Social Consequences of China's Hukou System," *China Quarterly*, no. 139 (1994): 644–668; K. W. Chan and L. Zhang, "The Hukou System and Rural-urban Migration in China: Processes and Changes," *China Quarterly*, no. 160 (1999): 818–855; F. L. Wang, "The Breakdown of a Great Wall: Recent Changes in the Household Registration System of China," in T. Scharping, ed., *Floating Population and Migration in China: The Impacts of Economic Reforms* (Hamburg: Institute of Asian Studies, 1997), 149–165; F. L. Wang, "Reformed Migration Control and New Targeted People: China's Hukou System in the 2000s," *China Quarterly*, no. 177 (2004): 115–132; F. L. Wang, *Organizing through Division and Exclusion: China's Hukou System* (Stanford, CA: Stanford University Press, 2005); Xiaogang Wu and Donald Treiman, "The Household Registration System and Social Stratification in China: 1955–1996," *Demography* 41, no. 2 (2004): 363–384; and Li Zhang, "Reform of the Hukou System and Rural-urban Migration in China: the Challenges Ahead," 2000, http://mumford.albany.edu/chinanet/conferences/Zhang.doc, accessed September 2006.

2. *Danwei* is one of the most-used Chinese words in contemporary Chinese studies. *Danwei* is a generic term denoting the Chinese socialist workplace and the specific range of practices that it embodies. It is a specific form of social organization that came to dominate socialist China's cities. To find more detailed discussion on *danwei*, see A. G. Walder, *Communist Neo-traditionalism: Work and Authority in Chinese Industry* (Berkeley: University of California Press, 1986); Lu Feng, *Danwei: Yizhong Teshu de Shehui Zuzhi Xingshi* [*Danwei*: a unique form of social organization], *Chinese Social Science* 1 (1989): 71–88; M. Li, F. Z. Zhou, and K. Li, *Danwei: Zhiduhua Zuzhi de Neibu Jizhi* [*Danwei*: the mechanism of institutional organization], *Chinese Social Science*, no. 16 (1996): 89–108; J. Q. Cao and Z. Y, Chen, *Zouchu Lixiang Chengbao: Zhongguo Danwei Xianxiang Yanjiu* [Walk out of the "ideal castle": research on the Chinese *danwei* phenomena] (Shenzhen: Hai-

tian Press, 1997); Y. H. Zhou and X. M. Yang, *Zhongguo Danwei Zhidu* [Chinese *danwei* system] (Beijing: Chinese Economy Press, 1999); D. Bray, *Social Space and Governance in Urban China: The Danwei System from Origins to Reform* (Stanford, CA: Stanford University Press, 2005); D. F. Lu, *Remaking Chinese Urban Form: Modernity, Scarcity, and Space, 1949–2005* (London and New York: Routledge, 2006).

3. W. L. Parish and M. K. Whyte, *Village and Family in Contemporary China* (Chicago: University of Chicago Press, 1978), Chapter 4; Walder, *Communist Neo-traditionalism*.

4. See, for example, Wu and Treiman, "The Household Registration System and Social Stratification."

5. NBS, "2005 *nian Quanguo Baifen Zhiyi Renkou Chouyang Diaocha Zhuyao Shuju Gongbao* [Comminique on China 2005 1 percent population survey data], NBS, March 16, 2006.

6. For information about the administration system of Chinese cities, see W. Hua, "*Danwei zhi Xiang Shequ zhi de Huigui: Zhongguo Chengshi Jiceng Guanli Tizhi Wushi Nian Bianqian*" [From the work-unit to community system: fifty years of change in China's urban local management system], *Zhanlue yu Guanli* [Strategy and management], (2000): 86–99; and F. L. Wu, "China's Changing Urban Governance in the Transition towards a more Market-oriented Economy," *Urban Studies* 39, no. 7(2002): 1071–1093.

7. S. M. Li and Y. M. Siu, "Residential Mobility and Urban Restructuring under Market Transition: A Study of Guangzhou, China," *Professional Geographer* 53 (2001): 219–229; S. M. Li and Y. M. Siu, "Commodity Housing Construction and Intra-urban Migration in Beijing: An Analysis of Survey Data," *Third World Planning Review* 23, no. 1 (2001): 39–60; S. M. Li, "Housing Tenure and Residential Mobility in Urban China: Analysis of Survey Data," *Urban Affairs Review* 38, no. 4 (2003): 510–534; S. M. Li, "Life Course and Residential Mobility in Beijing, China," *Environment and Planning A* 36 (2004): 27–43; and S. M. Li, "Residential Mobility and Urban Change in China: What Have We Learned So Far?", in L. J. C. Ma and F. Wu, eds., *Restructuring the Chinese City: Changing Society, Economy and Space* (Oxford: Routledge, 2005), 175–192.

8. F. L. Wu, "Intraurban Residential Relocation in Shanghai: Modes and Stratification," *Environment and Planning A* 36 (2004): 7–25.

9. The survey was supported by a project funded by the Research Grant Council of Hong Kong entitled "Rising Homeownership and Emerging Patterns of Residential Differentiation in Chinese Cites," which was investigated by Professor Li Si-ming of Hong Kong Baptist University. It was also part of a joint project in cooperation with a team of international scholars undertaking surveys covering Guangzhou, Shanghai, Nanjing, and Beijing.

10. Before 2000, Guangzhou had administered eight urban districts (Liwan, Yuexiu, Dongshan, Haizhu, Tianhe, Fangcun, Huangpu, and Baiyun) and four county-

level cities (Panyu, Huadu, Zengcheng, and Conghua). It enlarged its city proper by converting two county-level cities (Panyu and Huadu) into urban districts in 2000. On April 28, 2005, the State Council approved a new scheme of district administration in Guangzhou. The original urban districts of Dongshan and Fangcun were abolished and incorporated into Yuexiu and Liwan, respectively. The southern part of Panyu was upgraded into an independent urban district, Nansha district. The adjacent area between Baiyun, Zengcheng, Conghua, Huangpu, and Tianhe was designated as an independent urban district, Luogang District (see Figure 9.1). As a consequence, there are ten urban districts (Yuexiu, Liwan, Haizhu, Tianhe, Baiyun, Huangpu, Luogang, Panyu, Huadu, and Nansha, the former seven covering the same territory as the original eight urban districts), and two county-level cities (Zengcheng and Conghua) under Guangzhou's jurisdiction.

11. There was a slight oversampling in Panyu to get a sizable subsample so that a separate analysis could be implemented there.

12. P. F. Landry and M. M. Shen, "Reaching Migrants in Survey Research: The Use of the Global Positioning System to Reduce Coverage Bias in China," *Political Analysis* 13 (2005): 1–22.

13. Wang, *Organizing through Division and Exclusion*.

14. Urban villages, or villages in the city *(chengzhongcun)*, have emerged and flourished in many Chinese cities since economic reform. During rapid urbanization and urban expansion, large pieces of agricultural land of rural villages in the urban periphery have been expropriated by the government for nonagriculture use. But the villages still keep the rural administrative system, independent from their urban counterparts. These villages are allowed to retain a certain amount of land to develop secondary or tertiary industry. More often than not, these villages construct housing, hotels, and commercial and office buildings for lease. As a result, the former rural landscape has been transformed dramatically. The villages are now surrounded by the urban built-up area. For example, in 2000 there were 138 urban villages in the original eight urban districts in Guangzhou. The dual land system and *hukou* system are considered the most important factors contributing to the emergence of urban villages.

The peasants in urban villages keep their rural *hukou* status, although they are no longer engaged in any agricultural activities. The rural *hukou* of the urban village are entitled to the benefits of residential lots, collective redistribution, and more lenient family planning targets. Each peasant is allowed to keep a piece of residential land, where they can construct a building. The building may be as tall as ten floors. It is leased to migrants at a very low rent compared with other apartments in a similar location. The other important income source for urban village peasants is profit-sharing from the collective economy. For instance, the average household income for the peasant of Shipai village in Guangzhou can reach 100,000 yuan per year, including both profit-sharing and rents, which is much higher than the average income of the Guangzhou urban residents. The

peasants are relying greatly on the collective economy and redistribution; there-
fore, they are not willing to convert their *hukou* status from agricultural to nonagricultural. For more detailed analysis on urban villages in China, see J. M.
Zhang, *Guangzhou Dushi Cunzhuang Xingcheng Yanbian Jizhi: Yi Tianhe Qu
Haizhu Qu Weili* [The formation and evolution of the urban village in Guang-
zhou: the cases of Tianhe and Haizhu], (PhD diss., Sun Yat-Sen University,
Guangzhou, 1998); L. X. Li, *Guangzhou Chengzhongcun Xingcheng Ji Gaizao
Jizhi Yanjiu* [Research on the formation and alteration mechanism of urban vil-
lages in Guangzhou], (PhD diss., Sun Yat-Sen University, Guangzhou, 2001);
X. B. Cai, *Guangzhou Chengzhongcun Gaizao Celue Tantao* [Discussion on the
alteration strategies toward urban villages in Guangzhou], (Master's thesis, Sun
Yat-Sen University, Guangzhou, 2003); P. L. Li, *Cunluo de Zhongjie: Yangcheng-
cun de Gushi* [The end of villages: a tale of Yangchengcun] (Beijing: Commercial
Press, 2004); Y. Y. Lan, Dushi li de Cunzhuang: Yige "Xin Cunshe Gongtongti"
de Shidi Yanjiu [Village in the Metropolis: An Empirical Research on "Urban Village Community"] (Beijing: SDX Joint Publishing Company, 2005).

15. The "blue seal (lanyin) *hukou*" was formally endorsed in 1992 and has become
popular in large Chinese cities since the mid- and late 1990s. It aimed at attracting the most desirable elements of the migrant population by providing them
with a right of abode and certain welfare provisions in cities. The criteria for
obtaining a blue seal *hukou* include a large amount of investment or home purchase and age, education, and professional skills. See L. Wong and W. P. Huen,
"Reforming the Household Registration System: A Preliminary Glimpse of the
Blue Chop Household Registration System in Shanghai and Shenzhen," *International Migration Review* 32, no. 4 (1998): 974–994; Wang, "The Breakdown of a
Great Wall"; and Chan and Zhang, "The Hukou System and Rural-Urban Migration in China."

16. Wang, *Organizing through Division and Exclusion*.

17. The *hukou* acquisition scheme through commodity housing purchase was can-
celled in Guangzhou in 2004. But those who bought commodity housing before
2004 are still eligible to apply for the blue seal *hukou* of Guangzhou.

18. K. Xie, *"Woguo Renhufenli de Jiben Zhuangkuang"* [The basic condition of the
separation of registered *hukou* place and actual residence in China], *Renkou Yanjiu* [Population Research] 21, no. 5 (1997): 54–58; R. J. Wu, *"Dachengshi Neibu
Renhufenli Xianxiang Jiqi Duice Yanjiu: Yi Shanghai Weili"* [The phenomenon
of "people living away from their household registration places" in big cities: the
case of Shanghai], *Renkou Yanjiu* [Population Research] 23, no. 6 (1999): 16–20;
H. W. Zhou and X. Yang, *"Zhongguo Chengshi Renhu Fenli Zhuangkuang yanjiu"* [Studies on the separation of registered place and residence in Chinese cit-
ies], *Zhongguo Renkou Kexue* [Chinese Journal of Population Science] (2002):
29–34; H. Z. Geng, *"Dachengshi Renhufenli Tezheng Zongshu he Duice Sikao"*
[The characteristics and countermeasures of separation of registered and actual

residence in big cities], *Chengshi Guihua Xuekan* [Urban Planning Forum] 4 (2005): 67–71.

19. Y. X. Zhou and L. J. C. Ma, "Economic Restructuring and Suburbanization in China," *Urban Geography* 21 (2000): 205–236; and Y. X. Zhou and John R. Logan, "Growth on the Edge: The New Chinese Metropolis," in John R. Logan, ed., *Urban China in Transition* (London: Blackwell Publishers, 2008).

20. F. L. Wu and Anthony Gar-On Yeh, "Changing Spatial Distribution and Determinants of Land Development in Chinese Cities in the Transition from a Centrally Planned Economy to a Socialist Market Economy: A Case Study of Guangzhou," *Urban Studies*, 34 (1997): 1851–1880; Zhou and Ma, "Economic Restructuring and Suburbanization"; Li and Siu, "Residential Mobility and Urban Restructuring"; and Li and Siu, "Commodity Housing Construction and Intra-urban Migration."

21. P. Gaubatz, "China's Urban Transformation: Patterns and Processes of Morphological Change in Beijing, Shanghai and Guangzhou," *Urban Studies* 36 (1999): 1495–1521.

22. Wu, "China's Changing Urban Governance."

23. The urban infrastructure construction fee was abolished in Guangzhou on January 1, 2004.

24. Guangzhou Municipal Government, *Guanyu Gaige Woshi Changzhu Renkou Tiaokong Guanli Zhidu de Ruogan Yijian de Tongzhi* [Circular concerning the reform on management and control regulation of resident population] (Guangzhou: Guangzhou Municipal Government, 2003).

25. Chan and Zhang, "The Hukou System and Rural-Urban Migration."

26. On repeated occasions in recent years, the Chinese central government has called for an elimination of the discriminatory treatment of migrant children by urban public schools and in 2008 even pledged to supply funding to enable such schools to enroll migrant children on an equal basis with children of urban *hukou* holders. However, at the time of the 2005 survey systematic discrimination against migrant children was still very much in force in Guangzhou and other large cities, and even in 2008 it is unclear how fully these new measures will actually be implemented.

27. C. Ikels, *The Return of the God of Wealth: The Transformation to a Market Economy in Urban China* (Stanford, CA: Stanford University Press, 1996).

28. Guangzhou Municipal Education Bureau, *Guangzhoushi Zhongxiaoxue Zhaosheng Kaoshi Gongzuo Yijian* [Circular on the admission and examination of the primary and junior schools in Guangzhou in 2006], http://www.gzedu.gov.cn/file/InfoRead.asp?id=1760, accessed August 22, 2006.

29. Besides the requirement of holding a local *hukou*, evidence must be presented that the only residence of the child is in the urban district where the targeted prestigious school is located.

30. Zhou and Yang, "Zhongguo Chengshi Renhu Fenli Zhuangkuang Yanjiu."

31. According to the guidelines of the Panyu Urban Planning Bureau, the standard for setting up school for a commodity housing estate is as follows: there should

be one junior middle school for every 20,000 persons with an area ranging from 20,000 to 25,000 m² (215,278 to 269,098 ft²); a primary school for every 10,000 persons with an area from 12,000 to 15,000 m² (129,167 to 161,459 ft²); and a kindergarten for every 5,000 persons with an area 3,000 to 4,000 m² (32,292 to 43,056 ft²).

32. It is a common practice for public schools, especially prestigious ones, to charge high temporary enrollment fees *(zanzhu fei, zexiao fei)* for students who are not eligible for admission.

33. For instance, Beijing, Shanghai, and Guangzhou began to allow migrant children to attend the local public schools (primary and junior middle schools only) provided that the host schools have extra enrollment quota and a lump sum of temporary enrollment fee is paid. At present, only a few migrant children actually go to the local public schools.

34. The admission and examination committee of Guangzhou, *Guangzhoushi Gaozhong Jieduan Xuexiao Zhaosheng Baoming Redian Wenti Jieda* [Questions and answers about the admission of senior middle schools in Guangzhou in 2007], March 14, 2007, http://www.gzzk.com.cn/html/100002110.html, accessed April 4, 2007.

35. C. Froissart, "China's Household Registration (Hukou) System: Discrimination and Reform," 2005, http://www.cecc.gov/pages/roundtables/090205/Froissart .php, accessed August 16, 2006; and Wang, *Organizing through Division and Exclusion.*

36. L.P. Sun, *"Weishenme Zhongguoren Shangban Zheme Lei* [Why Chinese are so tired at work?], Feburary 28, 2007. http://www.chinaelections.org/NewsInfo.asp? NewsID=103614, accessed June 2, 2009.

37. W. S. Tang, "Urbanisation in China: A Review of Its Causal Mechanisms and Spatial Relations," *Progress in Planning* 48, no. 1 (1997): 1–65.

10. Boundaries of Inequality

1. Charles Tilly, *Durable Inequality* (Berkeley: University of California Press, 1998).

2. Neil C. Macrae and Galen V. Bodenhausen, "Social Cognition: Thinking Categorically about Others," *Annual Review of Psychology* 51 (2000): 93–120.

3. Michèle Lamont and Marcel Fournier, "Introduction," in Michèle Lamont and Marcel Fournier, eds., *Cultivating Differences: Symbolic Boundaries and the Making of Inequality* (Chicago: University of Chicago Press, 1992), 1–20.

4. These volumes were, respectively, William Parish and Martin Whyte, *Village and Family in Contemporary China* (Chicago: University of Chicago Press, 1978), and Martin Whyte and William Parish, *Urban Life in Contemporary China* (Chicago: University of Chicago Press, 1984).

5. Examples of such works include Deborah Davis's work on the urban elderly (Deborah Davis-Friedman, *Long Lives: Chinese Elderly and the Communist*

Revolution [Cambridge, MA: Harvard University Press, 1983]); Andrew Walder's study of urban factories (Andrew Walder, *Communist Neo-traditionalism* [Berkeley: University of California Press, 1986]); and Yanjie Bian's book on urban inequality and stratification (Yanjie Bian, *Work and Inequality in Urban China* [Albany, NY: SUNY Press, 1994]). For Chinese villages they include Anita Chan, Richard Madsen, and Jonathan Unger, *Chen Village* (Berkeley: University of California Press, 1984); Jean C. Oi, *State and Peasant in Contemporary China* (Berkeley: University of California Press, 1989); and Edward Friedman, Paul Pickowicz, and Mark Selden, *Revolution, Resistance and Reform in Village China* (New Haven, CT: Yale University Press, 2005).

6. Discussions of China's past urban-rural relations can be found in Gary D. Hamilton, *Commerce and Capitalism in Chinese Societies* (Oxford: Routledge, 2006). On urbanization in other developing country settings, see Michael Lipton, *Why Poor People Stay Poor* (London: Temple Smith, 1977).

7. This invisible wall and the urban-rural inequality associated with the *hukou* system are well documented and analyzed. See, for example, Kam Wing Chan, *Cities with Invisible Walls: Reinterpreting Urbanization in Post-1949 China* (Hong Kong: Oxford University Press, 1994); John Knight and Lina Song, *Rural Urban Divide: Economic Disparity and Interactions in China* (Oxford: Oxford University Press, 1999); Xiaogang Wu and Donald Treiman, "The Household Registration System and Social Stratification in China, 1955–1996," *Demography* 41 (2004): 363–384; and Martin K. Whyte, "City Versus Countryside in China's Development," *Problems of Post-Communism* 43 (1996): 9–22.

8. Zai Liang and Zhongdong Ma, "China's Floating Population," *Population and Development Review* 30 (2004): 467.

9. Kam Wing Chan, "Recent Migration in China: Patterns, Trends, and Policies," *Asian Perspectives* 25 (2001): 127–155.

10. Zai Liang, "Internal Migration in China: Policy Changes, Recent Trends, and New Challenges," in Zhongwei Zhao and Fei Guo, eds., *Transition and Change: China's Population at the Turn of the Twenty-First Century* (Oxford: Oxford University Press, 2007), 197–215.

11. The remainder of the growth was roughly equally attributed to rural-to-urban reclassification and urban natural population growth. See Kam Wing Chan and Ying Hu, "Urbanization in China in the 1990s: New Definition, Different Series, and Revised Trends," *China Review* 3 (2003): 49–71.

12. Using a Chinese government definition of poverty as a per capita income of less than 101 yuan (US$12.50 by official exchange rates) per year in 1978 and 626 yuan (US$77.90) per year in 2000, the poverty headcount fell from 31 percent of the population or 250 million people in 1978 to under 4 percent or 32 million in 2000 (Albert Park and Sangui Wang, "China's Poverty Statistics," *China Economic Review* 12 [2001]: 384–398). Raising the bar above this draconian definition to the World Bank's more conventional measure of one purchasing power

parity dollar a day, the results are equally impressive. In 1980, 76 percent of China's rural population had incomes of under a dollar a day; by 1988 the percentage had plummeted to 23 percent, by 1995 to 20 percent, and by 2003 only 9 percent lived at such extreme hardship (Deborah Davis and Wang Feng, "Poverty and Wealth in Post-socialist China: An Overview," in Deborah Davis and Wang Feng, eds., *Creating Wealth and Poverty in Post-Socialist China* [Stanford, CA: Stanford University Press, 2008]).

13. Barry Naughton, *The Chinese Economy: Transitions and Growth* (Cambridge, MA: MIT Press, 2007), 210–211.

14. Naughton, *The Chinese Economy*, 133. See also Figure 5.1 in this volume.

15. The World Bank, *Sharing Rising Incomes: Disparities in China* (Washington, DC: The World Bank, 1997), 3.

16. Inequality between urban and rural China is staggering, as the World Bank study comments, "Internationally, the urban-rural income ratio rarely exceeds 2.0—as it does in China—and in most countries it is below 1.5." In addition, because of the extensive urban public subsidies, "even China's high ratio fails to capture the full extent of disparities in living standards between city dwellers and rural residents" (World Bank, *Sharing Rising Incomes*, 3). See the attempt to capture the value of urban subsidies in Chapter 5 of this volume.

17. Azizur Rahman Khan and Carl Riskin, "Income and Inequality in China: Composition, Distribution and Growth of Household Income, 1988 to 1995," *China Quarterly* 154 (1998): 247.

18. Azizur Rahman Khan and Carl Riskin, "China's Household Income and Its Distribution, 1995 and 2002," *China Quarterly* 182 (2005): 358.

19. Dorothy J. Solinger, *Contesting Citizenship in Urban China: Peasant Migrants, the State, and the Logic of the Market* (Berkeley: University of California Press, 1999).

20. For labor market segregation, see John Knight and Lina Song, *Toward a Labor Market in China* (Oxford: Oxford University Press, 2005). For unequal citizenship rights, see Solinger, *Contesting Citizenship in Urban China*, and Chapter 3 in this volume. For unequal benefits in one Chinese city (Shanghai), see Wang Feng, Xuejin Zuo, and Danqing Ruan, "Rural Migrants in Shanghai: Living under the Shadows of Socialism," *International Migration Review* 36 (2002): 520–545; Wang Feng, Ping Ren, Zhan Shaokang, and Shen Anan, "Reproductive Health Status, Knowledge, and Access to Health Care among Female Migrants in Shanghai, China," *Journal of Biosocial Sciences* 37 (2004): 603–622.

21. *Southern Weekend*, August 4, 2005, B-14.

22. The survey was conducted by Peking University's Research Center on Contemporary China in 2004, with funding from the Smith-Richardson Foundation, supplemented by Harvard University, University of California—Irvine, and Peking University. Martin King Whyte is the principal investigator of the survey project. I would like to thank survey organizers and participants—in particular,

Martin Whyte, Shen Mingming, Yang Ming, Pierre Laundry, Jieming Chen, and Albert Park. I am also indebted to research assistants at Harvard University for data cleaning and organization, which made analyses for this study much easier.

23. Oversampling of the urban population was carried out to increase representation of urban respondents in the sample and has no consequences for most of the analyses in this chapter, as results to follow are divided into three groups and are not national averages.

24. In our multistage probability sampling, 40 half-degree grids were first selected following the probability proportional to size (PPS) principle based on the population density of all half-degree grids. At the second stage, two square-minute grids were selected from each of the selected half-degree grids, again following the PPS principle based on population density of the square-minute grids (each square-minute grid covers about 2.26 km² [.87 sq. miles]). At the third stage, within each selected square-minute grid, one half-minute grid was selected. These sampling procedures resulted in 80 half-minute grids. Oversampling of urban population added 21 city half-minute grid units, with a total number of half-minute grids of 101. At the fourth stage of sampling, within each selected half-minute grid, a number of square-second grids (each covering 90 by 90 meters, or 84.4 by 97.4 yards) were selected based on the population density of the half-minute grid. At the last stage, survey takers compiled lists of all residences in the selected grids. These lists formed the basis of selecting individual respondents, with one randomly selected person aged eighteen to seventy interviewed at each listed address. To enhance the representativeness of our sample, we also applied stratification across different macro-regions of China (Pierre Landry and Mingming Shen, "Reaching Migrants in Survey Research: The Use of the Global Positioning System to Reduce Coverage Bias in China," *Political Analysis* 13 (2005): 1–22.

25. The seemingly higher medical insurance coverage for rural population, at 15.3 percent, is mainly due to recently created rural cooperative health insurance programs, in which rural residents pay a small premium (in some locales at 20 yuan per person per month) and receive in return a very limited reimbursement for expenses. (See the discussion in Chapter 7 in this volume.)

26. Such a pattern is also well documented and discussed in Wenfang Tang, *Public Opinion and Political Change in China* (Stanford, CA: Stanford University Press, 2005), as well as in Martin Whyte, "Chinese Popular Views about Inequality," *Asia Program Special Report, Woodrow Wilson International Center* 104 (2002): 4–10; and in Chunping Han and Martin Whyte, "The Social Contours of Distributive Injustice Feelings in Contemporary China," in Deborah Davis and Wang Feng, eds., *Creating Wealth and Poverty in Post-Socialist China* (Stanford, CA: Stanford University Press, 2008).

27. The question on polarization was "In recent years, in our society the rich have become richer and the poor have become poorer. Do you agree with such a state-

ment?" The answers were coded into one of the five categories: strongly agree, somewhat agree, have no opinion, somewhat disagree, or strongly disagree.

28. Factor analysis is used to create summary measures of distrust in the system. The questions used to create the factors are those asking respondents what actually counted in determining a person's income level. The questions asked include those more based on merit, such as education, difficult working conditions, personal effort, job responsibilities, and contributions to one's work organization. They also include those based on status or connections, such as gender, relationship with superiors, having connections, or having urban households, and so on. A five-point scale was used for answers. With a factor analysis limiting to two factors using a Varimax rotation, one factor was created that has a high representation (factor loadings) of answers on merit-based items and another on non-merit-based items. The latter is used here as the "System Distrust" factor. Factor scores are standardized scores with a mean of zero.

29. See Tang, *Public Opinion and Political Change in China;* Whyte, "Chinese Popular Views about Inequality"; and Han and Whyte, "The Social Contours of Distributive Injustice Feelings."

30. Wang Feng, *Boundaries and Categories: Rising Inequality in Post-Socialist Urban China* (Stanford, CA: Stanford University Press, 2008).

31. Wang Feng, *Boundaries and Categories.*

11. Rural Prejudice and Gender Discrimination in China's Urban Job Market

This chapter was presented at the conference "Rethinking the Rural-Urban Cleavage in Contemporary China" held at the Fairbank Center for East Asian Research at Harvard University, October 6–8, 2006, and in a workshop sponsored by the Department of Organization and Management, National University of Singapore on October 11, 2006. The authors would like to thank the participants at the Fairbank conference and the NUS workshop, especially Professors Richard Avery, John Logan, and Martin Whyte, for comments and suggestions. Lei Guang also acknowledges research support from San Diego State University's Faculty Development Program and the Program in Agrarian Studies at Yale University in 2004–2005.

1. Kam Wing Chan, *Cities with Invisible Walls: Reinterpreting Urbanization in Post-1949 China* (Hong Kong: Oxford University Press, 1994); Gail E. Henderson et al., "Re-Drawing the Boundaries of Work: Views on the Meaning of Work *(Gongzuo)*," in *Re-Drawing Boundaries: Work, Households, and Gender in China,* ed. Barbara Entwisle and Gail E. Henderson (Berkeley: University of California Press, 2000); Emily Honig, *Creating Chinese Ethnicity* (New Haven, CT: Yale University Press, 1992); John Knight and Lina Song, *The Rural-Urban Divide: Economic Disparities and Interactions in China* (New York: Oxford University Press, 1999); Ching Kwan Lee, *Gender and the South China Miracle: Two Worlds of Factory Women* (Berkeley: University of California Press, 1998); Helen Siu,

"Cultural Identity and the Politics of Difference in South China," *Daedalus* 122, no. 2 (1993); Dorothy Solinger, *Contesting Citizenship in Urban China* (Berkeley: University of California Press, 1999); Martin King Whyte, "Town and Country in Contemporary China," *Comparative Urban Research* 10, no. 1 (1983).

2. C. Cindy Fan, "The Elite, the Natives, and the Outsiders: Migration and Labor Market Segmentation in Urban China," *Annals of the Association of American Geographers* 92, no. 1 (2002); C. Cindy Fan, "Rural-Urban Migration and Gender Division of Labor in Transitional China," *International Journal of Urban and Regional Research* 27, no. 1 (2003); Xin Meng and Junsen Zhang, "The Two-tier Labor Market in Urban China," *Journal of Comparative Economics* 29, no. 3 (2001); Li Qiang, *Nongmingong yu Zhongguo shehui fenceng* [Peasant migrants and social stratification in China] (Beijing: shehui kexue wenxian chubanshe, 2004); Yang Yunyan, et al., *Chengshi jiuye yu laodongli shichang zhuanxing* [Urban employment and transition of labor market] (Beijing: Zhongguo tongji chubanshe, 2004).

3. Edward X. Gu, "Forging a Labor Market in Urban China: The Legacies of the Past and the Dynamics of Institutional Transformation," *Asian Affairs* 28, no. 2 (2001); John Knight, Lina Song, and Huaibin Jia, "Chinese Rural Migrants in Urban Enterprises: Three Perspectives," *Journal of Development Studies* 35, no. 3 (1999).

4. Zou Ping, "Guanyu jianli chengxiang tongyi laodongli shichang de sikao" [Reflections on building a unified rural-urban labor market], *Jingji yanjiu cankao* [Economic research reference], no. 27 (2004): 17.

5. *Hukou* migrants are also termed "permanent migrants." This term refers to those who are allowed to transfer their *hukou* registration along with their employment to the new city of residence. They are in contrast to the "temporary migrants" whose *hukou* is not transferred and who are thus regarded as "outsiders," no matter how long they have lived and worked in a city. See Fan, "The Elite, the Natives, and the Outsiders"; Yang Yunyan, Kam Wing Chan, and Liu Ta, "Wailai laodongli dui chengshi bendi laodongli shichang de yingxiang—Wuhan diaocha de jiben kuangjia yu zhuyao faxian" [Rural migrant workers and impact on local labor market—research framework and main findings from Wuhan research], *Zhongguo renkou kexue* [Chinese population science], no. 2 (2001).

6. Yunyan Yang, "Urban Labor Market Segmentation: Some Observations Based on Wuhan Census Data," *China Review* 3, no. 2 (2003): 154.

7. Fan, "The Elite, the Natives, and the Outsiders"; Yang Yunyan, Kam Wing Chan, and Liu Ta, "Wailai laodongli dui chengshi bendi laodongli shichang de yingxiang."

8. Ching Kwan Lee, "Engendering the Worlds of Labor: Women Workers, Labor Markets, and Production Politics in the South China Economic Miracle," *American Sociological Review* 60, no. 3 (1995); Wailai nongmingong ketizu, "Zhujiang sanjiaozhou wailai nongmingong zhuangkuang" [Conditions of rural migrant

workers in the Pearl River Delta area], *Zhongguo shehui kexue* [Chinese social science], no. 4 (1995).

9. Meng and Zhang, "The Two-tier Labor Market in Urban China."

10. Qi Zhongxi and Li Jianghong, "Duoshao mingong na budao qian?" [How many rural migrant workers do not get paid?] *Beijing rencai shichang bao* [Beijing talent market news], January 18, 2003, 22.

11. Pan Jinchang, "Jingji zhuangui zhong de Zhongguo nuxing jiuye yu shehui baozhang" [Chinese economic transition and women's employment and social security], *Guanli shijie* [Management world], no. 7 (2002).

12. Yang Yunyan, et al., *Chengshi jiuye yu laodongli shichang zhuanxing*, 190.

13. Guojia tongji ju, *Zhongguo laodong tongji nianjian* [China labor statistics almanac] (Beijing: Zhongguo tongji chubanshe, 2003), 18, 130, 38, 41.

14. Shi Meixia, "Zhongguo xianjieduan nv daxuesheng jiuye wenti yanjiu" [Research on the employment of female college graduates], *Funu yanjiu luncong* [Research on women series], no. 69 (2005).

15. Cai Fang, Zhang Chewei and Du Yang, eds., *2002 nian: Zhongguo renkou yu laodong wenti baogao* [2002 report on population and labor issues] (Beijing: shehui kexue wenxian chubanshe, 2002), 274.

16. Yang Yunyan, et al., *Chengshi jiuye yu laodongli shichang zhuanxing*, 190.

17. Fan, "Rural-Urban Migration and Gender Division of Labor in Transitional China," 39.

18. Yang Cao and Chiung-Yin Hu, "Gender and Job Mobility in Postsocialist China: A Longitudinal Study of Job Changes in Six Coastal Cities" (Charlotte, NC: University of North Carolina-Charlotte, 2006).

19. Cai Fang, Zhang Chewei, and Du Yang, *2002 nian: Zhongguo renkou yu laodong wenti baogao*, 274.

20. John Knight and Lina Song, "Towards a Labor Market in China," *Oxford Review of Economic Policy* 11, no. 4 (1995): 106.

21. Margaret Maurer-Fazio, Thomas G. Rawski, and Wei Zhang, "Inequality in the Rewards for Holding up Half the Sky: Gender Wage Gaps in China's Urban Labor Market, 1988–1994," *China Journal*, no. 41 (1999).

22. Xiaoling Shu and Yanjie Bian, "Market Transition and Gender Gap in Earnings in Urban China," *Social Forces* 81, no. 4 (2003). Nevertheless, Cai Fang and his colleagues found overall wage differentials between men and women to be insignificant, even though they acknowledge that gender discrimination exists in other areas, such as in unequal job opportunities, occupational segregation, and limits on promotion for women in the workplace. Cai Fang, Zhang Chewei and Du Yang, *2002 nian: Zhongguo renkou yu laodong wenti baogao*, 277, 86.

23. Michael Fix and Raymond Struyk, eds., *Clear and Convincing Evidence: Measurement of Discrimination in America* (Washington, DC: The Urban Institute Press, 1993).

24. Michael Fix, George Galster, and Raymond Struyk, "An Overview of Auditing for Discrimination," in *Clear and Convincing Evidence: Measurement of Discrimination in America*, ed. Michael Fix and Raymond Struyk (Washington, DC: The Urban Institute Press, 1993).

25. James J. Heckman, "Detecting Discrimination," *Journal of Economic Perspectives* 12, no. 2 (1998); James J. Heckman and Peter Siegelman, "The Urban Institute Audit Studies: Their Methods and Findings," in *Clear and Convincing Evidence: Measurement of Discrimination in America*, ed. Michael Fix and Raymond Struyk (Washington, DC: The Urban Institute Press, 1993).

26. Fix, Galster, and Struyk, "An Overview of Auditing for Discrimination," 12.

27. Peter A. Riach and Judith Rich, "Measuring Discrimination by Direct Experimental Methods: Seeking Gunsmoke," *Journal of Post Keynesian Economics* 14, no. 2 (1991–1992).

28. Fix, Galster, and Struyk, "An Overview of Auditing for Discrimination," 2.

29. Devah Pager, "The Mark of a Criminal Record," *American Journal of Sociology* 108, no. 5 (2003): 945.

30. Roger Jowell and Patricia Prescott-Clarke, "Racial Discrimination and White-Collar Workers in Britain," *Race: A Journal of Race and Group Relations* 11, no. 4 (1970); Neil McIntosh and David J. Smith, "The Extent of Racial Discrimination," *Political and Economic Planning Broadsheet* 15, no. 547 (1974); Riach and Rich, "Measuring Discrimination by Direct Experimental Methods," 144.

31. Devah Pager, "Double Jeopardy: Race, Crime, and Getting a Job," *Wisconsin Law Review* 2 (2005): 629.

32. Fix and Struyk, *Clear and Convincing Evidence: Measurement of Discrimination in America.*

33. David Neumark, *Sex Differences in Labor Markets* (New York: Routledge, 2004), 185–205; Pager, "The Mark of a Criminal Record."

34. All four were unemployed at the time of our contact, but one student had to make arrangements to put off starting a temporary position he was due to start a few days after our initial contact.

35. Wang Jicheng, "Zhongguo qiye renyuan zhaopin xianzhuang diaocha baogao" [Report on employee recruitment by Chinese enterprises], in Lin Zeyan, ed., *Zhuanxing Zhongguo qiye renli ziyuan guanli* [Human resource management in transitional China] (Beijing: Zhongguo laodong shehui baozhan chubanshe, 2004), 58–59.

36. By 2003, there were 3,305 talent markets at various levels of government in China. They held scheduled job fairs at regular intervals as well as specialized job fairs targeting certain segments of the population (for example, spring college-graduate job fairs).

37. The job fairs we surveyed in the district were run by labor or personnel agencies at various levels of governments, including the District Labor Bureau, the Municipal Personnel Department, and even the Central Personnel Ministry.

38. Employers generally pay 300 to 400 yuan for a small booth to display information materials and conduct interviews. Admission tickets for job seekers cost about 3 to 5 yuan for the day.

39. In contemporary China, "ruralness" is not fully captured by one's agricultural *hukou* status. In this study we use "rural" loosely to include not only people with agricultural *hukou* (who may come from the Beijing suburbs), but also people with nonagricultural *hukou* who are from so-called "rural" areas—small towns and even small cities in largely rural provinces, say Jiangxi or Anhui, which are far from Beijing. In the questionnaire, we ask our testers to furnish at least two pieces of information to establish their "rural" personhood: one is that their *Jiguan* (where they are from) is in a rural town; the other is that they have had work experience in a rural town or county seat.

40. Gary Becker, *The Economics of Discrimination* (Chicago: University of Chicago Press, 1971).

41. Fix, Galster, and Struyk, "An Overview of Auditing for Discrimination," 15.

42. Interview, Senior Editor of BTMN, July 22, 2004.

43. Interview, Staff of marketing department of BTMN, July 22, 2004.

44. One must not be misled by the number of "managerial" positions, as the word *manager* is used loosely so that it may include low-level supervisory positions, especially in the private sector. It is hard to discern the ownership status of these companies, but interviews with the newspaper staff confirm that most advertisers were from the private sector.

45. Wang Ruilin and Xu Jianxue, "Changshe xing biyesheng jiuye shichang shou huanying" [Permanent graduate labor markets welcomed], in *Beijing rencai shichang bao* [Beijing talent market news], July 24, 2002.

46. Xu Jianxue, "Fei jingji daxuesheng jinjing jiuye jiang shenpi" [Non-Beijing *hukou* college graduates need approval for employment in Beijing], in *Beijing rencai shichang bao* [Beijing talent market news], March 5, 2003.

47. *Beijing rencai shichang bao* [Beijing talent market news], September 3, 2003, 11.

48. Dorothy Solinger, "Labor Market Reform and the Plight of the Laid-Off Proletariat," *China Quarterly* 170 (2002).

49. Interview, Human Resource manager, July 28 2004.

50. *Beijing rencai shichang bao* [Beijing talent market news], August 2, 2003, 7.

51. We included "SOE work" and "laid-off/unemployment status" in our query to see if HR managers would regard these items as relevant to their hiring decisions. Lei Guang found in his fieldwork in the late 1990s that many businesses preferred hiring laid-off SOE workers because of government incentives. For example, employers of laid-off SOE workers were exempted from mandatory contribution to the unemployment fund, health-care account, and pension plan for those workers.

52. A "unified" national labor market here usually refers to the repeal of all government restrictions on labor mobility. In such a market, *hukou* would no longer be

a formal criterion for exclusion of individuals from employment opportunities in a given locality.

53. In spite of its unique strengths, the audit methodology in general, and the present study in particular, suffers from several limitations. Critics of the audit methodology have pointed out the ethical issues involved in the audit test design, the difficulties of exact matches of testers, the so-called experimenter effect whereby testers are predisposed to find discrimination, the problem of inference and cross-pair comparison, and other definitional and conceptual issues. Designing such a study in China has its special challenges. For one thing, hiring by blind interviews was still not widely practiced in China at the time, so a large number of jobs were not accessible to our testers. For another, variations in local, regional, and even sectoral (e.g. construction) recruitment practices tended to make it difficult to generalize our findings beyond service and low-end jobs in metropolitan cities.

12. Gender and Citizenship Inequality

Thanks to Martin K. Whyte for inviting me to participate in this edited volume and the workshop on which it is based and for editorial advice. Thanks also to Rachel Murphy and Emily Hannum for helpful feedback on an earlier draft.

1. Despite the easing of migration restrictions and the erosion of *hukou* functions in recent years, labor migrants in China's large cities were still excluded from certain privileges based on their outsider status. See chapters in this volume by Lei Guang and Fanmin Kong (Chapter 11), Li Limei and Li Si-ming (Chapter 9), and Fei-Ling Wang (Chapter 15), and also the following: Fei-Ling Wang, "Reformed Migration Control and New Targeted People: China's Hukou System in the 2000s," *China Quarterly* 177 (2004): 115–132; Fei-Ling Wang, "Brewing Tensions While Maintaining Stabilities: The Dual Role of the Hukou System in Contemporary China," *Asian Perspective* 29, no. 4 (2005): 85–134; Amnesty International Report on the People's Republic of China, "Internal Migrants: Discrimination and Abuse: The Human Cost of an Economic 'Miracle'" (2007); Centre for Women's Law Studies and Legal Services of Peking University, *Theory and Practice of Women's Rights and Interests in Contemporary China: Investigation and Study on the Enforcement of UN CEDAW in China* (Beijing: Worker's Publishing House of China, 2001); and Tan Shen, "Nüxing liudong yu xingbie pingdeng" [Rural women's migration and gender equality], (paper presented at the conference on "Rural-Urban Migrants: Situations, Trends, and What We Can Do," Beijing, August 19–20, 2006).

2. Wang, "Brewing Tensions," 101.

3. Research Team on Migration and Gender Relationship, Chinese Academy of Social Sciences (Zheng Zhenzhen and Zhan Shaohua) and Sichuan Academy of So-

cial Science (Gao Hua), "Impact of Migration on Gender Relationships and Rural Women's Status in China," UNESCO Research Project Report, March 2006, 1.

4. See Delia Davin, *Internal Migration in China* (New York: St. Martin's Press, 1999); Arianne M. Gaetano and Tamara Jacka, eds., *On the Move: Women and Rural-to-Urban Migration in Contemporary China* (New York: Columbia University Press, 2004); Tamara Jacka, *Rural Women in Urban China: Gender, Migration, and Social Change* (Armonk, NY: M. E. Sharpe, 2006); *Nongmin liudong yu xingbie* [Peasant migration and gender] (Zhengzhou: Zhongyuan nongmin chubanshe, 2000); Zheng Zhenzhen and Xie Zhenming, *Renkou liudong yu nongcun funü fazhan* [Migration and rural women's development] (Beijing: Social Sciences Academic Press, 2004).

5. Tamara Jacka and Arianne M. Gaetano, "Introduction: Focusing on Migrant Women," in Gaetano and Jacka, *On the Move*: 1–38; Ching Kwan Lee, *Gender and the South China Miracle: Two Worlds of Factory Women* (Berkeley: University of California Press, 1998); Pun Ngai, *Made in China: Women Factory Workers in a Global Workplace* (Durham, NC: Duke University Press, 2005); Li Zhang, "The Interplay of Gender, Space, and Work in China's Floating Population," in Barbara Entwisle and Gail E. Henderson, eds., *Re-Drawing Boundaries: Work, Households, and Gender in China* (Berkeley: University of California Press, 2000), 171–196.

6. C. Cindy Fan, "Rural-Urban Migration and Gender Division of Labor in Transitional China," *International Journal of Urban and Regional Research* 27, no. 1 (2003): 24–47.

7. See Arianne M. Gaetano, " 'Filial Daughters, Modern Women': Migrant Domestic Workers in Post-Mao Beijing," in Gaetano and Jacka, *On the Move*, 41–79; Tiantian Zheng, "From Peasant Women to Bar Hostesses: Gender and Modernity in Post-Mao Dalian," in Gaetano and Jacka, *On the Move*, 80–108; Pun, *Made in China*; Tan Shen, "Leaving Home and Coming Back: The Experiences of Rural Migrant Women," in Tao Jie, Zheng Bijun, and Shirley L. Mow, eds., *Holding Up Half the Sky: Chinese Women Past, Present, and Future* (New York: The Feminist Press at the City University of New York, 2004), 248–258; Tan Shen, "The Relationship Between Foreign Enterprises, Local Governments, and Women Migrant Workers in the Pearl River Delta," in Loraine A. West and Yaohui Zhao, eds., *Rural Labor Flows in China* (Berkeley: Institute of East Asian Studies, University of California, 2000), 292–309; Feng Xu, *Women Migrant Workers in China's Economic Reform* (New York: St. Martin's Press, 2000); Zhang, "The Interplay"; and Heather Xiaoquan Zhang, "Female Migration and Urban Labour Markets in Tianjin," *Development and Change* 30 (1999): 21–41.

8. See C. Cindy Fan, "Out to the City and Back to the Village: The Experiences and Contributions of Rural Women Migrating from Sichuan and Anhui," in Gaetano and Jacka, *On the Move*, 177–206; Arianne Gaetano, "Sexuality in Diasporic Space: Rural-to-Urban Migrant Women Negotiating Gender and Marriage in Contempo-

rary China," *Gender, Place, and Culture* 15, no. 6 (2008), special issue on hetero-sexuality and migration in Asia edited by Katie Walsh, Hsiu-hua Shen, and Katie Willis; Jacka, *Rural Women;* Zhang, "The Interplay"; Louise Beynon, "Dilemmas of the Heart," in Gaetano and Jacka, *On the Move,* 131–150; Zheng and Xie, "Renkou liudong"; and Binbin Lou, Zhenzhen Zheng, Rachel Connelly, and Kenneth D. Roberts, "The Migration Experiences of Young Women from Four Counties in Sichuan and Anhui," in Gaetano and Jacka, *On the Move,* 207–241.

9. Bai Nansheng and Song Hong, eds., *Huixiang, haishi jincheng? Zhongguo nong-cun waichu laodongli huiliu yanjiu* [Return to the countryside, or enter the city? Research on the return migration of China's migrant labor force] (Beijing: China Financial and Economic Press, 2002), 104–105; Jacka and Gaetano, "Introduction," 24.

10. Compare with Scott Rozelle, Li Guo, Minggao Shen, Amelia Hughart and John Giles, "Leaving China's Farms: Survey Results of New Paths and Remaining Hurdles to Rural Migration," *China Quarterly* 58 (1999): 367–393.

11. See Bai and Song, *"Huixiang."*

12. Employers often demand a deposit *(yajin)* from migrant workers at the start of their employment period as a guarantee that a worker will not quit without giving advance notice.

13. According to the manager of hotel housekeeping services at that time, hiring migrants through a contractor was a cost-cutting measure that did not violate existing Labor Bureau regulations, which stipulated that hotel chambermaids must have local, Beijing *hukou.* Indeed, more than 100 occupations were closed to migrant workers in the 1990s. For more information, see Wang Huaxin, ed., *Nongmin jincheng jiuye zhinan* [Problems of peasants entering cities] (Beijing: Zhonguo Nongye Press, 1998), 50.

14. Gaetano, " 'Filial Daughters' "; Jacka, *Rural Women.*

15. C. Cindy Fan, *China on the Move: Migration, the State, and the Household* (New York: Routledge, 2007).

16. World Bank East Asia Environment and Social Development Unit, *China Country Gender Review 2002* (June); and Elizabeth Rosenthal, "School a Rare Luxury for Rural Chinese Girls," *New York Times,* November 1, 1999.

17. Tan, *"Nüxing liudong."*

18. Bai and Song, *"Huixiang,"* 119.

19. Ibid., 121; Qian Cai, "Migrant Remittances and Family Ties: A Case Study in China," *International Journal of Population Geography* 9 (2003): 471–483. The situation is opposite for remitting overseas migrants from the Philippines, according to Maruja M. B. Asis, "The Return Migration of Filipino Women Migrants: Home, But Not for Good?", in Dr. Supang Chantavanich et al., eds., *Female Labor Migration in South-East Asia: Change and Continuity* (Bangkok: Asian Research Centre for Migration, Institute of Asian Studies, Chulalongkorn University, 2001).

20. Fan, "The State, the Migrant," 186.

21. Cai, "Migrant Remittances." In contrast, Thai and Javanese daughters are expected to remit more than sons do in order to fulfill their filial obligations to parents. See Mary Beth Mills, *Thai Women in the Global Labor Force: Consuming Desires, Contested Selves* (New Brunswick, NJ: Rutgers University Press, 1999); Pilipa Esara, "'Women Will Keep the Household': The Mediation of Work and Family by Female Labor Migrants in Bangkok," *Critical Asian Studies* 36, no. 2 (2004): 199–216; and Juliette Koning, "The Impossible Return: The Post-Migration Narratives of Young Women in Rural Java," *Asian Journal of Social Science* 32, no. 2 (2005): 165–185.

22. Sally Sargeson, "Building for the Future Family," in Anne E. McLaren, ed., *Chinese Women: Living and Working* (New York: Routledge/Curzon Press, 2004), 149–168. In resource-poor villages and among disadvantaged rural bachelors. there is a shortage of prospective brides, which is attributed to the unbalanced sex ratio and the spatial economics (and sexual politics) of marriage migration. This shortage gives bachelors from more developed regions and wealthier households a comparative advantage. See Li Shuzhuo et al., "Son Preference and the Marriage Market Squeeze in China: An Integrated Analysis of the First Marriage and Remarriage Market," Abstract (2005), www.popline.org (accessed July 17, 2008).

23. Janet W. Salaff, *Working Daughters of Hong Kong: Filial Piety or Power in the Family?* (Cambridge: Cambridge University Press, 1981).

24. Nana Oishi, *Women in Motion: Globalization, State Policies, and Labor Migration in Asia* (Stanford, CA: Stanford University Press, 2005).

25. Mills, *Thai Women.*

26. Gaetano, "Sexuality."

27. See Asis, "The Return Migration"; and Esara, "'Women Will Keep the Household'."

28. Official employment agencies (for example, those run by the Ministry of Labor or Women's Federation) are far too few, and in addition these often levy fees that many migrants are unable or unwilling to afford. Furthermore, a lack of oversight has also allowed illicit agents to set up shop and take advantage of potential migrants.

29. Gaetano, "'Filial Daughters'," 49.

30. Pun, *Made in China.*

31. Large foreign investment enterprises in south China, for example, routinely replace women workers at marriage or pregnancy. See Tan, "The Relationship," and Pun, *Made in China.* Dismissal at pregnancy may even be written into labor contracts. See Zhenzhen Zheng and Pengling Lian, "Health Vulnerability among Temporary Migrants in Urban China" (paper prepared for XXV International Population Conference, Tours, France, July 18–23, 2005), 5.

32. Fan, "Rural-Urban Migration."

33. Jacka and Gaetano, "Introduction," 25–26.
34. Fan, "Rural-Urban Migration," 35; Tan, "The Relationship"; and Pun, *Made in China.*
35. See Susan Mann, "Work and Households in Chinese Culture: Historical Perspectives," in Entwisle and Henderson, *Re-Drawing Boundaries,* 15–32.
36. Lee, *Gender and the South China;* and Pun, *Made in China.*
37. Gaetano, "'Filial Daughters'"; and Zhang, "The Interplay."
38. Huang Ping, "China's Rural Labor Migrants under Uneven Development," *Social Sciences in China* (Winter 2003): 102–117.
39. Lei Guang and Fanmin Kong, Chapter 11 of this volume.
40. China has robust legislation protecting rights of workers and women, mainly in the form of the 1994 Labor and 1992 Women's laws. However, these were generated to protect rights of urban state-sector workers in response to restructuring. Only since 2001 has the government taken steps to extend these protections to the private sector, where migrants congregate (see Fei-Ling Wang's chapter in this volume, Chapter 15).
41. See reports in Amnesty International, "Report"; Centre for Women's Law, "Theory and Practice," 179–181; Jacka, *Rural Women,* 100–101; and Tan, "Rural Women's Migration."
42. See Amnesty International, "Report"; and Centre for Women's Law, "Theory and Practice," 179–181.
43. Mei-Ling Ellerman, *Gender and Rights: Research Report on Chinese Female Migrant Domestic Workers* (UNESCO Action Research Project on Domestic Workers, 2007).
44. See, for example, Centre for Women's Law, "Theory and Practice," 183–184.
45. Tan, "The Relationship" and "Leaving Home."
46. Centre for Women's Law, "Theory and Practice," 184–185.
47. Diana Fu, "China's Paradox Passage into Modernity: A Study on the Portrayal of Sexual Harassment in Chinese Media," *Stanford Journal of East Asian Affairs* (April 2005): 45–57. Exceptions include Ellerman, *Gender and Rights;* and Tang Can, "Sexual Harassment: The Dual Status of and Discrimination against Female Migrant Workers in Urban Areas," *Social Sciences in China* 19, no. 3 (1998): 64–71.
48. See Wu Jieh-min's chapter in this volume, Chapter 3.
49. For example, Lina and her coworkers were told by their supervisor in June that migrants would be prohibited from entering and exiting Beijing during the games.
50. Jacka, *Rural Women;* and Pun, *Made in China.*
51. Zheng and Lian, "Health Vulnerability," 5; and Zheng and Xie, *Renkou liudong,* 8.
52. Amnesty International, "Report," 16.
53. Oishi, *Women in Motion.*
54. See also Beynon, "Dilemmas"; Gaetano, "Sexuality"; and Jacka, *Rural Women.*

55. Wang Feng, "Gendered Migration and the Migration of Genders in Contemporary China," in Entwisle and Henderson, *Re-Drawing Boundaries*, 231–242.

56. Oishi, *Women in Motion.*

57. Rhacel Salazar Parreñas, *Servants of Globalization: Women, Migration and Domestic Work* (Stanford, CA: Stanford University Press, 2001); Koning, "Impossible Return"; Mills, *Thai Women;* Esara, "'Women Will Keep the Household'"; Bernadette P. Resurreccion, "Women In-Between: Gender, Transnational and Rural-Urban Mobility in the Mekong Region," *Gender, Technology, and Development* 9, no. 1 (2005): 31–56; and Anru Lee, "Between Filial Daughter and Loyal Sister: Global Economy and Family Politics in Taiwan," in Catherine Farrer, Anru Lee, and Murray Rubenstein, eds., *Women in the New Taiwan: Gender Roles and Gender Consciousness in a Changing Society* (Armonk, NY: M. E. Sharpe, 2004): 101–119.

58. Male migrants in China are likewise embedded in dual rural and urban social contexts. Yet they seem not to undergo a crisis in gender identity with migration, as it better enables them to fulfill gender expectations of a (future) household head, as I explained above. Thus they may remain homeward-oriented throughout the migration process. As Lei Guang remarks on migrant construction workers, who are mainly men: "They treat urban informal work as the source of accumulation for rural ends." Lei Guang, "Guerrilla Workfare: Migrant Renovators, State Power, and Informal Work in Urban China," *Politics and Society* 33, no. 3 (2005): 481–506 (quote from p. 501).

13. Ethnicity, Rurality, and Status

A version of this chapter was published in *China Journal*, no. 60 (July 2008): 1–21.

1. In this chapter, "Tibet" refers to the Tibet Autonomous Region (TAR) in China. This chapter does not address other areas populated with ethnic Tibetans or areas that are influenced by Tibetan Buddhism.

2. This and all quotations in this chapter are from interviews taken during the authors' fieldwork in Lhasa in 1999–2000, 2001, and 2003.

3. See, for example, Kam Wing Chan and Li Zhang, "The *Hukou* System and Rural-Urban Migration in China: Processes and Changes," *China Quarterly*, no. 160 (December 1999): 818–855; Tiejun Cheng and Mark Selden, "The Origins and Social Consequences of China's *Hukou* System," *China Quarterly*, no. 139 (September 1994): 646–668.

4. Dorothy Solinger, *Contesting Citizenship in Urban China: Peasant Migrants, the State, and the Logic of the Market* (Berkeley: University of California Press, 1999); and Jieh-min Wu, Chapter 3 in this volume.

5. Barbara Ching and Gerald Creed, eds., *Knowing Your Place: Rural Identity and Cultural Hierarchy* (New York: Routledge, 1997).

6. Katherine Palmer Kaup, *Creating the Zhuang: Ethnic Politics in China* (Boulder, CO: Lynne Rienner Publishers, 2000).

7. Barry Sautman, "Affirmative Action, Ethnic Minorities and China's Universities" (paper presented at the Fifth Conference of the Chinese Studies Association of Australia, 1997).

8. Hugh E. Richardson, *Tibet and Its History* (Boulder, CO: Shambhala Publications, 1984), 15.

9. Ping Xu, "Zangzu de hunyin guize he daode guannian" [Tibetan Rules of Marriage and Moral Views], *Zhongguo Xizang* [China Tibet], Issue 2 (2001).

10. Tsering Shakya, "Politicisation and the Tibetan Language," in R. Barnett and S. Akiner, eds., *Resistance and Reform in Tibet* (London: Hurst & Company, 1994), 157–165.

11. Åshild Kolås, "'Class' in Tibet: Creating Social Order Before and During the Mao Era," *Identities: Global Studies in Culture and Power* 10 (2003), 181–200.

12. Melvyn C. Goldstein and Cynthia M. Beall, "The Impact of China's Reform Policy on the Nomads of Western Tibet," *Asian Survey* 29 (1989): 619–641.

13. For details, see Yasheng Huang, "China's Cadre Transfer Policy toward Tibet in the 1980s," *Modern China* 21 (1995): 184–204; Rong Ma, "Han and Tibetan Residential Patterns in Lhasa," *China Quarterly*, no. 128 (December 1991): 814–835; and Lixiong Wang, *Tianzang—Xizang de mingyun* [Sky Burial: The Fate of Tibet] (Hong Kong: Mirror Press, 1998).

14. The only figures available for this period are about cadres, namely, "public administrators." Other Han residents included technical personnel and their family members. There were very few unskilled Han. In 1980 the total Han population of all kinds with formal *hukou* in TAR was around 120,000.

15. Yasheng Huang, "China's Cadre Transfer Policy."

16. "Work for the state" has a technical meaning in China's bureaucratic system. It includes those working in government agencies, state-owned enterprises, schools, hospitals, research institutes, art troupes, and so on. "Work for the state" means an urban *hukou*, a stable income, permanent job security, and full social welfare. These commonalities, rather than differences among various jobs, are the focus of this chapter.

17. Rong Ma, "Han and Tibetan Residential Patterns."

18. Li Luo and Lasan, *Xizang 50 nian: jingji juan* [50 Years of Tibet: Economic Volume] (Beijing: Minzu Chubanshe, 2001); Rong Ma, "Xizang de jingji xingtai ji qi bianqian" [Tibet's Economic Pattern and Its Changes], in *Xizang shehui fazhan yanjiu* [Studies of Social Development in Tibet], edited by the Sociology and Anthropology Institute of Beijing University and the National Center for Tibetan Studies (Beijing: Zhongguo Zangxue Chubanshe, 1997), 46–48.

19. Barry Sautman, "Ethnic Law and Minority Rights in China: Progress and Constraints," *Law & Policy* 21 (1999): 283–314.

20. Barry Sautman, "The New Tibetan Middle Class" (unpublished manuscript, 2004).

21. Judith Banister, "Impacts of Migration to China's Border Regions," in Myron Weiner and Sharon S. Russell, eds., *Moving Targets: Demography and Security* (Oxford: Berghahn Press, 2001), 101–142; Yasheng Huang, "China's Cadre Transfer Policy"; Barry Sautman, "Is Tibet China's Colony? The Claim of Demographic Catastrophe," *Columbia Journal of Asia Law* 15 (2001): 82–131; Lixiong Wang, *Tianzang;* and Tibet Statistical Bureau, *Xizang tongji nianjian* [Tibet Statistical Yearbook] (Beijing: Zhongguo Tongji Chubanshe, 1990–2000).

22. Jiangcunluobu, *Huihuang de ershi shiji xin Zhongguo dajilu: xizang juan* [Complete Records of the Twentieth Century New China: Tibet Volume] (Beijing: Hongqi Chubanshe, 1999).

23. "Xizang shaoshu minzu ganbu zai dang de huaibao li zhuozhuang chengzhang" [Tibet's Ethnic Minority Cadres Are Growing Strong with the Party's Support], *Xizang Ribao* [Tibet Daily], 12 December 2007. Available at: http://www.chinati betnews.com/pinglun/2007-2/12/content_71717.htm (accessed 21 June 2009).

24. After the initial influx of rural Han and Hui migrants into Lhasa, rural Tibetans also entered the city to look for nonagricultural work. In the 1990s, the overall ratio between "local" business (owned by people with TAR *hukou*) and "outsider" businesses (people without TAR *hukou*) was around 3:7. This statistic can be viewed as more or less the "ethnic ratio" in Lhasa's market (with the caveat that there are a significant number of ethnic Tibetans in Lhasa who come from Sichuan and Qinghai Provinces). Gradually, rural Tibetan market niches were formed along lines of kinship and home region, just as for Han and Hui migrants. In addition, these market niches rarely overlapped among the ethnic groups. Because the local productivity of Tibet is low, a competitive commercial edge depends heavily on whether one has access (usually through kin networks) to manufacturing from the producing areas. Han and Hui rural migrants tend to concentrate on niches that depend on manufactures from inland China. Rural Tibetans, lacking such networks in inland areas, do not enter those niches. Tibetans instead control portions of Lhasa's hotel business, Internet cafes, real estate, precious stones, and antiques or do business in a number of specialized niches, such as sutras and *thangkas*, incense, prayer flags, yak butter, barley beer brewing, fashion jewelry, pirated music, and other products from India and Nepal where Tibetan networks give them an advantage. Although Han and Tibetan migrants do not compete directly in small businesses, the situation may not be the same in the construction and service work labor markets.

25. For details of migrant business people in the Lhasa market, see Xiaojiang Hu, *The Little Shops in Lhasa: Migrant Businesses and the Formation of Markets in a Transitional Economy* (PhD diss., Harvard University, 2003); Xiaojiang Hu and Miguel Salazar, "Market Formation and Transformation: Private Businesses in Lhasa," in Barry Sautman and June Dreyer, eds., *Contemporary Tibet: Politics, Development and Society in a Disputed Region* (Armonk, NY: M. E. Sharpe,

2005); Xiaojiang Hu and Miguel Salazar, "The Dynamics of Migrant Networks: How Networks Change under Changing Market Environment" (paper presented at 2007 Annual Meeting of American Sociological Association, New York City, 2007). For more details on migrant business networks in China, see Biao Xiang, *Kuayue bianjing de shequ: Beijing Zhejiangcun de shenghuoshi* [Community Beyond Borders: Life History of Zhejiang Village in Beijing] (Beijing: Sanlian Chubanshe, 2000).

26. For a detailed discussion on the number of Han migrants in Tibet, the jobs in which they engage, the style of competition, and the high turnover rate among migrant businesses, see Xiaojiang Hu, *Little Shops in Lhasa*.

27. Åshild Kolås, "'Class' in Tibet."

28. This seems to be a misunderstanding of language. Tibetan language has terms for "reverence" toward male and female interlocutors. When translated into Chinese, these reverence words inaccurately carry a "generational" reference.

29. State media also interviewed some of the injured, witnesses, and perpetrators, but we have chosen not to use such information to avoid selection bias. Foreign tourists and journalists presented a similar general picture, but no individual level of information has been collected.

30. For example, although there were no Hui Muslim fatalities reported, there is no doubt that the Hui group was consciously targeted by rioters. A mosque was also burnt down.

31. See the transcript of the CNN interview with *The Economist* correspondent James Miles on March 20, 2008, http://edition.cnn.com/2008/WORLD/asiapcf/03/20/tibet.miles.interview/ (accessed 11 July 2008).

14. Bringing the City Back In

The author acknowledges research support from San Diego State University's Faculty Development Program and the Program in Agrarian Studies at Yale University in 2004–2005.

1. Li Chang Ping, *Wo xiang zongli shuo shihua* [I share truth with the Premier] (Beijing: Guangming Daily Press, 2002).

2. Zhu Rongji, *Guanyu guomin jingji he shehui fazhan di shige wunian jihua gangyao de baogao* [Report on the Tenth Five-year Plan on national economic and social development], http://www.people.com.cn/GB/shizheng/16/20010317/419313.html (accessed May 20, 2005). An earlier reference to the three rural issues (without explicitly invoking the term *sannong*) can be found in the resolution on agricultural and rural issues passed by the Central Committee of the Chinese Communist Party in October 1998. But the resolution was not followed by focused discussion and debate on the issue; nor was there any indication of a clear shift in the orientation of rural policies that continued to stress agricultural production.

3. Lu Xueyi, "Zhongguo sannong wenti de youlai he fazhan" [Origins and development of China's *sannong* issues], *Dangdai zhongguoshi yanjiu* [Journal of contemporary Chinese history] 11, no. 3 (2004): 4.

4. The 2006 No. 1 Document contains a reference to the term "socialist new countryside" for the first time. It reiterates the importance of reducing the rural tax burden, raising peasant incomes, and increasing fiscal outlays for agriculture. But the accent is on *comprehensive* socioeconomic development, rural governance, and transfer of urban resources to rural areas. The 2006 Document thus represents a shift in rural development discourse from one that centered around economic and production issues to one that emphasizes the need for social development.

5. Editorial, "Xin gaige gongshi" [New reform consensus], *Zhongguo jingji shibao* [China Economic Times], March 9, 2005.

6. Ji Bin and He Jiazheng, "Zhonggong zhongyang zhaokai nongcun gongzuo huiyi quanmian bushu jinnian nongye nongcun gongzuo" [CCP Central Committee convenes rural work conference on this year's rural and agricultural issues], *Renmin ribao* [People's Daily], March 24, 1994.

7. Yang Yongzhe, "Jianchi wending he wanshan liangshi gouxiao zhengce" [Stabilize and improve policies on grain purchase and sale], *Renmin ribao* [People's Daily], December 12, 1995.

8. Gale D. Johnson, "Does China Have a Grain Problem?" *China Economic Review* 5, no. 1 (1994); and Justin Lin, "Yi tang juti de shichang jingji ke" [A concrete lesson on market economy], *Liaowang* [Outlook], no. 3 (1994).

9. Lester Brown, *Who Will Feed China?* (New York: Norton, 1995); Jikun Huang, *China's Food Economy to the 21st Century: Supply, Demand, and Trade* (Adelaide, S.A.: Australia Centre for International Economic Studies, University of Adelaide, 1996); and Vaclav Smil, "Who Will Feed China," *China Quarterly*, no. 143 (1995).

10. Zhonggong zhongyang, "Zhonggong zhongyang guanyu nongye he nongcun gongzuo ruogang zhongda wenti de jueding" [CCP Central Committee decisions on several major issues concerning agriculture and rural work], *Renmin ribao* [People's Daily], October 19, 1998; and Chen Xiwen, "'Jiuwu' shiqi nongye nongcun jingji de fazhan he wenti" [Development and problems of agriculture and rural economy during the Ninth Five-Year Plan] in *Zhongguo jingji nianjian* [China's economic almanac] (Beijing: Zhongguo jingji nianjian she, 2001), 818.

11. Lu Xueyi, "Zhongguo sannong wenti de youlai he fazhan," 6–7.

12. Chen Xiwen, "Xin shiji de sannong wenti" [*Sannong* issues in the new century], *Shanghai nongcun jingji* [Shanghai rural economy], no. 8 (2003): 4.

13. Editorial Board of China Agricultural Yearbook, *China Agricultural Yearbook, 2003 (English Edition)* (Beijing: China Agricultural Press, 2003), 320.

14. Lu Xueyi, ed., *Dangdai zhongguo shehui liudong* [Social mobility in contemporary China] (Beijing: shehui kexue wenxian chubanshe, 2004), 1–32.

15. Wen Tiejun, "Guanzhu jincheng nongmin de shengcun zhuangtai" [Paying attention to rural migrants' livelihood], *Shidai chao* [Tide], no. 7 (2001).

16. Sun Zifa and Hu Angang, *Zhongguo cunzai sinong wenti* [China has four rural crises], http://finance.sina.com.cn (accessed May 25 2005).

17. Note that in 2008 when the World Bank appointed a new chief economist, the post went to Prof. Lin, a symbolically important recognition of China's success at economic development over the last thirty years.

18. Justin Lin, "Rang zhongguo nongmin yu shichang jingji jieyuan" [Connect China's peasants to the market], *Zhongguo gaige* [China's reform], no. 5 (1994).

19. Justin Lin, "Yi tang juti de shichang jingji ke"; Justin Lin and Li Zhou, "Danqian woguo nongcun de zhuyao wenti he duice" [Main rural problems and policy responses in today's China], *Lilun zhanxian* [Theoretical front], no. 9 (1995).

20. Justin Lin, "Youguan dangqian nongcun zhengce de jidian yijian" [Notes on the present rural policies], *Sannong zhongguo* [Rural China] 2, no. 1 (2004): 2–3.

21. Justin Lin, "Sannong wenti yu woguo nongcun de weilai fazhan" [*Sannong* issues and the future of China's countryside], *Beijing daxue zhongguo yanjiu zhongxin taolun gao xilie* [Workshop papers series of Beijing University's China Center for Economic Research], No. C2002005 (2002), 4.

22. Justin Lin, "Zhongguo chengshi fazhan yu nongcun xiandaihua" [China's urban development and rural modernization], *Beijing daxue xuebao* [Beijing University Journal] 39, no. 4 (2002).

23. Laodong he shehui baozhang bu ketizu, *Guanyu mingong duanque de diaocha baogao* [Report on migrant labor shortage], http://news.xinhuanet.com/zhengfu/ 2004–09/14/content_1979817.htm (accessed March 31, 2005).

24. N.A., "Yixie hangye tuoqian mingong gongzi xianxiang yanzhong" [Serious wage arrears for migrant workers exist in some industries], *Beijing rencai shichang bao* [Beijing talent market news], January 18, 2003, 22.

25. Qi Zhongxi and Li Jianghong, "Duoshao mingong na budao qian?" [How many migrants do not get paid], *Beijing rencai shichang bao* (Beijing talent market news), January 18, 2003, 22.

26. Ching Kwan Lee, "'Made in China': Politics of Labor, Law and Legitimacy," in *Asia Program Special Report, No. 124* (Washington, DC: Woodrow Wilson International Center for Scholars, 2004), 9.

27. Liu Xiaoyue, "Nongcun jumin shouru fenpei chaju jixu kuoda" [Income gap continues to enlarge among rural residents], *Zhejiang tongji* [Zhejiang statistics], no. 1 (2005): 19.

28. Keith Griffin, Azizur Rahman Khan, and Amy Ickowitz, "In Defense of Neo-Classical Neo-Populism," *Journal of Agrarian Change* 4, no. 3 (2004): 380.

29. Chris Bramall, "Chinese Land Reform in Long-Run Perspective and in the Wider East Asian Context," *Journal of Agrarian Change* 4, no. 1–2 (2004): 129; and Griffin, Khan, and Ickowitz, "In Defense of Neo-Classical Neo-Populism," 380.

30. Ge Rujiang, Pan Haiping, and Wang Xinya, "Shui zhizao le 2000 wan shidi nongmin?" [Who is responsible for the 20 million landless peasants?], *Zhongguo gaige* [China's reform], no. 1 (2004).

31. Thomas P. Bernstein and Xiaobo Lu, *Taxation without Representation in Rural China* (Cambridge: Cambridge University Press, 2003).

32. Howard W. French, "Girl, 13, Dies as Police Battle Chinese Villagers," *New York Times,* January 16, 2006; and Joseph Kahn, "Police Fire on Protesters in China, Killing Several," *New York Times,* December 9, 2005.

33. Lu Xueyi, "Zhongguo sannong wenti de youlai he fazhan," 10–11.

34. Wen Tiejun, "Sannong wenti yu jiejue banfa" [*Sannong* issues and their solutions], *Zhongguo gaige* [China's reform], no. 2 (2003): 32.

35. Wen Tiejun, "Shichang shiling+zhengfu shiling shuangchong kunjing xia de sannong wenti" [*Sannong* issues under the double predicament of market and government failures], *Dushu* [Reading], no. 10 (2001): 23

36. Ibid., 24.

37. Wen Tiejun, "Zhiyue sannong wenti de liangge jiben maodun" [Two basic contradictions pressuring *sannong* issues], *Jingji wenti yanjiu* [Research on economic issues], no. D5 (1996); and Wen Tiejun, "Shichang shiling+zhengfu shiling shuangchong kunjing xia de sannong wenti," 23.

38. Wen Tiejun, "Sannong wenti yu jiejue banfa," 33.

39. Ibid.; and Wen Tiejun, "Shichang shiling+zhengfu shiling shuangchong kunjing xia de sannong wenti."

40. Wen Tiejun, "Zhiyue sannong wenti de liangge jiben maodun," 21; and Wen Tiejun, et al., "*Zhongguo dalu de xiangcun jianshe*" [Rural reconstruction in mainland China], *Kaifang shidai* [Open times], no. 2 (2003).

41. Wen Tiejun, "21 shiji de zhongguo rengran shi xiaonong jingji" [China will remain a small peasant economy in the twenty-first century], *Sannong zhongguo* [Rural China] 2, no. 1 (2004): 19.

42. Wen Tiejun, "Sannong wenti yu jiejue banfa," 34.

43. Ibid.

44. Wen Tiejun, "21 shiji de zhongguo rengran shi xiaonong jingji," 9.

45. Wu Li and Zheng Yougui, eds., *Jiejue sannong wenti zhilu: zhongguo gongchandang sannong sixiang zhengce shi* [Solutions to *sannong* issues: history of CCP's thinking and policy on *sannong*] (Beijing: Zhongguo jingji chubanshe, 2004), 719–723.

46. Xiaotong Fei, *Rural Development in China: Prospect and Retrospect* (Chicago: University of Chicago Press, 1989), 66; and G. William Skinner, *Marketing and Social Structure in Rural China* (Tucson: University of Arizona Press, 1965).

47. Fei, *Rural Development in China: Prospect and Retrospect;* Zhou Erliu and Zhang Yulin, *Chengxiang xietiao fazhan yanjiu* [Research on rural-urban coordinated development] (Nanjing: Jiangsu renmin chubanshe, 1991); and Wu Li and

Zheng Yougui, eds., *Jiejue sannong wenti zhilu: zhongguo gongchandang sannong sixiang zhengce shi*, 706–709.

48. Jae Ho Chung and Tao-chiu Lam, "China's 'City System' in Flux: Explaining Post-Mao Administrative Changes," *China Quarterly*, no. 180 (2004): 952.

49. Ren Jin, "Urbanization on Fast Track," *Beijing Review*, October 16, 2003, 27.

50. Chung and Lam, "China's 'City System' in Flux: Explaining Post-Mao Administrative Changes," 954–955.

51. Zhonggong zhongyan and Guowuyuan, *Guanyu tuijin shehui zhuyi xin nongcun jianshe de ruogan yijian* [Directives on promoting the reconstruction of socialist new countryside], http://www.gov.cn/jrzg/2006–02/21/content_205958.htm (accessed March 8, 2006).

52. Michael Lipton, *Why Poor People Stay Poor: Urban Bias in World Development* (Cambridge, MA: Harvard University Press, 1977).

53. Kam Wing Chan, *Cities with Invisible Walls: Reinterpreting Urbanization in Post-1949 China* (Hong Kong: Oxford University Press, 1994); and R. J. R. Kirkby, *Urbanization in China* (New York: Columbia University Press, 1985).

54. Martin King Whyte, "Town and Country in Contemporary China," *Comparative Urban Research* 10, no. 1 (1983).

55. Kirkby, *Urbanization in China*; Dorothy Solinger, *Contesting Citizenship in Urban China* (Berkeley: University of California Press, 1999).

56. See the discussion in Peter Nolan and Gordon White, "Urban Bias, Rural Bias or State Bias? Urban-Rural Relations in Post-Revolutionary China," *Journal of Development Studies* 20 (1984): 52–81; and Jean Oi, "Reform and Urban Bias in China," *Journal of Development Studies* 29, no. 4 (1993): 145.

57. Cai Fan and Yang Tao, "Chengxiang shuru chaju de zhengzhi jingji xue," *Zhongguo shehui kexue* [Chinese Social Science], no. 4 (2000).

58. Oi, "Reform and Urban Bias in China," 144.

59. Chu Chengya, "Dangdai zhongguo chengshi pianxiang zhengce de zhengzhi gengyuan" [Political origins of China's urban bias policies in the present era], *Dangdai shijie shehui zhuyi yanjiu* [Research on today's world socialism] no. 4 (2002).

60. Daniel Kelliher, *Peasant Power in China* (New Haven, CT: Yale University Press, 1992); and Kate Xiao Zhou, *How the Farmers Changed China: Power of the People* (Boulder, CO: Westview Press, 1996).

61. Yu Depeng, "Lun xianxing huji zhidu yu chengxiang guanxi de gaige" [On the current household registration system and the reform of urban-rural relations], *Zhongguo nongcun jingji* [Chinese rural economy], no. 2 (1995): 176–180; Xu Zhiyong, "Cong sifen zhi yi xuanju quan kan woguo renda xuanju zhidu de gaige" [One-quarter of voting representation and reform of China's NPC electoral system], *Zhongnan daxue xuebao* [Central South University journal], 10, no. 2 (2004).

62. See http://news.xinhuanet.com/ziliao/2003–03/03/content_758170.htm (accessed March 6, 2006).

63. See http://www.ahrd.gov.cn/publishinfo/browser/index.asp (accessed March 6, 2006).

64. Chu Chengya, "Dangdai zhongguo chengshi pianxiang zhengce de zhengzhi gengyuan."

65. See http://www.ccyl.org.cn/number/index.htm (accessed March 6, 2006).

66. Beijing shi Deng Xiaoping lilun yanjiu zhongxin ketizu, "Zhongguo gongchandang dangyuan duiwu shehui chengfen de lishi kaocha" [Historical examination of the socioeconomic makeup of CCP party members], Zhongguo tese shehuizhuyi yanjiu [Research on socialism with Chinese characteristics], no. 1 (2002).

67. See http://www.people.com.cn/GB/shizheng/19/20021107/861171.html (accessed April 4, 2006).

68. Liu Siyang and Zhai Wei, Jicun zuzhi jianshe chengxiao mingxian [Significant achievements in grassroots organizational building], http://www.cctv.com/specials/80zhounian/sanji/zxbb061508.html (accessed March 14, 2006).

69. Yu Jianrong, "Nongcun hei'e shili he jicun zhengquan tuihua" [Criminal forces in rural areas and the decay of grassroots government organs], Zhanlue yu guanli [Strategy and management], no. 5 (2003); Wang Xiaodong, Yang Peng, and Ou Yanguo, "Nongcun jicun zuzhi kaocha baogao" [Report on rural grassroots organizations], Jingji guanli wenzhai [Selections on economic management], no. 7 (2003).

70. Wang Shaoguang and He Jianyu, "Zhongguo de shetuan geming" [China's NGO revolution], Zhejiang xuekan [Zhejiang journal], no. 11 (2004).

71. Minxin Pei, "Chinese Civic Associations: An Empirical Analysis," Modern China 24, no. 3 (1998).

72. Minggao Shen, Scott Rozelle, and Linxiu Zhang, "Farmer's Professional Associations in Rural China: State Dominated or New State-Society Partnership?" in FED Working Papers Series No. FE20050013 (Peking: Peking University, 2005), 5. See www.fed.org.cn. Accessed on May 24, 2005.

73. Kevin J. O'Brien and Lianjiang Li, Rightful Resistance in Rural China (Cambridge: Cambridge University Press, 2006); and Yu Jianrong, "Dangqian nongmin weiquan huodong de yige jieshi kuangjia" [A framework for explaining villager's rightful resistance], Shehuixue yanjiu [Sociological Study], no. 2 (2004).

74. Helen F. Siu, Agents and Victims in South China (New Haven, CT: Yale University Press, 1989); and Qin Hui, Chuantong shilun [Ten theses on tradition] (Shanghai: Fudan daxue chubanshe, 2003).

75. Yu Jianrong, "20 shiji zhongguo nonghui zhidu de bianqian ji qidi" [China's peasant union system in the 20th century: changes and re-thinking], Fujian shifang daxue xuebao [Fujian Normal University journal], no. 5 (2003).

76. Yu Jianrong, Wo weishenme zhuzhang chongjian nongmin xiehui [Why do I suggest re-building a peasant union system], http://www.zhinong.cn/data/detail.php?id=868 (accessed March 6, 2006).

77. Chu Chengya, "Dangdai zhongguo chengshi pianxiang zhengce de zhengzhi gengyuan."

15. Renovating the Great Floodgate

1. Li Shengbo, "Disici huji gaige huzhiyuchu" [The fourth *hukou* reform is coming], *Fazhi zaobao* [Legal morning news], Beijing, February 2, 2005. See the discussion of Li Changping's views in Chapter 14 in this volume.
2. "The Pain of China's Hukou System: The Pandora's Dilemma of Hukou Reform," *Guoji xianqu daobao* [International Herald Leader], November 8, 2005.
3. Fei-Ling Wang, *Organizing through Division and Exclusion: China's Hukou System* (Stanford, CA: Stanford University Press, 2005), 32–60. For earlier studies of the system, see Tiejun Cheng and Mark Selden, "The Origins and Social Consequences of China's *Hukou* System," *China Quarterly*, no. 139 (1994): 646–668; Dorothy J. Solinger, *Contesting Citizenship in Urban China: Peasant Migrants, the State, and the Logic of the Market* (Berkeley: University of California Press, 1999); Delia Davin, *Internal Migration in Contemporary China* (New York: Palgrave, 1999); and Michael R. Dutton, *Policing and Punishment in China: From Patriarchy to "The People"* (New York: Cambridge University Press, 1992).
4. Fei-Ling Wang, "Brewing Tensions While Maintaining Stabilities: The Dual Role of the *Hukou* System in Contemporary China," in Dali L. Yang, ed., "Interests, Institutions, and Contentions in China," a special issue of *Asian Perspectives* 29, no. 4 (2005): 85–124.
5. Kam Wing Chan and Will Buckingham, "Is China Abolishing the *Hukou* System?", *China Quarterly*, no. 195 (2008).
6. Sina News Net report, Beijing, August 8, 2003; and *Beijing chenbao* [Beijing morning news], Beijing, April 7, 2006.
7. For official but "internal" statements of the missions of the *hukou* system, see Jiang Xianjin and Luo Feng, eds., *Jingcha yewu shiyong quanshu—zhian guanli juan* [Complete guide of police works—volume on public security management] (Beijing: Qunzhong Press, 1996), 218, 220; Bureau of Personnel and Training-Ministry of Public Security, *Huzheng guanli jiaocheng* [Textbook on *hukou* management] (Beijing: Qunzhong Press, 2000), 5, 161–173. For an analysis of those functions, see Fei-Ling Wang, *Organizing through Division and Exclusion*.
8. Yang Jisheng, *Mobei: Zhongguo liushi niandai jihuang jishi* [Tombstone: Report on the Chinese famine in the 1960s] (Hong Kong: Tiandi Books, 2008).
9. CCP Central Commission and State Council, "Opinions on deepening the reform of medical and health care system." Beijing, April 6, 2009.
10. Hein Mallee, "China's Household Registration System under Reform," *Development and Change* 26 (1995); Lei Guang, "Reconstructing the Rural-Urban Divide: Peasant Migration and the Rise of 'Orderly Migration' in Contempo-

rary China," *Journal of Contemporary China* 10 (2001): 471–493; *Chinese Law and Government,* ed. Zhang Tingting, special issue, May–June, 2001; Fei-Ling Wang, "Reformed Migration Control and New List of the Targeted People: China's *Hukou* System in the 2000s," *China Quarterly,* no. 177 (2004): 115–132; and Chan and Buckingham, "Is China Abolishing the *Hukou* System?"

11. *Xinjing bao* [New Bejing news], Beijing, January 4 and 25, 2005; *Zhongguo qingnian bao* [Chinese youth daily], July–August, 2001; and author's interviews of education officials from Beijing, 2007.

12. Kam Wing Chan and Li Zhang, "The *Hukou* System and Rural-Urban Migration in China: Processes and Changes," *China Quarterly,* no. 160 (1999): 831–840.

13. Report by Wang Jianwei, Chief of Domestic Security Protection Unit, Huanggang City Public Security Bureau, Hubei, September 23, 2006.

14. *Wenhui bao* [Wenhui daily], Shanghai, September 2, 2004; *Yangcheng wanbao* [Yangcheng evening news], Guangzhou, August 23, 2006; and *Beijing qingnianbao* [Beijing youth daily], Beijing, September 7, 2006.

15. Kam Wing Chan and Li Zhang, "The *Hukou* System and Rural-Urban Migration," 836–840; and Chan and Buckingham, "Is China Abolishing the *Hukou* System?"

16. Author's interviews of officials in Shanghai 2002; *Nanfang dushibao* [Southern Metropolis news], Guangzhou, September 30, 2004; and *Yangcheng wanbao* [Guangzhou evening news], Guangzhou, August 23, 2006.

17. Chinese National People's Congress (NPC) deputies started to propose bills for a *hukou* law in 2001 (Associated Press, Beijing, March 15, 2001). Some have even called for a clause of "freedom of migration" to be added to the PRC Constitution. *Renmin ribao* [People's daily], Beijing, August 14, 2002. None of these proposals have yet been included as part of the legislative agenda. Accompanying such acts, senior *hukou* officials were seen making announcements about their "busy and hard work" and "near completion" of drafting such a law around the annual meeting of the NPC every spring in 2002–2008. *Zhongguo qingnian bao* [Chinese youth daily], Beijing, March 17, 2006; and *People's Net,* Beijing, March 4, 2008.

18. Department of Politics-Ministry of Public Security, *Gongan yewu jichu zhishi* [Basic knowledge of public security works] (Beijing: Qunzhong Press, 1999), 75–76; *Zhongguo qingnian bao* [Chinese youth daily], Beijing, January 5, 2002; and *Jinghua shibao* [Jinghua times], Beijing, August 30, 2005.

19. "E jingcha kaishi liangxian, huji dangan jiang dianzihua" [E-police starts to emerge and *hukou* files will be electronic], http://www.news.china.com (accessed February 19, 2002).

20. *Xinhua News Dispatch,* Fuzhou, February 17, 2005.

21. For discussion of some of these relaxations, see Kam Wing Chan and Li Zhang, "The *Hukou* System and Rural-Urban Migration," and the special issue of *Chinese Law and Government,* May–June, 2001.

22. *Renmin ribao* [People's daily], Beijing, September 24, 2001, 9.

23. *Zhongguo minzhen* [China civil affairs], Beijing, no. 11 (November 2001), 57.

24. *Renmin ribao* [People's daily], Beijing, September 4, 2001.

25. Shen Wenmin, "Guanyu huji zhidu gaige de wenda" [Q and A on the *hukou* system reforms], *Renmin ribao-huadong ban* [People's daily—Eastern China edition], Shanghai, August 29, 2001, 3.

26. Chinese Central TV, *Jingji banxiaoshi* [Half hour on the economy], Beijing, August 9, 2001; and Chan and Buckingham, "Is China Abolishing the *Hukou* System?".

27. Beijing Municipal Government, *Regulations on Encouraging Chinese Who Studied Overseas to Work or Open Business in Beijing*, May 1, 2000, in *Shengzhou xueren* [Chinese scholars], Beijing (June 2000): 47.

28. See http://www.news.china.com (accessed January 19, 2002).

29. China News Agency, Beijing, October 1, 2001.

30. *Business China*, Hong Kong, August 30, 1999, 4; *China Daily*, Beijing, April 24, 2001; and *Provisional Measure on the Management of Individual Housing Loans*, April 28, 1997.

31. A "low" price had attracted "too many" outsiders to the booming city, so in April 2002 the Shanghai government stopped issuing blue-seal *hukou* to those who purchased a commercial housing unit, but "talents" and other investors were still allowed to move in.

32. "Jiujing sui caishi zuixuyao beijing hukou de ren?" [Exactly who needs a Beijing *hukou* the most?], http://www.news.china.com (accessed January 6, 2002).

33. Chan and Buckingham, "Is China Abolishing the *Hukou* System?".

34. *Hunan ribao* [Hunan daily], Changsha, January 20, 2002; *Renmin ribao-huadongban* [People's daily—East China edition], Shanghai, January 9, 2002; *Nanfang dushi bao* [Southern urban daily], Guangzhou, September 8, 2001; *Xinhua Daily Telegraph*, Beijing, December 24, 2001; and *Xinwen chengbao* [Morning news], Shanghai, September 29, 2004.

35. *Xinhua Daily Telegraph*, Beijing, August 9, 2001.

36. Fei-Ling Wang, *Organizing through Division and* Exclusion, 99–100.

37. Zhang Yinghong, "Sun Zhigang zhisi yu zhidu zhier" [The death of Sun Zhigang and the evil of the (hukou) system], April 28, 2003, http://www.tecn.cn/data/detail.php?id=876, last accessed June 9, 2009; *Caijing shibao* [Financial and economic times], Beijing, June 15, 2003; *Changsha wanbao* [Changsha evening news], June 13, 2003; and *Xinhua Daily Telegraph*, Beijing, June 21, 2004.

38. Zheng Binwen, "China should carefully prevent Latin Americanization," http://www.yannan.cn/data/detail.php?id=5889, May 29, 2005, last accessed June 9, 2009 For a scholarly discussion from a different perspective, see George Gilboy and Eric Heginbotham, "The Latin Americanization of China?", *Current Affairs* 103 (2004): 256–261.

39. "Shenyang nuqingnian zhuangao shanghai jingfang huosheng" [Young woman from Shenyang wins suit against Shanghai police], *Shenyang wanbao* [Shenyang

evening news], January 14, 2004. The same story was then circulated in many media outlets, including the *Beijing Review* in August 2004.

40. Shi Feike, "Jia Fangjun: bei juya 11 ge xiaoshi de boshihou" [Jia Fangjun: Post-Doc detained for 11 hours], *21 shiji huanqiu baodao* [21st century global news], Beijing, March 2003; and Hu Ji, "Chumen weidaizheng, beiju 11 xiaoshi" (Out without ID, detained for 11 hours], *Xinjing bao* [New Beijing daily], Beijing, November 22, 2003.

41. Author's interview of *hukou* police, February 2007.

42. For anecdotal evidence for Beijing, see http://www.bjbbs.com/bbs/read.php?tid=8750, posted October 12, 2005; for Guangzhou, *Nanfang dushi bao* [Southern metropolis news], September 1, 2006); for Wuhan, http://legal.people.com.cn/GB/42733/4514687.html, posted October 22, 2006; for Guangdong, http://cache.tianya.cn/publicforum/Content/free/1/737231.shtml, posted June 23, 2006; and for Shanghai, http://bbs.2500sz.com/Dvbbs/dispbbs.asp?boardid=40andid=288214, posted on January 16, 2007.

43. "Beijing aoyun qijian kaolu kongzhi liudong renkou: quanfang bufen mingong" [Considering population control during the Beijing Olympics: to persuade migrant workers go home], *Huaxia shibao* [China times]; and *Beijing chenbao* [Beijing morning news], Beijing, September 15, 2006.

44. "The terrible secrets of Beijing's 'black jails'," *Spectator*, London, October 10, 2007; and "Unreported World: China's Olympic Lie," http://www.veoh.com/videos/v1357069DKZqmaty, July 2007.

45. *China News Weekly*, Beijing, and *Huaxi dushi bao* [Western China metro news], Chengdu, September 5, 2002.

46. Wu Fengying, "Zhengzhou huji xinzheng de shibai shuoming shimu" [What is meant by the failure of the new deal on *hukou* in Zhengzhou], *Zhongguo qingnianbao* [Chinese youth daily], Beijing, September 15, 2004.

47. *Beijing qingnian bao* [Beijing youth daily], Beijing, September 20, 2004; *Henan ribao* [Henan daily], Zhengzhou, September 22, 2004; and *Nanfang dushi bao* [Southern metropolis news], Guangzhou, September 23, 2004.

48. Chen Fang and Liang Peng, "Qu zhengfu baigong weihe cheng liao migong?" [Why the district government White House becomes a house of puzzles?], Xinhua News Net, Beijing, posted June 26, 2006. On January 30, 2007, the party chief of the district who supervised the construction of the complex was sentenced to jail for life on corruption charges. Xinhua News Net, posted January 30, 2007.

49. There has been no open discussion (other than indirect hints) about this in the PRC media, as the political role of the *hukou* system in the management of targeted people is strictly a taboo issue. Internally, however, the police have openly admitted such for a long time (Fei-Ling Wang, *Organizing through Division and Exclusion*, 106–111).

50. *Henan shangbao* [Henan business news], Zhengshou, September 15, 2006.

51. *Hubei ribao* [Hubei daily], Wuhan, October 16, 2004; *Cheng bao* [Morning news], Shanghai, October 2, 2004; *Yangcheng wanbao* [Yangcheng evening news], Guangzhou, December 26, 2004.

52. See the reports and articles on *hukou* issues in *Xinhua News Dispatch*, February 21, 2006; *Zhongguo qingnianbao* [Chinese youth daily], Beijing, January 17, 2006; *Huaxi dushi bao* [Western China metropolis news], January 18, 2006; *Liaowang* [Outlook weekly], Beijing, January 8, 2007; and *Beijing keji bao* [Beijing science & technology daily], Beijing, March 17, 2008.

53. Many of the contributors to this volume have reported in great detail the stubbornly persistent and ever-enlarging rural-urban income gap, which Qiu Xiaohua, chief of the PRC Statistical Bureau, openly admitted to be at the staggering ratio of 1:6 (rather than the "official" figure of 1:3 or even 1:2) shortly before he was abruptly arrested on corruption charges in late 2006. See the discussion in Chapter 5 of this volume.

54. Thomas Lum, *Social Unrest in China*, a CRS Report for Congress, Washington, DC, June 12, 2006; and Albert Keidel, *China's Social Unrest: The Story Behind the Stories*, a policy brief by the Carnegie Endowment for International Peace, Washington, DC, September, 2006.

55. Hu Xingdou, "Open Letter to the Chinese NPC Standing Committee on the Unconstitutionality of the Duality in the *Hukou* System," Beijing, November 6, 2004, http://www.huxingdou.com.cn. Reported by many local and Web-based Chinese media outlets, such as *Fazhi zaobao* [Morning legal news] Beijing November 18, 2004, and *Shidai xinbao* [Times news] Beijing, November 25, 2004.

56. Deputy Minister of MPS Liu Jinguo, report to the CCP's Central Commission on Comprehensive Management of Public Security, October 25, 2005, first reported by *Fazhi ribao* [Legal daily] on October 26, 2005, and then by the more influential Xinhua News Agency in *Liaowang* [Outlook weekly], Beijing, November 21, 2005.

57. *Xinwen chengbao* [Morning news], Shanghai, September 29, 2004; *Renmin ribao* [People's daily], March 20, 2006; and *Xinhua News Dispatch*, Hohhot, January 9, 2007.

58. He Qinglian, "The State's Role at Variance: Unconscionable Conduct of Governments in Current PRC," *Modern China Studies* 13 no. 93 (2006): 4–31.

59. Lu Dadao, member of the Chinese Science Academy and member of the advisory committee to the PRC Eleventh Five-Year Plan, "Zhongguo chengzhenhua cheng "dayuejin" shitou [China's urbanization shows a trend of "Great Leap Forward"], *Xian wanbao* [Xian evening news], Xian, January 14, 2007.

60. *Zhongguo qingnian bao* [Chinese youth daily], Beijing, October 27, 2005. For some anecdotal reports, see *Beijing keji bao* [Beijing science & technology daily], Beijing, March 17, 2008.

61. *Renmin ribao* [People's daily], Beijing, November 4, 2005, 10; *Xinbao* [News daily], Beijing, January 26, 2006; *Caijing ribao* [Financial daily], Beijing, June 26,

2006. As the practice of college admission shows (Fei-Ling Wang, *Organizing through Division and Exclusion,* 139–147), participating in civil-service exams does not necessarily mean equal chance of being accepted as a state employee.

62. *Shanghai shi juzhuzheng zhanxing guiding* [Provisional regulation on residential permit in Shanghai], Shanghai municipal government, October 1, 2004.

63. The PRC Supreme People's Court, *Legal Opinion on Compensation for Bodily Injuries,* Beijing, no. 2003-20, issued December 28, 2003.

64. There have been numerous reports about this *hukou*-based discrimination since the late 1990s. For a recent example, see *Gongren ribao* [Worker's daily], Beijing, December 7, 2005.

65. *Chen bao* [Morning news], Beijing, March 11, 2006; *Huaxi dushibao* [Western China urban news], Chengdu, July 10, 2006.

66. *Chongqing chenbao* [Chongqing morning news], Chongqing, December 13, 2006; and *Dongfang jinbao* [Dongfang news], Zhengzhou, December 20, 2006.

67. *Nanfang ribao* [Southern daily], Guangzhou, July 15, 2008.

68. *Liaowang zhoukan* [Outlook weekly], Beijing, November 21, 2005. Foreign researchers also noticed this local resistance, see Litao Zhao and Jianying Li, *China Reforming the Hukuo System: Reducing Discrimination against Rural Population,* Background Brief 284, EAI, National University of Singapore, May 10, 2006.

69. Li Zhongxin, *Shiqu jingwu yu paichusuo gongzuo gaige lunwenji* [Collection of essays on the reform of community policing and police stations] (Beijing: Qunzhong Press, for law enforcement use only, 1998); and Wang Taiyuan, *Huzheng yu renkou guanli lilun yanjiu zhongshu* [Comprehensive summary on the theoretical study on the *hukou* system and population management] (Beijing: Qunzhong Press, for law enforcement agencies use only, 1997). See also Fei-Ling Wang, *Organizing through Division and Exclusion,* 184–185, 196–197.

70. Cheng Honggen, "Huji gaige buneng yiqian liaozhi" [*Hukou* reform cannot be just a relocation], China News Net, Beijing, January 8, 2007.

71. *Zhongguo qingnianbao* [Chinese youth daily], March 7, 2006; and *Renmin ribao* [People's daily], Beijing, March 20, 2006.

72. Reported by *Xinhua News Net,* Beijing, March 20, 2006.

73. *Zhongguo jingying bao* [Chinese management news], Beijing, May 13, 2006.

74. *Liaowang zhoukan* [Outlook weekly], Beijing, January 8, 2007.

75. *Jinghua shibao* [Beijing times], Beijing, March 6, 2008.

76. *Xinhua news dispatch,* Beijing, October 20, 2008.

77. For an interesting discussion about reforming the *hukou* system in the context of land reform, property rights reform, and social security provision in the PRC, see Tao Ran and Xu Zhigang, "Urbanization, rural land system and social security in China" (unpublished paper, University of Oxford, 2006).

78. Li Yining, "Chenxiang eryuan tizhi gaige guanjian hezai?" [Where are the keys to the reform of the rural-urban duality system], *Guangming ribao* (Guangming daily), Beijing, March 2, 2008.

79. For a study on China's governmental control of the media, see He Qinglian, *Media Control in China* (New York: Human Rights in China, 2004).

80. Chan and Buckingham, "Is China Abolishing the *Hukou* System?".

81. Shu Shengxiang, *Huji xinzheng shi yichang zhidu youxi?* [*Hukou* new deal is an institutional game?], *Zhongguo qingnianbao* [Chinese youth daily], Beijing, March 7, 2006.

82. Reng Yuan, Chengxiang tongyi de huji gaige keneng shibai" [*Hukou* reform to unify rural-urban is likely to fail] (Shanghai: Demography Institute, Fudan University, November 2005).

83. Hong Wang, "Hukou zhidu chidi jiejue? Bie lede taizao le" [Complete solution of the *hukou* system? Don't celebrate too early], http://news.xinhuanet.com/com ments/2005-10/29/content_3698696.htm (accessed February 1, 2007).

84. *Laiowang* [Outlook weekly], Beijing, November 22, 2005.

85. *Xinhua News Net*, Beijing, November 21, 2005.

86. Hu's similar arguments and new criticisms, fairly harsh at times, were sporadically but continuously reported by various PRC Web sites and were still available in 2009.

87. Yu Jianrong, "Xiangzheng zizhi: genju he lujin" [Township self-governance: reasons and routes], *Zhanlu yu guanli* [Strategy and management], Beijing, no. 6 (2002); "Zhongguo xinfang zhidu pipan" [Critic of China's *xinfang* system] (public speech at Beijing University, December 2, 2004).

88. Yu Jianrong, "Buneng jiandandi feichu hukou zhidu" [We cannot simply abolish the *hukou* system], *Shehui kexue bao* [Social science daily], Shanghai, December 1, 2006.

89. Ge Jianxiong, "Feichu zhanzhu zheng de guanjian zaiyu xiaochu shengfen qishi" [The key to eliminating temporary residential permits is to eliminate discrimination based on personal identity], *Xin jingbao* [New Beijing news], Beijing, December 31, 2006; and interviews reported on China.net, Beijing, on January 22, 2007.

90. Liu Yazhou [Lt. General of the PLA], *Tan nongmin wenti* [On the issue of the peasants] (unpublished essay written in Beijing, 2005).

91. Zhou Qing, *Zhongguo zuida de renquan an: xianxing hukou zhidu* [China's Biggest Human Rights Case: The Current *Hukou* System] (Beijing, 2003), http://www.boxun.com/hero/zhouqing/2_1.shtml (accessed February 7, 2007).

92. *China Daily*, Beijing, February 2, 2007.

93. Fei-Ling Wang, "Reformed Migration Control and New List of the Targeted People"; and Fei-Ling Wang, *Organizing through Division and Exclusion*, 198–203.

94. In 2006 as a reform measure and a creative use of the *hukou* system, the government started to offer a much-desired Beijing *hukou* to those selected nonlocal college graduates who responded to the call of the CCP to work as assistant village heads in rural areas for at least two years with a good record. Du Ding,

"Dang liangnian haoguan nenglouhu Beijing" [One can get a Beijing *hukou* after serving as a good cadre for two years], *Beijing yulu xinbao* [Beijing entertainment news], Beijing, January 26, 2006.

95. Wang Qing, "Siwan yanjiusheng zheng siqian beijing hukou" [Forty thousand graduate students competing for four thousand Beijing *hukou*], *Jinghua shibao* [Jinghua times], Beijing, November 30, 2006.

96. *Jingji cankao bao* [Economic reference news], Beijing, November 28, 2005. Similar calls and acts are also reported in other places. Jim Yardley, "Guangzhou Journal: In City Ban, a Sign of Wealth and Its Discontents," *New York Times*, January 15, 2007.

97. For a vivid report about those white-collar floaters in Beijing, see He Xiaopeng and Sun Zhan, "Diqu chabie dailai renkou liudong, yuelaiyueduo" [Regional gaps brought increasing population movement], *Zhongguo xinwen zhoukan* [China news weekly], Beijing, September 14, 2006.

98. *Beijing wanbao* [Beijing evening news], Beijing, May 10, 2005.

99. *Beijing qingnian bao* [Beijing youth daily], Beijing, September 14, 2005.

100. One survey found that in 2007, "temporary residential permit" holders had been in Beijing for an average of 4.8 years, while nearly a fifth of them had been there for more than 10 years. Zai Zhengwu, et al., "Beijing shi liudong renkou de jiben tezheng" [Basic features of migrants in Beijing], *Hongqi wengao* [Red flag drafts], Beijing, no. 12 (2007).

101. Fei-Ling Wang, *Organizing through Division and Exclusion*, 60, 202, and 203.

102. Chan and Buckingham, "Is China Abolishing the *Hukou* System?".

103. Fei-Ling Wang, "Brewing tensions while Maintaining Stabilities," 99–113.

104. Ying Zhongqing, "Liudong renkou guanli" [Management of floating people], *Zhongguo dangzhen ganbu luntan* [Forum for Chinese party an government cadres], Beijing, no. 8, 2007; and Zheng Gongcheng, "Zhongguo liudong renkou de shehui baozhang wenti" [Social security for China's floating population], *Lilun shiye* [Theoretical spectrum], Beijing, no. 6 (2007).

105. "Ningbo hukou bilei hongran daota" [The *hukou* barriers collapsing], in *Nanfang zhoumu* [Southern weekend], Guangzhou, August 31, 2001; and *Zhongguo qingnianbao* [Chinese youth daily], September 17, 2001.

106. Josephine Ma, "Farmers Turn Noses up at Life in the City," *South China Morning Post*, Hong Kong, October 17, 2001; and *Jingji cankao bao* [Economic reference news], Beijing, November 28, 2005.

107. PRC State Council Center for Development Research, *Zhongguo nongcun laodongli zhuanyi zhidu huanjing yanjiu* [Study on the institutions and environment of China's rural labor reallocation], Beijing, January 26, 2005; China Labour Bulletin, *Falling through the Floor: Migrant Women Workers' Quest for Decent Work in Dongguan, China* (Hong Kong, 2006); and Zheng Gongcheng and Huang-Li Ruolian, "Zhongguo nonnmingong wenti" [China's issue of rural

migrant workers], *Zhongguo renimin daxue xuebao* [Journal of Chinese Renmin University], Beijing, no. 6 (2006).

108. Cary Huang, "Bleak future for millions of graduates," *South China Morning Post*, Hong Kong, November 23, 2006.

109. See http://news.sina.com.cn/c/2005-02-02/17225750760.shtml (accessed February 12, 2007). For a sarcastic but illustrating list of "Top ten reasons (for the urban elite) against abolishing the *hukou* system," see http://hi.baidu.com/%B6%F6%C0%C7/blog/item/bbdfbc011738db021d95831f.html (accessed July 18, 2008). For a Beijing resident's more thoughtful comment on why the *hukou* system should continue, see http://www.xiaolaotou.com/dianping/greencard.htm (accessed July 19, 2008).

110. Minxin Pei, *China's Trapped Transition: The Limits of Developmental Autocracy* (Cambridge, MA: Harvard University Press, 2006).

111. For the latest example of such misleading official promise, see Fu Jing and Wang Bo, "*Hukou* Should Be Scrapped," *China Daily*, Beijing, January 23, 2008.

Contributors

Jennifer Adams is Assistant Professor in the School of Education at Stanford University and co-director of the Rural Education Action Project.

Arianne Gaetano is Assistant Professor of Anthropology at Auburn University. She is currently Postdoctoral Fellow of Contemporary China at the Center for East and Southeast Asian Studies, Lund University.

Lei Guang is Associate Professor of Political Science at San Diego State University.

Björn A. Gustafsson is Professor at the Department of Social Work, University of Gothenburg, Sweden, and Research Fellow, Institute for the Study of Labor (IZA), Bonn, Germany.

Emily Hannum is Associate Professor of Sociology at the University of Pennsylvania.

Xiaojiang Hu is Associate Professor and Director of the Migration Center at the School of Social Development and Public Policy of Beijing Normal University.

Fanmin Kong is Associate Professor of Human Resources and Industrial Relations at Peking University.

Li Limei is Lecturer in the Center for Modern Chinese City Studies at East China Normal University, Shanghai.

Li Shi is Professor of Economics in the School of Economics and Business and Director of the Center for Income Distribution and Poverty Studies at Beijing Normal University.

Li Si-ming is Chair Professor of Geography and Director of the Centre for China Urban and Regional Studies at Hong Kong Baptist University.

Hanchao Lu is Professor of History and Director of Graduate Studies in the School of History, Technology, and Society at Georgia Institute of Technology.

Luo Chuliang is Associate Professor of Economics in the School of Economics and Business at Beijing Normal University.

Rachel Murphy is BICC University Lecturer in the Sociology of China and Director of the Asian Studies Centre, St Antony's College Oxford.

Miguel A. Salazar is Associate Professor at the School of Social Development and Public Policy of Beijing Normal University.

Terry Sicular is Professor of Economics at the University of Western Ontario.

Fei-Ling Wang is Professor of International Affairs at Georgia Institute of Technology.

Wang Feng is Professor of Sociology at the University of California, Irvine.

Meiyan Wang is Associate Professor of Institute of Population and Labor Economics, Chinese Academy of Social Sciences.

Martin King Whyte is Professor of Sociology and Associate of the Fairbank Center for Chinese Studies, Harvard University.

Wu Jieh-min is Associate Professor of Sociology and has served as director of the Center for Contemporary China at National Tsing Hua University in Taiwan.

Winnie Yip is Reader in Economics for Health Policy at Oxford University and is also an Adjunct Associate Professor at the Harvard School of Public Health.

Yue Ximing is Professor of Economics at the School of Finance, Renmin University of China.